Feature Extraction and Image Processing

Mark S. Nixon

Alberto S. Aguado

Newnes

OXFORD   AUCKLAND   BOSTON   JOHANNESBURG   MELBOURNE   NEW DELHI

Newnes
An imprint of Butterworth-Heinemann
Linacre House, Jordan Hill, Oxford OX2 8DP
225 Wildwood Avenue, Woburn, MA 01801-2041
A division of Reed Educational and Professional Publishing Ltd

 A member of the Reed Elsevier plc group

First edition 2002

British Library Cataloguing in Publication Data
A catalogue record for this book is available from the British Library

ISBN 0 7506 5078 8

Typeset at Replika Press Pvt Ltd, Delhi 110 040, India
Printed and bound in Great Britain

Contents

Preface

Why did we write this book?

We will no doubt be asked many times: why on earth write a new book on computer vision? Fair question: there are already many good books on computer vision already out in the bookshops, as you will find referenced later, so why add to them? Part of the answer is that any textbook is a snapshot of material that exists prior to it. Computer vision, the art of processing images stored within a computer, has seen a considerable amount of research by highly qualified people and the volume of research would appear to have increased in recent years. That means a lot of new techniques have been developed, and many of the more recent approaches have yet to migrate to textbooks.

But it is not just the new research: part of the speedy advance in computer vision technique has left some areas covered only in scant detail. By the nature of research, one cannot publish material on technique that is seen more to fill historical gaps, rather than to advance knowledge. This is again where a new text can contribute.

Finally, the technology itself continues to advance. This means that there is new hardware, new programming languages and new programming environments. In particular for computer vision, the advance of technology means that computing power and memory are now relatively cheap. It is certainly considerably cheaper than when computer vision was starting as a research field. One of the authors here notes that the laptop that his portion of the book was written on has more memory, is faster, has bigger disk space and better graphics than the computer that served the entire university of his student days. And he is not that old! One of the more advantageous recent changes brought by progress has been the development of mathematical programming systems. These allow us to concentrate on mathematical technique itself, rather than on implementation detail. There are several sophisticated flavours of which Mathcad and Matlab, the chosen vehicles here, are amongst the most popular. We have been using these techniques in research and in teaching and we would argue that they have been of considerable benefit there. In research, they help us to develop technique faster and to evaluate its final implementation. For teaching, the power of a modern laptop and a mathematical system combine to show students, in lectures and in study, not only how techniques are implemented, but also how and why they work with an explicit relation to conventional teaching material.

We wrote this book for these reasons. There is a host of material we could have included but chose to omit. Our apologies to other academics if it was your own, or your favourite, technique. By virtue of the enormous breadth of the subject of computer vision, we restricted the focus to feature extraction for this has not only been the focus of much of our research, but it is also where the attention of established textbooks, with some exceptions, can be rather scanty. It is, however, one of the prime targets of applied computer vision, so would benefit from better attention. We have aimed to clarify some of its origins and development, whilst also exposing implementation using mathematical systems. As such, we have written this text with our original aims in mind.

ix

The book and its support

Each chapter of the book presents a particular package of information concerning feature extraction in image processing and computer vision. Each package is developed from its origins and later referenced to more recent material. Naturally, there is often theoretical development prior to implementation (in Mathcad or Matlab). We have provided working implementations of most of the major techniques we describe, and applied them to process a selection of imagery. Though the focus of our work has been more in analysing medical imagery or in biometrics (the science of recognising people by behavioural or physiological characteristic, like face recognition), the techniques are general and can migrate to other application domains.

You will find a host of further supporting information at the book's website http://www.ecs.soton.ac.uk/~msn/book/. First, you will find the worksheets (the Matlab and Mathcad implementations that support the text) so that you can study the techniques described herein. There are also lecturing versions that have been arranged for display via a data projector, with enlarged text and more interactive demonstration. The website will be kept as up to date as possible, for it also contains links to other material such as websites devoted to techniques and to applications, as well as to available software and on-line literature. Finally, any errata will be reported there. It is our regret and our responsibility that these will exist, but our inducement for their reporting concerns a pint of beer. If you find an error that we don't know about (not typos like spelling, grammar and layout) then use the mailto on the website and we shall send you a pint of good English *beer*, free!

There is a certain amount of mathematics in this book. The target audience is for third or fourth year students in BSc/BEng/MEng courses in electrical or electronic engineering, or in mathematics or physics, and this is the level of mathematical analysis here. Computer vision can be thought of as a branch of applied mathematics, though this does not really apply to some areas within its remit, but certainly applies to the material herein. The mathematics essentially concerns mainly calculus and geometry though some of it is rather more detailed than the constraints of a conventional lecture course might allow. Certainly, not all the material here is covered in detail in undergraduate courses at Southampton.

The book starts with an overview of computer vision hardware, software and established material, with reference to the most sophisticated vision system yet 'developed': the *human vision* system. Though the precise details of the nature of processing that allows us to see have yet to be determined, there is a considerable range of *hardware* and *software* that allow us to give a computer system the capability to acquire, process and reason with imagery, the function of 'sight'. The first chapter also provides a comprehensive *bibliography* of material you can find on the subject, not only including textbooks, but also available software and other material. As this will no doubt be subject to change, it might well be worth consulting the website for more up-to-date information. The preference for journal references are those which are likely to be found in local university libraries, *IEEE Transactions* in particular. These are often subscribed to as they are relatively low cost, and are often of very high quality.

The next chapter concerns the basics of signal processing theory for use in computer vision. It introduces the Fourier transform that allows you to look at a signal in a new way, in terms of its frequency content. It also allows us to work out the minimum size of a picture to conserve information, to analyse the content in terms of frequency and even helps to speed up some of the later vision algorithms. Unfortunately, it does involve a few equations, but it is a new way of looking at data and at signals, and proves to be a rewarding topic of study in its own right.

We then start to look at *basic* image processing techniques, where image points are mapped into a new value first by considering a single point in an original image, and then by considering groups of points. Not only do we see common operations to make a picture's appearance better, especially for human vision, but also we see how to reduce the effects of different types of commonly encountered image noise. This is where the techniques are implemented as algorithms in Mathcad and Matlab to show precisely how the equations work.

The following chapter concerns *low-level features* which are the techniques that describe the content of an image, at the level of a whole image rather than in distinct regions of it. One of the most important processes we shall meet is called *edge detection*. Essentially, this reduces an image to a form of a caricaturist's sketch, though without a caricaturist's exaggerations. The major techniques are presented in detail, together with descriptions of their implementation. Other image properties we can derive include measures of *curvature* and measures of *movement*. These also are covered in this chapter.

These edges, the curvature or the motion need to be grouped in some way so that we can find shapes in an image. Our first approach to *shape extraction* concerns analysing the *match* of low-level information to a known template of a target shape. As this can be computationally very cumbersome, we then progress to a technique that improves computational performance, whilst maintaining an optimal performance. The technique is known as the *Hough transform* and it has long been a popular target for researchers in computer vision who have sought to clarify its basis, improve it speed, and to increase its accuracy and robustness. Essentially, by the Hough transform we estimate the parameters that govern a shape's appearance, where the shapes range from *lines* to *ellipses* and even to *unknown shapes*.

Some applications of shape extraction require to determine rather more than the parameters that control appearance, but require to be able to *deform* or *flex* to match the image template. For this reason, the chapter on shape extraction by matching is followed by one on *flexible shape* analysis. This is a topic that has shown considerable progress of late, especially with the introduction of *snakes* (*active contours*). These seek to match a shape to an image by analysing local properties. Further, we shall see how we can describe a shape by its *symmetry* and also how global constraints concerning the *statistics* of a shape's appearance can be used to guide final extraction.

Up to this point, we have not considered techniques that can be used to describe the shape found in an image. We shall find that the two major approaches concern techniques that describe a shape's perimeter and those that describe its area. Some of the *perimeter description* techniques, the Fourier descriptors, are even couched using Fourier transform theory that allows analysis of their frequency content. One of the major approaches to *area description*, statistical moments, also has a form of access to frequency components, but is of a very different nature to the Fourier analysis.

The final chapter describes *texture* analysis, prior to some introductory material on *pattern classification*. Texture describes patterns with no known analytical description and has been the target of considerable research in computer vision and image processing. It is used here more as a vehicle for the material that precedes it, such as the Fourier transform and area descriptions though references are provided for access to other generic material. There is also introductory material on how to classify these patterns against known data but again this is a window on a much larger area, to which appropriate pointers are given.

The *appendices* include material that is germane to the text, such as *co-ordinate geometry* and the method of *least squares*, aimed to be a short introduction for the reader. Other related material is referenced throughout the text, especially to on-line material. The appendices include a printout of one of the shortest of the Mathcad and Matlab *worksheets*.

In this way, the text covers all major areas of feature extraction in image processing and computer vision. There is considerably more material in the subject than is presented here: for example, there is an enormous volume of material in 3D computer vision and in 2D signal processing which is only alluded to here. But to include all that would lead to a monstrous book that no one could afford, or even pick up! So we admit we give a snapshot, but hope more that it is considered to open another window on a fascinating and rewarding subject.

In gratitude

We are immensely grateful to the input of our colleagues, in particular to Dr Steve Gunn and to Dr John Carter. The family who put up with it are Maria Eugenia and Caz and the nippers. We are also very grateful to past and present researchers in computer vision at the Image, Speech and Intelligent Systems Research Group (formerly the Vision, Speech and Signal Processing Group) under (or who have survived?) Mark's supervision at the Department of Electronics and Computer Science, University of Southampton. These include: Dr Hani Muammar, Dr Xiaoguang Jia, Dr Yan Chen, Dr Adrian Evans, Dr Colin Davies, Dr David Cunado, Dr Jason Nash, Dr Ping Huang, Dr Liang Ng, Dr Hugh Lewis, Dr David Benn, Dr Douglas Bradshaw, David Hurley, Mike Grant, Bob Roddis, Karl Sharman, Jamie Shutler, Jun Chen, Andy Tatem, Chew Yam, James Hayfron-Acquah, Yalin Zheng and Jeff Foster. We are also very grateful to past Southampton students on BEng and MEng Electronic Engineering, MEng Information Engineering, BEng and MEng Computer Engineering and BSc Computer Science who have pointed out our earlier mistakes, noted areas for clarification and in some cases volunteered some of the material herein. To all of you, our very grateful thanks.

Final message

We ourselves have already benefited much by writing this book. As we already know, previous students have also benefited, and contributed to it as well. But it remains our hope that it does inspire people to join in this fascinating and rewarding subject that has proved to be such a source of pleasure and inspiration to its many workers.

Mark S. Nixon   Alberto S. Aguado
University of Southampton   University of Surrey

1

Introduction

1.1 Overview

This is where we start, by looking at the human visual system to investigate what is meant by vision, then on to how a computer can be made to sense pictorial data and then how we can process it. The overview of this chapter is shown in Table **1.1**; you will find a similar overview at the start of each chapter. We have not included the references (citations) in any overview, you will find them at the end of each chapter.

Table 1.1 Overview of Chapter 1

Main topic	Sub topics	Main points
Human vision system	How the *eye* works, how visual *information* is *processed* and how it can *fail*.	Sight, lens, retina, image, colour, monochrome, processing, brain, illusions.
Computer vision systems	How electronic *images* are formed, how *video* is fed into a *computer* and how we can *process* the information using a computer.	Picture elements, pixels, video standard, camera technologies, pixel technology, performance effects, specialist cameras, video conversion, computer languages, processing packages.
Mathematical systems	How we can process images using *mathematical packages*; introduction to the *Matlab* and *Mathcad* systems.	Ease, consistency, support, visualisation of results, availability, introductory use, example worksheets.
Literature	Other *textbooks* and other places to find *information* on image processing, computer vision and feature extraction.	Magazines, textbooks, websites and this book's website.

1.2 Human and computer vision

A computer vision system processes images acquired from an electronic camera, which is like the human vision system where the brain processes images derived from the eyes. Computer vision is a rich and rewarding topic for study and research for electronic engineers, computer scientists and many others. Increasingly, it has a commercial future. There are now many vision systems in routine industrial use: cameras inspect mechanical parts to check size, food is inspected for quality, and images used in astronomy benefit from computer vision techniques. Forensic studies and biometrics (ways to recognise people) using computer vision include automatic face recognition and recognising people by the 'texture' of their irises. These studies are paralleled by biologists and psychologists who continue to study how our human vision system works, and how we see and recognise objects (and people).

A selection of (computer) images is given in Figure **1.1**, these images comprise a set of points or *picture elements* (usually concatenated to *pixels*) stored as an *array of numbers* in a *computer*. To recognise faces, based on an image such as Figure **1.1**(a), we need to be able to analyse constituent shapes, such as the shape of the nose, the eyes, and the eyebrows, to make some measurements to describe, and then recognise, a face. (Figure **1.1**(a) is perhaps one of the most famous images in image processing. It is called the Lena image, and is derived from a picture of Lena Sjööblom in *Playboy* in 1972.) Figure **1.1**(b) is an ultrasound image of the carotid artery (which is near the side of the neck and supplies blood to the brain and the face), taken as a cross-section through it. The top region of the image is near the skin; the bottom is inside the neck. The image arises from combinations of the reflections of the ultrasound radiation by tissue. This image comes from a study aimed to produce three-dimensional models of arteries, to aid vascular surgery. Note that the image is very *noisy*, and this obscures the shape of the (elliptical) artery. Remotely sensed images are often analysed by their *texture* content. The perceived texture is different between the road junction and the different types of foliage seen in Figure **1.1**(c). Finally, Figure **1.1**(d) is a Magnetic Resonance Image (MRI) of a cross-section near the middle of a human body. The chest is at the top of the image, and the lungs and blood vessels are the dark areas, the internal organs and the fat appear grey. MRI images are in routine medical use nowadays, owing to their ability to provide high quality images.

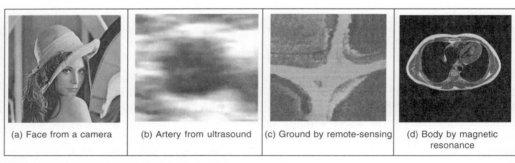

(a) Face from a camera   (b) Artery from ultrasound   (c) Ground by remote-sensing   (d) Body by magnetic resonance

Figure 1.1   Real images from different sources

There are many different image sources. In medical studies, MRI is good for imaging soft tissue, but does not reveal the bone structure (the spine cannot be seen in Figure **1.1**(d)); this can be achieved by using Computerised Tomography (CT) which is better at imaging bone, as opposed to soft tissue. Remotely sensed images can be derived from infrared (thermal) sensors or Synthetic-Aperture Radar, rather than by cameras, as in Figure **1.1**(c). Spatial information can be provided by two-dimensional arrays of sensors, including sonar arrays. There are perhaps more varieties of sources of spatial data in medical studies than in any other area. But computer vision techniques are used to analyse any form of data, not just the images from cameras.

Synthesised images are good for *evaluating* techniques and finding out how they work, and some of the bounds on *performance*. Two synthetic images are shown in Figure **1.2**. Figure **1.2**(a) is an image of circles that were specified *mathematically*. The image is an ideal case: the circles are perfectly defined and the brightness levels have been specified to be constant. This type of synthetic image is good for evaluating techniques which find the borders of the shape (its edges), the shape itself and even for making a description of the shape. Figure **1.2**(b) is a synthetic image made up of sections of real image data. The borders between the regions of image data are exact, again specified by a program. The image data comes from a well-known texture database, the Brodatz album of textures. This was scanned and stored as computer images. This image can be used to analyse how well computer vision algorithms can identify regions of differing texture.

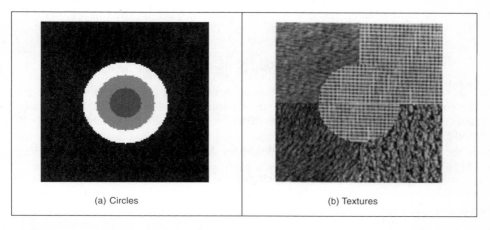

(a) Circles   (b) Textures

Figure 1.2   Examples of synthesised images

This chapter will show you how basic computer vision systems work, in the context of the human vision system. It covers the main elements of human vision showing you how your eyes work (and how they can be deceived!). For computer vision, this chapter covers the hardware and software used for image analysis, giving an introduction to Mathcad and Matlab, the software tools used throughout this text to implement computer vision algorithms. Finally, a selection of pointers to other material is provided, especially those for more detail on the topics covered in this chapter.

1.3   The human vision system

Human vision is a sophisticated system that senses and acts on *visual stimuli*. It has evolved for millions of years, primarily for defence or survival. Intuitively, computer and human vision appear to have the same function. The purpose of both systems is to interpret *spatial* data, data that is indexed by more than one dimension. Even though computer and human vision are functionally similar, you cannot expect a computer vision system to replicate exactly the function of the human eye. This is partly because we do not understand fully how the eye works, as we shall see in this section. Accordingly, we cannot design a system to replicate exactly its function. In fact, some of the properties of the human eye are useful when developing computer vision techniques, whereas others are actually undesirable in a computer vision system. But we shall see computer vision techniques which can to some extent replicate, and in some cases even improve upon, the human vision system.

You might ponder this, so put one of the fingers from each of your hands in front of your face and try to estimate the distance between them. This is difficult, and we are sure you would agree that your measurement would not be very accurate. Now put your fingers very close together. You can still tell that they are apart even when the distance between them is tiny. So human vision can distinguish *relative* distance well, but is poor for *absolute* distance. Computer vision is the other way around: it is good for estimating absolute difference, but with relatively poor resolution for relative difference. The number of pixels in the image imposes the accuracy of the computer vision system, but that does not come until the next chapter. Let us start at the beginning, by seeing how the human vision system works.

In human vision, the sensing element is the eye from which images are transmitted via the optic nerve to the brain, for further processing. The optic nerve has insufficient capacity to carry all the information sensed by the eye. Accordingly, there must be some pre-processing before the image is transmitted down the optic nerve. The human vision system can be modelled in three parts:

1. the eye – this is a physical model since much of its function can be determined by pathology;
2. the neural system – this is an experimental model since the function can be modelled, but not determined precisely;
3. processing by the brain – this is a psychological model since we cannot access or model such processing directly, but only determine behaviour by experiment and inference.

1.3.1 The eye

The function of the eye is to form an image; a cross-section of the eye is illustrated in Figure **1.3**. Vision requires an ability to focus selectively on objects of interest. This is achieved by the *ciliary muscles* that hold the *lens*. In old age, it is these muscles which become slack and the eye loses its ability to focus at short distance. The *iris*, or pupil, is like an *aperture* on a camera and controls the amount of light entering the eye. It is a delicate system and needs protection, this is provided by the cornea (sclera). The *choroid* has blood vessels that supply nutrition and is *opaque* to cut down the amount of light. The *retina* is on the inside of the eye, which is where light falls to form an image. By this system, muscles rotate the eye, and shape the lens, to form an image on the *fovea* (focal point) where the majority of sensors are situated. The *blind spot* is where the optic nerve starts; there are no sensors there.

Focusing involves *shaping* the lens, rather than positioning it as in a camera. The lens is shaped to refract close images greatly, and distant objects little, essentially by 'stretching' it. The distance of the focal centre of the lens varies from approximately 14 mm to around 17 mm depending on the lens shape. This implies that a world scene is translated into an area of about 2 mm^2. Good vision has high *acuity* (sharpness), which implies that there must be very many sensors in the area where the image is formed.

There are actually nearly 100 million sensors dispersed around the retina. Light falls on

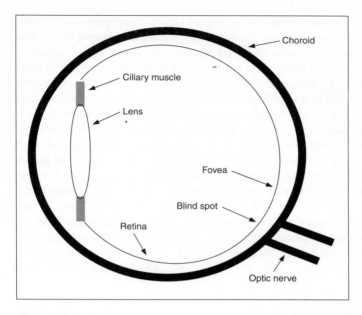

Figure 1.3 Human eye

these sensors to stimulate photochemical transmissions, which results in nerve impulses that are collected to form the signal transmitted by the eye. There are two types of sensor: first, the *rods*–these are used for *black and white* (*scotopic*) vision; and secondly, the *cones*–these are used for *colour* (*photopic*) vision. There are approximately 10 million cones and nearly all are found within 5° of the fovea. The remaining 100 million rods are distributed around the retina, with the majority between 20° and 5° of the fovea. Acuity is actually expressed in terms of spatial resolution (sharpness) and brightness/colour resolution, and is greatest within 1° of the fovea.

There is only one type of rod, but there are three types of cones. These types are:

1. α –these sense light towards the blue end of the visual spectrum;
2. β – these sense green light;
3. γ – these sense light in the red region of the spectrum.

The total response of the cones arises from summing the response of these three types of cones, this gives a response covering the whole of the visual spectrum. The rods are sensitive to light within the entire visual spectrum, and are more sensitive than the cones. Accordingly, when the light level is low, images are formed away from the fovea, to use the superior sensitivity of the rods, but without the colour vision of the cones. Note that there are actually very few of the α cones, and there are many more β and γ cones. But we can still see a lot of blue (especially given ubiquitous denim!). So, somehow, the human vision system compensates for the lack of blue sensors, to enable us to perceive it. The world would be a funny place with red water! The vision response is actually logarithmic and depends on brightness adaption from dark conditions where the image is formed on the rods, to brighter conditions where images are formed on the cones.

One inherent property of the eye, known as *Mach bands*, affects the way we perceive images. These are illustrated in Figure **1.4** and are the darker bands that appear to be where two stripes of constant shade join. By assigning values to the image brightness levels, the cross-section of plotted brightness is shown in Figure **1.4**(a). This shows that the picture is formed from stripes of constant brightness. Human vision *perceives* an image for which the cross-section is as plotted in Figure **1.4**(c). These Mach bands do not really exist, but are introduced by your eye. The bands arise from overshoot in the eyes' response at boundaries of regions of different intensity (this aids us to differentiate between objects in our field of view). The *real* cross-section is illustrated in Figure **1.4**(b). Note also that a human eye can distinguish only relatively few grey levels. It actually has a capability to discriminate between 32 levels (equivalent to five bits) whereas the image of Figure **1.4**(a) could have many more brightness levels. This is why your perception finds it more difficult to discriminate between the low intensity bands on the left of Figure **1.4**(a). (Note that that Mach bands cannot be seen in the earlier image of circles, Figure **1.2**(a), due to the arrangement of grey levels.) This is the limit of our studies of the first level of human vision; for those who are interested, Cornsweet (1970) provides many more details concerning visual perception.

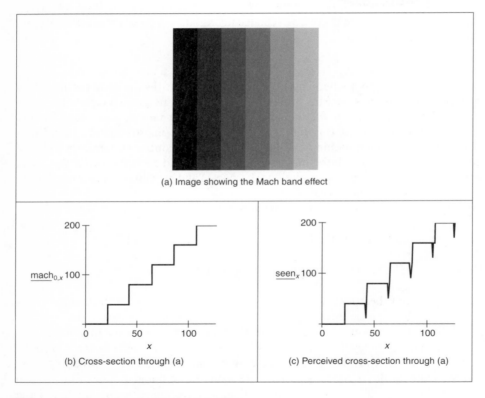

(a) Image showing the Mach band effect

(b) Cross-section through (a)

(c) Perceived cross-section through (a)

Figure 1.4   Illustrating the Mach band effect

So we have already identified two properties associated with the eye that it would be difficult to include, and would often be unwanted, in a computer vision system: Mach bands and sensitivity to unsensed phenomena. These properties are integral to human vision. At present, human vision is far more sophisticated than we can hope to achieve with a computer vision system. Infrared guided-missile vision systems can actually have difficulty in distinguishing between a bird at 100 m and a plane at 10 km. Poor birds! (Lucky plane?) Human vision can handle this with ease.

1.3.2 The neural system

Neural signals provided by the eye are essentially the transformed response of the wavelength dependent receptors, the cones and the rods. One *model* is to combine these transformed signals by addition, as illustrated in Figure **1.5**. The response is transformed by a logarithmic function, mirroring the known response of the eye. This is then multiplied by a weighting factor that controls the contribution of a particular sensor. This can be arranged to allow a combination of responses from a particular region. The weighting factors can be chosen to afford particular filtering properties. For example, in *lateral inhibition*, the weights for the centre sensors are much greater than the weights for those at the extreme. This allows the response of the centre sensors to dominate the combined response given by addition. If the weights in one half are chosen to be negative, whilst those in the other half are positive, then the output will show detection of contrast (change in brightness), given by the differencing action of the weighting functions.

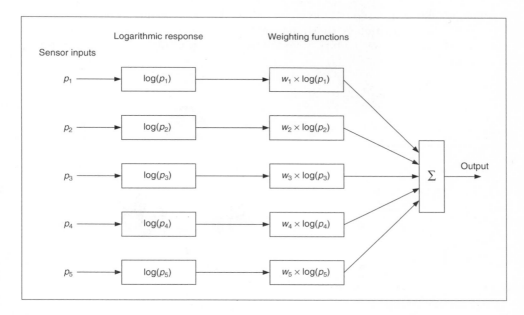

Figure 1.5 Neural processing

The signals from the cones can be combined in a manner that reflects *chrominance* (*colour*) and *luminance* (*brightness*). This can be achieved by subtraction of logarithmic functions, which is then equivalent to taking the logarithm of their ratio. This allows measures of chrominance to be obtained. In this manner, the signals derived from the sensors are combined prior to transmission through the optic nerve. This is an experimental model, since there are many ways possible to combine the different signals together. For further information on retinal neural networks, see Ratliff (1965); an alternative study of neural processing can be found in Overington (1992).

1.3.3 Processing

The neural signals are then transmitted to two areas of the brain for further processing. These areas are the *associative cortex*, where *links* between objects are made, and the *occipital cortex*, where *patterns* are processed. It is naturally difficult to determine precisely what happens in this region of the brain. To date, there have been no volunteers for detailed study of their brain's function (though progress with new imaging modalities such as Positive Emission Tomography or Electrical Impedance Tomography will doubtless help). For this reason, there are only psychological models to suggest how this region of the brain operates.

It is well known that one function of the eye is to use edges, or *boundaries*, of objects. We can easily read the word in Figure **1.6**(a), this is achieved by filling in the missing boundaries in the knowledge that the pattern most likely represents a printed word. But we can infer more about this image; there is a suggestion of illumination, causing shadows to appear in unlit areas. If the light source is bright, then the image will be washed out, causing the disappearance of the boundaries which are interpolated by our eyes. So there is more than just physical response, there is also knowledge, including prior knowledge of solid geometry. This situation is illustrated in Figure **1.6**(b) that could represent three 'Pacmen' about to collide, or a white triangle placed on top of three black circles. Either situation is possible.

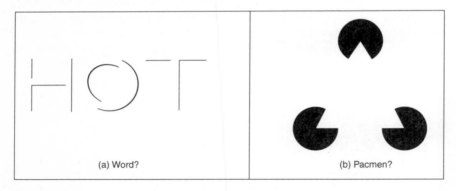

Figure 1.6 How human vision uses edges

It is also possible to deceive the eye, primarily by imposing a scene that it has not been trained to handle. In the famous *Zollner illusion*, Figure **1.7**(a), the bars appear to be *slanted*, whereas in reality they are *vertical* (check this by placing a pen between the lines): the small crossbars mislead your eye into perceiving the vertical bars as slanting. In the *Ebbinghaus illusion*, Figure **1.7**(b), the inner circle appears to be *larger* when surrounded by *small* circles, than it appears when surrounded by larger circles.

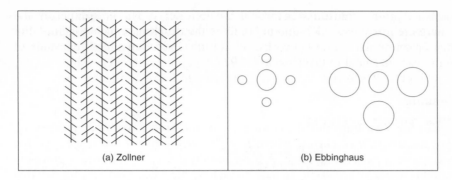

(a) Zollner   (b) Ebbinghaus

Figure 1.7   Static illusions

There are dynamic illusions too: you can always impress children with the 'see my wobbly pencil' trick. Just hold the pencil loosely between your fingers then, to whoops of childish glee, when the pencil is shaken up and down, the solid pencil will appear to bend. *Benham's disk*, Figure **1.8**, shows how hard it is to model vision accurately. If you make up a version of this disk into a spinner (push a matchstick through the centre) and spin it anti-clockwise, you do not see three dark rings, you will see three *coloured* ones. The outside one will appear to be *red*, the middle one a sort of *green*, and the inner one will appear deep *blue*. (This can depend greatly on lighting – and contrast between the black and white on the disk. If the colours are not clear, try it in a different place, with different lighting.) You can appear to explain this when you notice that the red colours are associated with the long lines, and the blue with short lines. But this is from physics, not psychology. Now spin the disk clockwise. The order of the colours reverses: *red* is associated with the *short* lines (inside), and *blue* with the *long* lines (outside). So the argument from physics is clearly incorrect, since red is now associated with short lines not long ones, revealing the need for psychological explanation of the eyes' function. This is not colour perception, see Armstrong (1991) for an interesting (and interactive!) study of colour theory and perception.

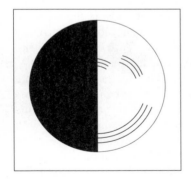

Figure 1.8   Benham's disk

Naturally, there are many texts on human vision. Marr's seminal text (Marr, 1982) is a computational investigation into human vision and visual perception, investigating it from a computer vision viewpoint. For further details on pattern processing in human vision, see Bruce (1990); for more illusions see Rosenfeld (1982). One text (Kaiser, 1999) is available on line (`http://www.yorku.ca/eye/thejoy.htm`) which is extremely convenient. Many of the properties of human vision are hard to include in a computer vision system, but let us now look at the basic components that are used to make computers see.

1.4 Computer vision systems

Given the progress in computer technology, computer vision hardware is now relatively inexpensive; a basic computer vision system requires a camera, a camera interface and a computer. These days, some personal computers offer the capability for a basic vision system, by including a camera and its interface within the system. There are specialised systems for vision, offering high performance in more than one aspect. These can be expensive, as any specialist system is.

1.4.1 Cameras

A *camera* is the *basic sensing element*. In simple terms, most cameras rely on the property of light to cause hole/electron pairs (the charge carriers in electronics) in a conducting material. When a potential is applied (to attract the charge carriers), this charge can be sensed as current. By Ohm's law, the voltage across a resistance is proportional to the current through it, so the current can be turned into a voltage by passing it through a resistor. The number of hole/electron pairs is proportional to the amount of incident light. Accordingly, greater charge (and hence greater voltage and current) is caused by an increase in brightness. In this manner cameras can provide as output, a voltage which is proportional to the brightness of the points imaged by the camera. Cameras are usually arranged to supply video according to a specified standard. Most will aim to satisfy the *CCIR standard* that exists for closed circuit television systems.

There are three main types of camera: *vidicons, charge coupled devices* (CCDs) and, more recently, *CMOS* cameras (Complementary Metal Oxide Silicon – now the dominant technology for logic circuit implementation). Vidicons are the *older* (analogue) technology, which though cheap (mainly by virtue of longevity in production) are now being replaced by the *newer* CCD and CMOS *digital* technologies. The digital technologies, currently CCDs, now dominate much of the camera market because they are *lightweight* and *cheap* (with other advantages) and are therefore used in the domestic video market.

Vidicons operate in a manner akin to a television in reverse. The image is formed on a screen, and then sensed by an electron beam that is scanned across the screen. This produces an output which is continuous, the output *voltage* is proportional to the *brightness* of points in the scanned line, and is a continuous signal, a voltage which varies continuously with time. On the other hand, CCDs and CMOS cameras use an array of sensors; these are regions where *charge* is collected which is proportional to the *light* incident on that region. This is then available in discrete, or *sampled*, form as opposed to the continuous sensing of a vidicon. This is similar to human vision with its array of cones and rods, but digital cameras use a *rectangular* regularly spaced lattice whereas human vision uses a *hexagonal* lattice with irregular spacing.

Two main types of semiconductor pixel sensors are illustrated in Figure **1.9**. In the *passive sensor*, the charge generated by incident light is presented to a bus through a pass transistor. When the signal *Tx* is activated, the pass transistor is enabled and the sensor provides a capacitance to the bus, one that is proportional to the incident light. An *active pixel* includes an amplifier circuit that can compensate for limited fill factor of the photodiode. The select signal again controls presentation of the sensor's information to the bus. A further reset signal allows the charge site to be cleared when the image is rescanned.

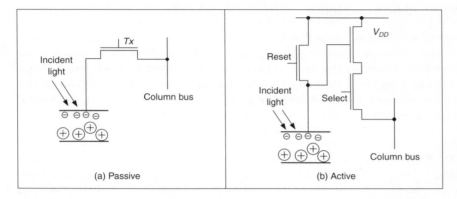

Figure 1.9 Pixel sensors

The basis of a CCD sensor is illustrated in Figure **1.10**. The number of charge sites gives the resolution of the CCD sensor; the contents of the charge sites (or buckets) need to be converted to an output (voltage) signal. In simple terms, the contents of the buckets are emptied into vertical transport registers which are shift registers moving information towards

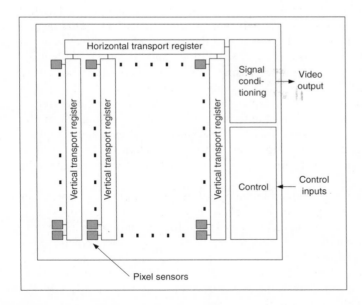

Figure 1.10 CCD sensing element

the horizontal transport registers. This is the column bus supplied by the pixel sensors. The horizontal transport registers empty the information row by row (point by point) into a signal conditioning unit which transforms the sensed charge into a voltage which is proportional to the charge in a bucket, and hence proportional to the brightness of the corresponding point in the scene imaged by the camera. CMOS cameras are like a form of memory: the charge incident on a particular site in a two-dimensional lattice is proportional to the brightness at a point. The charge is then read like computer memory. (In fact, a computer memory RAM chip can act as a rudimentary form of camera when the circuit – the one buried in the chip – is exposed to light.)

There are many more varieties of vidicon (Chalnicon etc.) than there are of CCD technology (Charge Injection Device etc.), perhaps due to the greater age of basic vidicon technology. Vidicons were cheap but had a number of intrinsic performance problems. The scanning process essentially relied on 'moving parts'. As such, the camera performance changed with time, as parts *wore*; this is known as *ageing*. Also, it is possible to *burn* an image into the scanned screen by using high incident light levels; vidicons also suffered *lag* that is a delay in response to moving objects in a scene. On the other hand, the digital technologies are dependent on the physical arrangement of charge sites and as such do not suffer from ageing, but can suffer from irregularity in the charge sites' (silicon) material. The underlying technology also makes CCD and CMOS cameras less sensitive to lag and burn, but the signals associated with the CCD transport registers can give rise to *readout effects*. CCDs actually only came to dominate camera technology when technological difficulty associated with *quantum efficiency* (the magnitude of response to incident light) for the shorter, blue, wavelengths was solved. One of the major problems in CCD cameras is *blooming*, where bright (incident) light causes a bright spot to grow and disperse in the image (this used to happen in the analogue technologies too). This happens much less in CMOS cameras because the charge sites can be much better defined and reading their data is equivalent to reading memory sites as opposed to shuffling charge between sites. Also, CMOS cameras have now overcome the problem of *fixed pattern noise* that plagued earlier MOS cameras. CMOS cameras are actually much more recent than CCDs. This begs a question as to which is best: CMOS or CCD? Given that they will both be subject to much continued development though CMOS is a cheaper technology and because it lends itself directly to intelligent cameras with on-board processing. This is mainly because the feature size of points (pixels) in a CCD sensor is limited to about 4 µm so that enough light is collected. In contrast, the feature size in CMOS technology is considerably smaller, currently at around 0.1 µm. Accordingly, it is now possible to integrate signal processing within the camera chip and thus it is perhaps possible that CMOS cameras will eventually replace CCD technologies for many applications. However, the more modern CCDs also have on-board circuitry, and their process technology is more mature, so the debate will continue!

Finally, there are specialist cameras, which include *high-resolution* devices (which can give pictures with a great number of points), *low-light level* cameras which can operate in very dark conditions (this is where vidicon technology is still found) and *infrared* cameras which sense heat to provide thermal images. For more detail concerning camera practicalities and imaging systems see, for example, Awcock and Thomas (1995) or Davies (1994). For practical minutiae on cameras, and on video in general, *Lenk's Video Handbook* (Lenk, 1991) has a wealth of detail. For more detail on sensor development, particularly CMOS, the article (Fossum, 1997) is well worth a look.

1.4.2 Computer interfaces

The basic computer *interface* needs to convert an analogue signal from a camera into a set of digital numbers. The interface system is called a *framegrabber* since it grabs frames of data from a *video sequence*, and is illustrated in Figure **1.11**. Note that intelligent cameras which provide digital information do not need this particular interface, just one which allows storage of their data. However, a conventional camera signal is *continuous* and is transformed into *digital* (discrete) format using an Analogue to Digital (A/D) converter. *Flash converters* are usually used due to the high speed required for conversion (say 11 MHz that cannot be met by any other conversion technology). The video signal requires conditioning prior to conversion; this includes DC restoration to ensure that the correct DC level is attributed to the incoming video signal. Usually, 8-bit A/D converters are used; at 6 dB/bit, this gives 48 dB which just satisfies the CCIR stated *bandwidth* of approximately 45 dB. The output of the A/D converter is often fed to *look-up tables* (LUTs) which implement designated conversion of the input data, but in hardware, rather than in software, and this is very fast. The outputs of the A/D converter are then stored in computer memory. This is now often arranged to be dual-ported memory that is shared by the computer and the framegrabber (as such the framestore is *memory-mapped*): the framegrabber only takes control of the image memory when it is acquiring, and storing, an image. Alternative approaches can use Dynamic Memory Access (DMA) or, even, external memory, but computer memory is now so cheap that such design techniques are rarely used.

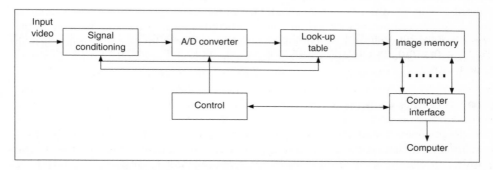

Figure 1.11 A computer interface – the framegrabber

There are clearly many different ways to design framegrabber units, especially for specialist systems. Note that the control circuitry has to determine exactly when image data is to be sampled. This is controlled by synchronisation pulses that are supplied within the video signal and can be extracted by a circuit known as a sync stripper (essentially a high gain amplifier). The sync signals actually control the way video information is constructed. Television pictures are constructed from a set of *lines*, those lines scanned by a camera. In order to reduce requirements on transmission (and for viewing), the 625 lines (in the *PAL system*) are transmitted in two *fields*, each of 312.5 lines, as illustrated in Figure **1.12**. (There was a big debate between the computer producers who don't want interlacing, and the television broadcasters who do.) If you look at a television, but not directly, the flicker due to *interlacing* can be perceived. When you look at the television directly, persistence in the human eye ensures that you do not see the *flicker*. These fields are called the *odd* and *even* fields. There is also an *aspect ratio* in picture transmission: pictures are arranged to be 1.33 times longer than they are high. These factors are chosen to make television images attractive to *human* vision, and can complicate the design of a framegrabber unit. Nowadays, *digital video cameras* can provide the digital output, in progressive scan (without interlacing). Life just gets easier!

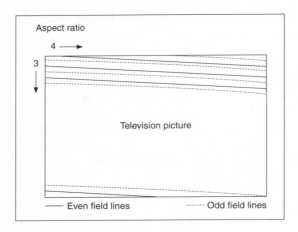

Figure 1.12 Interlacing in television pictures

This completes the material we need to cover for basic computer vision systems. For more detail concerning practicalities of computer vision systems see, for example, Davies (1994) and Baxes (1994).

1.4.3 Processing an image

Most image processing and computer vision techniques are implemented in computer *software*. Often, only the simplest techniques migrate to hardware; though coding techniques to maximise efficiency in image transmission are of sufficient commercial interest that they have warranted extensive, and very sophisticated, hardware development. The systems include the Joint Photographic Expert Group (JPEG) and the Moving Picture Expert Group (MPEG) image coding formats. C and C++ are by now the most popular languages for vision system implementation: C because of its strengths in integrating high- and low-level functions, and the availability of good compilers. As systems become more complex, C++ becomes more attractive when encapsulation and polymorphism may be exploited. Many people now use Java as a development language partly due to platform independence, but also due to ease in implementation (though some claim that speed/efficiency is not as good as in C/C++). There is considerable implementation advantage associated with use of the Java™ Advanced Imaging API (Application Programming Interface). There are some textbooks that offer image processing systems implemented in these languages. Also, there are many commercial packages available, though these are often limited to basic techniques, and do not include the more sophisticated shape extraction techniques. The Khoros image processing system has attracted much interest; this is a schematic (data-flow) image processing system where a user links together chosen modules. This allows for better visualisation of information flow during processing. However, the underlying mathematics is not made clear to the user, as it can be when a mathematical system is used. There is a new textbook, and a very readable one at that, by Nick Efford (Efford, 2000) which is based entirely on Java and includes, via a CD, the classes necessary for image processing software development.

A set of WWW links are shown in Table **1.2** for established freeware and commercial software image processing systems. What is perhaps the best selection can be found at the general site, from the computer vision homepage software site (repeated later in Table **1.5**).

Table 1.2 Software package websites

Packages (freeware or student version indicated by *)		
General Site	Carnegie Mellon	`http://www.cs.cmu.edu/afs/cs/` `project/cil/ftp/html/v-source.html`
Khoros	Khoral Research	`http://www.khoral.com/`
	Hannover U	`http://www.tnt.uni-hannover.de/` `soft/imgproc/khoros/`
AdOculos* (+ Textbook)	The Imaging Source	`http://www.theimagingsource.com/` `catalog/soft/dbs/ao.htm`
CVIPtools*	Southern Illinois U	`http://www.ee.siue.edu/CVIPtools/`
LaboImage*	Geneva U	`http://cuiwww.unige.ch/~vision/` `LaboImage/labo.html`
TN-Image*	Thomas J. Nelson	`http://las1.ninds.nih.gov/tnimage-` `manual/tnimage-manual.html`

1.5 Mathematical systems

In recent years, a number of *mathematical systems* have been developed. These offer what is virtually a word-processing system for mathematicians and many are screen-based using a Windows system. The advantage of these systems is that you can transpose mathematics pretty well directly from textbooks, and see how it works. Code functionality is not obscured by the use of data structures, though this can make the code appear cumbersome. A major advantage is that the system provides the low-level functionality and data visualisation schemes, allowing the user to concentrate on techniques alone. Accordingly, these systems afford an excellent route to understand, and appreciate, mathematical systems prior to development of application code, and to check the final code functions correctly.

1.5.1 Mathematical tools

Mathcad, Mathematica, Maple and Matlab are amongst the most popular of current tools. There have been surveys that compare their efficacy, but it is difficult to ensure precise comparison due to the impressive speed of development of techniques. Most systems have their protagonists and detractors, as in any commercial system. There are many books which use these packages for particular subjects, and there are often handbooks as addenda to the packages. We shall use both Matlab and Mathcad throughout this text as they are perhaps the two most popular of the mathematical systems. We shall describe Matlab later, as it is different from Mathcad, though the aim is the same. The website links for the main mathematical packages are given in Table **1.3**.

Table 1.3 Mathematical package websites

General		
Math-Net Links to the Mathematical World	Math-Net (Germany)	`http://www.math-net.de/`

Vendors		
Mathcad	MathSoft	`http://www.mathcad.com/`
Mathematica	Wolfram Research	`http://www.wri.com/`
Matlab	Mathworks	`http://www.mathworks.com/`

1.5.2 Hello Mathcad, Hello images!

The current state of evolution is Mathcad 2001; this adds much to version 6 which was where the system became useful as it included a programming language for the first time. Mathcad offers a compromise between many performance factors, and is available at low cost. If you do not want to buy it, there was a free worksheet viewer called Mathcad Explorer which operates in read-only mode. There is an image processing handbook available with Mathcad, but it does not include many of the more sophisticated feature extraction techniques.

Mathcad uses *worksheets* to implement mathematical analysis. The flow of calculation is very similar to using a piece of paper: calculation starts at the top of a document, and flows left-to-right and downward. Data is available to *later* calculation (and to calculation to the right), but is not available to prior calculation, much as is the case when calculation is written manually on paper. Mathcad uses the Maple mathematical library to extend its functionality. To ensure that equations can migrate easily from a textbook to application, Mathcad uses a WYSIWYG (What You See Is What You Get) notation (its equation editor is actually not dissimilar to the Microsoft Equation (Word) editor).

Images are actually spatial data, data which is indexed by two spatial co-ordinates. The camera senses the brightness at a point with co-ordinates x, y. Usually, x and y refer to the horizontal and vertical axes, respectively. Throughout this text we shall work in *orthographic projection*, ignoring *perspective*, where real world co-ordinates map directly to x and y co-ordinates in an image. The *homogeneous co-ordinate system* is a popular and proven method for handling three-dimensional co-ordinate systems (x, y and z where z is depth). Since it is not used directly in the text, it is included as Appendix 1 (Section 9.1). The brightness sensed by the camera is transformed to a signal which is then fed to the A/D converter and stored as a value within the computer, referenced to the co-ordinates x, y in the image. Accordingly, a computer image is a matrix of points. For a greyscale image, the value of each point is proportional to the brightness of the corresponding point in the scene viewed, and imaged, by the camera. These points are the picture elements, or *pixels*.

Consider, for example, the matrix of pixel values in Figure **1.13**(a). This can be viewed as a surface (or function) in Figure **1.13**(b), or as an image in Figure **1.13**(c). In Figure **1.13**(c) the brightness of each point is proportional to the value of its pixel. This gives the synthesised image of a bright square on a dark background. The square is bright where the pixels have a value around 40 brightness levels; the background is dark, these pixels have a value near 0 brightness levels. This image is first given a label, pic, and then pic is allocated, :=, to the matrix defined by using the matrix dialog box in Mathcad, specifying a matrix with 8 rows and 8 columns. The pixel values are then entered one by one until the matrix is complete (alternatively, the matrix can be specified by using a subroutine, but that comes later). Note that neither the background, nor the square, has a constant brightness. This is because noise has been added to the image. If we want to evaluate the performance of a computer vision technique on an image, but without the noise, we can simply remove it (one of the advantages to using synthetic images). The matrix becomes an image when it is viewed as a picture, as in Figure **1.13**(c). This is done either by presenting it as a surface plot, rotated by zero degrees and viewed from above, or by using Mathcad's picture facility. As a surface plot, Mathcad allows the user to select a greyscale image, and the patch plot option allows an image to be presented as point values.

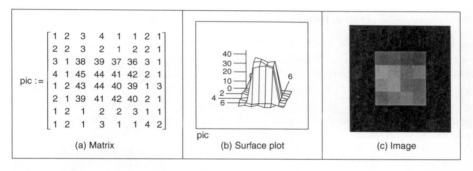

(a) Matrix (b) Surface plot (c) Image

Figure 1.13   Synthesised image of a square

Mathcad stores matrices in row-column format. The co-ordinate system used throughout this text has x as the horizontal axis and y as the vertical axis (as conventional). Accordingly, x is the column count and y is the row count so a point (in Mathcad) at co-ordinates x,y is actually accessed as $pic_{y,x}$. The origin is at co-ordinates $x = 0$ and $y = 0$ so $pic_{0,0}$ is the magnitude of the point at the origin and $pic_{2,2}$ is the point at the third row and third column and $pic_{3,2}$ is the point at the third column and fourth row, as shown in Code **1.1** (the points can be seen in Figure **1.13**(a)). Since the origin is at (0,0) the bottom right-hand point, at the last column and row, has co-ordinates (7,7). The number of rows and the number of columns in a matrix, the dimensions of an image, can be obtained by using the Mathcad rows and cols functions, respectively, and again in Code **1.1**.

```
pic2,2=38  pic3,2=45
rows(pic)=8  cols(pic)=8
```

Code 1.1   Accessing an image in Mathcad

This synthetic image can be processed using the Mathcad programming language, which can be invoked by selecting the appropriate dialog box. This allows for conventional `for`, `while` and `if` statements, and the earlier assignment operator which is `:=` in non-code sections is replaced by ← in sections of code. A subroutine that inverts the brightness level at each point, by subtracting it from the maximum brightness level in the original image, is illustrated in Code **1.2**. This uses `for` loops to index the rows and the columns, and then calculates a new pixel value by subtracting the value at that point from the maximum obtained by Mathcad's `max` function. When the whole image has been processed, the new picture is returned to be assigned to the label `newpic`. The resulting matrix is shown in Figure **1.14**(a). When this is viewed as a surface, Figure **1.14**(b), the inverted brightness levels mean that the square appears dark and its surroundings appear white, as in Figure **1.14**(c).

```
New_pic:=  for  x∈0..cols(pic)-1
               for  y∈0..rows(pic)-1
                    newpicture_{y,x} ←max(pic)-pic_{y,x}
               newpicture
```

Code 1.2   Processing image points in Mathcad

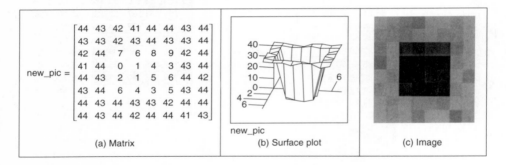

Figure 1.14   Image of a square after inversion

Routines can be formulated as *functions*, so they can be invoked to process a chosen picture, rather than restricted to a specific image. Mathcad functions are conventional, we simply add two arguments (one is the image to be processed, the other is the brightness to be added), and use the arguments as local variables, to give the `add` function illustrated in Code **1.3**. To add a value, we simply call the function and supply an image and the chosen brightness level as the arguments.

```
add_value(inpic,value):=  for  x  0..cols(inpic)-1
                               for  y  0..rows(inpic)-1
                                    newpicture_{y,x} ←inpic_{y,x}+value
                               newpicture
```

Code 1.3   Function to add a value to an image in Mathcad

Mathematically, for an image which is a matrix of $N \times N$ points, the brightness of the pixels in a new picture (matrix), $\mathbf{N}$, is the result of adding b brightness values to the pixels in the old picture, $\mathbf{O}$, given by:

$$\mathbf{N}_{x,y} = \mathbf{O}_{x,y} + b \qquad \forall x, y \in 1, N \tag{1.1}$$

Real images naturally have many points. Unfortunately, the Mathcad matrix dialog box only allows matrices that are 10 rows and 10 columns at most, i.e. a 10×10 matrix. Real images can be 512×512, but are often 256×256 or 128×128, this implies a storage requirement for 262 144, 65 536 and 16 384 pixels, respectively. Since Mathcad stores all points as high precision, complex floating point numbers, 512×512 images require too much storage, but 256×256 and 128×128 images can be handled with ease. Since this cannot be achieved by the dialog box, Mathcad has to be 'tricked' into accepting an image of this size. Figure **1.15** shows the image of a human face captured by a camera. This image has been stored in Windows bitmap (.BMP) format. This can be read into a Mathcad worksheet using the READBMP command (yes, capitals please! – Mathcad can't handle readbmp), and is assigned to a variable. It is inadvisable to attempt to display this using the Mathcad surface plot facility as it can be slow for images, and require a lot of memory.

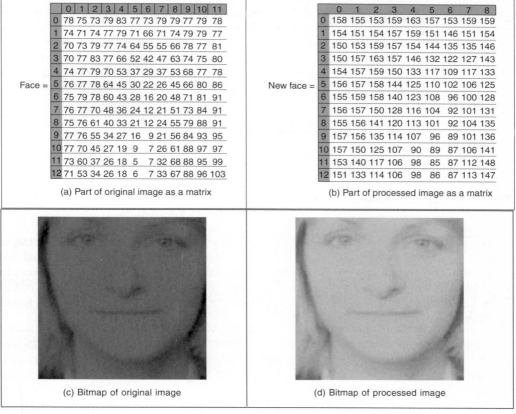

Figure 1.15 Processing an image of a face

It is best to view an image using Mathcad's picture facility or to store it using the WRITEBMP command, and then look at it using a bitmap viewer.

So if we are to make the image of the face brighter, by addition, by the routine in Code **1.3**, via the code in Code **1.4**, the result is as shown in Figure **1.15**. The matrix listings in Figure **1.15**(a) and Figure **1.15**(b) show that 80 has been added to each point (these only show the top left-hand section of the image where the bright points relate to the blonde hair, the dark points are the gap between the hair and the face). The effect will be to make each point appear brighter as seen by comparison of the (darker) original image, Figure **1.15**(c), with the (brighter) result of addition, Figure **1.15**(d). In Chapter 3 we will investigate techniques which can be used to manipulate the image brightness to show the face in a much better way. For the moment though, we are just seeing how Mathcad can be used, in a simple way, to process pictures.

```
face    :=READBMP(rhdark)
newface :=add_value(face,80)
WRITEBMP(rhligh) :=newface
```

Code 1.4   Processing an image

Naturally, Mathcad was used to generate the image used to demonstrate the *Mach band* effect; the code is given in Code **1.5**. First, an image is defined by copying the face image (from Code **1.4**) to an image labelled mach. Then, the floor function (which returns the nearest integer less than its argument) is used to create the bands, scaled by an amount appropriate to introduce sufficient contrast (the division by 21.5 gives six bands in the image of Figure **1.4**(a)). The cross-section and the perceived cross-section of the image were both generated by Mathcad's X-Y plot facility, using appropriate code for the perceived cross-section.

```
mach := face
mach := | for x∈0..cols(mach)-1
        |     for y∈0..rows(mach)-1
        |
        |         machy,x←40·floor( x / 21.5 )
        |
        | mach
```

Code 1.5   Creating the Image of Figure 1.4(a)

The translation of the Mathcad code into application can be rather prolix when compared with the Mathcad version by the necessity to include low-level functions. Since these can obscure the basic image processing functionality, Mathcad is used throughout this book to show you how the techniques work. The translation to application code is perhaps easier via Matlab (it offers direct compilation of the code). There is also an electronic version of this book which is a collection of worksheets to help you learn the subject; and an example Mathcad worksheet is given in Appendix 3 (Section 9.3). You can download these worksheets from this book's website (http://www.ecs.soton.ac.uk/~msn/book/) and there is a link to Mathcad Explorer there too. You can then use the algorithms as a basis for developing your own application code. This provides a good way to verify that your code actually works: you can compare the results of your final application code with those of the original mathematical description. If your final application code and the Mathcad implementation are both correct, the results should be the same. Naturally, your application code will be much faster than in Mathcad, and will benefit from the GUI you've developed.

1.5.3 Hello Matlab!

Matlab is rather different from Mathcad. It is not a WYSIWYG system but instead it is more screen-based. It was originally developed for matrix functions, hence the 'Mat' in the name. Like Mathcad, it offers a set of mathematical tools and visualisation capabilities in a manner arranged to be very similar to conventional computer programs. In some users' views, a WYSIWYG system like Mathcad is easier to start with but there are a number of advantages to Matlab, not least the potential speed advantage in computation and the facility for debugging, together with a considerable amount of established support. Again, there is an image processing toolkit supporting Matlab, but it is rather limited compared with the range of techniques exposed in this text. The current version is Matlab 5.3.1, but these systems evolve fast!

Essentially, Matlab is the set of instructions that process the data stored in a workspace, which can be extended by user-written commands. The workspace stores the different lists of data and these data can be stored in a MAT file; the user-written commands are functions that are stored in M-files (files with extension .M). The procedure operates by instructions at the command line to process the workspace data using either one of Matlab's own commands, or using your own commands. The results can be visualised as graphs, surfaces or as images, as in Mathcad.

The system runs on Unix/Linux or Windows and on Macintosh systems. A student version is available at low cost. There is no viewer available for Matlab, you have to have access to a system for which it is installed. As the system is not based around worksheets, we shall use a script which is the simplest type of M-file, as illustrated in Code **1.6**. To start the Matlab system, type MATLAB at the command line. At the Matlab prompt (>>) type chapter1 to load and run the script (given that the file chapter1.m is saved in the directory you are working in). Here, we can see that there are no text boxes and so comments are preceded by a %. The first command is one that allocates data to our variable pic. There is a more sophisticated way to input this in the Matlab system, but that is not available here. The points are addressed in row-column format and the origin is at co-ordinates $y = 1$ and $x = 1$. So we then access these point $pic_{3,3}$ as the third column of the third row and $pic_{4,3}$ is the point in the third column of the fourth row. Having set the display facility to black and white, we can view the array pic as a surface. When the surface, illustrated in Figure **1.16**(a), is plotted, then Matlab has been made to pause until you press Return before moving on. Here, when you press Return, you will next see the image of the array, Figure **1.16**(b).

We can use Matlab's own command to interrogate the data: these commands find use in the M-files that store subroutines. An example routine is called after this. This subroutine is stored in a file called invert.m and is a function that inverts brightness by subtracting the value of each point from the array's maximum value. The code is illustrated in Code **1.7**. Note that this code uses for loops which are best avoided to improve speed, using Matlab's vectorised operations (as in Mathcad), but are used here to make the implementations clearer to those with a C background. The whole procedure can actually be implemented by the command inverted=max(max(pic))-pic. In fact, one of Matlab's assets is

```
%Chapter 1 Introduction (Hello Matlab) CHAPTER1.M
%Written by: Mark S. Nixon

disp('Welcome to the Chapter1 script')
disp('This worksheet is the companion to Chapter 1 and is an
introduction.')
disp('It is the source of Section 1.4.3 Hello Matlab.')
disp('The worksheet follows the text directly and allows you to
process basic images.')

disp('Let us define a matrix, a synthetic computer image called
pic.')

pic =[1    2   3    4    1    1    2   1;
      2    2   3    2    1    2    2   1;
      3    1  38   39   37   36    3   1;
      4    1  45   44   41   42    2   1;
      1    2  43   44   40   39    1   3;
      2    1  39   41   42   40    2   1;
      1    2   1    2    2    3    1   1;
      1    2   1    3    1    1    4   2]

%Pixels are addressed in row-column format.
%Using x for the horizontal axis(a column count), and y for the
vertical axis (a row
%count) then picture points are addressed as pic(y,x). The origin
is at co-ordinates
%(1,1), so the point pic(3,3) is on the third row and third column;
the point pic(4,3)
%is on the fourth row, at the third column. Let's print them:
disp ('The element pic(3,3)is')
pic(3,3)
disp('The element pic(4,3)is')
pic(4,3)

%We'll set the output display to black and white
colormap(gray);
%We can view the matrix as a surface plot
disp ('We shall now view it as a surface plot (play with the
controls to see it in relief)')
disp('When you are ready to move on, press RETURN')
surface(pic);
%Let's hold a while so we can view it
pause;
%Or view it as an image
disp ('We shall now view the array as an image')
disp('When you are ready to move on, press RETURN)
imagesc(pic);
%Let's hold a while so we can view it
pause;

%Let's look at the array's dimensions
```

```
disp('The dimensions of the array are')
size(pic)

%now let's invoke a routine that inverts the image
inverted_pic=invert(pic);
%Let's print it out to check it
disp('When we invert it by subtracting each point from the
maximum, we get')
inverted_pic
%And view it
disp('And when viewed as an image, we see')
disp('When you are ready to move on, press RETURN')
imagesc(inverted_pic);
%Let's hold a while so we can view it pause;
disp('We shall now read in a bitmap image, and view it')
disp('When you are ready to move on, press RETURN')
face=imread('rhdark.bmp','bmp');
imagesc(face);
pause;
%Change from unsigned integer(unit8) to double precision so we can
process it
face=double(face);
disp('Now we shall invert it, and view the inverted image')
inverted_face=invert(face);
imagesc(inverted_face);
disp('So we now know how to process images in Matlab. We shall be
using this later!')
```

Code 1.6 Matlab script for chapter 1

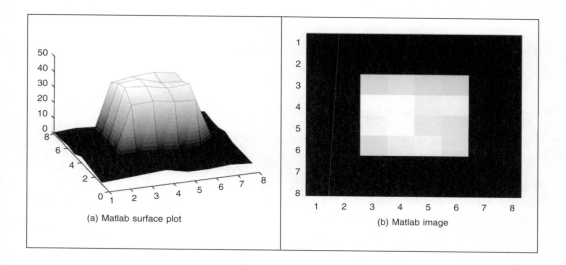

(a) Matlab surface plot

(b) Matlab image

Figure 1.16 Matlab image visualisation

a 'profiler' which allows you to determine exactly how much time is spent on different parts of your programs. Naturally, there is facility for importing graphics files, which is actually rather more extensive (i.e. it accepts a wider range of file formats) than available in Mathcad. When images are used, this reveals that unlike Mathcad which stores all variables as full precision real numbers, Matlab has a range of datatypes. We must move from the unsigned integer datatype, used for images, to the double precision datatype to allow processing as a set of real numbers. In these ways Matlab can, and will be used to process images throughout this book. As with the Mathcad worksheets, there are Matlab scripts available at the website for on-line tutorial support of the material in this book; an abbreviated example worksheet is given in Appendix 4 (Section 9.4).

```
function inverted=invert(image)
%Subtract image point brightness from maximum
%
% Usage: [new image]=invert(image)
%
% Parameters: image-array of points
%
% Author: Mark S. Nixon
%get dimensions
[rows,cols]=size(image);

%find the maximum
maxi=max(max(image));

%subtract image points from maximum
for x=1:cols %address all columns
  for y=1:rows %address all rows
    inverted(y,x)=maxi-image(y,x);
  end
end
```

Code 1.7 Matlab function (invert.m) to invert an image

1.6 Associated literature

1.6.1 Journals and magazines

As in any academic subject, there are many sources of literature. The *professional magazines* include those that are more systems oriented, like *Image Processing* and *Advanced Imaging*. These provide more general articles, and are often a good source of information about new computer vision products. For example, *Image Processing* often surveys available equipment, such as cameras and monitors, and provides a tabulated listing of those available, including some of the factors by which you might choose to purchase them. *Advanced Imaging* is another professional journal that can cover material of commercial and academic interest.

There is a wide selection of *research journals* – probably more than you can find in your nearest library unless it is particularly well stocked. These journals have different merits: some are targeted at short papers only, whereas some have short and long papers; some are more dedicated to the development of new theory whereas others are more pragmatic and focus more on practical, working, image processing systems. But it is rather naive to classify journals in this way, since all journals welcome good research, with new ideas, which has been demonstrated to satisfy promising objectives.

The main research journals include: *IEEE Transactions on*: *Pattern Analysis and Machine Intelligence* (in later references this will be abbreviated to *IEEE Trans. on PAMI*); *Image Processing (IP); Systems, Man and Cybernetics (SMC)*; and *Medical Imaging* (there are many more IEEE transactions, some of which sometimes publish papers of interest in image processing and computer vision). The *IEEE Transactions* are usually found in (university) libraries since they are available at comparatively low cost. *Computer Vision and Image Understanding* and *Graphical Models and Image Processing* arose from the splitting of one of the subject's earlier journals, *Computer Vision, Graphics and Image Processing (CVGIP)*, into two parts. Do not confuse *Pattern Recognition (Pattern Recog.)* with *Pattern Recognition Letters (Pattern Recog. Lett.)*, published under the aegis of the Pattern Recognition Society and the International Association of Pattern Recognition, respectively, since the latter contains shorter papers only. The *International Journal of Computer Vision* is a more recent journal whereas *Image and Vision Computing* was established in the early 1980s. Finally, do not miss out on the *IEE Proceedings – Vision, Image and Signal Processing* and *IEE Proceedings – Digital Techniques*.

Some of the journals are now on-line but usually to subscribers only, in the UK through Ingenta through BIDS (you need an account at Bath Information and Data Services at http://www.bids.ac.uk/). Academic Press appear to be mostly on-line now, including *Computer Vision and Image Understanding*, *Graphical Models and Image Processing* and *Real-Time Imaging* at http://www.apnet.com/www/journal/iv.htm, http://www.apnet.com/www/journal/ip.htm, and http://www.academicpress.com/rti respectively.

1.6.2 Textbooks

There are many textbooks in this area. Increasingly, there are web versions, or web support, as summarised in Table **1.4**. This text aims to start at the foundation of computer vision, and ends very close to a research level. Its content specifically addresses techniques for image analysis, considering shape analysis in particular. Mathcad and Matlab are used as a vehicle to demonstrate implementation, which is rarely considered in other texts. But there are other texts, and these can help you to develop your interest in other areas of computer vision.

This section includes only a selection of some of the texts. There are more than these, some of which will be referred to in later chapters; each offers a particular view or insight into computer vision and image processing. The *introductory texts* include: Fairhurst, M. C.: *Computer Vision for Robotic Systems* (Fairhurst, 1988); Low, A.: *Introductory Computer Vision and Image Processing* (Low, 1991); Teuber, J.: *Digital Image Processing* (Teuber, 1993); and Baxes, G. A.: *Digital Image Processing, Principles and Applications* (Baxes, (1994) which includes software and good coverage of image processing hardware.

Some of the *main textbooks* include: Marr, D.: *Vision* (Marr, 1982) which concerns vision and visual perception (as previously mentioned); Jain, A. K.: *Fundamentals of Computer Vision* (Jain, 1989) which is stacked with theory and technique, but omits implementation and some image analysis; Sonka, M., Hllavac, V. and Boyle, R. *Image Processing, Analysis and Computer Vision* (Sonka, 1998) offers more modern coverage of computer vision including many more recent techniques, together with pseudocode

Table 1.4 Web textbooks and homepages

This book's **homepage**	Southampton U	`http://www.ecs.soton.ac.uk/~msn/book/`
CVOnline	Edinburgh U	`http://www.dai.ed.ac.uk/CVonline/`
Ad Oculos	Imaging Source	`http://www.theimagingsource.com/prod/link/adoculos.htm`
Image Processing Fundamentals	Delft University	`http://www.ph.tn.tudelft.nl/Courses/FIP/noframes/fip.html`
World of Mathematics	Wolfram Research	`http://mathworld.wolfram.com`
Numerical Recipes	Cambridge University Press	`http://www.nr.com/`
The Joy of Visual Perception	York U	`http://www.yorku.ca/research/vision/eye/thejoy.htm`
Machine Vision **homepage**	Penn State	`http://vision.cse.psu.edu/`
Active Contours **homepage**	Oxford U	`http://www.robots.ox.ac.uk/~contours/`

implementation but omitting some image processing theory; Jain, R. C., Kasturi, R. and Schunk, B. G.: *Machine Vision* (Jain, 1995) offers concise and modern coverage of 3D and motion (there is an on-line website at `http://vision.cse.psu.edu/` with code and images, together with corrections); Gonzalez, R. C. and Wintz, P.: *Digital Image Processing* (Gonzalez, 1987) has more tutorial element than many of the basically theoretical texts; Rosenfeld, A. and Kak, A. C.: *Digital Picture Processing* (Rosenfeld and Kak, 1982) is rather dated now, but is a well-proven text for much of the basic material; and Pratt, W. K.: *Digital Image Processing* (Pratt, 1992) which was originally one of the earliest books on image processing and, like Rosenfeld and Kak, is a well-proven text for much of the basic material, particularly image transforms. Despite its name, the recent text called *Active Contours* (Blake, 1998) concentrates rather more on models of motion and deformation and probabalistic treatment of shape and motion, than on the active contours which we shall find here. As such it is a more research text, reviewing many of the advanced techniques to describe shapes and their motion. A recent text in this field, *Image Processing – The Fundamentals* (Petrou, 1999) surveys the subject (as its title implies) from an image processing viewpoint covering not only image transforms, but also restoration and enhancement before edge detection. The latter of these is most appropriate for one of the major contributors to that subject. Also, Kasturi, R. and Jain, R. C. (eds): *Computer Vision: Principles* (Kasturi, 1991a) and *Computer Vision: Advances and Applications* (Kasturi, 1991b) presents a collection of seminal papers in computer vision, many of which are cited in their original form (rather than in this volume) in later chapters. There are other interesting edited collections (Chellappa, 1992), one edition (Bowyer, 1996) honours Azriel Rosenfeld's many contributions.

Books which include a *software implementation* include: Lindley, C. A.: *Practical Image Processing in C* (Lindley, 1991) and Pitas, I.: *Digital Image Processing Algorithms* (Pitas, 1993) which both cover basic image processing and computer vision algorithms.

Parker, J. R.: *Practical Computer Vision Using C* (Parker, 1994) offers an excellent description and implementation of low-level image processing tasks within a well-developed framework, but again does not extend to some of the more recent and higher level processes in computer vision and includes little theory though there is more in his later text *Image Processing and Computer Vision* (Parker, 1996). A recent text *Computer Vision and Image Processing* (Umbaugh, 1998) takes an applications-oriented approach to computer vision and image processing, offering a variety of techniques in an engineering format, together with a working package with a GUI. One recent text concentrates on Java only, *Image Processing in Java* (Lyon, 1999), and concentrates more on image processing systems implementation than on feature extraction (giving basic methods only). As already mentioned, the newest textbook (Efford, 2000) offers Java implementation, though it omits much of the mathematical detail making it a lighter (more enjoyable?) read. Masters, T.: *Signal and Image Processing with Neural Networks – A C++ Sourcebook* (Masters, 1994) offers good guidance in combining image processing technique with neural networks and gives code for basic image processing technique, such as frequency domain transformation.

There are now a number of books on the *web* as given in Table **1.4**. This book's homepage has a link to these web-based texts, and will be kept as up to date as possible. The *CVOnline* site describes a great deal of technique, whereas the *Ad Oculos* page describes the book that supports the software. *Image Processing Fundamentals* is a textbook for image processing. The *World of Mathematics* comes from Wolfram research (the distributors of Mathematica) and gives an excellent web-based reference for mathematics. *Numerical Recipes* is one of the best established texts in signal processing. It is beautifully written, with examples and implementation and is on the web too. The *Joy of Perception* gives you web access to the processes involved in human vision (and the worst title?).

Other textbooks include: Russ, J. C.: *The Image Processing Handbook* (Russ, 1995) which contains much basic technique with excellent visual support, but without any supporting theory, and has many practical details concerning image processing systems; Davies, E. R.: *Machine Vision: Theory, Algorithms and Practicalities* (Davies, 1994) which is targeted primarily at (industrial) machine vision systems but covers much basic technique, with pseudocode to describe their implementation; and Awcock, G. J. and Thomas, R.: *Applied Image Processing* (Awcock, 1995) which again has much practical detail concerning image processing systems and implementation.

1.6.3 The web

The web entries continue to proliferate. A list of web pages is given in Table **1.5** and these give you a starting point from which to build up your own list of favourite bookmarks. All these links, and more are available at this book's homepage `http://www.ecs.soton.ac.uk/~msn/book/)`. This will be checked regularly and kept up to date. The web entries in Table **1.5** start with the Carnegie Mellon homepage (called the Computer Vision Homepage). The Computer Vision Online CVOnline homepage has been brought to us by Bob Fisher from the University of Edinburgh. There's a host of material there, including its description. Their group also proves the Hypermedia Image Processing Website and in their words: 'HIPR2 is a free www-based set of tutorial materials for the 50 most commonly used image processing operators. It contains tutorial text, sample results and Java demonstrations of individual operators and collections.' It covers a lot of basic material and shows you the results of various processing options. A big list of active groups can be

Table 1.5 Computer vision and image processing websites

Name/Scope	Host	Address
Vision and its Applications		
The Computer Vision Homepage	Carnegie Mellon U	`http://www.cs.cmu.edu/afs/cs/project/cil/ftp/html/vision.html`
Computer Vision Online	Edinburgh U	`http://www.dai.ed.ac.uk/CVonline/`
Hypermedia Image Processing Reference 2	Edinburgh U	`http://www.dai.ed.ac.uk/HIPR2`
Image Processing Archive	PEIPA	`http://peipa.essex.ac.uk/`
Pattern Recognition	Delft U	`http://www.ph.tn.tudelft.nl/PRInfo.html`
3D Reconstruction	Stanford U	`http://biocomp.stanford.edu/3dreconstruction/index.html`
Medical Imaging	Leeds U	`http://agora.leeds.ac.uk/comir/resources/links.html`
Face Recognition	Groningen U	`http://www.cs.rug.nl/~peterkr/FACE/face.html`
General		
Signal Processing Information Base	Rice	`http://spib.rice.edu/spib.html`
Image formats and reading software	Edinburgh U	`http://www.dcs.ed.ac.uk/%7Emxr/gfx/`
Computer Graphics	U of Southern California	`http://mambo.ucsc.edu/psl/cg.html`
Neural Networks	Southampton U	`http://www.isis.ecs.soton.ac.uk/resources/nninfo/`
Human and Animal Vision	VisionScience	`http://www.visionscience.com/VisionScience.html`
Newsgroups		
Computer Vision Image Processing	Vision List	`comp.ai.vision sci.image.processing`

found at the Computer Vision homepage and searchers like Google or Altavista can be a boon when trawling the web. If your university has access to the web-based indexes of published papers, the ISI index gives you journal papers (and allows for citation search), but unfortunately including medicine and science (where you can get papers with 30+ authors). Alternatively, Compendex and INSPEC include papers more related to engineering, together with papers in conferences, and hence vision (INSPEC in particular), but without the ability to search citations. Citeseer is increasingly useful. Two newsgroups can be found at the addresses given in Table **1.5** to give you what is perhaps the most up-to-date information.

1.7 References

Armstrong, T., *Colour Perception – A Practical Approach to Colour Theory*, Tarquin Publications, Diss UK, 1991

Awcock, G. J. and Thomas, R., *Applied Image Processing*, Macmillan Press Ltd, Basingstoke UK, 1995

Baxes, G. A., *Digital Image Processing, Principles and Applications*, Wiley & Sons Inc., NY USA, 1994

Blake, A. and Isard, M., *Active Contours*, Springer-Verlag London Limited, London UK, 1998

Bowyer, K. and Ahuja, N. (eds), *Advances in Image Understanding, A Festschrift for Azriel Rosenfeld*, IEEE Computer Society Press, Los Alamitos, CA USA, 1996

Bruce, V. and Green, P., *Visual Perception: Physiology, Psychology and Ecology*, 2nd Edition, Lawrence Erlbaum Associates, Hove UK, 1990

Chellappa, R., *Digital Image Processing*, 2nd Edition, IEEE Computer Society Press, Los Alamitos, CA USA, 1992

Cornsweet, T. N., *Visual Perception*, Academic Press Inc., NY USA, 1970

Davies, E. R., *Machine Vision: Theory, Algorithms and Practicalities*, Academic Press, London UK, 1990

Efford, N., *Digital Image Processing – a practical introduction using JAVA*, Pearson Education Ltd, Harlow, Essex UK, 2000

Fairhurst, M. C., *Computer Vision for Robotic Systems*, Prentice Hall International (UK) Ltd, Hemel Hempstead UK, 1988

Fossum, E. R., CMOS Image Sensors: Electronic Camera-On-A-Chip, *IEEE Trans. Electron Devices*, **44**(10), pp. 1689–1698, 1997

Gonzalez, R. C. and Wintz, P., *Digital Image Processing*, 2nd Edition, Addison Wesley Publishing Co. Inc., Reading MA USA, 1987

Jain, A. K., *Fundamentals of Computer Vision*, Prentice Hall International (UK) Ltd, Hemel Hempstead UK, 1989

Jain, R. C., Kasturi, R. and Schunk, B. G., *Machine Vision*, McGraw-Hill Book Co., Singapore, 1995

Kaiser, P. F., The Joy of Visual Perception, http://www.yorku.ca/eye/thejoy.htm (as at 20/01/2000)

Kasturi, R. and Jain, R. C., *Computer Vision: Principles*, IEEE Computer Society Press, Los Alamitos, CA USA, 1991

Kasturi, R. and Jain, R. C., *Computer Vision: Advances and Applications*, IEEE Computer Society Press, Los Alamitos, CA USA, 1991

Lindley, C. A., *Practical Image Processing in C*, Wiley & Sons Inc., NY USA, 1991

Lenk, J. D., *Lenk's Video Handbook – Operation and Troubleshooting*, McGraw-Hill Inc., NY USA, 1991

Low, A., *Introductory Computer Vision and Image Processing*, McGraw-Hill Book Co. (UK) Ltd, Maidenhead UK, 1991

Lyon, D. A., *Image Processing in Java*, Prentice Hall, 1999

Maple V, Waterloo Maple Software Inc., Ontario Canada

Marr, D., *Vision*, W. H. Freeman and Co., NY USA, 1982

Masters, T., *Signal and Image Processing with Neural Networks – A C++ Sourcebook*, Wiley and Sons Inc., NY USA, 1994

MATLAB, The MathWorks Inc., 24 Prime Way Park, Natick, MA USA

Mathcad Plus 6.0, Mathsoft Inc., 101 Main St, Cambridge, MA USA

Mathematica, Wolfram Research Inc., 100 Trade Center Drive, Champaign, IL USA

Overington, I., *Computer Vision – A Unified, Biologically-Inspired Approach*, Elsevier Science Press, Holland, 1992

Parker, J. R., *Practical Computer Vision using C*, Wiley & Sons Inc., NY USA, 1994

Parker, J. R., *Algorithms for Image Processing and Computer Vision*, Wiley & Sons Inc., NY USA, 1996

Petrou, M. and Bosdogianni, P., *Image Processing – The Fundamentals*, John Wiley & Sons Ltd, London UK, 1999

Pitas, I., *Digital Image Processing Algorithms*, Prentice-Hall International (UK) Ltd, Hemel Hempstead UK, 1993

Pratt, W. K., *Digital Image Processing*, Wiley, 1992

Ratliff, F., *Mach Bands: Quantitative Studies on Neural Networks in the Retina*, Holden-Day Inc., SF USA, 1965

Rosenfeld, A. and Kak, A. C., *Digital Picture Processing*, 2nd Edition, Vols 1 and 2, Academic Press Inc., Orlando, FL USA, 1982

Russ, J. C., *The Image Processing Handbook*, 2nd Edition, CRC Press (IEEE Press), Boca Raton, FL USA, 1995

Sonka, M., Hllavac, V. and Boyle, R., *Image Processing, Analysis and Computer Vision*, 2nd Edition, Chapman Hall, London UK, 1998

Teuber, J., *Digital Image Processing*, Prentice Hall International (UK) Ltd, Hemel Hempstead UK, 1993

Umbaugh, S. E., *Computer Vision and Image Processing*, Prentice-Hall International (UK) Ltd, Hemel Hempstead UK, 1998

2

Images, sampling and frequency domain processing

2.1 Overview

In this chapter, we shall look at the basic theory which underlies image formation and processing. We shall start by investigating what makes up a picture and then look at the consequences of having a different number of points in the image. We shall also look at images in a different representation, known as the frequency domain. In this, as the name implies, we consider an image as a collection of frequency components. We can actually operate on images in the frequency domain and we shall also consider different transformation processes. These allow us different insights into images and image processing which will be used in later chapters not only as a means to develop techniques, but also to give faster (computer) processing.

Table 2.1 Overview of Chapter 2

Main topic	Sub topics	Main points
Images	Effects of differing *numbers* of points and of number *range* for those points.	Greyscale, colour, resolution, dynamic range, storage.
Fourier transform theory	What is meant by the *frequency domain*, how it applies to *discrete* (sampled) images, how it allows us to *interpret* images and the *sampling resolution* (number of points).	Continuous Fourier transform and properties, sampling criterion, discrete Fourier transform and properties, image transformation, transform duals.
Consequences of transform approach	Basic *properties* of Fourier transforms, *other transforms*, frequency domain *operations*.	Translation (shift), rotation and scaling. Walsh, Hartley, discrete cosine and wavelet transforms. Filtering and other operations.

2.2 Image formation

A computer image is a matrix (a two-dimensional array) of *pixels*. The value of each pixel is proportional to the *brightness* of the corresponding point in the scene; its value is often derived from the output of an A/D converter. The matrix of pixels, the image, is usually square and we shall describe an image as $N \times N$ m-bit pixels where N is the number of points along the axes and m controls the number of brightness values. Using m bits gives a range of 2^m values, ranging from 0 to $2^m - 1$. If m is 8 this gives brightness levels ranging between 0 and 255, which are usually displayed as black and white, respectively, with shades of grey in between, as they are for the *greyscale image* of a walking man in Figure **2.1**(a). Smaller values of m give fewer available levels reducing the available contrast in an image.

The ideal value of m is actually related to the signal to noise ratio (bandwidth) of the camera. This is stated as approximately 45 dB and since there are 6 dB per bit, then 8 bits will cover the available range. Choosing 8-bit pixels has further advantages in that it is very convenient to store pixel values as *bytes*, and 8-bit A/D converters are cheaper than those with a higher resolution. For these reasons images are nearly always stored as 8-bit bytes, though some applications use a different range. The relative influence of the 8 bits is shown in the image of the walking subject in Figure **2.1**. Here, the least significant bit, bit 0 (Figure **2.1**(b)), carries the least information (it changes most rapidly). As the order of the bits increases, they change less rapidly and carry more information. The most information is carried by the most significant bit, bit 7 (Figure **2.1**(i)). Clearly, the fact that there is a walker in the original image can be recognised much better from the high order bits, much more reliably than it can from the other bits (notice too the odd effects in the bits which would appear to come from lighting at the top left corner).

Colour images follow a similar storage strategy to specify pixels' intensities. However, instead of using just one image plane, colour images are represented by three intensity components. These components generally correspond to red, green, and blue (the RGB model) although there are other colour schemes. For example, the CMYK colour model is defined by the components cyan, magenta, yellow and black. In any colour mode, the pixel's colour can be specified in two main ways. First, you can associate an integer value, with each pixel, that can be used as an index to a table that stores the intensity of each colour component. The index is used to recover the actual colour from the table when the pixel is going to be displayed, or processed. In this scheme, the table is known as the image's *palette* and the display is said to be performed by *colour mapping*. The main reason for using this colour representation is to reduce memory requirements. That is, we only store a single image plane (i.e. the indices) and the palette. This is less than storing the red, green and blue components separately and so makes the hardware cheaper and it can have other advantages, for example when the image is transmitted. The main disadvantage is that the quality of the image is reduced since only a reduced collection of colours is actually used. An alternative to represent colour is to use several image planes to store the colour components of each pixel. This scheme is known as *true colour* and it represents an image more accurately, essentially by considering more colours. The most common format uses 8 bits for each of the three RGB components. These images are known as *24-bit* true colour and they can contain 16 777 216 different colours simultaneously. In spite of requiring significantly more memory, the image quality and the continuing reduction in cost of computer memory make this format a good alternative, even for storing the image frames from a video sequence. Of course, a good compression algorithm is always helpful in these cases, particularly if images need to be transmitted on a network. Here we will consider the processing of grey level images only since they contain enough information to perform feature extraction and image analysis. Should the image be originally colour, we will

(a) Original image   (b) Bit 0 (LSB)   (c) Bit 1

(d) Bit 2   (e) Bit 3   (f) Bit 4

(g) Bit 5   (h) Bit 6   (i) Bit 7 (MSB)

Figure 2.1   Decomposing an image into its bits

consider processing its luminance only, often computed in a standard way. In any case, the amount of memory used is always related to the image size.

Choosing an appropriate value for the image size, N, is far more complicated. We want N to be sufficiently large to resolve the required level of spatial detail in the image. If N is too *small*, the image will be coarsely quantised: lines will appear to be very 'blocky' and some of the detail will be *lost*. Larger values of N give more *detail*, but need more storage space and the images will take longer to process, since there are more pixels. For example, with reference to the image of the walking subject in Figure **2.1**(a), Figure **2.2** shows the effect of taking the image at different resolutions. Figure **2.2**(a) is a 64×64 image, that shows only the broad structure. It is impossible to see any detail in the subject's face. Figure **2.2**(b) is a 128×128 image, which is starting to show more of the detail, but it would be hard to determine the subject's identity. The original image, repeated in Figure **2.2**(c), is a 256×256 image which shows a much greater level of detail, and the subject can be recognised from the image. (These images actually come from a research programme aimed to use computer vision techniques to recognise people by their gait; face recognition would be of little potential for the low resolution image which is often the sort of image that security cameras provide.) If the image was a pure photographic image, some of the much finer detail like the hair would show up in much greater detail. This is because the grains in film are very much smaller than the pixels in a computer image. Note that the images in Figure **2.2** have been scaled to be the same size. As such, the pixels in Figure **2.2**(a) are much larger than in Figure **2.2**(c) which emphasises its blocky structure. The most common choices are for 256×256 or 512×512 images. These require 64 and 256 Kbytes of storage, respectively. If we take a sequence of, say, 20 images for motion analysis, we will need more than 1 Mbyte to store the 20 256×256 images, and more than 5 Mbytes if the images were 512×512. Even though memory continues to become cheaper, this can still impose high cost. But it is not just cost which motivates an investigation of the appropriate image size, the appropriate value for N. The main question is: are there theoretical guidelines for choosing it? The short answer is 'yes'; the long answer is to look at digital signal processing theory.

Figure 2.2   Effects of differing image resolution

The choice of sampling frequency is dictated by the *sampling criterion*. Presenting the sampling criterion requires understanding how we interpret signals in the *frequency domain*.

The way in is to look at the Fourier transform. This is a highly theoretical topic, but do not let that put you off. The Fourier transform has found many uses in image processing and understanding; it might appear to be a complex topic (that's actually a horrible pun!) but it is a very rewarding one to study. The particular concern is the appropriate sampling frequency of (essentially, the value for N), or the rate at which pixel values are taken from, a camera's video signal.

2.3 The Fourier transform

The *Fourier transform* is a way of mapping a signal into its component frequencies. *Frequency* measures in hertz (Hz) the rate of repetition with *time*, measured in seconds (s); time is the *reciprocal* of frequency and vice versa (hertz = 1/second; s = 1/Hz).

Consider a music centre: the sound comes from a CD player (or a tape) and is played on the speakers after it has been processed by the amplifier. On the amplifier, you can change the bass or the treble (or the loudness which is a combination of bass and treble). *Bass* covers the *low* frequency components and *treble* covers the *high* frequency ones. The Fourier transform is a way of mapping the signal from the CD player, which is a signal varying continuously with time, into its frequency components. When we have transformed the signal, we know which frequencies made up the original sound.

So why do we do this? We have not changed the signal, only its representation. We can now visualise it in terms of its frequencies, rather than as a voltage which changes with time. But we can now change the frequencies (because we can see them clearly) and this will change the sound. If, say, there is hiss on the original signal then since hiss is a high frequency component, it will show up as a high frequency component in the Fourier transform. So we can see how to remove it by looking at the Fourier transform. If you have ever used a graphic equaliser, then you have done this before. The graphic equaliser is a way of changing a signal by interpreting its frequency domain representation; you can selectively control the frequency content by changing the positions of the controls of the graphic equaliser. The equation which defines the *Fourier transform*, Fp, of a signal p, is given by a complex integral:

$$Fp(\omega) = \int_{-\infty}^{\infty} p(t)e^{-j\omega t} dt \qquad (2.1)$$

where: $Fp(\omega)$ is the Fourier transform;

ω is the *angular* frequency, $\omega = 2\pi f$ measured in *radians/s* (where the frequency f is the reciprocal of time t, $f = (1/t)$;

j is the complex variable (electronic engineers prefer j to i since they cannot confuse it with the symbol for current – perhaps they don't want to be mistaken for mathematicians!)

$p(t)$ is a *continuous* signal (varying continuously with time); and

$e^{-j\omega t} = \cos(\omega t) - j \sin(\omega t)$ gives the frequency components in $x(t)$.

We can derive the Fourier transform by applying Equation 2.1 to the signal of interest. We can see how it works by constraining our analysis to simple signals. (We can then say that complicated signals are just made up by adding up lots of simple signals.) If we take a pulse which is of amplitude (size) A between when it starts at time $t = -T/2$ and when it ends at $t = T/2$, and is zero elsewhere, the pulse is:

$$p(t) = \begin{vmatrix} A & \text{if } -T/2 \le t \le T/2 \\ 0 & \text{otherwise} \end{vmatrix} \tag{2.2}$$

To obtain the Fourier transform, we substitute for $p(t)$ in Equation 2.1. $p(t) = A$ only for a specified time so we choose the limits on the integral to be the start and end points of our pulse (it is zero elsewhere) and set $p(t) = A$, its value in this time interval. The Fourier transform of this pulse is the result of computing:

$$Fp(\omega) = \int_{-T/2}^{T/2} Ae^{-j\omega t}\, dt \tag{2.3}$$

When we solve this we obtain an expression for $Fp(\omega)$:

$$Fp(\omega) = -\frac{Ae^{-j\omega T/2} - Ae^{j\omega T/2}}{j\omega} \tag{2.4}$$

By simplification, using the relation $\sin(\theta) = (e^{j\theta} - e^{-j\theta})/2j$, then the Fourier transform of the pulse is:

$$Fp(\omega) = \begin{vmatrix} \dfrac{2A}{\omega}\sin\left(\dfrac{\omega T}{2}\right) & \text{if} & \omega \ne 0 \\ AT & \text{if} & \omega = 0 \end{vmatrix} \tag{2.5}$$

This is a version of the *sinc* function, $\text{sinc}(x) = \sin(x)/x$. The original pulse and its transform are illustrated in Figure **2.3**. Equation 2.5 (as plotted in Figure **2.3**(a)) suggests that a pulse is made up of a lot of low frequencies (the main body of the pulse) and a few higher frequencies (which give us the edges of the pulse). (The range of frequencies is symmetrical around zero frequency; negative frequency is a necessary mathematical abstraction.) The plot of the Fourier transform is actually called the *spectrum* of the signal, which can be considered akin with the spectrum of light.

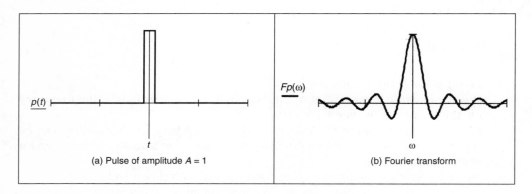

Figure 2.3 A pulse and its Fourier transform

So what actually is this Fourier transform? It tells us what frequencies make up a time domain signal. The magnitude of the transform at a particular frequency is the amount of that frequency in the original signal. If we collect together sinusoidal signals in amounts specified by the Fourier transform, then we should obtain the originally transformed signal. This process is illustrated in Figure **2.4** for the signal and transform illustrated in Figure **2.3**. Note that since the Fourier transform is actually a *complex* number it has real and imaginary parts, and we only plot the *real* part here. A low frequency, that for $\omega = 1$, in Figure **2.4**(a) contributes a large component of the original signal; a higher frequency, that for $\omega = 2$, contributes less as in Figure **2.4**(b). This is because the transform coefficient is less for $\omega = 2$ than it is for $\omega = 1$. There is a very small contribution for $\omega = 3$, Figure **2.4**(c), though there is more for $\omega = 4$, Figure **2.4**(d). This is because there are frequencies for which there is no contribution, where the transform is zero. When these signals are integrated, we achieve a signal that looks similar to our original pulse, Figure **2.4**(e). Here we have only considered frequencies from $\omega = -6$ to $\omega = 6$. If the frequency range in integration

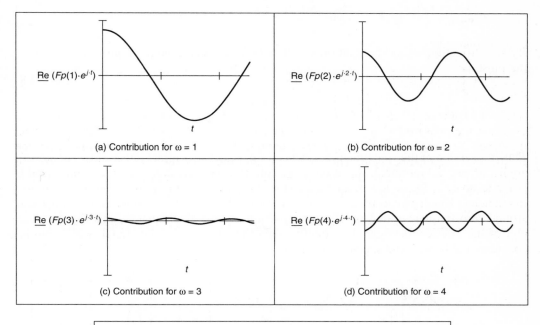

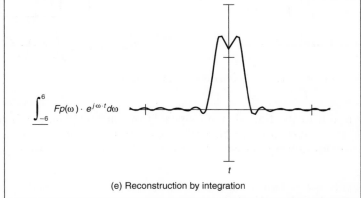

(e) Reconstruction by integration

Figure 2.4 Reconstructing a signal from its transform

was larger, more high frequencies would be included, leading to a more faithful reconstruction of the original pulse.

The result of the Fourier transform is actually a *complex* number. As such, it is usually represented in terms of its *magnitude* (or size, or modulus) and *phase* (or argument). The transform can be represented as:

$$\int_{-\infty}^{\infty} p(t)e^{-j\omega t}\,dt = \mathrm{Re}[\,Fp(\omega)] + j\,\mathrm{Im}[\,Fp(\omega)] \tag{2.6}$$

where $\mathrm{Re}(\omega)$ and $\mathrm{Im}(\omega)$ are the real and imaginary parts of the transform, respectively. The *magnitude* of the transform is then:

$$\left| \int_{-\infty}^{\infty} p(t)e^{-j\omega t}\,dt \right| = \sqrt{\mathrm{Re}\,[\,Fp(\omega)]^2 + \mathrm{Im}[\,Fp(\omega)]^2} \tag{2.7}$$

and the *phase* is:

$$\left\langle \int_{-\infty}^{\infty} p(t)e^{-j\omega t}\,dt = \tan^{-1}\frac{\mathrm{Im}[\,Fp(\omega)]}{\mathrm{Re}[\,Fp(\omega)]} \tag{2.8}$$

where the signs of the real and the imaginary components can be used to determine which quadrant the phase is in (since the phase can vary from 0 to 2π radians). The *magnitude* describes the *amount* of each frequency component, the *phase* describes *timing*, when the frequency components occur. The magnitude and phase of the transform of a pulse are shown in Figure **2.5** where the magnitude returns a positive transform, and the phase is either 0 or 2π radians (consistent with the sine function).

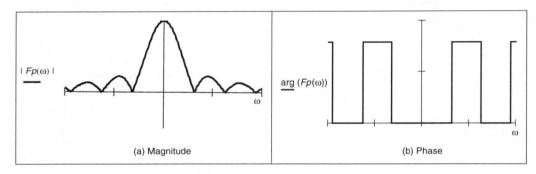

(a) Magnitude   (b) Phase

Figure 2.5   Magnitude and phase of Fourier transform of pulse

In order to return to the time domain signal, from the frequency domain signal, we require the *inverse Fourier transform*. Naturally, this is the process by which we reconstructed the pulse from its transform components. The inverse FT calculates $p(t)$ from $Fp(\omega)$ according to:

$$p(t) = \frac{1}{2\pi}\int_{-\infty}^{\infty} Fp(\omega)e^{j\omega t}\,d\omega \tag{2.9}$$

Together, Equation 2.1 and Equation 2.9 form a relationship known as a *transform pair* that allows us to transform into the frequency domain, and back again. By this process, we can perform operations in the frequency domain or in the time domain, since we have a way of changing between them. One important process is known as *convolution*. The convolution of one signal $p_1(t)$ with another signal $p_2(t)$, where the convolution process denoted by *, is given by the integral

$$p_1(t) * p_2(t) = \int_{-\infty}^{\infty} p_1(\tau) p_2(t - \tau)d\tau \qquad (2.10)$$

This is actually the basis of systems theory where the output of a system is the convolution of a stimulus, say p_1, and a system's *response*, p_2. By inverting the time axis of the system response, to give $p_2(t - \tau)$ we obtain a *memory* function. The convolution process then sums the effect of a stimulus multiplied by the memory function: the current output of the system is the cumulative response to a stimulus. By taking the Fourier transform of Equation 2.10, where the Fourier transformation is denoted by F, the Fourier transform of the convolution of two signals is

$$\begin{aligned} F[p_1(t) * p_2(t)] &= \int_{-\infty}^{\infty} \left\{ \int_{-\infty}^{\infty} p_1(\tau) p_2(t - \tau)d\tau \right\} e^{-j\omega t} dt \\ &= \int_{-\infty}^{\infty} \left\{ \int_{-\infty}^{\infty} p_2(t - \tau) e^{-j\omega t} dt \right\} p_1(\tau)d\tau \end{aligned} \qquad (2.11)$$

Now since $F[p_2(t - \tau)] = e^{-j\omega\tau} Fp_2(\omega)$ (to be considered later in Section 2.6.1), then

$$\begin{aligned} F[p_1(t) * p_2(t)] &= \int_{-\infty}^{\infty} Fp_2(\omega) p_1(\tau) e^{-j\omega\tau} d\tau \\ &= Fp_2(\omega) \int_{-\infty}^{\infty} p_1(\tau) e^{-j\omega\tau} d\tau \\ &= Fp_2(\omega) \times Fp_1(\omega) \end{aligned} \qquad (2.12)$$

As such, the frequency domain dual of convolution is multiplication; the *convolution integral* can be performed by *inverse* Fourier transformation of the *product* of the transforms of the two signals. A frequency domain representation essentially presents signals in a different way but it also provides a different way of processing signals. Later we shall use the duality of convolution to speed up the computation of vision algorithms considerably.

Further, *correlation* is defined to be

$$p_1(t) \otimes p_2(t) = \int_{-\infty}^{\infty} p_1(\tau) p_2(t + \tau)d\tau \qquad (2.13)$$

where $\otimes$ denotes correlation ($\odot$ is another symbol which is used sometimes, but there is not much consensus on this symbol). Correlation gives a measure of the *match* between the two signals $p_2(\omega)$ and $p_1(\omega)$. When $p_2(\omega) = p_1(\omega)$ we are correlating a signal with itself and the process is known as *autocorrelation*. We shall be using correlation later, to *find* things in images.

Before proceeding further, we also need to define the *delta function*, which can be considered to be a function occurring at a particular time interval:

$$\text{delta}(t - \tau) = \begin{vmatrix} 1 & \text{if} \quad t = \tau \\ 0 & \text{otherwise} \end{vmatrix} \tag{2.14}$$

The relationship between a signal's time domain representation and its frequency domain version is also known as a *transform pair*: the transform of a pulse (in the time domain) is a sinc function in the frequency domain. Since the transform is symmetrical, the Fourier transform of a sinc function is a pulse.

There are other Fourier transform pairs, as illustrated in Figure **2.6**. First, Figures **2.6**(a) and (b) show that the Fourier transform of a cosine function is two points in the frequency domain (at the same value for positive and negative frequency) – we expect this since there is only one frequency in the cosine function, the frequency shown by its transform. Figures **2.6**(c) and (d) show that the transform of the *Gaussian function* is another Gaussian function; this illustrates linearity. Figure **2.6**(e) is a single point (the delta function) which has a transform that is an infinite set of frequencies, Figure **2.6**(f), an alternative interpretation is that a delta function contains an equal amount of all frequencies. This can be explained by using Equation 2.5 where if the pulse is of shorter duration (T tends to zero), then the sinc function is wider; as the pulse becomes infinitely thin, the spectrum becomes infinitely flat.

Finally, Figures **2.6**(g) and (h) show that the transform of a set of uniformly spaced delta functions is another set of uniformly spaced delta functions, but with a different spacing. The spacing in the frequency domain is the reciprocal of the spacing in the time domain. By way of a (non-mathematical) explanation, let us consider that the Gaussian function in Figure **2.6**(c) is actually made up by summing a set of closely spaced (and very thin) Gaussian functions. Then, since the spectrum for a delta function is infinite, as the Gaussian function is stretched in the time domain (eventually to be a set of pulses of uniform height) we obtain a set of pulses in the frequency domain, but spaced by the reciprocal of the time domain spacing. This transform pair is actually the basis of sampling theory (which we aim to use to find a criterion which guides us to an appropriate choice for the image size).

2.4 The sampling criterion

The *sampling criterion* specifies the condition for the *correct choice* of sampling frequency. *Sampling* concerns taking *instantaneous* values of a continuous signal, physically these are the outputs of an A/D converter sampling a camera signal. Clearly, the samples are the values of the signal at sampling instants. This is illustrated in Figure **2.7** where Figure **2.7**(a) concerns taking samples at a *high* frequency (the spacing between samples is low), compared with the amount of change seen in the signal of which the samples are taken. Here, the samples are taken sufficiently fast to notice the slight dip in the sampled signal. Figure **2.7**(b) concerns taking samples at a *low* frequency, compared with the rate of change of (the maximum frequency in) the sampled signal. Here, the slight dip in the sampled signal is *not* seen in the samples taken from it.

We can understand the process better in the frequency domain. Let us consider a time-variant signal which has a range of frequencies between $-f_{max}$ and f_{max} as illustrated in Figure **2.9**(b). This range of frequencies is shown by the Fourier transform where the

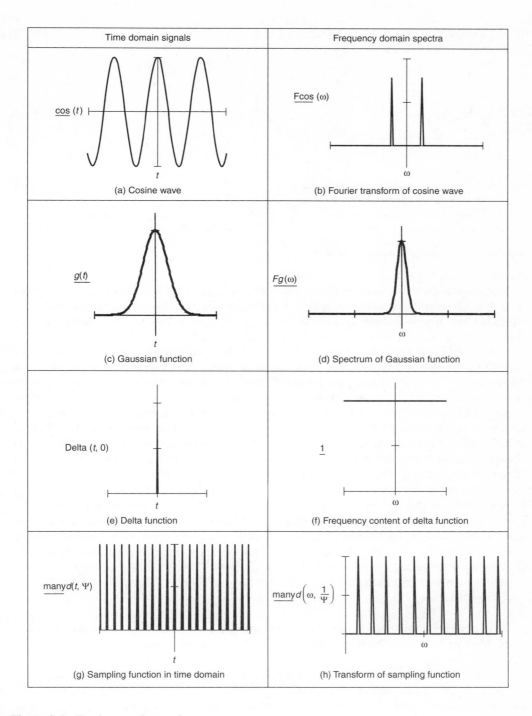

Time domain signals	Frequency domain spectra
$\underline{\cos}\,(t)$	$\underline{F\cos}\,(\omega)$
(a) Cosine wave	(b) Fourier transform of cosine wave
$\underline{g}(t)$	$Fg(\omega)$
(c) Gaussian function	(d) Spectrum of Gaussian function
Delta $(t, 0)$	$\underline{1}$
(e) Delta function	(f) Frequency content of delta function
$\underline{\mathrm{many}}d(t, \Psi)$	$\underline{\mathrm{many}}d\left(\omega, \dfrac{1}{\Psi}\right)$
(g) Sampling function in time domain	(h) Transform of sampling function

Figure 2.6   Fourier transform pairs

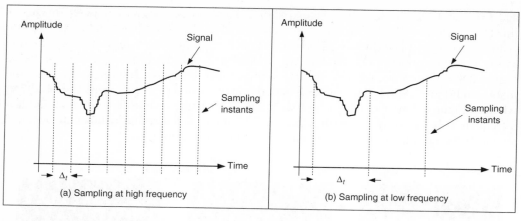

Figure 2.7 Sampling at different frequencies

signal's *spectrum* exists only between these frequencies. This function is sampled every Δ_t s: this is a sampling function of spikes occurring every Δ_t s. The Fourier transform of the sampling function is a series of spikes separated by $f_{sample} = 1/\Delta_t$ Hz. The Fourier pair of this transform was illustrated earlier, Figures **2.6**(g) and (h).

The sampled signal is the result of multiplying the time-variant signal by the sequence of spikes, this gives samples that occur every Δ_t s, and the sampled signal is shown in Figure **2.9**(a). These are the outputs of the A/D converter at sampling instants. The frequency domain analogue of this sampling process is to *convolve* the spectrum of the time-variant signal with the spectrum of the sampling function. Convolving the signals, the convolution process, implies that we take the spectrum of one, *flip* it along the horizontal axis and then *slide* it across the other. Taking the spectrum of the time-variant signal and sliding it over the spectrum of the spikes, results in a spectrum where the spectrum of the original signal is *repeated* every $1/\Delta_t$ Hz, f_{sample} in Figures **2.9**(b–d). If the spacing between samples is Δ_t, the repetitions of the time-variant signal's spectrum are spaced at intervals of $1/\Delta_t$, as in Figure **2.9**(b). If the sample spacing is *small*, then the time-variant signal's spectrum is replicated close together and the spectra *collide*, or interfere, as in Figure **2.9**(d). The spectra just *touch* when the sampling frequency is *twice* the maximum frequency in the signal. If the frequency domain spacing, f_{sample}, is *more* than twice the maximum frequency, f_{max}, the spectra do *not* collide or interfere, as in Figure **2.9**(c). If the sampling frequency exceeds twice the maximum frequency then the spectra cannot collide. This is the Nyquist sampling criterion:

> **In order to reconstruct a signal from its samples, the sampling frequency must be at least twice the highest frequency of the sampled signal.**

If we do not obey Nyquist's sampling theorem the spectra collide. When we inspect the sampled signal, whose spectrum is within $-f_{max}$ to f_{max}, wherein the spectra collided, the corrupt spectrum implies that by virtue of sampling we have *ruined* some of the information. If we were to attempt to reconstruct a signal by inverse Fourier transformation of the sampled signal's spectrum, processing Figure **2.9**(d) would lead to the wrong signal whereas inverse Fourier transformation of the frequencies between $-f_{max}$ and f_{max} in Figures **2.9**(b) and (c) would lead back to the original signal. This can be seen in computer images as illustrated in Figure **2.8** which show a texture image (a chain-link fence) taken at different spatial resolutions. The lines in an original version are replaced by indistinct information in the version sampled at low frequency. Indeed, it would be difficult to imagine what Figure **2.8**(c) represents, whereas it is much more clear in Figures **2.8**(a) and (b). Also, the texture in Figure **2.8**(a) appears to have underlying distortion (the fence appears to be bent) whereas Figures **2.8**(b) and (c) do not show this. This is the result of sampling at too low a frequency. If we sample at high frequency, the interpolated result matches the original signal. If we sample at too low a frequency we get the wrong signal.

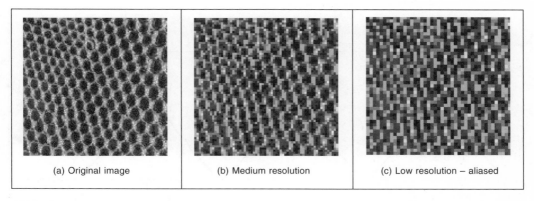

| (a) Original image | (b) Medium resolution | (c) Low resolution – aliased |

Figure 2.8 Aliasing in sampled imagery

Obtaining the wrong signal is called *aliasing*: our interpolated signal is an alias of its proper form. Clearly, we want to *avoid* aliasing, so according to the sampling theorem we must sample at twice the maximum frequency of the signal coming out of the camera. The maximum frequency is defined to be 5.5 MHz so we must sample the camera signal at 11 MHz. (For information, when using a computer to analyse speech we must sample the speech at a minimum frequency of 12 kHz since the maximum speech frequency is 6 kHz.) Given the timing of a video signal, sampling at 11 MHz implies a minimum image resolution of 576×576 pixels. This is unfortunate: 576 is not an integer power of two which has poor implications for storage and processing. Accordingly, since many image processing systems have a maximum resolution of 512×512, they must anticipate aliasing. This is mitigated somewhat by the observations that:

1. globally, the *lower* frequencies carry *more* information whereas *locally* the *higher* frequencies contain more information so the corruption of high frequency information is of less importance; and
2. there is *limited* depth of focus in imaging systems (reducing high frequency content).

But aliasing can, and does, occur and we must remember this when interpreting images. A different form of this argument applies to the images derived from digital cameras. The basic argument that the precision of the estimates of the high order frequency components is dictated by the relationship between the effective sampling frequency (the number of image points) and the imaged structure, naturally still applies.

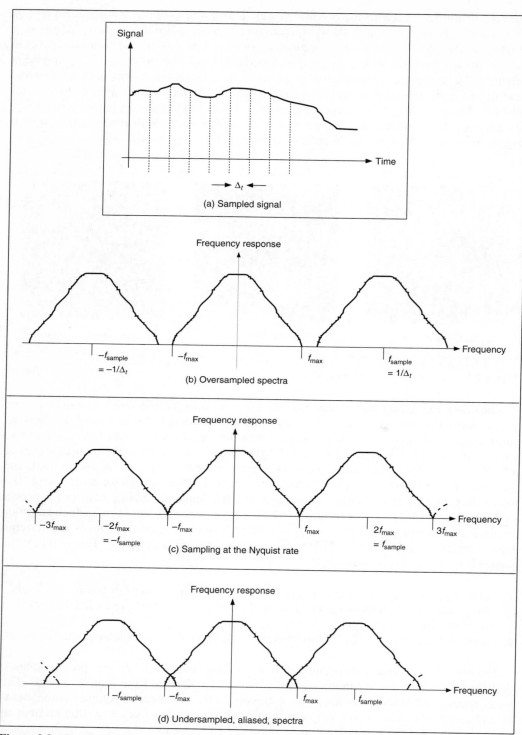

Figure 2.9 Sampled spectra

The effects of sampling can often be seen in films, especially in the rotating wheels of cars, as illustrated in Figure **2.10**. This shows a wheel with a single spoke, for simplicity. The film is a sequence of frames starting on the left. The sequence of frames plotted in Figure **2.10**(a) is for a wheel which rotates by 20° between frames, as illustrated in Figure **2.10**(b). If the wheel is rotating much faster, by 340° between frames, as in Figure **2.10**(c) and Figure **2.10**(d) then the wheel will appear to rotate the other way. If the wheel rotates by 360° between frames, then it will appear to be stationary. In order to perceive the wheel as rotating forwards, then the rotation between frames must be 180° at most. This is consistent with sampling at at least twice the maximum frequency. Our eye can resolve this in films (when watching a film, I bet you haven't thrown a wobbly because the car's going forwards whereas the wheels say it's going the other way) since we know that the direction of the car must be consistent with the motion of its wheels, and we expect to see the wheels appear to go the wrong way, sometimes.

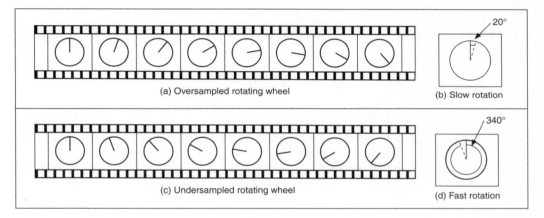

(a) Oversampled rotating wheel   (b) Slow rotation

(c) Undersampled rotating wheel   (d) Fast rotation

Figure 2.10   Correct and incorrect apparent wheel motion

2.5   The discrete Fourier transform (DFT)

2.5.1   One-dimensional transform

Given that image processing concerns sampled data, we require a version of the Fourier transform which handles this. This is known as the *discrete Fourier transform* (DFT). The DFT of a set of N points $\mathbf{p}_x$ (sampled at a frequency which at least equals the Nyquist sampling rate) into sampled frequencies $\mathbf{Fp}_u$ is:

$$\mathbf{Fp}_u = \frac{1}{\sqrt{N}} \sum_{x=0}^{N-1} \mathbf{p}_x e^{-j\left(\frac{2\pi}{N}\right)xu} \tag{2.15}$$

This is a discrete analogue of the continuous Fourier transform: the continuous signal is replaced by a set of samples, the continuous frequencies by sampled ones, and the integral is replaced by a summation. If the DFT is applied to samples of a pulse in a window from sample 0 to sample $N/2 - 1$ (when the pulse ceases), then the equation becomes:

$$\mathbf{Fp}_u = \frac{1}{\sqrt{N}} \sum_{x=0}^{\frac{N}{2}-1} A e^{-j\left(\frac{2\pi}{N}\right)xu}$$ (2.16)

And since the sum of a geometric progression can be evaluated according to:

$$\sum_{k=0}^{n} a_0 r^k = \frac{a_0(1 - r^{n+1})}{1 - r}$$ (2.17)

the discrete Fourier transform of a sampled pulse is given by:

$$\mathbf{Fp}_u = \frac{A}{\sqrt{N}} \left(\frac{1 - e^{-j\left(\frac{2\pi}{N}\right)\left(\frac{N}{2}\right)u}}{1 - e^{-j\left(\frac{2\pi}{N}\right)u}} \right)$$ (2.18)

By rearrangement, we obtain:

$$\mathbf{Fp}_u = \frac{A}{\sqrt{N}} e^{-j\left(\frac{\pi u}{2}\right)\left(1 - \frac{2}{N}\right)} \frac{\sin(\pi u/2)}{\sin(\pi u/N)}$$ (2.19)

The modulus of the transform is:

$$|\mathbf{Fp}_u| = \frac{A}{\sqrt{N}} \left| \frac{\sin(\pi u/2)}{\sin(\pi u/N)} \right|$$ (2.20)

since the magnitude of the exponential function is 1. The original pulse is plotted in Figure **2.11**(a) and the magnitude of the Fourier transform plotted against frequency is given in Figure **2.11**(b).

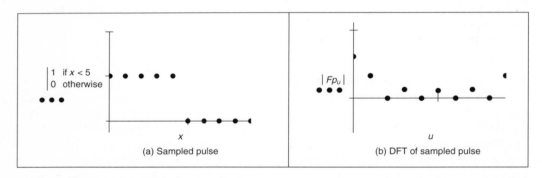

Figure 2.11 Transform pair for sampled pulse

This is clearly comparable with the result of the continuous Fourier transform of a pulse, Figure **2.3**, since the transform involves a similar, sinusoidal, signal. The spectrum is equivalent to a set of sampled frequencies; we can build up the sampled pulse by adding up the frequencies according to the Fourier description. Consider a signal such as that shown in Figure **2.12**(a). This has no explicit analytic definition, as such it does not have a closed Fourier transform; the Fourier transform is generated by direct application of Equation 2.15. The result is a set of samples of frequency, Figure **2.12**(b).

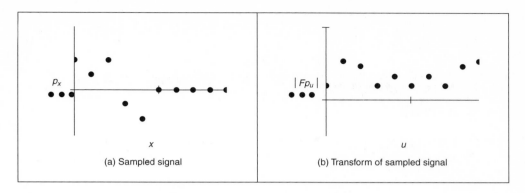

| (a) Sampled signal | (b) Transform of sampled signal |

Figure 2.12   A sampled signal and its discrete transform

The Fourier transform in Figure **2.12**(b) can be used to reconstruct the original signal in Figure **2.12**(a), as illustrated in Figure **2.13**. Essentially, the coefficients of the Fourier transform tell us how much there is of each of a set of sinewaves (at different frequencies), in the original signal. The lowest frequency component $\mathbf{Fp}_0$, for zero frequency, is called the *d.c. component* (it is constant and equivalent to a sinewave with no frequency) and it represents the *average* value of the samples. Adding the contribution of the first coefficient $\mathbf{Fp}_0$, Figure **2.13**(b), to the contribution of the second coefficient $\mathbf{Fp}_1$, Figure **2.13**(c), is shown in Figure **2.13**(d). This shows how addition of the first two frequency components approaches the original sampled pulse. The approximation improves when the contribution due to the fourth component, $\mathbf{Fp}_3$, is included, as shown in Figure **2.13**(e). Finally, adding up all six frequency components gives a close approximation to the original signal, as shown in Figure **2.13**(f).

This process is, of course, the *inverse DFT*. This can be used to reconstruct a sampled signal from its frequency components by:

$$\mathbf{p}_x = \sum_{u=0}^{N-1} \mathbf{Fp}_u e^{j\left(\frac{2\pi}{N}\right)ux} \tag{2.21}$$

Note that there are several assumptions made prior to application of the DFT. The first is that the sampling criterion has been satisfied. The second is that the sampled function replicates to infinity. When generating the transform of a pulse, Fourier theory assumes that the pulse repeats outside the window of interest. (There are window operators that are designed specifically to handle difficulty at the ends of the sampling window.) Finally, the maximum frequency corresponds to half the sampling period. This is consistent with the assumption that the sampling criterion has not been violated, otherwise the high frequency spectral estimates will be corrupt.

2.5.2   Two-dimensional transform

Equation 2.15 gives the DFT of a one-dimensional signal. We need to generate Fourier transforms of images so we need a *two-dimensional discrete Fourier transform*. This is a transform of pixels (sampled picture points) with a two-dimensional spatial location indexed by co-ordinates x and y. This implies that we have two dimensions of frequency, u and v,

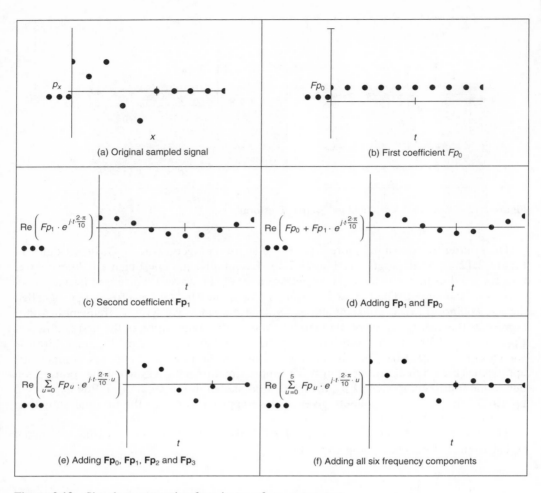

Figure 2.13 Signal reconstruction from its transform components

which are the horizontal and vertical spatial frequencies, respectively. Given an image of a set of vertical lines, the Fourier transform will show only horizontal spatial frequency. The vertical spatial frequencies are zero since there is no vertical variation along the y axis. The two-dimensional Fourier transform evaluates the frequency data, $\mathbf{FP}_{u,v}$, from the $N \times N$ pixels $\mathbf{P}_{x,y}$ as:

$$\mathbf{FP}_{u,v} = \frac{1}{N} \sum_{x=0}^{N-1} \sum_{y=0}^{N-1} \mathbf{P}_{x,y} e^{-j\left(\frac{2\pi}{N}\right)(ux + vy)} \tag{2.22}$$

The Fourier transform of an image can actually be obtained *optically* by transmitting a laser through a photographic slide and forming an image using a lens. The Fourier transform of the image of the slide is formed in the front focal plane of the lens. This is still restricted to transmissive systems whereas reflective formation would widen its application potential considerably (since optical computation is just slightly faster than its digital counterpart). The magnitude of the 2D DFT to an image of vertical bars (Figure **2.14**(a)) is shown in

Figure **2.14**(b). This shows that there are only horizontal spatial frequencies; the image is constant in the vertical axis and there are no vertical spatial frequencies.

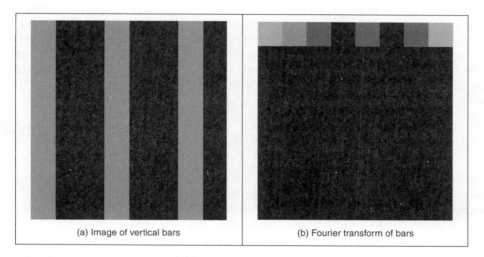

(a) Image of vertical bars   (b) Fourier transform of bars

Figure 2.14   Applying the 2D discrete fourier transform

The *two-dimensional (2D) inverse DFT* transforms from the frequency domain back to the image domain. The 2D inverse DFT is given by:

$$\mathbf{P}_{x,y} = \sum_{u=0}^{N-1} \sum_{v=0}^{N-1} \mathbf{FP}_{u,v} e^{j\left(\frac{2\pi}{N}\right)(ux+vy)} \qquad (2.23)$$

One of the important properties of the FT is *replication* which implies that the transform *repeats* in frequency up to *infinity*, as indicated in Figure **2.9** for 1D signals. To show this for 2D signals, we need to investigate the Fourier transform, originally given by $\mathbf{FP}_{u,v}$, at integer multiples of the number of sampled points $\mathbf{FP}_{u+mM,v+nN}$ (where m and n are integers). The Fourier transform $\mathbf{FP}_{u+mM,v+nN}$ is, by substitution in Equation 2.22:

$$\mathbf{FP}_{u+mN,v+nN} = \frac{1}{N} \sum_{x=0}^{N-1} \sum_{y=0}^{N-1} \mathbf{P}_{x,y} e^{-j\left(\frac{2\pi}{N}\right)((u+mN)x+(v+nN)y)} \qquad (2.24)$$

so,

$$\mathbf{FP}_{u+mN,v+nN} = \frac{1}{N} \sum_{x=0}^{N-1} \sum_{y=0}^{N-1} \mathbf{P}_{x,y} e^{-j\left(\frac{2\pi}{N}\right)(ux+vy)} \times e^{-j2\pi(mx+ny)} \qquad (2.25)$$

and since $e^{-j2\pi(mx+ny)} = 1$ (since the term in brackets is always an integer and then the exponent is always an integer multiple of 2π) then

$$\mathbf{FP}_{u+mN,\ v+nN} = \mathbf{FP}_{u,v} \qquad (2.26)$$

which shows that the replication property does hold for the Fourier transform. However, Equation 2.22 and Equation 2.23 are very slow for large image sizes. They are usually implemented by using the *Fast Fourier Transform* (FFT) which is a splendid rearrangement of the Fourier transform's computation which improves speed dramatically. The FFT algorithm is beyond the scope of this text but is also a rewarding topic of study (particularly for computer scientists or software engineers). The FFT can only be applied to square images whose size is an integer power of 2 (without special effort). Calculation actually involves the *separability* property of the Fourier transform. Separability means that the Fourier transform is calculated in two stages: the rows are first transformed using a 1D FFT, then this data is transformed in columns, again using a 1D FFT. This process can be achieved since the sinusoidal basis functions are orthogonal. Analytically, this implies that the 2D DFT can be decomposed as in Equation 2.27

$$\frac{1}{N}\sum_{x=0}^{N-1}\sum_{y=0}^{N-1}\mathbf{P}_{x,y}e^{-j\left(\frac{2\pi}{N}\right)(ux+vy)} = \frac{1}{N}\sum_{x=0}^{N-1}\left\{\sum_{y=0}^{N-1}\mathbf{P}_{x,y}e^{-j\left(\frac{2\pi}{N}\right)(vy)}\right\}e^{-j\left(\frac{2\pi}{N}\right)(ux)} \tag{2.27}$$

showing how separability is achieved, since the inner term expresses transformation along one axis (the y axis), and the outer term transforms this along the other (the x axis).

Since the computational cost of a 1D FFT of N points is $O(N \log(N))$, the cost (by separability) for the 2D FFT is $O(N^2 \log(N))$ whereas the computational cost of the 2D DFT is $O(N^3)$. This implies a considerable saving since it suggests that the FFT requires much less time, particularly for large image sizes (so for a 128×128 image, if the FFT takes minutes, the DFT will take days). The 2D FFT is available in Mathcad using the `icfft` function which gives a result equivalent to Equation 2.22. The inverse 2D FFT, Equation 2.23, can be implemented using the Mathcad `cfft` function. (The difference between many Fourier transform implementations essentially concerns the chosen scaling factor.) The Mathcad implementations of the 2D DFT, the inverse 2D DFT, are given in Code **2.1**(a) and Code **2.1**(b), respectively. The implementations using the Mathcad functions using the FFT are given in Code **2.1**(c) and Code **2.1**(d), respectively.

$$FP_{u,v} := \frac{1}{\text{rows}(P)} \sum_{y=0}^{\text{rows}(P)-1} \sum_{x=0}^{\text{cols}(P)-1} P_{y,x} \cdot e^{\frac{-j \cdot 2 \cdot \pi \cdot (u \cdot y + v \cdot x)}{\text{rows}(P)}}$$

(a) 2D DFT, Equation 2.22

$$IFP_{y,x} := \sum_{u=0}^{\text{rows}(FP)-1} \sum_{v=0}^{\text{cols}(FP)-1} FP_{u,v} \cdot e^{\frac{j \cdot 2 \cdot \pi \cdot (u \cdot y + v \cdot x)}{\text{rows}(FP)}}$$

(b) Inverse 2D DFT, Equation 2.23

```
Fourier(pic):=icfft(pic)
```

(c) 2D FFT

```
inv_Fourier(trans):=cfft(trans)
```

(d) Inverse 2D FFT

Code 2.1 Implementing Fourier transforms

For reasons of speed, the 2D FFT is the algorithm commonly used in application. One (unfortunate) difficulty is that the nature of the Fourier transform produces an image which, at first, is difficult to interpret. The Fourier transform of an image gives the frequency components. The position of each component reflects its frequency: *low* frequency components are *near* the origin and *high* frequency components are further *away*. As before, the lowest frequency component – for zero frequency – the d.c. component represents the *average* value of the samples. Unfortunately, the arrangement of the 2D Fourier transform places the low frequency components at the *corners* of the transform. The image of the square in Figure **2.15**(a) shows this in its transform, Figure **2.15**(b). A spatial transform is easier to visualise if the d.c. (zero frequency) component is in the *centre*, with frequency increasing towards the edge of the image. This can be arranged either by rotating each of the four quadrants in the Fourier transform by 180°. An alternative is to *reorder* the original image to give a transform which shifts the transform to the centre. Both operations result in the image in Figure **2.15**(c) wherein the transform is much more easily seen. Note that this is aimed to improve visualisation and does not change any of the frequency domain information, only the way it is displayed.

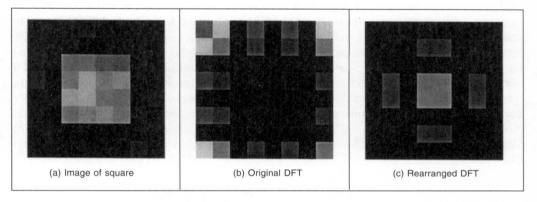

| (a) Image of square | (b) Original DFT | (c) Rearranged DFT |

Figure 2.15   Rearranging the 2D DFT for display purposes

To rearrange the image so that the d.c. component is in the centre, the frequency components need to be reordered. This can be achieved simply by multiplying each image point $\mathbf{P}_{x,y}$ by $-1^{(x+y)}$. Since $\cos(-\pi) = -1$, then $-1 = e^{-j\pi}$ (the minus sign in the exponent keeps the analysis neat) so we obtain the transform of the multiplied image as:

$$\frac{1}{N}\sum_{x=0}^{N-1}\sum_{y=0}^{N-1}\mathbf{P}_{x,y}e^{-j\left(\frac{2\pi}{N}\right)(ux+vy)} \times -1^{(x+y)} = \frac{1}{N}\sum_{x=0}^{N-1}\sum_{y=0}^{N-1}\mathbf{P}_{x,y}e^{-j\left(\frac{2\pi}{N}\right)(ux+vy)}e^{-j\pi(x+y)}$$

$$= \frac{1}{N}\sum_{x=0}^{N-1}\sum_{y=0}^{N-1}\mathbf{P}_{x,y}e^{-j\left(\frac{2\pi}{N}\right)\left(\left(u+\frac{N}{2}\right)x+\left(v+\frac{N}{2}\right)y\right)} \quad (2.28)$$

$$= \mathbf{FP}_{u+\frac{N}{2},v+\frac{N}{2}}$$

According to Equation 2.28, when pixel values are multiplied by $-1^{(x+y)}$, the Fourier transform becomes shifted along each axis by half the number of samples. According to the replication theorem, Equation 2.26, the transform replicates along the frequency axes. This implies that the centre of a transform image will now be the d.c. component. (Another way of interpreting this is rather than look at the frequencies centred on where the image is, our viewpoint has been shifted so as to be centred on one of its corners – thus invoking the replication property.) The operator `rearrange`, in Code **2.2**, is used prior to transform calculation and results in the image of Figure **2.15**(c), and all later transform images.

`rearrange(picture) :=`	`for y∈0..rows(picture)-1`
	`    for x∈0..cols(picture)-1`
	`        rearranged_pic`$_{y,x}$`←picture`$_{y,x}$`·(-1)`$^{(y+x)}$
	`rearranged_pic`

Code 2.2 Reordering for transform calculation

The full effect of the Fourier transform is shown by application to an image of much higher resolution. Figure **2.16**(a) shows the image of a face and Figure **2.16**(b) shows its transform. The transform reveals that much of the information is carried in the *lower* frequencies since this is where most of the spectral components concentrate. This is because the face image has many regions where the brightness does not change a lot, such as the cheeks and forehead. The *high* frequency components reflect *change* in intensity. Accordingly, the higher frequency components arise from the hair (and that feather!) and from the borders of features of the human face, such as the nose and eyes.

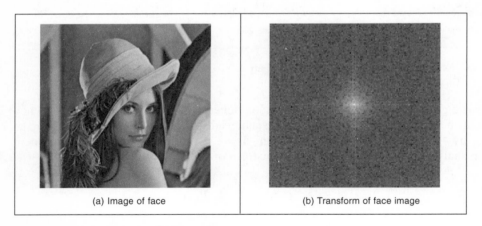

(a) Image of face   (b) Transform of face image

Figure 2.16 Applying the Fourier transform to the image of a face

As with the 1D Fourier transform, there are 2D Fourier transform pairs, illustrated in Figure **2.17**. The 2D Fourier transform of a two-dimensional pulse, Figure **2.17**(a), is a two-dimensional sinc function, in Figure **2.17**(b). The 2D Fourier transform of a Gaussian function, in Figure **2.17**(c), is again a two-dimensional Gaussian function in the frequency domain, in Figure **2.17**(d).

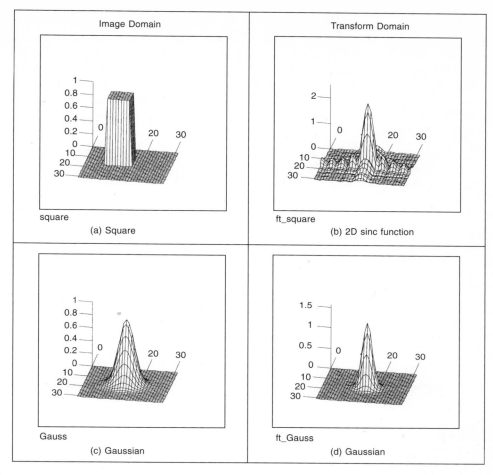

Figure 2.17 2D Fourier transform pairs

2.6 Other properties of the Fourier transform

2.6.1 Shift invariance

The decomposition into spatial frequency does not depend on the position of features within the image. If we shift all the features by a fixed amount, or acquire the image from a different position, the magnitude of its Fourier transform does not change. This property is known as *shift invariance*. By denoting the delayed version of $p(t)$ as $p(t - \tau)$, where τ is the delay, and the Fourier transform of the shifted version is $F[p(t - \tau)]$, we obtain the relationship between a time domain shift in the time and frequency domains as:

$$F[p(t - \tau)] = e^{-j\omega\tau} P(\omega) \tag{2.29}$$

Accordingly, the magnitude of the Fourier transform is:

$$|F[p(t-\tau)]| = |e^{-j\omega\tau} P(\omega)| = |e^{-j\omega\tau}| |P(\omega)| = |P(\omega)| \qquad (2.30)$$

and since the magnitude of the exponential function is 1.0 then the magnitude of the Fourier transform of the shifted image equals that of the original (unshifted) version. We shall use this property later in Chapter 7 when we use Fourier theory to describe shapes. There, it will allow us to give the same description to different instances of the same shape, but a different description to a different shape. You do not get something for nothing: even though the magnitude of the Fourier transform remains constant, its phase does not. The phase of the shifted transform is:

$$\langle F[p(t-\tau)] = \langle e^{-j\omega\tau} P(\omega) \qquad (2.31)$$

The Mathcad implementation of a `shift` operator, Code **2.3**, uses the modulus operation to enforce the cyclic shift. The arguments fed to the function are: the image to be shifted (`pic`), the horizontal shift along the x axis (`x_val`), and the vertical shift down the y axis (`y_val`).

```
shift(pic,y_val,x_val):=   NC←cols(pic)
                           NR←rows(pic)
                           for y∈0..NR-1
                             for x∈0..NC-1
                               shifted_y,x←pic_mod(y+y_val, NR),mod(x+x_val,NC)
                           shifted
```

Code 2.3   Shifting an image

This process is illustrated in Figure **2.18**. An original image, Figure **2.18**(a), is shifted by 30 pixels along the x and the y axes, Figure **2.18**(d). The shift is cyclical, so parts of the image wrap around; those parts at the top of the original image appear at the base of the shifted image. The Fourier transform of the original image and the shifted image are identical: Figure **2.18**(b) appears the same as Figure **2.18**(e). The phase differs: the phase of the original image, Figure **2.18**(c), is clearly different from the phase of the shifted image, Figure **2.18**(f).

The differing phase implies that, in application, the magnitude of the Fourier transform of a face, say, will be the same irrespective of the position of the face in the image (i.e. the camera or the subject can move up and down), assuming that the face is much larger than its image version. This implies that if the Fourier transform is used to analyse an image of a human face, to describe it by its spatial frequency, then we do not need to control the position of the camera, or the face, precisely.

2.6.2   Rotation

The Fourier transform of an image *rotates* when the source image *rotates*. This is to be expected since the decomposition into spatial frequency reflects the orientation of features within the image. As such, orientation dependency is built into the Fourier transform process.

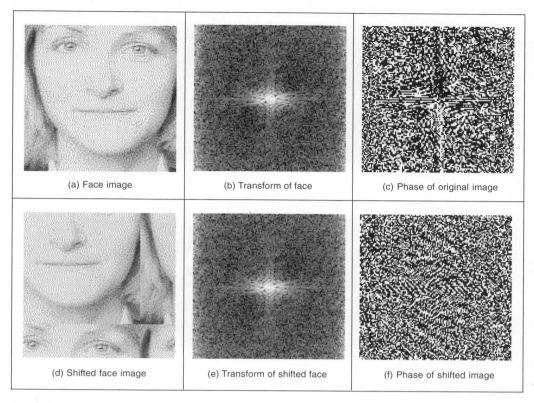

(a) Face image	(b) Transform of face	(c) Phase of original image
(d) Shifted face image	(e) Transform of shifted face	(f) Phase of shifted image

Figure 2.18   Illustrating shift invariance

This implies that if the frequency domain properties are to be used in image analysis, via the Fourier transform, then the orientation of the original image needs to be known, or fixed. It is often possible to fix orientation, or to estimate its value when a feature's orientation cannot be fixed. Alternatively, there are techniques to impose invariance to rotation, say by translation to a polar representation, though this can prove to be complex.

The effect of rotation is illustrated in Figure **2.19**. A face image, Figure **2.19**(a), is rotated by 90° to give the image in Figure **2.19**(b). Comparison of the transform of the original image, Figure **2.19**(c), with the transform of the rotated image, Figure **2.19**(d), shows that the transform has been rotated by 90°, by the same amount as the image. In fact, close inspection of Figure **2.19**(c) shows that the major axis is almost vertical, and is consistent with the major axis of the face in Figure **2.19**(a).

2.6.3   Frequency scaling

By definition, time is the reciprocal of frequency. So if an image is compressed, equivalent to reducing time, then its frequency components will spread, corresponding to increasing frequency. Mathematically the relationship is that the Fourier transform of a function of time multiplied by a scalar λ, $p(\lambda t)$, gives a frequency domain function $P(\omega/\lambda)$, so:

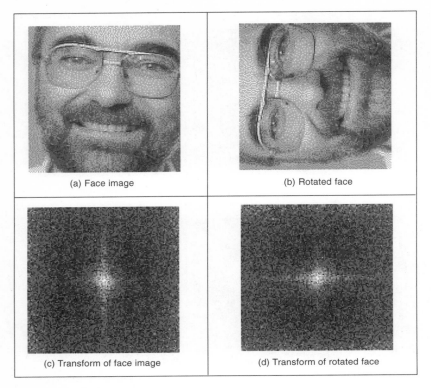

(a) Face image

(b) Rotated face

(c) Transform of face image

(d) Transform of rotated face

Figure 2.19 Illustrating rotation

$$F[p(\lambda t)] = \frac{1}{\lambda} P\left(\frac{\omega}{\lambda}\right)$$ (2.32)

This is illustrated in Figure **2.20** where the texture image (of a chain-link fence), Figure **2.20**(a), is reduced in scale, Figure **2.20**(b), thereby increasing the spatial frequency. The DFT of the original texture image is shown in Figure **2.20**(c) which reveals that the large spatial frequencies in the original image are arranged in a star-like pattern. As a consequence of scaling the original image, the spectrum will spread from the origin consistent with an increase in spatial frequency, as shown in Figure **2.20**(d). This retains the star-like pattern, but with points at a greater distance from the origin.

The implications of this property are that if we reduce the scale of an image, say by imaging at a greater distance, then we will alter the frequency components. The relationship is linear: the amount of reduction, say the proximity of the camera to the target, is directly proportional to the scaling in the frequency domain.

2.6.4 Superposition (linearity)

The *principle of superposition* is very important in systems analysis. Essentially, it states that a system is linear if its response to two combined signals equals the sum of the responses to the individual signals. Given an output O which is a function of two inputs I_1

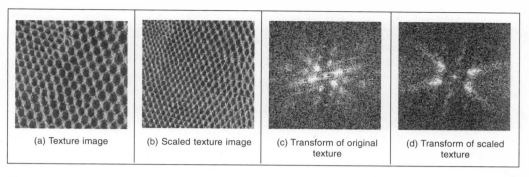

| (a) Texture image | (b) Scaled texture image | (c) Transform of original texture | (d) Transform of scaled texture |

Figure 2.20 Illustrating frequency scaling

and I_2, the response to signal I_1 is $O(I_1)$, that to signal I_2 is $O(I_2)$, and the response to I_1 and I_2, when applied together, is $O(I_1 + I_2)$, the superposition principle states:

$$O(I_1 + I_2) = O(I_1) + O(I_2) \tag{2.33}$$

Any system which satisfies the principle of superposition is termed linear. The Fourier transform is a linear operation since, for two signals p_1 and p_2:

$$F[p_1 + p_2] = F[p_1] + F[p_2] \tag{2.34}$$

In application this suggests that we can separate images by looking at their frequency domain components. Given the image of a fingerprint in blood on cloth, it is very difficult to separate the fingerprint from the cloth by analysing the combined image. However, by translation to the frequency domain, the Fourier transform of the combined image shows strong components due to the texture (this is the spatial frequency of the cloth's pattern) and weaker, more scattered, components due to the fingerprint. If we suppress the frequency components due to the cloth's texture, and invoke the inverse Fourier transform, then the cloth will be removed from the original image. The fingerprint can now be seen in the resulting image.

2.7 Transforms other than Fourier

2.7.1 Discrete cosine transform

The *Discrete Cosine Transform* (DCT) (Ahmed, 1974) is a real transform that has great advantages in *energy compaction*. Its definition for spectral components $\mathbf{DP}_{u,v}$ is:

$$\mathbf{DP}_{u,v} = \left| \begin{array}{l} \dfrac{1}{N^2} \displaystyle\sum_{x=0}^{N-1} \sum_{y=0}^{N-1} \mathbf{P}_{x,y} \quad \text{if} \quad u = 0 \quad \text{and} \quad v = 0 \\[2em] \dfrac{2}{N^2} \displaystyle\sum_{x=0}^{N-1} \sum_{y=0}^{N-1} \mathbf{P}_{x,y} \times \cos\!\left(\dfrac{(2x+1)u\pi}{2N} \right) \times \cos\!\left(\dfrac{(2y+1)v\pi}{2N} \right) \text{otherwise} \end{array} \right. \tag{2.35}$$

The inverse DCT is defined by

$$\mathbf{P}_{x,y} = \dfrac{1}{N^2} \sum_{u=0}^{N-1} \sum_{v=0}^{N-1} \mathbf{DP}_{u,v} \times \cos\!\left(\dfrac{(2x+1)u\pi}{2N} \right) \times \cos\!\left(\dfrac{(2y+1)v\pi}{2N} \right) \tag{2.36}$$

A fast version of the DCT is available, like the FFT, and calculation can be based on the FFT. Both implementations offer about the same speed. The Fourier transform is not actually optimal for *image coding* since the Discrete Cosine transform can give a higher compression rate, for the same image quality. This is because the cosine basis functions can afford for high energy compaction. This can be seen by comparison of Figure **2.21**(b) with Figure **2.21**(a), which reveals that the DCT components are much more concentrated around the origin, than those for the Fourier transform. This is the compaction property associated with the DCT. The DCT has actually been considered as optimal for image coding, and this is why it is found in the JPEG and MPEG standards for coded image transmission.

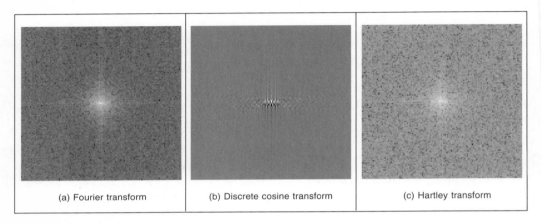

| (a) Fourier transform | (b) Discrete cosine transform | (c) Hartley transform |

Figure 2.21   Comparing transforms of lena

The DCT is actually shift variant, due to its cosine basis functions. In other respects, its properties are very similar to the DFT, with one important exception: it has not yet proved possible to implement convolution with the DCT. It is actually possible to calculate the DCT via the FFT. This has been performed in Figure **2.21**(b) since there is no fast DCT algorithm in Mathcad and, as shown earlier, fast implementations of transform calculation can take a fraction of the time of the conventional counterpart.

The Fourier transform essentially decomposes, or *decimates*, a signal into sine and cosine components, so the natural partner to the DCT is the Discrete Sine Transform (DST). However, the DST transform has odd basis functions (sine) rather than the even ones in the DCT. This lends the DST transform some less desirable properties, and it finds much less application than the DCT.

2.7.2   Discrete Hartley transform

The Hartley transform (Hartley, 1942) is a form of the Fourier transform, but without complex arithmetic, with result for the face image shown in Figure **2.21**(c). Oddly, though it sounds like a very rational development, the Hartley transform was first invented in 1942, but not rediscovered and then formulated in discrete form until 1983 (Bracewell, 1983). One advantage of the Hartley transform is that the forward and inverse transform are the same operation; a disadvantage is that phase is built into the order of frequency components since it is not readily available as the argument of a complex number. The definition of the Discrete Hartley Transform (DHT) is that transform components $\mathbf{HP}_{u,v}$ are:

$$\mathbf{HP}_{u,v} = \frac{1}{N} \sum_{x=0}^{N-1} \sum_{y=0}^{N-1} \mathbf{P}_{x,y} \times \left(\cos\left(\frac{2\pi}{N} \times (ux + vy) \right) + \sin\left(\frac{2\pi}{N} \times (ux + vy) \right) \right) \quad (2.37)$$

The inverse Hartley transform is the same process, but applied to the transformed image.

$$\mathbf{P}_{x,y} = \frac{1}{N} \sum_{u=0}^{N-1} \sum_{v=0}^{N-1} \mathbf{HP}_{u,v} \times \left(\cos\left(\frac{2\pi}{N} \times (ux + vy) \right) + \sin\left(\frac{2\pi}{N} \times (ux + vy) \right) \right) \quad (2.38)$$

The implementation is then the same for both the forward and the inverse transforms, as given in Code **2.4**.

```
Hartley(pic):= NC←cols(pic)
               NR←rows(pic)
               for v∈0.. NR-1
                 for u∈0.. NC-1

                   trans_{v,u} ← 1/NC · Σ_{y=0}^{NR-1} Σ_{x=0}^{NC-1} pic_{y,x} · [ cos[ 2·π·(u·x+v·y) / NR ]
                                                                                  +sin[ 2·π·(u·x+v·y) / NC ] ]

               trans
```

Code 2.4   Implementing the Hartley transform

Again, a fast implementation is available, the fast Hartley transform (Bracewell, 1984) (though some suggest that it should be called the Bracewell transform, eponymously). It is actually possible to calculate the DFT of a function, $F(u)$, from its Hartley transform, $H(u)$. The analysis here is based on one-dimensional data, but only for simplicity since the argument extends readily to two dimensions. By splitting the Hartley transform into its odd and even parts, $O(u)$ and $E(u)$, respectively we obtain:

$$H(u) = O(u) + E(u) \quad (2.39)$$

where:

$$E(u) = \frac{H(u) + H(N - u)}{2} \quad (2.40)$$

and

$$O(u) = \frac{H(u) - H(N - u)}{2} \quad (2.41)$$

The DFT can then be calculated from the DHT simply by

$$F(u) = E(u) - j \times O(u) \quad (2.42)$$

Conversely, the Hartley transform can be calculated from the Fourier transform by:

$$H(u) = \text{Re}[F(u)] - \text{Im}[F(u)] \tag{2.43}$$

where Re[ ] and Im[ ] denote the real and the imaginary parts, respectively. This emphasises the natural relationship between the Fourier and the Hartley transform. The image of Figure **2.21**(c) has been calculated via the 2D FFT using Equation 2.43. Note that the transform in Figure **2.21**(c) is the complete transform whereas the Fourier transform in Figure **2.21**(a) shows magnitude only. Naturally, as with the DCT, the properties of the Hartley transform mirror those of the Fourier transform. Unfortunately, the Hartley transform does not have shift invariance but there are ways to handle this. Also, convolution requires manipulation of the odd and even parts.

2.7.3 Introductory wavelets; the Gabor wavelet

Wavelets are a comparatively recent approach to signal processing, being introduced only in the last decade (Daubechies, 1990). Their main advantage is that they allow multi-resolution analysis (analysis at different scales, or resolution). Furthermore, wavelets allow decimation in space and frequency *simultaneously*. Earlier transforms actually allow decimation in frequency, in the forward transform, and in time (or position) in the inverse. In this way, the Fourier transform gives a measure of the frequency content of the whole image: the contribution of the image to a particular frequency component. Simultaneous decimation allows us to describe an image in terms of frequency which occurs at a position, as opposed to an ability to measure frequency content across the whole image. Clearly this gives us a greater descriptional power, which can be used to good effect.

First though we need a basis function, so that we can decompose a signal. The basis functions in the Fourier transform are sinusoidal waveforms at different frequencies. The function of the Fourier transform is to convolve these sinusoids with a signal to determine how much of each is present. The *Gabor wavelet* is well suited to introductory purposes, since it is essentially a sinewave modulated by a Gaussian envelope. The Gabor wavelet *gw* is given by

$$gw(t) = e^{-jf_0t} \, e^{-\left(\frac{t-t_0}{a}\right)^2} \tag{2.44}$$

where f_0 is the modulating frequency, t_0 dictates position and a controls the width of the Gaussian envelope which embraces the oscillating signal. An example Gabor wavelet is shown in Figure **2.22** which shows the real and the imaginary parts (the modulus is the Gaussian envelope). Increasing the value of f_0 increases the frequency content within the envelope whereas increasing the value of a spreads the envelope without affecting the frequency. So why does this allow simultaneous analysis of time and frequency? Given that this function is the one convolved with the test data, then we can compare it with the Fourier transform. In fact, if we remove the term on the right-hand side of Equation 2.44 then we return to the sinusoidal basis function of the Fourier transform, the exponential in Equation 2.1. Accordingly, we can return to the Fourier transform by setting a to be very large. Alternatively, setting f_0 to zero removes frequency information. Since we operate in between these extremes, we obtain position and frequency information simultaneously.

Actually, an infinite class of wavelets exists which can be used as an expansion basis in signal decimation. One approach (Daugman, 1988) has generalised the Gabor function to

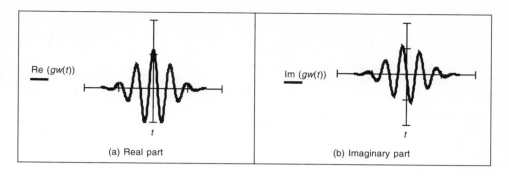

Figure 2.22   An example Gabor wavelet

a 2D form aimed to be optimal in terms of spatial and spectral resolution. These 2D Gabor wavelets are given by

$$gw2D(x, y) = \frac{1}{\sigma\sqrt{\pi}} e^{-\left(\frac{(x-x_0)^2 + (y-y_0)^2}{2\sigma^2}\right)} e^{-j2\pi f_0 ((x-x_0)\cos(\theta) + (y-y_0)\sin(\theta))} \qquad (2.45)$$

where x_0, y_0 control position, f_0 controls the frequency of modulation along either axis, and θ controls the *direction* (orientation) of the wavelet (as implicit in a two-dimensional system). Naturally, the shape of the area imposed by the 2D Gaussian function could be elliptical if different variances were allowed along the x and y axes (the frequency can also be modulated differently along each axis). Figure **2.23**, of an example 2D Gabor wavelet, shows that the real and imaginary parts are even and odd functions, respectively; again, different values for f_0 and σ control the frequency and envelope's spread respectively, the extra parameter θ controls rotation.

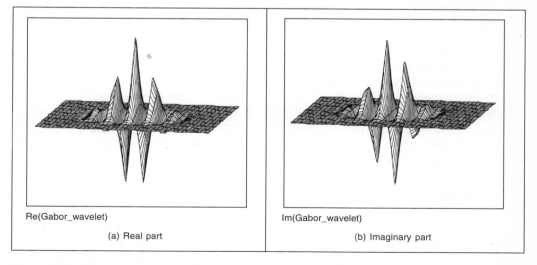

Figure 2.23   Example two-dimensional Gabor wavelet

The function of the wavelet transform is to determine where and how each wavelet specified by the range of values for each of the free parameters occurs in the image. Clearly, there is a wide choice which depends on application. An example transform is given in Figure **2.24**. Here, the Gabor wavelet parameters have been chosen in such a way as to select face features: the eyes, nose and mouth have come out very well. These features are where there is local frequency content with orientation according to the head's inclination. Naturally, these are not the only features with these properties, the cuff of the sleeve is highlighted too! But this does show the Gabor wavelet's ability to select and analyse localised variation in image intensity.

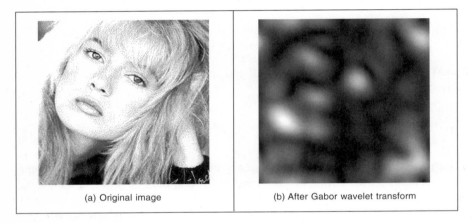

(a) Original image   (b) After Gabor wavelet transform

Figure 2.24   An example Gabor wavelet transform

However, the conditions under which a set of continuous Gabor wavelets will provide a complete representation of any image (i.e. that any image can be reconstructed) have only recently been developed. However, the theory is naturally very powerful, since it accommodates frequency and position simultaneously, and further it facilitates multi-resolution analysis. Amongst applications of Gabor wavelets, we can find measurement of iris texture to give a very powerful security system (Daugman, 1993) and face feature extraction for automatic face recognition (Lades, 1993). Wavelets continue to develop (Debauchies, 1990) and have found applications in image texture analysis (Laine, 1993), in coding (daSilva, 1996) and in image restoration (Banham, 1996). Unfortunately, the discrete wavelet transform is not shift invariant, though there are approaches aimed to remedy this (see, for example, Donoho (1995)). As such, we shall not study it further and just note that there is an important class of transforms that combine spatial and spectral sensitivity, and that this importance will continue to grow.

2.7.4 Other transforms

Decomposing a signal into sinusoidal components was actually one of the first approaches to transform calculus, and this is why the Fourier transform is so important. The sinusoidal functions are actually called *basis functions*, the implicit assumption is that the basis functions map well to the signal components. There is (theoretically) an infinite range of basis functions. Discrete signals can map better into collections of binary components rather than sinusoidal ones. These collections (or sequences) of binary data are called sequency components and form the basis functions of the *Walsh transform* (Walsh, 1923). This has found wide application in the interpretation of digital signals, though it is less widely used in image processing. The Karhunen–Loéve transform (Karhunen, 1947) (Loéve, 1948) (also called the *Hotelling* transform from which it was derived, or more popularly *Principal Components Analysis* (Jain, 1989) is a way of analysing (statistical) data to reduce it to those data which are *informative*, discarding those which are not.

2.8 Applications using frequency domain properties

Filtering is a major use of Fourier transforms, particularly because we can understand an image, and how to process it, much better in the frequency domain. An analogy is the use of a graphic equaliser to control the way music sounds. In images, if we want to remove high frequency information (like the hiss on sound) then we can filter, or remove, it by inspecting the Fourier transform. If we retain low frequency components, then we implement a *low-pass filter*. The low-pass filter describes the area in which we retain spectral components, the size of the area dictates the range of frequencies retained, and is known as the filter's *bandwidth*. If we retain components within a circular region centred on the d.c. component, and inverse Fourier transform the filtered transform then the resulting image will be *blurred*. Higher spatial frequencies exist at the sharp *edges* of features, so removing them causes blurring. But the amount of fluctuation is reduced too; any high frequency noise will be removed in the filtered image.

The implementation of a low-pass filter which retains frequency components within a circle of specified radius is the function `low_filter`, given in Code **2.5**. This operator assumes that the radius and centre co-ordinates of the circle are specified prior to its use. Points within the circle remain unaltered, whereas those outside the circle are set to zero, black.

$$
\text{low\_filter(pic)} := \begin{array}{l} \text{for } y \in 0..\text{rows(pic)}-1 \\ \quad \text{for } x \in 0..\text{cols(pic)}-1 \\ \quad\quad \text{filtered}_{y,x} \leftarrow \\ \\ \quad\quad \left| \begin{array}{l} \text{pic}_{y,x} \text{ if} \left(y - \dfrac{\text{rows(pic)}}{2}\right)^2 + \left(x - \dfrac{\text{cols(pic)}}{2}\right)^2 \\ \hspace{8cm} -\text{radius}^2 \leq 0 \\ 0 \text{ otherwise} \end{array} \right. \\ \\ \text{filtered} \end{array}
$$

Code 2.5   Implementing low-pass filtering

When applied to an image we obtain a low-pass filtered version. In application to an image of a face, the low spatial frequencies are the ones which change slowly as reflected in the resulting, blurred image, Figure **2.25**(a). The high frequency components have been removed as shown in the transform, Figure **2.25**(b). The radius of the circle controls how much of the original image is retained. In this case, the radius is 10 pixels (and the image resolution is 256×256). If a larger circle were to be used, more of the high frequency detail would be retained (and the image would look more like its original version); if the circle was very small, an even more blurred image would result, since only the lowest spatial frequencies would be retained. This differs from the earlier Gabor wavelet approach which allows for *localised* spatial frequency analysis. Here, the analysis is *global*: we are filtering the frequency across the *whole* image.

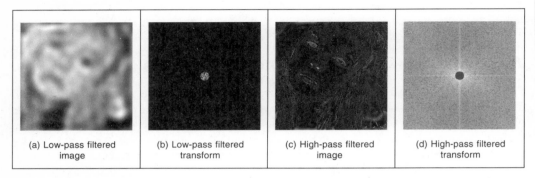

| (a) Low-pass filtered image | (b) Low-pass filtered transform | (c) High-pass filtered image | (d) High-pass filtered transform |

Figure 2.25 Illustrating low- and high-pass filtering

Alternatively, we can retain high frequency components and remove low frequency ones. This is a *high-pass filter*. If we remove components near the d.c. component and retain all the others, the result of applying the inverse Fourier transform to the filtered image will be to emphasise the features that were removed in low-pass filtering. This can lead to a popular application of the high-pass filter: to 'crispen' an image by emphasising its high frequency components. An implementation using a circular region merely requires selection of the set of points outside the circle, rather than inside as for the low-pass operator. The effect of high-pass filtering can be observed in Figure **2.25**(c) which shows removal of the low frequency components: this emphasises the hair and the borders of a face's features since these are where brightness varies rapidly. The retained components are those which were removed in low-pass filtering, as illustrated in the transform, Figure **2.25**(d).

It is also possible to retain a specified range of frequencies. This is known as *band-pass filtering*. It can be implemented by retaining frequency components within an annulus centred on the d.c. component. The width of the annulus represents the bandwidth of the band-pass filter.

This leads to digital signal processing theory. There are many considerations to be made in the way you select, and the manner in which frequency components are retained or excluded. This is beyond a text on computer vision. For further study in this area, Rabiner and Gold (Rabiner, 1975), and Oppenheim and Schafer (Oppenheim, 1996), although published (in their original form) a long time ago, remain as popular introductions to digital signal processing theory and applications.

It is actually possible to recognise the object within the low-pass filtered image. Intuitively, this implies that we could just store the frequency components selected from the transform data, rather than all the image points. In this manner a fraction of the information would be stored, and still provide a recognisable image, albeit slightly blurred. This concerns *image coding* which is a popular target for image processing techniques; for further information see Clarke (1985).

2.9 Further reading

For further study (and entertaining study too!) of the Fourier transform, try *The Fourier Transform and its Applications* by R. N. Bracewell (Bracewell, 1986). A number of the standard image processing texts include much coverage of transform calculus, such as Jain (Jain, 1989), Gonzalez and Wintz (Gonzalez, 1987), and Pratt (Pratt, 1992). For more coverage of the DCT try Jain (Jain, 1989); for an excellent coverage of the Walsh transform try Beauchamp's superb text (Beauchamp, 1975). For wavelets, try the new book by Wornell that introduces wavelets from a signal processing standpoint (Wornell, 1996). For general signal processing theory there are introductory texts (see, for example, Meade and Dillon (Meade, 1986), or Bob Damper's book (Damper, 1995), for more complete coverage try Rabiner and Gold (Rabiner, 1975) or Oppenheim and Schafer (Oppenheim, 1996) (as mentioned earlier). Finally, on the implementation side of the FFT (and for many other signal processing algorithms) *Numerical Recipes in C* (Press, 1992) is an excellent book. It is extremely readable, full of practical detail – well worth a look. Numerical Recipes is on the web too, together with other signal processing sites, as listed in Table **1.4**.

2.10 References

Ahmed, N., Natarajan, T. and Rao, K. R., Discrete Cosine Transform, *IEEE Trans. on Computers*, pp. 90–93, 1974

Banham, M. R. and Katsaggelos, K., Spatially Adaptive Wavelet-Based Multiscale Image Restoration, *IEEE Trans. on Image Processing*, **5**(4), pp. 619–634, 1996

Beauchamp, K. G., *Walsh Functions and Their Applications*, Academic Press, London UK, 1975

Bracewell, R. N., The Fast Hartley Transform, *Proc. IEEE*, **72**(8), pp. 1010–1018, 1984

Bracewell, R. N., The Discrete Hartley Transform, *J. Opt. Soc. Am.*, **73**(12), pp. 1832–1835, 1984

Bracewell, R. N., *The Fourier Transform and its Applications,* Revised 2nd Edition, McGraw-Hill Book Co., Singapore, 1986

Clarke, R. J., *Transform Coding of Images*, Addison Wesley, Reading, MA USA, 1985

Damper, R. I., *Introduction to Discrete-Time Signals and Systems*, Chapman and Hall, London UK, 1995

da Silva, E. A. B. and Ghanbari, M., On the Performance of Linear Phase Wavelet Transforms in Low Bit-Rate Image Coding, *IEEE Trans. on Image Processing*, **5**(5), pp. 689–704, 1996

Daubechies, I., The Wavelet Transform, Time Frequency Localisation and Signal Analysis, *IEEE Trans. on Information Theory*, **36**(5), pp. 961–1004, 1990

Daugman, J. G., Complete Discrete 2D Gabor Transforms by Neural Networks for Image Analysis and Compression, *IEEE Trans. on Acoustics, Speech and Signal Processing*, **36**(7), pp. 1169–1179, 1988

Daugman, J. G., High Confidence Visual Recognition of Persons by a Test of Statistical Independence, *IEEE Trans. on PAMI*, **15**(11), pp. 1148–1161, 1993

Donoho, D. L., Denoising by Soft Thresholding, *IEEE Trans. on Information Theory*, **41**(3), pp. 613–627, 1995

Gonzalez, R. C. and Wintz P.: *Digital Image Processing*, 2nd Edition, Addison Wesley Publishing Co. Inc., Reading, MA USA, 1987

Hartley, R. L. V., A More Symmetrical Fourier Analysis Applied to Transmission Problems, *Proc. IRE*, **144**, pp. 144–150, 1942

Jain, A. K., *Fundamentals of Computer Vision*, Prentice Hall International (UK) Ltd, Hemel Hempstead UK, 1989

Karhunen, K., Über Lineare Methoden in der Wahrscheinlich-Keitsrechnung, *Ann. Acad. Sci. Fennicae*, Ser A.I.37, 1947 (Translation in I. Selin, On Linear Methods in Probability Theory, Doc. T-131, The RAND Corp., Santa Monica CA, 1960.)

Lades, M., Vorbruggen, J. C., Buhmann, J. Lange, J., Madsburg, C. V. D., Wurtz, R. P. and Konen, W., Distortion Invariant Object Recognition in the Dynamic Link Architecture, *IEEE Trans. on Computers*, **42**, pp. 300–311, 1993

Laine, A. and Fan, J., Texture Classification by Wavelet Packet Signatures, *IEEE Trans. on PAMI*, **15**, pp. 1186–1191, 1993

Loéve, M., Fonctions Alétoires de Seconde Ordre, in: P: Levy (ed.), *Processus Stochastiques et Mouvement Brownien*, Hermann, Paris, 1948

Meade, M. L. and Dillon, C. R., *Signals and Systems, Models and Behaviour*, Van Nostrand Reinhold (UK) Co. Ltd, Wokingham UK, 1986

Oppenheim, A. V. and Schafer, R. W., *Digital Signal Processing,* 2nd Edition, Prentice Hall International (UK) Ltd, Hemel Hempstead UK, 1996

Pratt, W. K., *Digital Image Processing*, Wiley, New York USA, 1992

Press, W. H., Teukolsky, S. A., Vettering, W. T. and Flannery, B. P., *Numerical Recipes in C – The Art of Scientific Computing*, 2nd Edition, Cambridge University Press, Cambridge UK, 1992

Rabiner, L. R. and Gold, B., *Theory and Application of Digital Signal Processing*, Prentice Hall Inc., Englewood Cliffs, NJ USA, 1975

Walsh, J. L., A Closed Set of Normal Orthogonal Functions, *Am. J. Math.*, **45**(1), pp. 5–24, 1923

Wornell, G. W., *Signal Processing with Fractals, a Wavelet-Based Approach*, Prentice Hall Inc., Upper Saddle River, NJ USA, 1996

3
Basic image processing operations

3.1 Overview

We shall now start to process digital images as described in Table 3.1. First, we shall describe the brightness variation in an image using its histogram. We shall then look at operations which manipulate the image so as to change the histogram, processes that shift and scale the result (making the image brighter or dimmer, in different ways). We shall also consider thresholding techniques that turn an image from grey level to binary. These are called single point operations. After, we shall move to group operations where the group is those points found inside a template. Some of the most common operations on the groups of points are statistical, providing images where each point is the result of, say, averaging the neighbourhood of each point in the original image. We shall see how the statistical operations can reduce noise in the image, which is of benefit to the feature extraction techniques to be considered later. As such, these basic operations are usually for pre-processing for later feature extraction or to improve display quality.

3.2 Histograms

The intensity *histogram* shows how individual brightness levels are occupied in an image; the *image contrast* is measured by the range of brightness levels. The histogram plots the number of pixels with a particular brightness level against the brightness level. For 8-bit pixels, the brightness ranges from zero (black) to 255 (white). Figure **3.1** shows an image of an eye and its histogram. The histogram, Figure **3.1**(b), shows that not all the grey levels are used and the lowest and highest intensity levels are close together, reflecting moderate contrast. The histogram has a region between 100 and 120 brightness values which contains the dark portions of the image, such as the hair (including the eyebrow) and the eye's iris. The brighter points relate mainly to the skin. If the image was darker, overall, then the histogram would be concentrated towards black. If the image was brighter, but with lower contrast, then the histogram would be thinner and concentrated near the whiter brightness levels.

This histogram shows us that we have not used all available grey levels. Accordingly, we can stretch the image to use them all, and the image would become clearer. This is essentially cosmetic attention to make the image's appearance better. Making the appearance better, especially in view of later processing, is the focus of many basic image processing operations, as will be covered in this chapter. The histogram can also reveal if there is noise in the

Table 3.1 Overview of Chapter 3

Main topic	Sub topics	Main points
Image description	Portray *variation* in image brightness content as a graph/*histogram.*	Histograms, image contrast.
Point operations	Calculate *new* image points as a *function* of the point at the same place in the original image. The functions can be *mathematical*, or can be computed from the image itself and will change the image's histogram. Finally, *thresholding* turns an image from *grey* level to a *binary* (black and white) representation.	Histogram manipulation; intensity mapping: addition, inversion, scaling, logarithm, exponent. Intensity normalisation; histogram equalisation. Thresholding and optimal thresholding.
Group operations	Calculate new image points as a function of *neighbourhood* of the point at the same place in the original image. The functions can be *statistical* including: mean (average); median and mode.	Template convolution (including frequency domain implementation): direct averaging, median filter, mode filter.

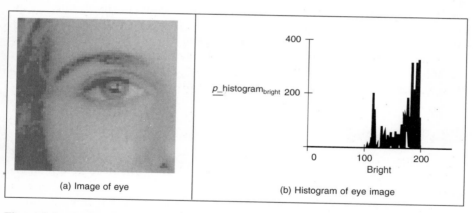

(a) Image of eye   (b) Histogram of eye image

Figure 3.1   An image and its histogram

image, if the ideal histogram is known. We might want to remove this noise, not only to improve the appearance of the image, but to ease the task of (and to present the target better for) later feature extraction techniques. This chapter concerns these basic operations which can improve the appearance and quality of images.

The histogram can be evaluated by the operator histogram, in Code **3.1**. The operator first initialises the histogram to zero. Then the operator works by counting up the number of image points that have an intensity at a particular value. These counts for the different values form the overall histogram. The counts are then returned as the two-dimensional histogram (a vector of the count values) which can be plotted as a graph, Figure **3.1**(b).

```
histogram(pic)  :=    for  bright∈0..255
                          pixels_at_level_bright←0
                      for  x∈0..cols(pic)-1
                        for  y∈0..rows(pic)-1
                          │ level←pic_y,x
                          │ pixels_at_level_level←pixels_at_level_level+1
                      pixels_at_level
```

Code 3.1 Evaluating the histogram

3.3 Point operators

3.3.1 Basic point operations

The most basic operations in image processing are point operations where each pixel value is replaced with a new value obtained from the old one. If we want to increase the brightness to stretch the contrast we can simply multiply all pixel values by a scalar, say by 2 to double the range. Conversely, to reduce the contrast (though this is not usual) we can divide all point values by a scalar. If the overall brightness is controlled by a *level*, l (e.g. the brightness of global light), and the range is controlled by a *gain*, k, the brightness of the points in a new picture, $\mathbf{N}$, can be related to the brightness in old picture, $\mathbf{O}$, by:

$$\mathbf{N}_{x,y} = k \times \mathbf{O}_{x,y} + l \quad \forall x, y \in 1, N \tag{3.1}$$

This is a point operator that replaces the brightness at points in the picture according to a linear brightness relation. The level controls overall brightness and is the minimum value of the output picture. The gain controls the contrast, or range, and if the gain is greater than unity, the output range will be increased, this process is illustrated in Figure **3.2**. So the image of the eye, processed by $k = 1.2$ and $l = 10$ will become brighter, Figure **3.2**(a), and with better contrast, though in this case the brighter points are mostly set near to white (255). These factors can be seen in its histogram, Figure **3.2**(b).

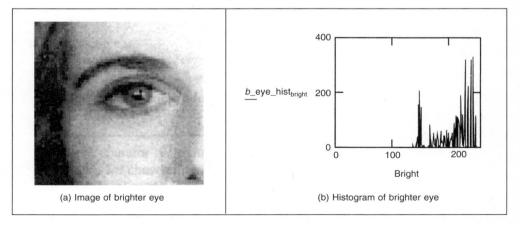

(a) Image of brighter eye   (b) Histogram of brighter eye

Figure 3.2 Brightening an image

The basis of the implementation of point operators was given earlier, for addition in Code **1.3**. The stretching process can be displayed as a mapping between the input and output ranges, according to the specified relationship, as in Figure **3.3**. Figure **3.3**(a) is a mapping where the output is a direct copy of the input (this relationship is the dotted line in Figures **3.3**(c) and (d)); Figure **3.3**(b) is the mapping for brightness *inversion* where dark parts in an image become bright and vice versa. Figure **3.3**(c) is the mapping for *addition* and Figure **3.3**(d) is the mapping for *multiplication* (or *division*, if the slope was less than that of the input). In these mappings, if the mapping produces values that are smaller than the expected minimum (say negative when zero represents black), or larger than a specified maximum, then a *clipping* process can be used to set the output values to a chosen level. For example, if the relationship between input and output aims to produce output points with intensity value greater than 255, as used for white, the output value can be set to white for these points, as it is in Figure **3.3**(c).

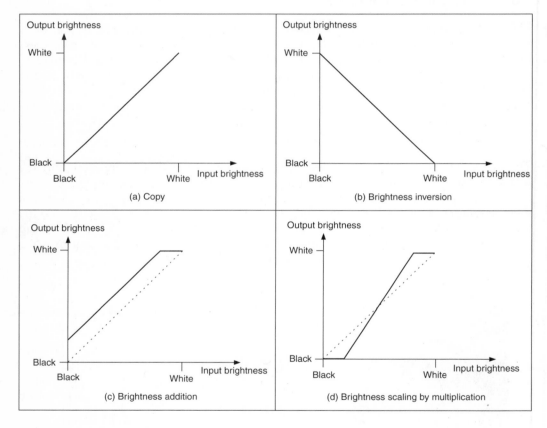

Figure 3.3 Intensity mappings

The *sawtooth* operator is an alternative form of the linear operator and uses a repeated form of the linear operator for chosen intervals in the brightness range. The sawtooth operator is actually used to emphasise local contrast change (as in images where regions of interest can be light or dark). This is illustrated in Figure **3.4** where the range of brightness levels is mapped into four linear regions by the sawtooth operator, Figure **3.4**(b). This remaps the intensity in the eye image to highlight local intensity variation, as opposed to global variation, in Figure **3.4**(a). The image is now presented in regions, where the region selection is controlled by its pixels' intensities.

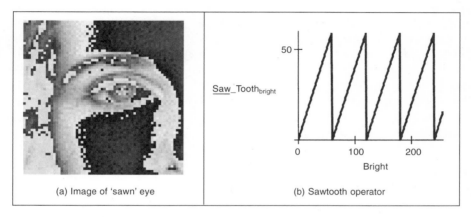

| (a) Image of 'sawn' eye | (b) Sawtooth operator |

Figure 3.4 Applying the sawtooth operator

Finally, rather than simple multiplication we can use arithmetic functions such as logarithm to reduce the range or exponent to increase it. This can be used, say, to equalise the response of a camera, or to compress the range of displayed brightness levels. If the camera has a known exponential performance, and outputs a value for brightness which is proportional to the exponential of the brightness of the corresponding point in the scene of view, the application of a *logarithmic point operator* will restore the original range of brightness levels. The effect of replacing brightness by a scaled version of its natural logarithm (implemented as $N_{x,y} = 20\ln(100O_{x,y})$) is shown in Figure **3.5**(a); the effect of a scaled version of the exponent (implemented as $N_{x,y} = 20\exp(O_{x,y}/100)$) is shown in Figure

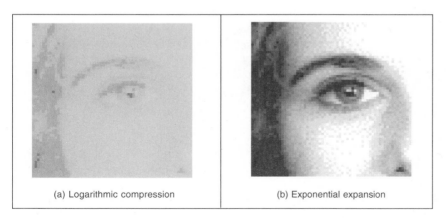

| (a) Logarithmic compression | (b) Exponential expansion |

Figure 3.5 Applying exponential and logarithmic point operators

3.5(b). The scaling factors were chosen to ensure that the resulting image can be displayed since the logarithm or exponent greatly reduces or magnifies pixel values, respectively. This can be seen in the results: Figure **3.5**(a) is dark with a small range of brightness levels whereas Figure **3.5**(b) is much brighter, with greater contrast. Naturally, application of the logarithmic point operator will change any *multiplicative* changes in brightness to become *additive*. As such, the logarithmic operator can find application in reducing the effects of multiplicative intensity change. The logarithm operator is often used to compress Fourier transforms, for display purposes. This is because the d.c. component can be very large with contrast too large to allow the other points to be seen.

In hardware, point operators can be implemented using look-up tables (LUTs) which exist in some framegrabber units. LUTs give an output that is programmed, and stored, in a table entry that corresponds to a particular input value. If the brightness response of the camera is known, then it is possible to pre-program a LUT to make the camera response equivalent to a uniform or flat response across the range of brightness levels (in software, this can be implemented as a CASE function).

3.3.2 Histogram normalisation

Popular techniques to stretch the range of intensities include *histogram (intensity) normalisation*. Here, the original histogram is stretched, and shifted, to cover all the 256 available levels. If the original histogram of old picture $\mathbf{O}$ starts at $\mathbf{O}_{min}$ and extends up to $\mathbf{O}_{max}$ brightness levels, then we can scale up the image so that the pixels in the new picture $\mathbf{N}$ lie between a minimum output level $\mathbf{N}_{min}$ and a maximum level $\mathbf{N}_{max}$, simply by scaling up the input intensity levels according to:

$$\mathbf{N}_{x,y} = \frac{\mathbf{N}_{max} - \mathbf{N}_{min}}{\mathbf{O}_{max} - \mathbf{O}_{min}} \times (\mathbf{O}_{x,y} - \mathbf{O}_{min}) + \mathbf{N}_{min} \qquad \forall x, y \in 1, N \qquad (3.2)$$

A Matlab implementation of intensity normalisation, appearing to mimic Matlab's `imagesc` function, the `normalise` function in Code **3.2**, uses an output ranging from $\mathbf{N}_{min} = 0$ to $\mathbf{N}_{max} = 255$. This is scaled by the input range that is determined by applying the `max` and the `min` operators to the input picture. Note that in Matlab, a 2-D array needs double application of the `max` and `min` operators whereas in Mathcad `max(image)` delivers the maximum. Each point in the picture is then scaled as in Equation 3.2 and the `floor` function is used to ensure an integer output.

The process is illustrated in Figure **3.6**, and can be compared with the original image and histogram in Figure **3.1**. An intensity normalised version of the eye image is shown in Figure **3.6**(a) which now has better contrast and appears better to the human eye. Its histogram, Figure **3.6**(b), shows that the intensity now ranges across all available levels (there is actually one black pixel!).

3.3.3 Histogram equalisation

Histogram equalisation is a **non-linear** process aimed to highlight image brightness in a way particularly suited to human visual analysis. Histogram equalisation aims to change a picture in such a way as to produce a picture with a *flatter* histogram, where all levels are equiprobable. In order to develop the operator, we can first inspect the histograms. For a range of *M* levels then the histogram plots the points per level against level. For the input

```
function normalised=normalise(image)
%Histogram normalisation to stretch from black to white

%Usage: [new image]=normalise(image)
%Parameters: image-array of integers
%Author: Mark S. Nixon

%get dimensions
[rows, cols]=size(image);

%set minimum
minim=min(min(image));

%work out range of input levels
range=max(max(image))-minim;

%normalise the image
for x=1:cols %address all columns
  for y=1:rows %address all rows
    normalised(y, x)=floor((image(y,x)-minim)*255/range);
  end
end
```

Code 3.2 Intensity normalisation

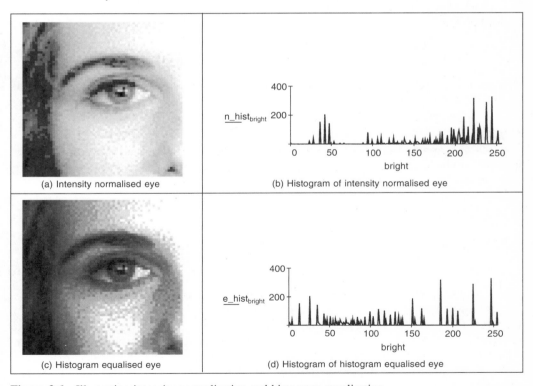

(a) Intensity normalised eye

(b) Histogram of intensity normalised eye

(c) Histogram equalised eye

(d) Histogram of histogram equalised eye

Figure 3.6 Illustrating intensity normalisation and histogram equalisation

(old) and the output (new) image, the number of points per level is denoted as $\mathbf{O}(l)$ and $\mathbf{N}(l)$ (for $0 < l < M$), respectively. For square images, there are N^2 points in the input and the output image, so the sum of points per level in each should be equal:

$$\sum_{l=0}^{M} \mathbf{O}(l) = \sum_{l=0}^{M} \mathbf{N}(l) \tag{3.3}$$

Also, this should be the same for an arbitrarily chosen level p, since we are aiming for an output picture with a uniformly flat histogram. So the cumulative histogram up to level p should be transformed to cover up to the level q in the new histogram:

$$\sum_{l=0}^{p} \mathbf{O}(l) = \sum_{l=0}^{q} \mathbf{N}(l) \tag{3.4}$$

Since the output histogram is uniformly flat, the cumulative histogram up to level p should be a fraction of the overall sum. So the number of points per level in the output picture is the ratio of the number of points to the range of levels in the output image:

$$\mathbf{N}(l) = \frac{N^2}{\mathbf{N}_{max} - \mathbf{N}_{min}} \tag{3.5}$$

So the cumulative histogram of the output picture is:

$$\sum_{l=0}^{q} \mathbf{N}(l) = q \times \frac{N^2}{\mathbf{N}_{max} - \mathbf{N}_{min}} \tag{3.6}$$

By Equation 3.4 this is equal to the cumulative histogram of the input image, so:

$$q \times \frac{N^2}{\mathbf{N}_{max} - \mathbf{N}_{min}} = \sum_{l=0}^{p} \mathbf{O}(l) \tag{3.7}$$

This gives a mapping for the output pixels at level q, from the input pixels at level p as:

$$q = \frac{\mathbf{N}_{max} - \mathbf{N}_{min}}{N^2} \times \sum_{l=0}^{p} \mathbf{O}(l) \tag{3.8}$$

This gives a mapping function that provides an output image that has an approximately flat histogram. The mapping function is given by phrasing Equation 3.8 as an equalising function (E) of the level (q) and the image ($\mathbf{O}$) as

$$E(q, \mathbf{O}) = \frac{\mathbf{N}_{max} - \mathbf{N}_{min}}{N^2} \times \sum_{l=0}^{p} \mathbf{O}(l) \tag{3.9}$$

The output image is then

$$\mathbf{N}_{x,y} = E(\mathbf{O}_{x,y}, \mathbf{O}) \tag{3.10}$$

The result of equalising the eye image is shown in Figure **3.6**. The intensity equalised image, Figure **3.6**(c) has much better defined features (especially around the eyes) than in the original version (Figure **3.1**). The histogram, Figure **3.6**(d), reveals the non-linear mapping process whereby white and black are not assigned equal weight, as they were in intensity normalisation. Accordingly, more pixels are mapped into the darker region and the brighter intensities become better spread, consistent with the aims of histogram equalisation.

Its performance can be very convincing since it is well mapped to the properties of human vision. If a linear brightness transformation is applied to the original image then the equalised histogram will be the same. If we replace pixel values with ones computed according to Equation 3.1 then the result of histogram equalisation will not change. An alternative interpretation is that if we equalise images (prior to further processing) then we need not worry about any brightness transformation in the original image. This is to be expected, since the linear operation of the brightness change in Equation 3.2 does not change the overall shape of the histogram, only its size and position. However, noise in the image acquisition process will affect the shape of the original histogram, and hence the equalised version. So the equalised histogram of a picture will not be the same as the equalised histogram of a picture with some noise added to it. You cannot avoid noise in electrical systems, however well you design a system to reduce its effect. Accordingly, histogram equalisation finds little use in generic image processing systems, though it can be potent in *specialised* applications. For these reasons, intensity normalisation is often preferred when a picture's histogram requires manipulation.

In implementation, the function `equalise` in Code **3.3**, we shall use an output range where $N_{min} = 0$ and $N_{max} = 255$. The implementation first determines the cumulative histogram for each level of the brightness histogram. This is then used as a look-up table for the new output brightness at that level. The look-up table is used to speed implementation of Equation 3.9, since it can be precomputed from the image to be equalised.

```
equalise(pic)  :=      range←255
                       number←rows(pic)·cols(pic)
                       for bright∈0..255
                          pixels_at_level_bright←0
                       for x∈0..rows(pic)-1
                          for y∈0..rows(pic)-1
                              pixels_at_level_pic_{y,x}←pixels_at_level_pic_{y,x}+1

                       sum←0
                       for level∈0..255
                          | sum←sum+pixels_at_level_level
                          |
                          | hist_level←floor[ ( range/number )·sum+0.00001 ]
                       for x∈0..cols(pic)-1
                          for y∈0..rows(pic)-1
                              newpic_{y,x}←hist_pic_{y,x}

                       newpic
```

Code 3.3 Histogram equalisation

An alternative argument against use of histogram equalisation is that it is a non-linear process and is irreversible. We cannot return to the original picture after equalisation, and we cannot separate the histogram of an unwanted picture. On the other hand, intensity normalisation is a linear process and we can return to the original image, should we need to, or separate pictures, if required.

3.3.4 Thresholding

The last point operator of major interest is called *thresholding*. This operator selects pixels which have a particular value, or are within a specified range. It can be used to find objects within a picture if their brightness level (or range) is known. This implies that the object's brightness must be known as well. There are two main forms: uniform and adaptive thresholding. In *uniform thresholding*, pixels above a specified level are set to white, those below the specified level are set to black. Given the original eye image, Figure **3.7** shows a thresholded image where all pixels *above* 160 brightness levels are set to white, and those below 160 brightness levels are set to black. By this process, the parts pertaining to the facial skin are separated from the background; the cheeks, forehead and other bright areas are separated from the hair and eyes. This can therefore provide a way of isolating points of interest.

Figure 3.7 Thresholding the eye image

Uniform thresholding clearly requires knowledge of the grey level, or the target features might not be selected in the thresholding process. If the level is not known, then histogram equalisation or intensity normalisation can be used, but with the restrictions on performance stated earlier. This is, of course, a problem of image interpretation. These problems can only be solved by simple approaches, such as thresholding, for very special cases. In general, it is often prudent to investigate the more sophisticated techniques of feature selection and extraction, to be covered later. Prior to that, we shall investigate group operators, which are a natural counterpart to point operators.

There are more advanced techniques, known as *optimal thresholding*. These usually seek to select a value for the threshold that separates an object from its background. This suggests that the object has a different range of intensities to the background, in order that an appropriate threshold can be chosen, as illustrated in Figure **3.8**. Otsu's method (Otsu, 1979) is one of the most popular techniques of optimal thresholding; there have been surveys (Sahoo, 1988; Lee 1990; Glasbey, 1993) which compare the performance different methods can achieve. Essentially, Otsu's technique maximises the likelihood that the threshold is chosen so as to split the image between an object and its background. This is achieved by selecting a threshold that gives the best separation of classes, for all pixels in an image. The theory is beyond the scope of this section and we shall merely survey its results and give their implementation. The basis is use of the normalised histogram where the number of points at each level is divided by the total number of points in the image. As such, this represents a probability distribution for the intensity levels as

$$p(l) = \frac{\mathbf{N}(l)}{N^2} \tag{3.11}$$

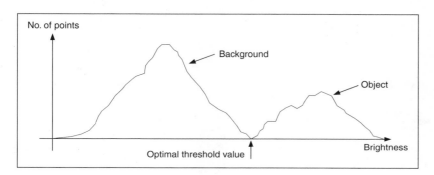

Figure 3.8 Optimal thresholding

This can be used to compute then zero- and first-order cumulative moments of the normalised histogram up to the kth level as

$$\omega(k) = \sum_{l=1}^{k} p(l) \tag{3.12}$$

and $$\mu(k) = \sum_{l=1}^{k} l \cdot p(l) \tag{3.13}$$

The total mean level of the image is given by

$$\mu T = \sum_{l=1}^{\mathbf{N}_{max}} l \cdot p(l) \tag{3.14}$$

The variance of the class separability is then the ratio

$$\sigma_B^2(k) = \frac{(\mu T \cdot \omega(k) - \mu(k))^2}{\omega(k)(1 - \omega(k))} \quad \forall k \in 1, \mathbf{N}_{max} \tag{3.15}$$

The optimal threshold is the level for which the variance of class separability is at its maximum, namely the optimal threshold T_{opt} is that for which the variance

$$\sigma_B^2(T_{opt}) = \max_{1 \le k < \mathbf{N}max} (\sigma_B^2(k)) \tag{3.16}$$

A comparison of uniform thresholding with optimal thresholding is given in Figure **3.9** for the eye image. The threshold selected by Otsu's operator is actually slightly lower than the value selected manually, and so the thresholded image does omit some detail around the eye, especially in the eyelids. However, the selection by Otsu is *automatic*, as opposed to *manual* and this can be to application advantage in automated vision. Consider, for example, the need to isolate the human figure in Figure **3.10**(a). This can be performed automatically by Otsu as shown in Figure **3.10**(b). Note, however, that there are some extra points, due to illumination, which have appeared in the resulting image together with the human subject. It is easy to remove the isolated points, as we will see later, but more difficult to remove the connected ones. In this instance, the size of the human shape could be used as information to remove the extra points, though you might like to suggest other factors that could lead to their removal.

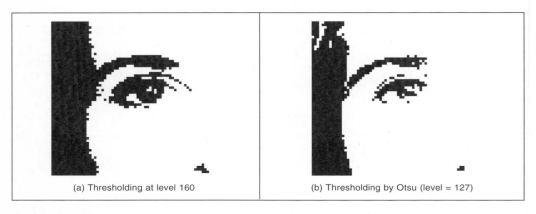

| (a) Thresholding at level 160 | (b) Thresholding by Otsu (level = 127) |

Figure 3.9 Thresholding the eye image: manual and automatic

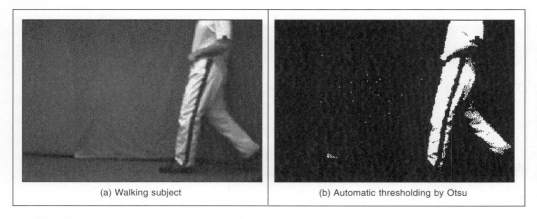

| (a) Walking subject | (b) Automatic thresholding by Otsu |

Figure 3.10 Thresholding an image of a walking subject

The code implementing Otsu's technique is given in Code **3.4** which follows Equations 3.11 to 3.16 to directly to provide the results in Figures **3.9** and **3.10**. Here, the histogram function of Code **3.1** is used to give the normalised histogram. The remaining code refers directly to the earlier description of Otsu's technique.

$$\omega(k, \text{histogram}) := \sum_{I=1}^{k} \text{histogram}_{I-1}$$

$$\mu(k, \text{histogram}) := \sum_{I=1}^{k} I \cdot \text{histogram}_{I-1}$$

$$\mu T(\text{histogram}) := \sum_{I=1}^{256} I \cdot \text{histogram}_{I-1}$$

```
Otsu(image):=
    |  image_hist ← histogram(image) / (rows(image)·cols(image))
    |
    |  for k∈1..255
    |
    |     values_k ← (μT(image_hist)·ω(k, image_hist)-μ(k, image_hist))² / (ω(k, image_hist)·(1-ω(k, image_hist)))
    |
    |  find_value(max(values),values)
```

Code 3.4 Optimal thresholding by Otsu's technique

Also, we have so far considered *global* techniques, methods that operate on the entire image. There are also *locally adaptive* techniques that are often used to binarise document images prior to character recognition. A recent survey (Trier, 1995) compares global and local techniques with reference to document image analysis. These techniques are often used in statistical pattern recognition: the thresholded object is classified according to its statistical properties. However, these techniques find less use in image interpretation, where a common paradigm is that there is more than one object in the scene, such as Figure **3.7** where the thresholding operator has selected many objects of potential interest. As such, only uniform thresholding is used in many vision applications, since objects are often occluded (hidden), and many objects have similar ranges of pixel intensity. Accordingly, more sophisticated metrics are required to separate them, by using the uniformly thresholded image, as discussed in later chapters.

3.4 Group operations

3.4.1 Template convolution

Group operations calculate new pixel values from pixels' neighbourhoods by using a 'grouping' process. The group operation is usually expressed in terms of *template convolution* where the template is a set of weighting coefficients. The template is usually square, and its size is usually odd to ensure that it can be positioned appropriately. The size is normally used to describe the template; a 3 × 3 template is three pixels wide by three pixels long. New pixel values are calculated by placing the template at the point of interest. Pixel values are multiplied by the corresponding weighting coefficient and added to an overall sum. The sum (usually) evaluates a new value for the centre pixel (where the template is centred) and this becomes the pixel in a new output image. If the template's position has not yet reached the end of a line, the template is then moved horizontally by one pixel and the process repeats.

This is illustrated in Figure **3.11** where a new image is calculated from an original one, by template convolution. The calculation obtained by template convolution for the centre pixel of the template in the original image becomes the point in the output image. Since the template cannot extend beyond the image, the new image is smaller than the original image since a new value cannot be computed for points in the border of the new image. When the template reaches the end of a line, it is repositioned at the start of the next line. For a 3×3 neighbourhood, nine weighting coefficients w_t are applied to points in the original image to calculate a point in the new image. To calculate the value in new image **N** at point with co-ordinates x, y, the template in Figure **3.12** operates on an original image **O** according to:

$$
\mathbf{N}_{x,y} =
\begin{aligned}
& w_0 \times \mathbf{O}_{x-1,y-1} + w_1 \times \mathbf{O}_{x,y-1} + w_2 \times \mathbf{O}_{x+1,y-1} + \\
& w_3 \times \mathbf{O}_{x-1,y} + w_4 \times \mathbf{O}_{x,y} + w_5 \times \mathbf{O}_{x+1,y} + \qquad \forall x,y \in 2, N-1 \\
& w_6 \times \mathbf{O}_{x-1,y+1} + w_7 \times \mathbf{O}_{x,y+1} + w_8 \times \mathbf{O}_{x+1,y+1} +
\end{aligned}
\qquad (3.17)
$$

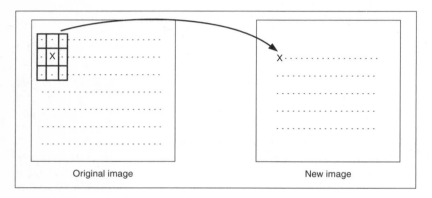

Figure 3.11   Template convolution process

w_0	w_1	w_2
w_3	w_4	w_5
w_6	w_7	w_8

Figure 3.12 3×3 template and weighting coefficents

Note that we cannot ascribe values to the picture's borders. This is because when we place the template at the border, parts of the template fall outside the image and we have no information from which to calculate the new pixel value. The width of the border equals half the size of the template. To calculate values for the border pixels, we now have three choices:

1. set the border to black (or deliver a smaller picture);
2. assume (as in Fourier) that the image replicates to infinity along both dimensions and calculate new values by cyclic shift from the far border; or
3. calculate the pixel value from a smaller area.

None of these approaches is optimal. The results here use the first option and set border pixels to black. Note that in many applications the object of interest is imaged centrally or, at least, imaged within the picture. As such, the border information is of little consequence to the remainder of the process. Here, the border points are set to black, by starting functions with a zero function which sets all the points in the picture initially to black (0).

The Matlab implementation of a general template convolution operator `convolve` is given in Code **3.5**. This function accepts, as arguments, the picture `image` and the template to be convolved with it, `template`. The result of template convolution is a picture `convolved`. The operator first initialises the temporary image `temp` to black (zero brightness levels). Then the size of the template is evaluated. These give the range of

```
function convolved=convolve(image,template)
%New image point brightness convolution of template with image
%Usage: [new image]=convolve(image,template of point values)
%Parameters: image-array of points
% template-array of weighting coefficients
%Author: Mark S. Nixon

%get image dimensions
[irows,icols]=size(image);

%get template dimensions
[trows,tcols]=size(template);

%set a temporary image to black
temp(1:irows,1:icols)=0;

%half of template rows is
trhalf=floor(trows/2);
%half of template cols is
tchalf=floor(tcols/2);

%then convolve the template
for x=trhalf+1:icols-trhalf %address all columns except border
  for y=tchalf+1:irows-tchalf %address all rows except border
    sum=0;
    for iwin=1:trows %address template columns
      for jwin=1:tcols %address template rows
        sum=sum+image(y+jwin-tchalf-1,x+iwin-trhalf-1)*
                       template(jwin,iwin);
      end
    end
    temp(y,x)=sum;
  end
end

%finally, normalise the image
convolved=normalise(temp);
```

Code 3.5 Template convolution operator

picture points to be processed in the outer `for` loops that give the co-ordinates of all points resulting from template convolution. The template is convolved at each picture point by generating a running summation of the pixel values within the template's window multiplied by the respective template weighting coefficient. Finally, the resulting image is normalised to ensure that the brightness levels are occupied appropriately.

Template convolution is usually implemented in software. It can of course be implemented in hardware and requires a two-line store, together with some further latches, for the (input) video data. The output is the result of template convolution, summing the result of multiplying weighting coefficients by pixel values. This is called pipelining, since the pixels essentially move along a pipeline of information. Note that two line stores can be used if the video fields only are processed. To process a full frame, one of the fields must be stored if it is presented in interlaced format.

Processing can be analogue, using operational amplifier circuits and a Charge Coupled Device (CCD) for storage along bucket brigade delay lines. Finally, an alternative implementation is to use a parallel architecture: for Multiple Instruction Multiple Data (MIMD) architectures, the picture can be split into blocks (spatial partitioning); Single Instruction Multiple Data (SIMD) architectures can implement template convolution as a combination of shift and add instructions.

3.4.2 Averaging operator

For an *averaging operator*, the template weighting functions are unity (or 1/9 to ensure that the result of averaging nine white pixels is white, not more than white!). The template for a 3×3 averaging operator, implementing Equation 3.17, is given by the template in Figure **3.13**. The result of averaging the eye image with a 3×3 operator is shown in Figure **3.14**. This shows that much of the detail has now disappeared revealing the broad image structure. The eyes and eyebrows are now much clearer from the background, but the fine detail in their structure has been removed.

1/9	1/9	1/9
1/9	1/9	1/9
1/9	1/9	1/9

Figure 3.13 3×3 averaging operator template coefficients

For a general implementation, Code **3.6**, we can define the width of the operator as `winsize`, the template size is `winsize × winsize`. We then form the average of all points within the area covered by the template. This is normalised (divided by) the number of points in the template's window. This is a direct implementation of a general averaging operator (i.e. without using the template convolution operator in Code **3.5**).

In order to implement averaging by using the template convolution operator, we need to define a template. This is illustrated for direct averaging in Code **3.7**, even though the simplicity of the direct averaging template usually precludes such implementation. The application of this template is also shown in Code **3.7**. (Note that there are averaging operators in Mathcad and Matlab that can be used for this purpose too.)

Figure 3.14 Applying direct averaging

```
ave(pic,winsize)  :=
            │new←zero(pic)
            │
            │half←floor(winsize/2)
            │
            │for x∈half..cols(pic)-half-1
            │   for y∈half..rows(pic)-half-1
            │
            │           new_{y,x}←floor[ (Σ_{iwin=0}^{winsize-1} Σ_{jwin=0}^{winsize-1} pic_{y+iwin-half,x+jwin-half}) / (winsize·winsize) ]
            │
            │new
```

Code 3.6 Direct averaging

```
averaging_template(winsize):=  │ sum←winsize·winsize
                               │ for y∈0..winsize-1
                               │    for x∈0..winsize-1
                               │       template_{y,x}←1
                               │ template
                               │ ‾‾‾‾‾‾‾‾
                               │   sum
smoothed := tm_conv(p, averaging_template(3))
```

Code 3.7 Direct averaging by template convolution

The effect of averaging is to reduce noise, this is its advantage. An associated disadvantage is that averaging causes blurring which reduces detail in an image. It is also a *low-pass* filter since its effect is to allow low spatial frequencies to be retained, and to suppress high frequency components. A larger template, say 5×5, will remove more noise (high frequencies) but reduce the level of detail. The size of an averaging operator is then equivalent to the reciprocal of the bandwidth of a low-pass filter it implements.

Since smoothing was earlier achieved by low-pass filtering the Fourier transform (Section 2.8), the Fourier transform actually gives an alternative method to implement template convolution. In Fourier transforms, the dual process to convolution is multiplication (as in Section 2.3). So template convolution can be implemented by multiplying the Fourier transform of the template with the Fourier transform of the picture to which the template is to be applied. The result needs to be inverse transformed to return to the picture domain. The transform of the template and the picture need to be the same size. Accordingly, the image containing the template is zero-padded prior to its transform. The process is illustrated in Code **3.8** and starts by calculation of the transform of the zero-padded template. The convolution routine then multiplies the transform of the template by the transform of the picture point by point (using the vectorize operator). When the routine is invoked, it is supplied with a transformed picture. The resulting transform is re-ordered prior to inverse transformation, to ensure that the image is presented correctly. (Theoretical study of this process is presented in Section 5.3.2 where we show how the same process can be used to find shapes in images.)

```
conv(pic,temp):=   pic_spectrum←Fourier(pic)
                   temp_spectrum←Fourier(temp)

                   convolved_spectrum←(pic_spectrum.temp_spectrum)
                   result←inv_Fourier(rearrange(convolved_spectrum))
                   result

new_smooth  :=conv(p,  square)
```

Code 3.8   Template convolution by the Fourier transform

Code **3.8** is simply a different implementation of direct averaging. It achieves the same result, but by transform domain calculus. It can be faster to use the transform rather than the direct implementation. The computational cost of a 2D FFT is of the order of $N^2 \log(N)$. If the transform of the template is precomputed, there are two transforms required and there is one multiplication for each of the N^2 transformed points. The total cost of the Fourier implementation of template convolution is then of the order of

$$C_{FFT} = 4N^2 \log(N) + N^2 \tag{3.18}$$

The cost of the direct implementation for an $m \times m$ template is then m^2 multiplications for each image point, so the cost of the direct implementation is of the order of

$$C_{dir} = N^2 m^2 \tag{3.19}$$

For $C_{dir} < C_{FFT}$, we require:

$$N^2 m^2 < 4N^2 \log(N) + N^2 \tag{3.20}$$

If the direct implementation of template matching is faster than its Fourier implementation, we need to choose m so that

$$m^2 < 4 \log(N) + 1 \tag{3.21}$$

This implies that, for a 256×256 image, a direct implementation is fastest for 3×3 and

5×5 templates, whereas a transform calculation is faster for larger ones. An alternative analysis (Campbell, 1969) has suggested that (Gonzalez, 1987) 'if the number of non-zero terms in (the template) is less than 132 then a direct implementation . . . is more efficient than using the FFT approach'. This implies a considerably larger template than our analysis suggests. This is in part due to higher considerations of complexity than our analysis has included. There are, naturally, further considerations in the use of transform calculus, the most important being the use of windowing (such as Hamming or Hanning) operators to reduce variance in high-order spectral estimates. This implies that template convolution by transform calculus should perhaps be used when large templates are involved, and then only when speed is critical. If speed is indeed critical, then it might be better to implement the operator in dedicated hardware, as described earlier.

3.4.3 On different template size

Templates can be larger than 3×3. Since they are usually centred on a point of interest, to produce a new output value at that point, they are usually of odd dimension. For reasons of speed, the most common sizes are 3×3, 5×5 and 7×7. Beyond this, say 9×9, many template points are used to calculate a single value for a new point, and this imposes high computational cost, especially for large images. (For example, a 9×9 operator covers nine times more points than a 3×3 operator.) Square templates have the same properties along both image axes. Some implementations use vector templates (a line), either because their properties are desirable in a particular application, or for reasons of speed.

The effect of larger averaging operators is to smooth the image more, to remove more detail whilst giving greater emphasis to the large structures. This is illustrated in Figure **3.15**. A 5×5 operator, Figure **3.15**(a), retains more detail than a 7×7 operator, Figure **3.15**(b), and much more than a 9×9 operator, Figure **3.15**(c). Conversely, the 9×9 operator retains only the largest structures such as the eye region (and virtually removing the iris) whereas this is retained more by the operators of smaller size. Note that the larger operators leave a larger border (since new values cannot be computed in that region) and this can be seen in the increase in border size for the larger operators, in Figures **3.15**(b) and (c).

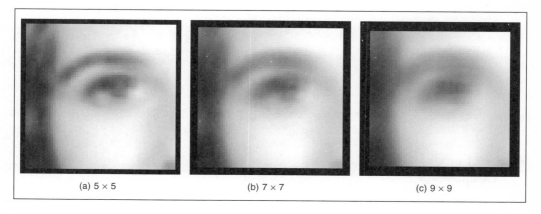

(a) 5×5 (b) 7×7 (c) 9×9

Figure 3.15 Illustrating the effect of window size

3.4.4 Gaussian averaging operator

The *Gaussian averaging operator* has been considered to be optimal for image smoothing. The template for the Gaussian operator has values set by the Gaussian relationship. The Gaussian *function g* at co-ordinates x, y is controlled by the variance σ^2 according to:

$$g(x, y) = e^{-\left(\frac{x^2+y^2}{2\sigma^2}\right)} \tag{3.22}$$

Equation 3.22 gives a way to calculate coefficients for a Gaussian template which is then convolved with an image. The effects of selection of Gaussian templates of differing size are shown in Figure **3.16**. The Gaussian function essentially removes the influence of points greater than 3σ in (radial) distance from the centre of the template. The 3×3 operator, Figure **3.16**(a), retains many more of the features than those retained by direct averaging (Figure **3.14**). The effect of larger size is to remove more detail (and noise) at the expense of losing features. This is reflected in the loss of internal eye component by the 5 $\times$ 5 and 7×7 operators in Figures **3.16**(b) and (c), respectively.

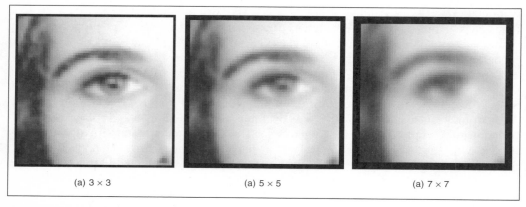

(a) 3 × 3	(a) 5 × 5	(a) 7 × 7

Figure 3.16   Applying Gaussian averaging

A surface plot of the 2D Gaussian function of Equation 3.22 has the famous bell shape, as shown in Figure **3.17**. The values of the function at discrete points are the values of a Gaussian template. Convolving this template with an image gives Gaussian averaging: the point in the averaged picture is calculated from the sum of a region where the central parts of the picture are weighted to contribute more than the peripheral points. The size of the template essentially dictates appropriate choice of the variance. The variance is chosen to ensure that template coefficients drop to near zero at the template's edge. A common choice for the template size is 5×5 with variance unity, giving the template shown in Figure **3.18**.

This template is then convolved with the image to give the Gaussian blurring function. It is actually possible to give the Gaussian blurring function antisymmetric properties by scaling the x and y co-ordinates. This can find application when an object's shape, and orientation, is known prior to image analysis.

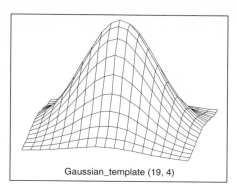

Gaussian_template (19, 4)

Figure 3.17 Gaussian function

0.02	0.08	0.14	0.08	0.02
0.08	0.37	0.61	0.37	0.08
0.14	0.61	1.0	0.61	0.14
0.08	0.37	0.61	0.37	0.08
0.02	0.08	0.14	0.08	0.02

Figure 3.18 Template for the 5 × 5 Gaussian averaging operator σ = 1.0)

By reference to Figure **3.16** it is clear that the Gaussian filter can offer improved performance compared with direct averaging: more features are retained whilst the noise is removed. This can be understood by Fourier transform theory. In Section 2.4.2 (Chapter 2) we found that the Fourier transform of a *square* is a two-dimensional *sinc* function. This has a non-even frequency response (the magnitude of the transform does not reduce in a smooth manner) and has regions where the transform becomes negative, called sidelobes. These can have undesirable effects since there are high frequencies that contribute *more* than some lower ones, a bit paradoxical in low-pass filtering to remove noise. In contrast, the Fourier transform of a Gaussian function is another Gaussian function, which decreases smoothly without these sidelobes. This can lead to better performance since the contributions of the frequency components reduce in a controlled manner.

In a software implementation of the Gaussian operator, we need a function implementing Equation 3.22, the `Gaussian_template` function in Code **3.9**. This is used to calculate the coefficients of a template to be centred on an image point. The two arguments are `winsize`, the (square) operator's size, and the standard deviation σ that controls its width, as discussed earlier. The operator coefficients are normalised by the sum of template values, as before. This summation is stored in `sum`, which is initialised to zero. The centre of the square template is then evaluated as half the size of the operator. Then, all template coefficients are calculated by a version of Equation 3.22 which specifies a weight relative to the centre co-ordinates. Finally, the normalised template coefficients are returned as the Gaussian template. The operator is used in template convolution, via `convolve`, as in direct averaging (Code **3.5**).

```
function template=gaussian_template(winsize,sigma)
%Template for Gaussian averaging

%Usage:[template]=gaussian_template(number, number)

%Parameters: winsize-size of template (odd, integer)
%sigma-variance of Gaussian function
%Author: Mark S. Nixon

%centre is half of window size
centre=floor(winsize/2)+1;

%we'll normalise by the total sum
sum=0;

%so work out the coefficients and the running total
for i=1:winsize
  for j=1:winsize
    template(j,i)=exp(-(((j-centre)*(j-centre))+((i-centre)*
      (i-centre)))/(2*sigma*sigma))
    sum=sum+template(j,i);
  end
end

%and then normalise
template=template/sum;
```

Code 3.9   Gaussian template specification

3.5   Other statistical operators

3.5.1   More on averaging

The averaging process is actually a statistical operator since it aims to estimate the mean of a local neighbourhood. The error in the process is naturally high, for a population of N samples, the statistical error is of the order of:

$$\text{error} = \frac{\text{mean}}{\sqrt{N}} \tag{3.23}$$

Increasing the averaging operator's size improves the error in the estimate of the mean, but at the expense of fine detail in the image. The average is of course an estimate optimal for a signal corrupted by additive *Gaussian noise* (see Appendix 2.1, Section 8.2). The estimate of the mean maximised the probability that the noise has its mean value, namely zero. According to the *central limit theorem*, the result of adding many noise sources together is a Gaussian distributed noise source. In images, noise arises in sampling, in quantisation, in transmission and in processing. By the central limit theorem, the result of these (independent) noise sources is that image noise can be assumed to be Gaussian. In fact, image noise is *not* necessarily Gaussian-distributed, giving rise to more statistical operators. One of these is the *median* operator which has demonstrated capability to reduce noise whilst retaining feature boundaries (in contrast to smoothing which blurs both noise and the boundaries), and the *mode* operator which can be viewed as optimal for a number of noise sources, including *Rayleigh noise*, but is very difficult to determine for small, discrete, populations.

3.5.2 Median filter

The *median* is another frequently used statistic; the median is the centre of a rank-ordered distribution. The median is usually taken from a template centred on the point of interest. Given the arrangement of pixels in Figure **3.19**(a), the pixel values are arranged into a vector format, Figure **3.19**(b). The vector is then sorted into ascending order, Figure **3.19**(c). The median is the central component of the sorted vector, this is the fifth component since we have nine values.

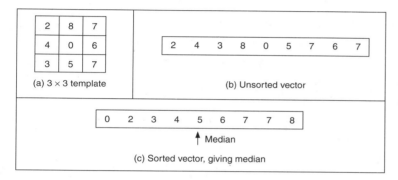

Figure 3.19   Finding the median from a 3 × 3 template

The median operator is usually implemented using a template, here we shall consider a 3 × 3 template. Accordingly, we need to process the nine pixels in a template centred on a point with co-ordinates (x, y). In a Mathcad implementation, these nine points can be extracted into vector format using the operator `unsorted` in Code **3.10**. This requires an integer pointer to nine values, `x1`. The modulus operator is then used to ensure that the correct nine values are extracted.

```
x1 := 0..8
unsorted_x1 := p_{x+mod(x1,3)-1, x+floor(x1/3)-1}
```

Code 3.10   Reformatting a neighbourhood into a vector

We then arrange the nine pixels, within the template, in ascending order using the Mathcad `sort` function, Code **3.11**:

This gives the rank ordered list and the median is the central component of the sorted vector, in this case the fifth component, Code **3.12**.

```
sorted := sort (unsorted)
```

Code 3.11   Using the Mathcad sort function

```
our_median := sorted₄
```

Code 3.12   Determining the median

These functions can then be grouped to give the full median operator as in Code **3.13**.

```
med(pic) := | newpic←zero(pic)
            | for x∈1..cols(pic)-2
            |    for y∈1..rows(pic)-2
            |       for x1∈0..8
            |          unsorted_{x1}←pic_{y+mod(x1,3)-1,x+floor(x1/3)-1}
            |          sorted←sort(unsorted)
            |          newpic_{y,x}←sorted₄
            |
            | newpic
```

Code 3.13   Determining the median

The median can of course be taken from *larger* template sizes. It is available as the `median` operator in Mathcad, but only for square matrices. The development here has aimed not only to demonstrate how the median operator works, but also to provide a basis for further development. The rank ordering process is computationally demanding (*slow*) and this has motivated use of template shapes other than a square. A selection of alternative shapes is shown in Figure **3.20**. Common alternative shapes include a cross or a line (horizontal or vertical), centred on the point of interest, which can afford much faster operation since they cover fewer pixels. The basis of the arrangement presented here could be used for these alternative shapes, if required.

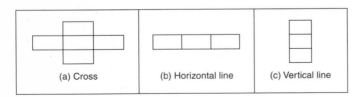

    (a) Cross   (b) Horizontal line   (c) Vertical line

Figure 3.20   Alternative template shapes for median operator

The median has a well-known ability to remove *salt and pepper noise*. This form of noise, arising from, say, decoding errors in picture transmission systems, can cause isolated white and black points to appear within an image. It can also arise when rotating an image, when points remain unspecified by a standard rotation operator (Appendix 1), as in a texture image, rotated by 10° in Figure **3.21**(a). When a median operator is applied, the salt and pepper noise points will appear at either end of the rank ordered list and are removed by the median process, as shown in Figure **3.21**(b). The median operator has practical advantage, due to its ability to retain edges (the boundaries of shapes in images) whilst suppressing the noise contamination. As such, like direct averaging, it remains a worthwhile member of the stock of standard image processing tools. For further details concerning properties and implementation, have a peep at Hodgson (1985). (Note that practical implementation of image rotation is a computer graphics issue, and is usually by *texture mapping*; further details can be found in Hearn (1997)).

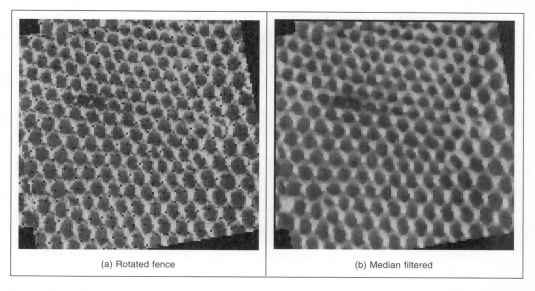

(a) Rotated fence
(b) Median filtered

Figure 3.21 Illustrating median filtering

Finding the *background* to an image is an example application of statistical operators. Say we have a sequence of images of a walking subject, and we want to be able to find the background (so we can then separate the walking subject from it), such as the sequence of images shown in Figures **3.22**(a)–(f) where a subject is walking from left to right. We can average the images so as to find the background. If we form a *temporal average*, an image where each point is the average of the points in the same position in each of the six images, then we achieve a result where the walking subject appears to be in the background, but very faintly as in Figure **3.22**(g). The shadow occurs since the walking subject's influence on image brightness is reduced by one-sixth, but it is still there. We could of course use more images, the ones in between the ones we already have and then the shadow will become much fainter. We can also include spatial averaging as in Section 3.3.2, to further reduce the effect of the walking subject, as shown in Figure **3.22**(h). This gives *spatiotemporal averaging*. For this, we have not required any more images, but the penalty paid for the better improvement in the estimate of the background is lack of detail. We cannot see the numbers in the clock, due to the nature of spatial averaging. However, if we form the background image by taking the median of the six images, a *temporal median*, we then get a much better estimate of the background as shown in Figure **3.22**(i). A lot of the image detail is retained, whilst the walking subject disappears. In this case, for a *sequence* of images where the target walks in front of a *static* background, the median is the most appropriate operator. If we did not have a sequence, we could just average the single image with a large operator and that could provide some estimate of the background.

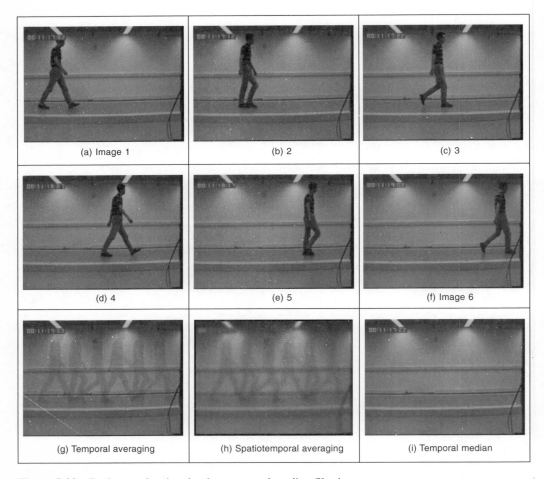

(a) Image 1   (b) 2   (c) 3

(d) 4   (e) 5   (f) Image 6

(g) Temporal averaging   (h) Spatiotemporal averaging   (i) Temporal median

Figure 3.22 Background estimation by mean and median filtering

3.5.3 Mode filter

The *mode* is the final statistic of interest. This is of course very difficult to determine for small populations and theoretically does not even exist for a continuous distribution. Consider, for example, determining the mode of the pixels within a square 5×5 template. Naturally, it is possible for all 25 pixels to be different, so each could be considered to be the mode. As such we are forced to estimate the mode: the truncated median filter, as introduced by

Davies (1988) aims to achieve this. The *truncated median filter* is based on the premise that for many non-Gaussian distributions, the order of the mean, the median and the mode is the same for many images, as illustrated in Figure **3.23**. Accordingly, if we truncate the distribution (i.e. remove part of it, where the part selected to be removed in Figure **3.23** is from the region beyond the mean) then the median of the truncated distribution will approach the mode of the original distribution.

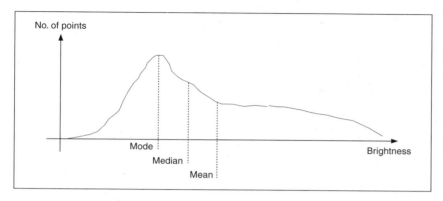

Figure 3.23 Arrangement of mode, median and mean

The implementation of the truncated median, `trun_med`, operator is given in Code **3.14**. The operator first finds the mean and the median of the current window. The distribution of intensity of points within the current window is truncated on the side of the mean so that the median now bisects the distribution of the remaining points (as such not affecting symmetrical distributions). So that the median bisects the remaining distribution, if the median is less than the mean then the point at which the distribution is truncated, *upper*, is

$$upper = median + (median - \min(distribution))$$

$$= 2 \cdot median - \min(distribution)$$

(3.24)

If the median is greater than the mean, then we need to truncate at a lower point (before the mean), *lower*, given by

$$lower = 2 \cdot median - \max(distribution)$$

(3.25)

The median of the remaining distribution then approaches the mode. The truncation is performed by storing pixel values in a vector `trun`. A pointer, `cc`, is incremented each time a new point is stored. The median of the truncated vector is then the output of the truncated median filter at that point. Naturally, the window is placed at each possible image point, as in template convolution. However, there can be several iterations at each position to ensure that the mode is approached. In practice only few iterations are usually required for the median to converge to the mode. The window size is usually large, say 7 × 7 or 9 × 9 or more.

The action of the operator is illustrated in Figure **3.24** when applied to a 128 × 128 part of the ultrasound image (Figure **1.1**(c)), from the centre of the image and containing a cross-sectional view of an artery. Ultrasound results in particularly noisy images, in part

```
trun_med(p,wsze) :=  newpic←zero(p)

                     ha←floor( wsze )
                               ( ──── )
                               (   2  )

                     for x∈ha..cols(p)-ha-1
                       for y∈ha..rows(p)-ha-1
                          win←submatric(p, y-ha, y+ha, x-ha, x+ha)
                          med←median(win)
                          ave←mean(win)
                          upper←2.med-min(win)
                          lower←2.med-max(win)
                          cc←0
                          for i∈0..wsze-1
                             for j∈0..wsze-1
                               trun_cc←win_{j,i} if (win_{j,i}<upper)·(med<ave)
                               trun_cc←win_{j,i} if (win_{j,i}>lower)·(med>ave)
                               cc←cc+1
                          newpic_{y,x}←median(turn)

                     newpic
```

Code 3.14   The truncated median operator

because the scanner is usually external to the body. The noise is actually multiplicative Rayleigh noise for which the mode is the optimal estimate. This noise obscures the artery which appears in cross-section in Figure **3.24**(a); the artery is basically elliptical in shape. The action of the 9×9 truncated median operator, Figure **3.24**(b) is to remove noise whilst retaining feature boundaries whilst a larger operator shows better effect, Figure **3.24**(c).

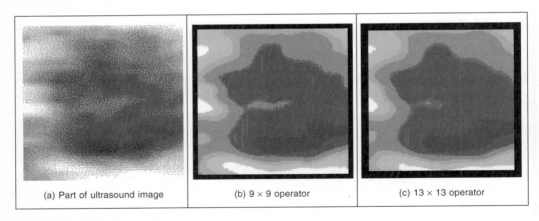

(a) Part of ultrasound image   (b) 9×9 operator   (c) 13×13 operator

Figure 3.24   Applying truncated median filtering

Close examination of the result of the truncated median filter is that a selection of boundaries is preserved which is not readily apparent in the original ultrasound image.

This is one of the known properties of median filtering: an ability to reduce noise whilst retaining feature boundaries. Indeed, there have actually been many other approaches to speckle filtering; the most popular include direct averaging (Shankar, 1986), median filtering, adaptive (weighted) median filtering (Loupas, 1987) and unsharp masking (Bamber, 1986).

3.5.4 Comparison of statistical operators

The different image filtering operators are shown by way of comparison in Figure **3.25**. All operators are 5×5 and are applied to the earlier ultrasound image, Figure **3.24**(a). Figure **3.25**(a), (b), (c), and (d) are the result of the mean (direct averaging), Gaussian averaging, median and truncated median, respectively. Each shows a different performance: the mean operator removes much noise but blurs feature boundaries; Gaussian averaging retains more features, but shows little advantage over direct averaging (it is not Gaussian-distributed noise anyway); the median operator retains some noise but with clear feature boundaries; whereas the truncated median removes more noise, but along with picture detail. Clearly, the increased size of the truncated median template, by the results in Figures **3.24**(b) and (c), can offer improved performance. This is to be expected since by increasing the size of the truncated median template, we are essentially increasing the size of the distribution from which the mode is found.

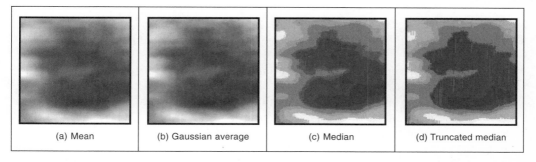

| (a) Mean | (b) Gaussian average | (c) Median | (d) Truncated median |

Figure 3.25   Comparison of filtering operators

As yet, however, we have not yet studied any quantitative means to evaluate this comparison. We can only perform subjective appraisal of the images in Figure **3.25**. This appraisal has been phrased in terms of the contrast boundaries perceived in the image, and on the basic shape that the image presents. Accordingly, better appraisal is based on the use of feature extraction. Boundaries are the low-level features studied in the next chapter; shape is a high-level feature studied in Chapter 5.

3.6 Further reading

Many texts cover basic point and group operators in much detail, in particular the introductory texts such as Fairhurst (Fairhurst, 1988) and Baxes (Baxes, 1994) (which includes more detail about hardware implementation); other texts give many more examples (Russ, 1995). Books with a C implementation often concentrate on more basic techniques including low-level image processing (Lindley, 1991) and (Parker, 1994). Some of the more advanced texts include more coverage of low-level operators, such as Rosenfeld and Kak (Rosenfeld, 1982) and Castleman (Castleman, 1996). Parker (1994) includes C code for nearly all the low-level operations in this chapter. For study of the effect of the median operator on image data, see Bovik (1987). The Truncated Median Filter is covered again in Davies (1994). For further study of the effects of different statistical operators on ultrasound images, see Evans (1995, 1996).

3.7 References

Baxes, G. A., *Digital Image Processing, Principles and Applications*, Wiley & Sons Inc., NY USA, 1994

Bamber, J. C. and Daft, C., Adaptive Filtering for Reduction of Speckle in Ultrasonic Pulse-Echo Images, *Ultrasonics*, **24**(3), pp. 41–44, 1986

Bovik, A. C., Huang, T. S. and Munson, D. C., The Effect of Median Filtering on Edge Estimation and Detection, *IEEE Trans. on PAMI*, **9**(2), pp. 181–194, 1987

Campbell, J. D., *Edge Structure and the Representation of Pictures*, PhD Thesis, University Missouri, Columbia USA, 1969

Castleman, K. R., *Digital Image Processing*, Prentice Hall Inc., Englewood Cliffs, NJ, USA, 1996

Davies, E. R., On the Noise Suppression Characteristics of the Median, Truncated Median and Mode Filters, *Pattern Recog. Lett.*, **7**(2), pp. 87–97, 1988

Davies, E. R., *Machine Vision: Theory, Algorithms and Practicalities*, Academic Press, London UK, 1990

Evans, A. N. and Nixon, M. S., Mode Filtering to Reduce Ultrasound Speckle for Feature Extraction, *Proc. IEE-Vision, Image and Signal Processing*, **142**(2), pp. 87–94, 1995

Evans, A. N. and Nixon, M. S., Biased Motion-Adaptive Temporal Filtering for Speckle Reduction in Echocardiography, *IEEE Trans. Medical Imaging*, **15**(1), pp. 39–50, 1996

Fairhurst, M. C., *Computer Vision for Robotic Systems*, Prentice Hall International (UK) Ltd, Hemel Hempstead UK, 1988

Glasbey, C. A., An Analysis of Histogram-Based Thresholding Algorithms, *CVGIP-Graphical Models and Image Processing*, **55**(6), pp. 532–537, 1993

Gonzalez, R. C. and Wintz, P., *Digital Image Processing*, 2nd Edition, Addison Wesley Publishing Co. Inc., Reading, MA USA, 1987

Hearn, D. and Baker, M. P., *Computer Graphics C Version*, 2nd Edition, Prentice Hall, Inc., Upper Saddle River, NJ USA, 1997

Hodgson, R. M., Bailey, D. G., Naylor, M. J., Ng, A. and Mcneill, S. J., Properties, Implementations and Applications of Rank Filters, *Image and Vision Computing*, **3**(1), pp. 3–14, 1985

Lee, S. A., Chung, S. Y. and Park, R. H., A Comparative Performance Study of Several Global Thresholding Techniques for Segmentation, *CVGIP*, **52**, pp. 171–190, 1990

Lindley, C. A., *Practical Image Processing in C*, Wiley & Sons Inc., NY USA, 1991

Loupas, T. and McDicken, W. N., Noise Reduction in Ultrasound Images by Digital Filtering, *British Journal of Radiology*, **60**, pp. 389–392, 1987

Otsu, N., A Threshold Selection Method from Gray-Level Histograms, *IEEE Trans. on SMC*, **9**(1) pp. 62–66, 1979

Parker, J. R., *Practical Computer Vision using C*, Wiley & Sons Inc., NY USA, 1994

Rosenfeld, A. and Kak, A. C., *Digital Picture Processing*, 2nd Edition, Vols 1 and 2, Academic Press Inc., Orlando, FL USA, 1982

Russ, J. C., *The Image Processing Handbook*, 2nd Edition, CRC Press (IEEE Press), Boca Raton, FL USA, 1995

Sahoo, P. K., Soltani, S., Wong, A. K. C. and Chen, Y. C., Survey of Thresholding Techniques, *CVGIP*, **41**(2), pp. 233–260, 1988

Shankar, P. M., Speckle Reduction in Ultrasound B Scans using Weighted Averaging in Spatial Compounding, *IEEE Trans. on Ultrasonics, Ferroelectrics and Frequency Control*, **33**(6), pp. 754–758, 1986

Trier, O. D. and Jain, A. K., Goal-Directed Evaluation of Image Binarisation Methods, *IEEE Trans. on PAMI*, **17**(12), pp. 1191–1201, 1995

4
Low-level feature extraction (including edge detection)

4.1 Overview

We shall define *low-level features* to be those basic features that can be extracted automatically from an image without any shape information (information about *spatial* relationships) as shown in Table 4.1. As such, thresholding is actually a form of low-level feature extraction performed as a point operation. Naturally, all of these approaches can be used in high-level feature extraction, where we find shapes in images. It is well known that we can recognise people from caricaturists' portraits. That is the first low-level feature we shall encounter. It is called *edge detection* and it aims to produce a *line drawing*, like one of a face in Figures **4.1**(a) and (d), something akin to a caricaturist's sketch though without the exaggeration a caricaturist would imbue. There are very basic techniques and more advanced ones and we shall look at some of the most popular approaches. The first-order detectors are equivalent to first-order differentiation and, naturally, the second-order edge detection operators are equivalent to a one-higher level of differentiation.

We shall also consider corner detection which can be thought of as detecting those points where lines bend very sharply with high *curvature*, as for the aeroplane in Figures **4.1**(b) and (e). These are another low-level feature that again can be extracted automatically from the image. Finally, we shall investigate a technique that describes *motion*, called optical flow. This is illustrated in Figures **4.1**(c) and (f) with the optical flow from images of a walking man: the bits that are moving fastest are the brightest points, like the hands and the feet. All of these can provide a set of points, albeit points with different properties, but all are suitable for grouping for shape extraction. Consider a square box moving though a sequence of images. The edges are the perimeter of the box; the corners are the apices; the flow is how the box moves. All these can be collected together to find the moving box. We shall start with the edge detection techniques, with the first-order operators which accord with the chronology of development. The first-order techniques date back more than 30 years.

4.2 First-order edge detection operators

4.2.1 Basic operators

Many approaches to image interpretation are based on edges, since analysis based on edge

99

Table 4.1 Overview of Chapter 4

Main topic	Sub topics	Main points
First-order edge detection	What is an edge and how we *detect* it. The *equivalence* of operators to first-order differentiation and the insight this brings. The need for *filtering* and more *sophisticated* first-order operators.	Difference operation; Roberts Cross, Smoothing, Prewitt, Sobel, Canny.
Second-order edge detection	Relationship between first- and second-order differencing operations. The *basis* of a second-order operator. The need to include *filtering* and better operations.	Second-order differencing; Laplacian, Zero-crossing detection; Marr–Hildreth, Laplacian of Gaussian.
Other edge operators	*Alternative* approaches and *performance* aspects. *Comparing* different operators.	Other noise models: Spacek. Other edge models; Petrou.
Detecting image curvature	Nature of *curvature*. Computing curvature from: *edge* information; by using *curve approximation*; by *change* in intensity; and by *correlation*.	Planar curvature; corners. Curvature estimation by: change in edge direction; curve fitting; intensity change; Harris corner detector.
Optical flow estimation	*Movement* and the nature of optical flow. Estimating the optical flow by *differential* approach. Need for *other* approaches (including matching regions).	Detection by differencing. Optical flow; aperture problem; smoothness constraint. Differential approach; Horn and Schunk method; correlation.

detection is insensitive to change in the overall illumination level. Edge detection. highlights image *contrast*. Detecting contrast, which is difference in intensity, can emphasise the boundaries of features within an image, since this is where image contrast occurs. This is, naturally, how human vision can perceive the perimeter of an object, since the object is of different intensity to its surroundings. Essentially, the boundary of an object is a step-change in the intensity levels. The edge is at the position of the step-change. To detect the edge position we can use *first-order* differentiation since this emphasises change; first-order differentiation gives no response when applied to signals that do not change. The first edge detection operators to be studied here are group operators which aim to deliver an output which approximates the result of first-order differentiation.

A change in intensity can be revealed by differencing adjacent points. Differencing horizontally adjacent points will detect *vertical* changes in intensity and is often called a *horizontal edge detector* by virtue of its action. A horizontal operator will not show up *horizontal* changes in intensity since the difference is zero. When applied to an image **P** the action of the horizontal edge detector forms the difference between two horizontally adjacent points, as such detecting the vertical edges, **Ex**, as:

$$\mathbf{Ex}_{x,y} = |\mathbf{P}_{x,y} - \mathbf{P}_{x+1,y}| \quad \forall x \in 1, N-1; \, y \in 1, N \tag{4.1}$$

In order to detect horizontal edges we need a *vertical edge detector* which differences

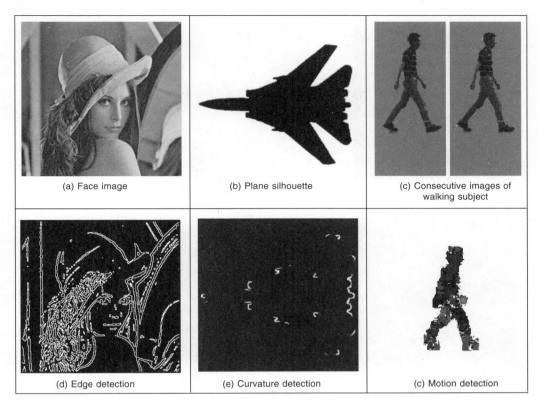

| (a) Face image | (b) Plane silhouette | (c) Consecutive images of walking subject |
| (d) Edge detection | (e) Curvature detection | (c) Motion detection |

Figure 4.1 Low-level feature detection

vertically adjacent points. This will determine *horizontal* intensity changes, but not *vertical* ones so the vertical edge detector detects the *horizontal* edges, **Ey**, according to:

$$\mathbf{Ey}_{x,y} = |\mathbf{P}_{x,y} - \mathbf{P}_{x,y+1}| \quad \forall x \in 1, N; \, y \in 1, N-1 \tag{4.2}$$

Figures **4.2**(b) and (c) show the application of the vertical and horizontal operators to the synthesised image of the square in Figure **4.2**(a). The left-hand vertical edge in Figure **4.2**(b) appears to be beside the square by virtue of the forward differencing process. Likewise, the upper edge in Figure **4.2**(b) appears above the original square.

Combining the two gives an operator **E** that can detect vertical and horizontal edges *together*. That is

$$\mathbf{E}_{x,y} = |\mathbf{P}_{x,y} - \mathbf{P}_{x+1,y} + \mathbf{P}_{x,y} - \mathbf{P}_{x,y+1}| \quad \forall x, y \in 1, N-1 \tag{4.3}$$

which gives:

$$\mathbf{E}_{x,y} = |2 \times \mathbf{P}_{x,y} - \mathbf{P}_{x+1,y} - \mathbf{P}_{x,y+1}| \quad \forall x, y \in 1, N-1 \tag{4.4}$$

Equation 4.4 gives the coefficients of a differencing template which can be convolved with an image to detect all the edge points, such as those shown in Figure **4.2**(d). Note that the bright point in the lower right corner of the edges of the square in Figure **4.2**(d) is much brighter than the other points. This is because it is the only point to be detected as an edge

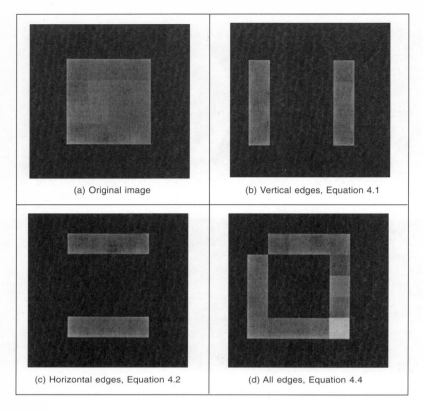

(a) Original image

(b) Vertical edges, Equation 4.1

(c) Horizontal edges, Equation 4.2

(d) All edges, Equation 4.4

Figure 4.2 First-order edge detection

by both the vertical and the horizontal operators and is therefore much brighter than the other edge points. In contrast, the top left hand corner point is detected by neither operator and so does not appear in the final image.

2	−1
−1	0

Figure 4.3 Template for first-order difference

The template in Figure **4.3** is convolved with the image to detect edges. The direct implementation of this operator, i.e. using Equation 4.4 rather than template convolution, is given in Code **4.1**. Naturally, template convolution could be used, but it is unnecessarily complex in this case.

Uniform thresholding (Section 3.3.4) is often used to select the brightest points, following application of an edge detection operator. The threshold level controls the number of selected points; too high a level can select too few points, whereas too low a level can

```
edge(pic)  =  │ newpic←zero(pic)
              │ for  x∈0..cols(pic)-2
              │   for  y∈0..rows(pic)-2
              │     newpic_{y,x}←|2·pic_{y,x}-pic_{y,x+1}-pic_{y+1,x}|
              │
              │ newpic
```

Code 4.1 First-order edge detection

select too much noise. Often, the threshold level is chosen by experience or by experiment, but it can be determined automatically by considering edge data (Venkatesh, 1995), or empirically (Haddon, 1988). For the moment, let us concentrate on the development of edge detection operators, rather than on their application.

4.2.2 Analysis of the basic operators

Taylor series analysis reveals that differencing adjacent points provides an estimate of the first order derivative at a point. If the difference is taken between points separated by Δx then by Taylor expansion for $f(x + \Delta x)$ we obtain:

$$f(x + \Delta x) = f(x) + \Delta x \times f'(x) + \frac{\Delta x^2}{2!} \times f''(x) + O(\Delta x^3) \tag{4.5}$$

By rearrangement, the first-order derivative $f'(x)$ is:

$$f'(x) = \frac{f(x + \Delta x) - f(x)}{\Delta x} - O(\Delta x^2) \tag{4.6}$$

This shows that the difference between adjacent points is an estimate of the first-order derivative, with error $O(\Delta x^2)$. This error depends on the size of the interval Δx and on the complexity of the curve. When Δx is large this error can be significant. The error is also large when the high-order derivatives take large values. In practice, the close sampling of image pixels and the reduced high frequency content make this approximation adequate. However, the error can be reduced by spacing the differenced points by one pixel. This is equivalent to computing the first-order difference delivered by Equation 4.1 at two adjacent points, as a new horizontal difference **Exx** where

$$\mathbf{Exx}_{x,y} = \mathbf{E}_{x+1,y} + \mathbf{E}_{x,y} = \mathbf{P}_{x+1,y} - \mathbf{P}_{x,y} + \mathbf{P}_{x,y} - \mathbf{P}_{x-1,y} = \mathbf{P}_{x+1,y} - \mathbf{P}_{x-1,y} \tag{4.7}$$

This is equivalent to incorporating spacing to detect the edges **Exx** by:

$$\mathbf{Exx}_{x,y} = |\mathbf{P}_{x+1,y} - \mathbf{P}_{x-1,y}| \quad \forall x \in 2, N-1; y \in 1, N \tag{4.8}$$

To analyse this, again by Taylor series, we expand $f(x - \Delta x)$ as:

$$f(x - \Delta x) = f(x) - \Delta x \times f'x + \frac{\Delta x^2}{2!} \times f''(x) - O(\Delta x^3) \tag{4.9}$$

By differencing Equation 4.9 from Equation 4.5, we obtain the first-order derivative as:

$$f'(x) = \frac{f(x + \Delta x) - f(x - \Delta x)}{2\Delta x} - O(\Delta x^2) \tag{4.10}$$

Equation 4.10 suggests that the estimate of the first order difference is now the difference

Low-level feature extraction (including edge detection)   103

between points separated by one pixel, with error $O(\Delta x^2)$. If $\Delta x < 1$ then this error is clearly smaller than the error associated with differencing adjacent pixels, in Equation 4.6. Again, averaging has reduced noise, or error. The template for a horizontal edge detection operator is given in Figure **4.4**(a). This template gives the vertical edges detected at its centre pixel. A transposed version of the template gives a vertical edge detection operator, Figure **4.4**(b).

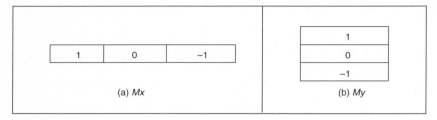

Figure 4.4   Templates for improved first-order difference

The *Roberts cross operator* (Roberts, 1965) was one of the earliest edge detection operators. It implements a version of basic first-order edge detection and uses two templates which difference pixel values in a diagonal manner, as opposed to along the axes' directions. The two templates are called M^+ and M^- and are given in Figure **4.5**.

+1	0
0	−1

(a) M^-

0	+1
−1	0

(b) M^+

Figure 4.5   Templates for Roberts cross operator

In implementation, the maximum value delivered by application of these templates is stored as the value of the edge at that point. The edge point $\mathbf{E}_{x,y}$ is then the maximum of the two values derived by convolving the two templates at an image point $\mathbf{P}_{x,y}$:

$$\mathbf{E}_{x,y} = \max \{|M^+ * \mathbf{P}_{x,y}|, |M^- * \mathbf{P}_{x,y}|\} \quad \forall x, y \in 1, N-1 \tag{4.11}$$

The application of the Roberts cross operator to the image of the square is shown in Figure **4.6**. The two templates provide the results in Figures **4.6**(a) and (b) and the result delivered by the Roberts operator is shown in Figure **4.6**(c). Note that the corners of the square now appear in the edge image, by virtue of the diagonal differencing action, whereas they were less apparent in Figure **4.2**(d) (where the top left corner did not appear).

An alternative to taking the maximum is to simply *add* the results of the two templates together to combine horizontal and vertical edges. There are of course more varieties of edges and it is often better to consider the two templates as providing components of an *edge vector*: the strength of the edge along the horizontal and vertical axes. These give components of a vector and can be added in a vectorial manner (which is perhaps more usual for the Roberts operator). The *edge magnitude* is the *length* of the vector, the *edge direction* is the vector's *orientation*, as shown in Figure **4.7**.

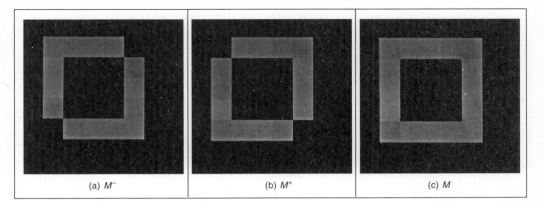

(a) M^- (b) M^+ (c) M

Figure 4.6 Applying the Roberts cross operator

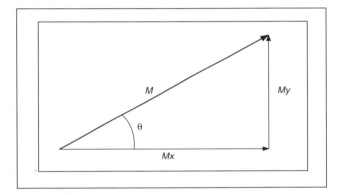

Figure 4.7 Edge detection in vectorial format

4.2.3 Prewitt edge detection operator

Edge detection is akin to differentiation. Since it detects change it is bound to respond to *noise*, as well as to step-like changes in image intensity (its frequency domain analogue is high-pass filtering as illustrated in Figure **2.25**(c)). It is therefore prudent to incorporate *averaging* within the edge detection process. We can then extend the vertical template, Mx, along three rows, and the horizontal template, My, along three columns. These give the *Prewitt edge detection operator* (Prewitt, 1966) that consists of two templates, Figure **4.8**.

This gives two results: the rate of change of brightness along each axis. As such, this is the vector illustrated in Figure **4.7**: the edge magnitude, M, is the length of the vector and the edge direction, θ, is the angle of the vector:

$$M = \sqrt{Mx(x, y)^2 + My(x, y)^2} \qquad (4.12)$$

$$\theta(x, y) = \tan^{-1}\left(\frac{My(x, y)}{Mx(x, y)}\right) \qquad (4.13)$$

Again, the signs of Mx and My can be used to determine the appropriate quadrant for the

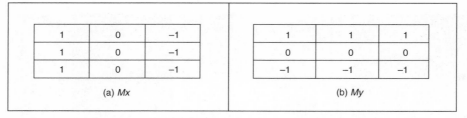

Figure 4.8 Templates for Prewitt operator

edge direction. A Mathcad implementation of the two templates of Figure **4.8** is given in Code **4.2**. In this code, both templates operate on a 3 × 3 sub-picture (which can be supplied, in Mathcad, using the `submatrix` function). Again, template convolution could be used to implement this operator, but (as with direct averaging and basic first-order edge detection) it is less suited to simple templates. Also, the provision of edge magnitude and direction would require extension of the template convolution operator given earlier (Code **3.5**).

Prewitt33_x(pic)	Prewitt33_y(pic)
$:= \displaystyle\sum_{y=0}^{2} pic_{y,0} - \sum_{y=0}^{2} pic_{y,2}$	$:= \displaystyle\sum_{x=0}^{2} pic_{0,x} - \sum_{x=0}^{2} pic_{2,x}$
(a) *Mx*	(b) *My*

Code 4.2 Implementing the Prewitt operator

When applied to the image of the square, Figure **4.9**(a), we obtain the edge magnitude and direction, Figures **4.9**(b) and (d), respectively (where (d) does not include the border points, only the edge direction at processed points). The edge direction in Figure **4.9**(d) is shown measured in degrees where 0° and 360° are horizontal, to the right, and 90° is vertical, upwards. Though the regions of edge points are wider due to the operator's averaging properties, the edge data is clearer than the earlier first-order operator, highlighting the regions where intensity changed in a more reliable fashion (compare, for example, the upper left corner of the square which was not revealed earlier). The direction is less clear in an image format and is better exposed by Mathcad's *vector* format in Figure **4.9**(c). In vector format, the edge direction data is clearly less well defined at the corners of the square (as expected, since the first-order derivative is discontinuous at these points).

4.2.4 Sobel edge detection operator

When the weight at the central pixels, for both Prewitt templates, is doubled, this gives the famous *Sobel edge detection operator* which, again, consists of two masks to determine the edge in vector form. The Sobel operator was the most popular edge detection operator until the development of edge detection techniques with a theoretical basis. It proved popular because it gave, overall, a better performance than other contemporaneous edge detection operators, such as the Prewitt operator.

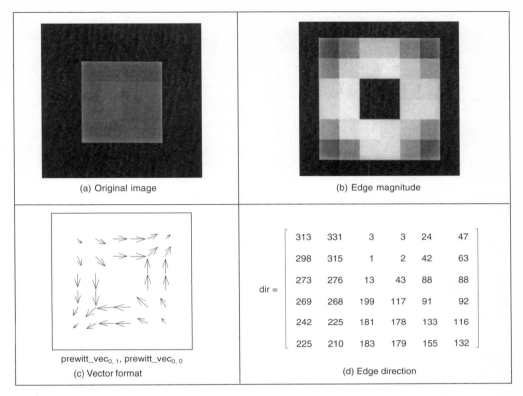

(a) Original image

(b) Edge magnitude

$$dir = \begin{bmatrix} 313 & 331 & 3 & 3 & 24 & 47 \\ 298 & 315 & 1 & 2 & 42 & 63 \\ 273 & 276 & 13 & 43 & 88 & 88 \\ 269 & 268 & 199 & 117 & 91 & 92 \\ 242 & 225 & 181 & 178 & 133 & 116 \\ 225 & 210 & 183 & 179 & 155 & 132 \end{bmatrix}$$

prewitt_vec$_{0,1}$, prewitt_vec$_{0,0}$

(c) Vector format

(d) Edge direction

Figure 4.9   Applying the Prewitt operator

The Mathcad implementation of these masks is very similar to the implementation of the Prewitt operator, Code **4.2**, again operating on a 3×3 sub-picture. This is the standard formulation of the Sobel templates, but how do we form larger templates, say for 5×5 or 7×7. Few textbooks state its original derivation, but it has been attributed (Heath, 1997) as originating from a PhD thesis (Sobel, 1970). Unfortunately a theoretical basis, which can be used to calculate the coefficients of larger templates, is rarely given. One approach to a theoretical basis is to consider the optimal forms of averaging and of differencing. Gaussian averaging has already been stated to give optimal averaging. The binomial expansion gives the integer coefficients of a series that, in the limit, approximates the normal distribution. Pascal's triangle gives sets of coefficients for a smoothing operator which, in the limit, approach the coefficients of a Gaussian smoothing operator. Pascal's triangle is then:

Window size								
2				1		1		
3			1		2		1	
4		1		3		3		1
5	1		4		6		4		1

This gives the (unnormalised) coefficients of an optimal discrete smoothing operator (it is essentially a Gaussian operator with integer coefficients). The rows give the coefficients for increasing template, or window, size. The coefficients of smoothing within the Sobel operator, Figure **4.10**, are those for a window size of 3. In Mathcad, by specifying the size of the smoothing window as `winsize`, then the template coefficients $smooth_{x\_win}$ can be calculated at each window point `x_win` according to Code **4.3**.

1	0	−1
2	0	−2
1	0	−1

(a) *Mx*

1	2	1
0	0	0
−1	−2	−1

(b) *My*

Figure 4.10 Templates for Sobel operator

$$smooth_{x\_win} := \frac{(winsize-1)!}{(winsize-1-x\_win)! \cdot x\_win!}$$

Code 4.3 Smoothing function

The differencing coefficients are given by Pascal's triangle for subtraction:

Window size

2				1	−1		
3			1	0	−1		
4		1	1	−1	−1		
5	1	2	0	−2	−1		

This can be implemented by subtracting the templates derived from two adjacent expansions for a smaller window size. Accordingly, we require an operator which can provide the coefficients of Pascal's triangle for arguments which are a window size n and a position k. The operator is the `Pascal(k,n)` operator in Code **4.4**.

$$Pascal\ (k,n) := \begin{vmatrix} \dfrac{n!}{(n-k)!\cdot k!} & \text{if } (k{\geq}0){\cdot}(k{\leq}n) \\ \\ 0 & \text{otherwise} \end{vmatrix}$$

Code 4.4 Pascal's triangle

The differencing template, $diff_{x\_win}$, is then given by the difference between two Pascal expansions, as given in Code **4.5**.

These give the coefficients of optimal differencing and optimal smoothing. This *general* form of the Sobel operator combines optimal smoothing along one axis, with optimal differencing along the other. This general form of the Sobel operator is then given in Code

```
diff_x_win=Pascal(x_win, winsize-2)-Pascal(x_win-1, winsize-2)
```

Code 4.5 Differencing function

4.6 which combines the differencing function along one axis, with smoothing along the other.

$$\text{Sobel\_x(pic)} := \sum_{x\_win=0}^{winsize-1} \sum_{y\_win=0}^{winsize-1} \text{smooth}_{y\_win} \cdot \text{diff}_{x\_win} \cdot \text{pic}_{y\_win, \, x\_win}$$

(a) Mx

$$\text{Sobel\_y(pic)} := \sum_{x\_win=0}^{winsize-1} \sum_{y\_win=0}^{winsize-1} \text{smooth}_{x\_win} \cdot \text{diff}_{y\_win} \cdot \text{pic}_{y\_win, \, x\_win}$$

(b) My

Code 4.6 Generalised Sobel templates

This generates a template for the Mx template for a Sobel operator, given for 5×5 in Code **4.7**.

$$\text{Sobel\_template\_x} = \begin{bmatrix} 1 & 2 & 0 & -2 & -1 \\ 4 & 8 & 0 & -8 & -4 \\ 6 & 12 & 0 & -12 & -6 \\ 4 & 8 & 0 & -8 & -4 \\ 1 & 2 & 0 & -2 & -1 \end{bmatrix}$$

Code 4.7 5×5 Sobel template Mx

All template-based techniques can be larger than 5×5 so, as with any group operator, there is a 7×7 Sobel and so on. The virtue of a larger edge detection template is that it involves more smoothing to reduce noise but edge blurring becomes a great problem. The estimate of edge direction can be improved with more smoothing since it is particularly sensitive to noise. There are circular edge operators designed specifically to provide accurate edge direction data.

The Sobel templates can be invoked by operating on a matrix of dimension equal to the window size, from which edge magnitude and gradient are calculated. The Sobel function (Code **4.8**) convolves the generalised Sobel template (of size chosen to be winsize) with the picture supplied as argument, to give outputs which are the images of edge magnitude and direction, in vector form.

The results of applying the 3×3 Sobel operator can be seen in Figure **4.11**. The original face image Figure **4.11**(a) has many edges in the hair and in the region of the eyes. This is

```
Sobel(pic,winsize):=

    w2←floor( winsize / 2 )

    edge_mag←zero(pic)
    edge_dir←zero(pic)
    for x∈w2..cols(pic)-1-w2
      for y∈w2..rows(pic)-1-w2
        x_mag←Sobel_x(submatrix(pic,y-w2,y+w2,x-w2,x+w2))
        y_mag←Sobel_y(submatrix(pic,y-w2,y+w2,x-w2,x+w2))

        edge_mag_y_x←floor( magnitude(x_mag, y_mag) / mag_normalise )

        edge_dir_y,x←direction(x_mag,y_mag)

    (edge_mag edge_dir)
```

Code 4.8   Generalised Sobel operator

shown in the edge magnitude image, Figure **4.11**(b). When this is thresholded at a suitable value, many edge points are found, as shown in Figure **4.11**(c). Note that in areas of the image where the brightness remains fairly constant, such as the cheek and shoulder, there is little change which is reflected by low edge magnitude and few points in the thresholded data.

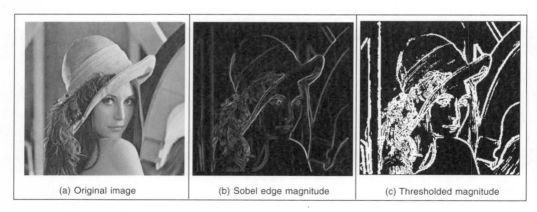

| (a) Original image | (b) Sobel edge magnitude | (c) Thresholded magnitude |

Figure 4.11   Applying the Sobel operator

The Sobel edge direction data can be arranged to point in different ways, as can the direction provided by the Prewitt operator. If the templates are inverted to be of the form shown in Figure **4.12**, the edge direction will be inverted around both axes. If only one of the templates is inverted, then the measured edge direction will be inverted about the chosen axis.

This gives *four* possible directions for measurement of the edge direction provided by the Sobel operator, two of which (for the templates of Figures **4.10** and **4.12**) are illustrated

−1	0	1
−2	0	2
−1	0	1

(a) −Mx

−1	−2	−1
0	0	0
1	2	1

(b) −My

Figure 4.12   Inverted templates for Sobel operator

in Figures **4.13**(a) and (b), respectively, where inverting the *Mx* template does not highlight discontinuity at the corners. (The edge magnitude of the Sobel applied to the square is not shown, but is similar to that derived by application of the Prewitt operator, Figure **4.9**(b).)

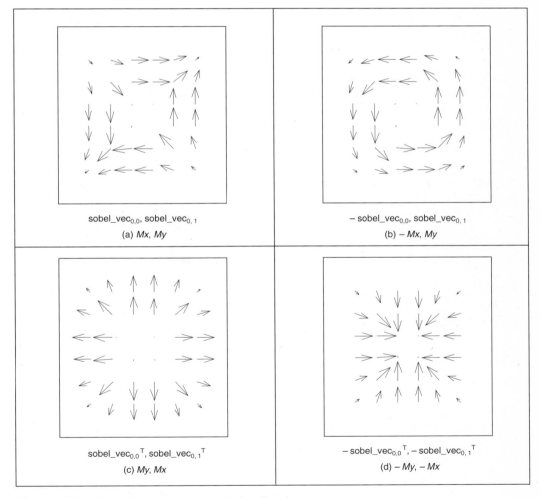

sobel_vec$_{0,0}$, sobel_vec$_{0,1}$

(a) *Mx, My*

− sobel_vec$_{0,0}$, sobel_vec$_{0,1}$

(b) − *Mx, My*

sobel_vec$_{0,0}^{T}$, sobel_vec$_{0,1}^{T}$

(c) *My, Mx*

− sobel_vec$_{0,0}^{T}$, − sobel_vec$_{0,1}^{T}$

(d) − *My*, − *Mx*

Figure 4.13   Alternative arrangements of edge direction

Low-level feature extraction (including edge detection)   111

By swapping the Sobel templates, the measured edge direction can be arranged to be normal to the edge itself (as opposed to tangential data along the edge). This is illustrated in Figures **4.13**(c) and (d) for swapped versions of the templates given in Figures **4.10** and **4.12**, respectively. The rearrangement can lead to simplicity in algorithm construction when finding shapes, to be shown later. Any algorithm which uses edge direction for finding shapes must know precisely which arrangement has been used, since the edge direction can be used to speed algorithm performance, but it must map precisely to the expected image data if used in that way.

Detecting edges by *template convolution* again has a frequency domain interpretation. The Fourier transform of a 7×7 Sobel template of Code **4.7** is given in Figure **4.14**. The Fourier transform is given in relief in Figure **4.14**(a) and as a contour plot in Figure **4.14**(b). The template is for the horizontal differencing action, My, which highlights vertical change. Accordingly, its transform reveals that it selects vertical spatial frequencies, whilst smoothing the horizontal ones. The horizontal frequencies are selected from a region near the origin (*low-pass* filtering), whereas the vertical frequencies are selected away from the origin (*high-pass*). This highlights the action of the Sobel operator; combining smoothing of the spatial frequencies along one axis with differencing of the other. In Figure **4.14**, the smoothing is of horizontal spatial frequencies whilst the differencing is of vertical spatial frequencies.

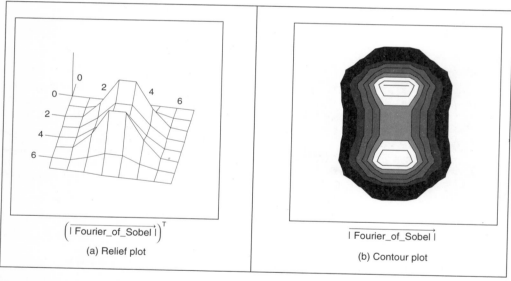

(a) Relief plot $\qquad$ (b) Contour plot

Figure 4.14 Fourier transform of the Sobel operator

4.2.5 The Canny edge detector

The *Canny edge detection operator* (Canny, 1986) is perhaps the most popular edge detection technique at present. It was formulated with three main objectives:

1. *optimal* detection with no spurious responses;

2. good localisation with minimal distance between detected and true edge position;
3. single response to eliminate multiple responses to a single edge.

The first requirement aims to *reduce* the response to noise. This can be effected by optimal smoothing; Canny was the first to demonstrate that Gaussian filtering is optimal for edge detection (within his criteria). The second criterion aims for accuracy: edges are to be detected, in the right place. This can be achieved by a process of *non-maximum suppression* (which is equivalent to peak detection). Non-maximum suppression retains only those points at the top of a ridge of edge data, whilst suppressing all others. This results in thinning: the output of non-maximum suppression is thin lines of edge points, in the right place. The third constraint concerns location of a single edge point in response to a change in brightness. This is because more than one edge can be denoted to be present, consistent with the output obtained by earlier edge operators.

Recalling that the Gaussian operator $g(x, y)$ is given by:

$$g(x, y) = e^{\frac{-(x^2 + y^2)}{2\sigma^2}} \qquad (4.14)$$

By differentiation, for unit vectors $U_x = [1, 0]$ and $U_y = [0, 1]$ along the co-ordinate axes, we obtain:

$$\nabla g(x, y) = \frac{\partial g(x, y)}{\partial x} U_x + \frac{\partial g(x, y)}{\partial y} U_y$$

$$= -\frac{x}{\sigma^2} e^{\frac{-(x^2 + y^2)}{2\sigma^2}} U_x - \frac{y}{\sigma^2} e^{\frac{-(x^2 + y^2)}{2\sigma^2}} U_y \qquad (4.15)$$

Equation 4.15 gives a way to calculate the coefficients of a template that combines first-order differentiation with Gaussian smoothing. This is a smoothed image, and so the edge will be a ridge of data. In order to mark an edge at the correct point (and to reduce multiple response), we can convolve an image with an operator which gives the first derivative in a direction normal to the edge. The maximum of this function should be the peak of the edge data, where the gradient in the original image is sharpest, and hence the location of the edge. Accordingly, we seek an operator, G_n, which is a first derivative of a Gaussian function g in the direction of the normal, $\mathbf{n}_\perp$:

$$G_n = \frac{\partial y}{\partial \mathbf{n}_\perp} \qquad (4.16)$$

where $\mathbf{n}_\perp$ can be estimated from the first-order difference of the Gaussian function g convolved with the image $\mathbf{P}$, and scaled appropriately as:

$$\mathbf{n}_\perp = \frac{\nabla(\mathbf{P} * g)}{|\nabla(\mathbf{P} * g)|} \qquad (4.17)$$

The location of the true edge point is then at the maximum point of G_n convolved with the image. This maximum is when the differential (along $\mathbf{n}_\perp$) is zero:

$$\frac{\partial(G_n * \mathbf{P})}{\partial \mathbf{n}_\perp} \qquad (4.18)$$

By substitution of Equation 4.16 in Equation 4.18,

$$\frac{\partial^2 (G * \mathbf{P})}{\partial \mathbf{n}_\perp{}^2} = 0 \tag{4.19}$$

Equation 4.19 provides the basis for an operator which meets one of Canny's criteria, namely that edges should be detected in the correct place. This is non-maximum suppression, which is equivalent to retaining peaks (a.k.a. differentiation perpendicular to the edge), which thins the response of the edge detection operator to give edge points which are in the right place, without multiple response and with minimal response to noise. However, it is virtually impossible to achieve an exact implementation of Canny given the requirement to estimate the normal direction.

A common approximation is, as illustrated in Figure **4.15**:

1. use Gaussian smoothing (as in Section 3.4.4), Figure **4.15**(a);
2. use the Sobel operator, Figure **4.15**(b);
3. use non-maximal suppression, Figure **4.15**(c);
4. threshold with hysteresis to connect edge points, Figure **4.15**(d).

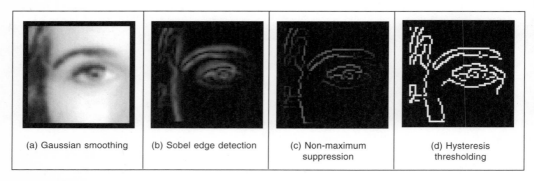

(a) Gaussian smoothing (b) Sobel edge detection (c) Non-maximum suppression (d) Hysteresis thresholding

Figure 4.15   Stages in Canny edge detection

Note that the first two stages can be combined using a version of Equation 4.15, but are separated here so that all stages in the edge detection process can be shown clearly. An alternative implementation of Canny's approach (Deriche, 1987) used Canny's criteria to develop two-dimensional recursive filters, claiming performance and implementation advantage over the approximation here.

Non-maximum suppression essentially locates the highest points in the edge magnitude data. This is performed by using edge direction information, to check that points are at the peak of a ridge. Given a 3×3 region, a point is at a maximum if the gradient at either side of it is less than the gradient at the point. This implies that we need values of gradient along a line which is normal to the edge at a point. This is illustrated in Figure **4.16**, which shows the neighbouring points to the point of interest, $\mathbf{P}_{x,y}$, the edge direction at $\mathbf{P}_{x,y}$ and the normal to the edge direction at $\mathbf{P}_{x,y}$. The point $\mathbf{P}_{x,y}$ is to be marked as a maximum if its gradient, $M(x, y)$, exceeds the gradient at points 1 and 2, M_1 and M_2, respectively. Since we have a discrete neighbourhood, M_1 and M_2 need to be interpolated. First-order interpolation using Mx and My at $\mathbf{P}_{x,y}$, and the values of Mx and My for the neighbours gives:

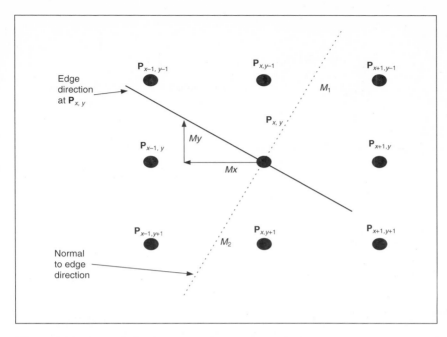

Figure 4.16 Interpolation in non-maximum suppression

$$M_1 = \frac{M_y}{M_x} M(x+1, y-1) + \frac{M_x - M_y}{M_x} M(x, y-1) \tag{4.20}$$

and

$$M_2 = \frac{M_y}{M_x} M(x-1, y+1) + \frac{M_x - M_y}{M_x} M(x, y+1) \tag{4.21}$$

The point $\mathbf{P}_{x,y}$ is then marked as a maximum if $M(x, y)$ exceeds both M_1 and M_2, otherwise it is set to zero. In this manner the peaks of the ridges of edge magnitude data are retained, whilst those not at the peak are set to zero. The implementation of non-maximum suppression first requires a function which generates the co-ordinates of the points between which the edge magnitude is interpolated. This is the function get_coords in Code **4.9** which requires the angle of the normal to the edge direction, returning the co-ordinates of the points beyond and behind the normal.

The non-maximum suppression operator, non_max in Code **4.10** then interpolates the edge magnitude at the two points either side of the normal to the edge direction. If the edge magnitude at the point of interest exceeds these two then it is retained, otherwise it is discarded. Note that the potential singularity in Equations 4.20 and 4.21 can be avoided by use of multiplication in the magnitude comparison, as opposed to division in interpolation, as it is in Code **4.10**. In practice, however, this implementation, Codes **4.9** and **4.10**, can suffer from numerical imprecision and ill-conditioning. Accordingly, it is better to implement a hand-crafted interpretation of Equations 4.20 and 4.21 applied separately to the four quadrants. This is too lengthy to be included here, but a version is included with the worksheet for Chapter 4 (to be found on the website, p. 26).

The transfer function associated with *hysteresis thresholding* is shown in Figure **4.17**. Points are set to white once the upper threshold is exceeded and set to black when the lower

```
get_coords(angle) :=  | δ←0.000000000000001
                      |
                      | x1←ceil[(cos(angle+π/8)·√2)-0.5-δ]
                      |
                      | y1←ceil[(-sin(angle+π/8)·√2)-0.5-δ]
                      |
                      | x2←ceil[(cos(angle-π/8)·√2)-0.5-δ]
                      |
                      | y2←ceil[(-sin(angle-π/8)·√2)-0.5-δ]
                      |
                      | (x1 y1 x2 y2)
```

Code 4.9 Generating co-ordinates for interpolation

```
Non_max(edges) :=  | for i∈1..cols(edges_{0,0})-2
                   |    for j∈1..rows(edges_{0,0})-2
                   |       Mx←(edges_{0,0})_{j,i}
                   |       My←(edges_{0,1})_{j,i}
                   |
                   |       0←atan(Mx/My) if My≠0
                   |
                   |       (0←π/2) if (My=0)·(Mx>0)
                   |
                   |       0←-π/2 otherwise
                   |       adds←get_coords(0)
                   |       M1←[ My·(edges_{0,2})_{j+adds_{0,1},i+adds_{0,0}} ···
                   |            + (Mx-My)·(edges_{0,2})_{j+adds_{0,3}, i+adds_{0,2}} ]
                   |       adds←get_coords(0+π)
                   |       M2←[ My·(edges_{0,2})_{j+adds_{0,1}, i+adds_{0,0}}  ···
                   |            + (Mx-My)·(edges_{0,2})_{j+adds_{0,3}, i+adds_{0,2}} ]
                   |       isbigger←[[Mx·(edges_{0,2})_{j,i}>M1]·[Mx·(edges_{0,2})_{j,i}
                   |       ≥M2]]+[[Mx·(edges_{0,2})_{j,i}<M1]·[Mx·(edges_{0,2})_{j,i}
                   |       ≤M2]]
                   |       new_edge_{j,i}←(edges_{0,2})_{j,i} if isbigger
                   |       new_edge_{j,i}←0 otherwise
                   |
                   | new_edge
```

Code 4.10 Non-maximum suppression

threshold is reached. The arrows reflect possible movement: there is only one way to change from black to white and vice versa.

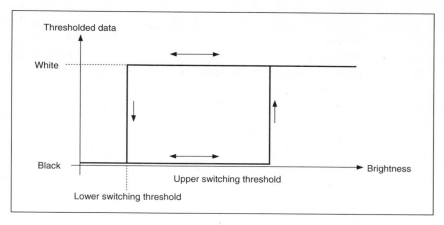

Figure 4.17   Hysteresis thresholding transfer function

The application of non-maximum suppression and hysteresis thresholding is illustrated in Figure **4.18**. This contains a ridge of edge data, the edge magnitude. The action of non-maximum suppression is to select the points along the top of the ridge. Given that the top of the ridge initially exceeds the upper threshold, the thresholded output is set to white until the peak of the ridge falls beneath the lower threshold. The thresholded output is then set to black until the peak of the ridge exceeds the upper switching threshold.

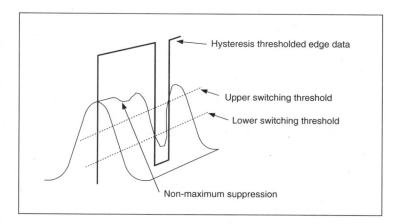

Figure 4.18   Action of non-maximum suppression and hysteresis thresholding

Hysteresis thresholding requires two thresholds, an *upper* and a *lower* threshold. The process starts when an edge point from non-maximum suppression is found to exceed the upper threshold. This is labelled as an edge point (usually white, with a value 255) and forms the first point of a line of edge points. The neighbours of the point are then searched to determine whether or not they exceed the lower threshold, as in Figure **4.19**. Any neighbour that exceeds the lower threshold is labelled as an edge point and its neighbours are then searched to determine whether or not they exceed the lower threshold. In this manner, the first edge point found (the one that exceeded the upper threshold) becomes a *seed* point for a search. Its neighbours, in turn, become seed points if they exceed the lower threshold, and so the search extends, along branches arising from neighbours that exceeded the lower threshold. For each branch, the search terminates at points that have no neighbours above the lower threshold.

seed ≥ lower	seed ≥ lower	seed ≥ lower
seed ≥ lower	seed ≥ upper	seed ≥ lower
seed ≥ lower	seed ≥ lower	seed ≥ lower

Figure 4.19 Neighbourhood search for hysteresis thresholding

In implementation, hysteresis thresholding clearly requires *recursion*, since the length of any branch is unknown. Having found the initial *seed* point, the seed point is set to white and its neighbours are searched. The co-ordinates of each point are checked to see whether it is within the picture size, according to the operator check, given in Code **4.11**.

$$\text{check}(xc, yc, pic) := \left| \begin{array}{l} 1 \text{ if}(xc{\geq}1)\cdot(xc{\leq}\text{cols}(pic)-2)\cdot(yc{\geq}1)\cdot(yc{\leq}\text{rows}(pic)-2) \\ 0 \text{ otherwise} \end{array} \right.$$

Code 4.11 Checking points are within an image

The neighbourhood (as in Figure **4.19**) is then searched by a function connect (Code **4.12**) which is fed with the non-maximum suppressed edge image, the co-ordinates of the seed point whose connectivity is under analysis and the lower switching threshold. Each of the neighbours is searched if its value exceeds the lower threshold, and the point has not

```
connect(x,y,nedg,low):=     for x1∈x-1..x+1
                              for y1∈y-1..y+1
                                if (nedg_{y1,x1}≥low)·(nedg_{y1,x1}≠255)·
                                    check(x1, y1, nedg)
                                  | nedg_{y1,x1}←255
                                  | nedg←connect(x1,y1,nedg,low)

                            nedg
```

Code 4.12 Connectivity analysis after seed point location

already been labelled as white (otherwise the function would become an infinite loop). If both conditions are satisfied (and the point is within the picture) then the point is set to white and becomes a seed point for further analysis. This implementation tries to check the seed point as well, even though it has already been set to white. The operator could be arranged not to check the current seed point, by direct calculation without the `for` loops, and this would be marginally faster. Including an extra Boolean constraint to inhibit check of the seed point would only slow the operation. The `connect` routine is recursive: it is called again by the new seed point.

The process starts with the point that exceeds the upper threshold. When such a point is found, it is set to white and it becomes a seed point where connectivity analysis starts. The calling operator for the connectivity analysis, `hyst_thr`, which starts the whole process is given in Code **4.13**. When `hyst_thr` is invoked, its arguments are the co-ordinates of the point of current interest, the non-maximum suppressed edge image, n_edg (which is eventually delivered as the hysteresis thresholded image), and the upper and lower switching thresholds, upp and `low`, respectively. For *display* purposes, this operator requires a later operation to remove points which have not been set to white (to remove those points which are below the upper threshold and which are not connected to points above the lower threshold). This is rarely used in application since the points set to white are the only ones of interest in later processing.

```
hyst_thr(n_edg,upp,low):=      for  x∈1..cols(n_edg)-2
                                  for  y∈1..rows(n_edg)-2
                                    if[(n_edg_{y,x}≥upp)·(n_edg_{y,x}≠255)]
                                      n_edg_{y,x}←255
                                      n_edg←connect(x,y,n_edg,low)

                                n_edg
```

Code 4.13 Hysteresis thresholding operator

A comparison with the results of *uniform* thresholding is shown in Figure **4.20**. Figure **4.20**(a) shows the result of hysteresis thresholding of a Sobel edge detected image of the eye with an upper threshold set to 40 pixels, and a lower threshold of 10 pixels. Figures **4.20**(b) and (c) show the result of uniform thresholding applied to the image with thresholds of 40 pixels and 10 pixels, respectively. Uniform thresholding can select too few points if the threshold is too high, and too many if it is too low. Hysteresis thresholding naturally selects *all* the points in Figure **4.20**(b), and *some* of those in Figure **4.20**(c), those connected to the points in (b). In particular, part of the nose is partly present in Figure **4.20**(a), whereas it is absent in Figure **4.20**(b) and masked by too many edge points in Figure **4.20**(c). Also, the eyebrow is more complete in (a) whereas it is only partial in (b) and complete (but obscured) in (c). Hysteresis thresholding therefore has an ability to detect major features of interest in the edge image, in an improved manner to uniform thresholding.

The action of the Canny operator on a larger image is shown in Figure **4.21**, in comparison with the result of the Sobel operator. Figure **4.21**(a) is the original image of a face, Figure **4.21**(b) is the result of the Canny operator (using a 5×5 Gaussian operator with $\sigma = 1$ and with upper and lower thresholds set appropriately) and Figure **4.21**(c) is the result of a

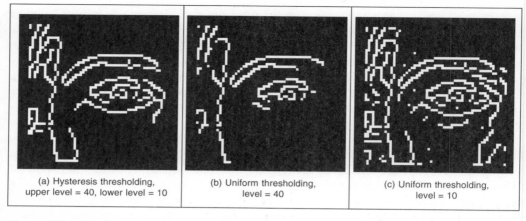

| (a) Hysteresis thresholding, upper level = 40, lower level = 10 | (b) Uniform thresholding, level = 40 | (c) Uniform thresholding, level = 10 |

Figure 4.20   Comparing hysteresis thresholding with uniform thresholding

3×3 Sobel operator with uniform thresholding. The retention of major detail by the Canny operator is very clear; the face is virtually recognisable in Figure **4.21**(b) whereas it is less clear in Figure **4.21**(c).

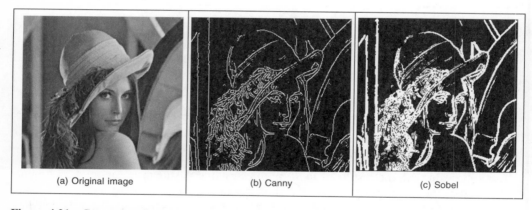

| (a) Original image | (b) Canny | (c) Sobel |

Figure 4.21   Comparing Canny with Sobel

4.3   Second-order edge detection operators

4.3.1   Motivation

First-order edge detection is based on the premise that differentiation highlights change; image intensity changes in the region of a feature boundary. The process is illustrated in Figure **4.22** where Figure **4.22**(a) is a cross-section through image data. The result of *first-order* edge detection, $f'(x) = \mathrm{d}f/\mathrm{d}x$ in Figure **4.22**(b), is a *peak* where the rate of change of the original signal, $f(x)$ in Figure **4.22**(a), is greatest. There are of course higher order derivatives; applied to the same cross-section of data, the *second-order* derivative, $f''(x) =$

$d^2 f/dx^2$ in Figure **4.22**(c), is greatest where the rate of change of the signal is greatest and zero when the rate of change is constant. The rate of change is constant at the peak of the first-order derivative. This is where there is a *zero-crossing* in the second-order derivative, where it changes sign. Accordingly, an alternative to first-order differentiation is to apply second-order differentiation and then find zero-crossings in the second-order information.

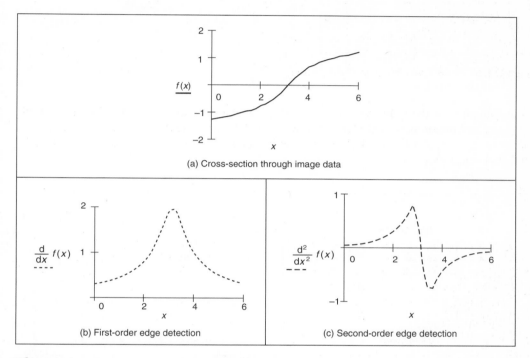

Figure 4.22   First- and second-order edge detection

4.3.2   Basic operators: the Laplacian

The *Laplacian operator* is a template which implements second-order differencing. The second-order differential can be approximated by the difference between two adjacent first-order differences:

$$f''(x) \cong f'(x) - f'(x + 1) \tag{4.22}$$

Which, by Equation 4.6, gives

$$f''(x) \cong -f(x) + 2f(x + 1) - f(x + 2) \tag{4.23}$$

This gives a horizontal second-order template as given in Figure **4.23**.

−1	2	−1

Figure 4.23   Horizontal second-order template

When the horizontal second-order operator is combined with a vertical second-order difference we obtain the full Laplacian template, given in Figure **4.24**.

0	−1	0
−1	4	−1
0	−1	0

Figure 4.24 Laplacian edge detection operator

Application of the Laplacian operator to the image of the square is given in Figure **4.25**. The original image is provided in numeric form in Figure **4.25**(a). The detected edges are the *zero-crossings* in Figure **4.25**(b) and can be seen to lie between the edge of the square and its background.

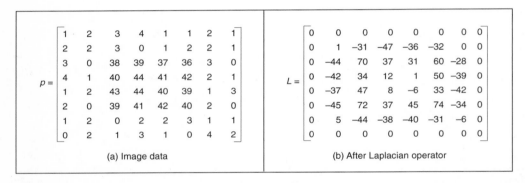

$$p = \begin{bmatrix} 1 & 2 & 3 & 4 & 1 & 1 & 2 & 1 \\ 2 & 2 & 3 & 0 & 1 & 2 & 2 & 1 \\ 3 & 0 & 38 & 39 & 37 & 36 & 3 & 0 \\ 4 & 1 & 40 & 44 & 41 & 42 & 2 & 1 \\ 1 & 2 & 43 & 44 & 40 & 39 & 1 & 3 \\ 2 & 0 & 39 & 41 & 42 & 40 & 2 & 0 \\ 1 & 2 & 0 & 2 & 2 & 3 & 1 & 1 \\ 0 & 2 & 1 & 3 & 1 & 0 & 4 & 2 \end{bmatrix}$$

(a) Image data

$$L = \begin{bmatrix} 0 & 0 & 0 & 0 & 0 & 0 & 0 & 0 \\ 0 & 1 & -31 & -47 & -36 & -32 & 0 & 0 \\ 0 & -44 & 70 & 37 & 31 & 60 & -28 & 0 \\ 0 & -42 & 34 & 12 & 1 & 50 & -39 & 0 \\ 0 & -37 & 47 & 8 & -6 & 33 & -42 & 0 \\ 0 & -45 & 72 & 37 & 45 & 74 & -34 & 0 \\ 0 & 5 & -44 & -38 & -40 & -31 & -6 & 0 \\ 0 & 0 & 0 & 0 & 0 & 0 & 0 & 0 \end{bmatrix}$$

(b) After Laplacian operator

Figure 4.25 Edge detection via the Laplacian operator

An alternative structure to the template in Figure **4.24** is one where the central weighting is 8 and the neighbours are all weighted as −1. Naturally, this includes a different form of image information, so the effects are slightly different. (In both structures, the central weighting can be negative and that of the four or the eight neighbours can be positive, without loss of generality.) Actually, it is important to ensure that the sum of template coefficients is zero, so that edges are not detected in areas of uniform brightness. One advantage of the Laplacian operator is that it is *isotropic* (like the Gaussian operator): it has the same properties in each direction. However, as yet it contains *no* smoothing and will again respond to noise, more so than a first-order operator since it is differentiation of a higher order. As such, the Laplacian operator is rarely used in its basic form. Smoothing can use the averaging operator described earlier but a more optimal form is Gaussian smoothing. When this is incorporated with the Laplacian we obtain a Laplacian of Gaussian (LoG) operator which is the basis of the Marr–Hildreth approach, to be considered next. A clear disadvantage with the Laplacian operator is that edge direction is *not* available. It does, however, impose low computational cost, which is its main advantage. Though interest in the Laplacian operator abated with rising interest in the Marr–Hildreth approach, a nonlinear Laplacian operator was developed (Vliet, 1989) and shown to have good performance, especially in low-noise situations.

4.3.3 The Marr–Hildreth operator

The *Marr–Hildreth* approach (Marr, 1980) again uses Gaussian filtering. In principle, we require an image which is the second differential ∇^2 of a Gaussian operator $g(x, y)$ convolved with an image **P**. This convolution process can be separated as:

$$\nabla^2(g(x, y) * \mathbf{P}) = \nabla^2(g(x, y)) * \mathbf{P} \tag{4.24}$$

Accordingly, we need to compute a template for $\nabla^2(g(x, y))$ and convolve this with the image. By further differentiation of Equation 4.15, we achieve a *Laplacian of Gaussian* (LoG) operator:

$$
\begin{aligned}
\nabla^2 g(x, y) &= \frac{\partial^2 g(x, y)}{\partial x^2} U_x + \frac{\partial^2 g(x, y)}{\partial^2 y} U_y \\[2mm]
&= \frac{\partial \nabla g(x, y)}{\partial x} U_x + \frac{\partial \nabla g(x, y)}{\partial y} U_y \\[2mm]
&= \left(\frac{x^2}{\sigma^2} - 1 \right) \frac{e^{\frac{-(x^2 + y^2)}{2\sigma^2}}}{\sigma^2} + \left(\frac{y^2}{\sigma^2} - 1 \right) \frac{e^{\frac{-(x^2 + y^2)}{2\sigma^2}}}{\sigma^2} \\[2mm]
&= \frac{1}{\sigma^2} \left(\frac{(x^2 + y^2)}{\sigma^2} - 2 \right) e^{\frac{-(x^2 + y^2)}{2\sigma^2}}
\end{aligned} \tag{4.25}
$$

This is the basis of the Marr–Hildreth operator. Equation 4.25 can be used to calculate the coefficients of a template which, when convolved with an image, combines Gaussian smoothing with second-order differentiation. The operator is sometimes called a 'Mexican hat' operator, since its surface plot is the shape of a sombrero, as illustrated in Figure **4.26**.

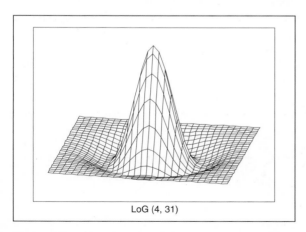

LoG (4, 31)

Figure 4.26 Shape of Laplacian of Gaussian operator

The implementation of Equation 4.25 to calculate template coefficients for the LoG operator is given in Code **4.14**. The function includes a normalisation function which ensures that the sum of the template coefficients is unity, so that edges are not detected in area of uniform brightness. This is in contrast with the earlier Laplacian operator (where the template coefficients summed to zero) since the LoG operator includes smoothing within the differencing action, whereas the Laplacian is pure differencing. The template generated by this function can then be used within template convolution. The Gaussian operator again suppresses the influence of points away from the centre of the template, basing differentiation on those points nearer the centre; the standard deviation, σ, is chosen to ensure this action. Again, it is isotropic consistent with Gaussian smoothing.

$$
\text{LoG}(\sigma, \text{size}) := \left|
\begin{array}{l}
\text{cx} \leftarrow \dfrac{\text{size}-1}{2} \\[2mm]
\text{cy} \leftarrow \dfrac{\text{size}-1}{2} \\[2mm]
\text{for } x \in 0 .. \text{size}-1 \\
\quad \text{for } y \in 0 .. \text{size}-1 \\
\qquad \text{nx} \leftarrow x - \text{cx} \\
\qquad \text{ny} \leftarrow y - \text{cy} \\[2mm]
\qquad \text{template}_{y,x} \leftarrow \dfrac{1}{\sigma^2} \cdot \left(\dfrac{nx^2 + ny^2}{\sigma^2} - 2 \right) \cdot e^{-\left(\frac{nx^2 + ny^2}{2 \cdot \sigma^2} \right)} \\[2mm]
\text{template} \leftarrow \text{normalize (template)} \\[2mm]
\text{template}
\end{array}
\right.
$$

Code 4.14 Implementation of the Laplacian of Gaussian operator

Determining the zero-crossing points is a major difficulty with this approach. There is a variety of techniques which can be used, including manual determination of zero-crossing or a least squares fit of a plane to local image data, which is followed by determination of the point at which the plane crosses zero, if it does. The former is too simplistic, whereas the latter is quite complex.

The approach here is much simpler: given a local 3×3 area of an image, this is split into quadrants. These are shown in Figure **4.27** where each quadrant contains the centre pixel.

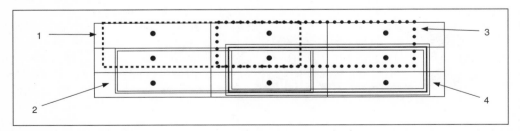

Figure 4.27 Regions for zero-crossing detection

The first quadrant contains the four points in the upper left corner and the third quadrant contains the four points in the upper right. If the average of the points in any quadrant differs in sign from the average in any other quadrant, then there must be a zero-crossing at the centre point. In `zerox`, Code **4.16**, the average intensity in each quadrant is then evaluated, giving four values and `int0`, `int1`, `int2`, and `int3`. If the maximum value of these points is positive, and the minimum value is negative, then there must be a zero-crossing within the neighbourhood. If one exists, then the output image at that point is marked as white, otherwise it is set to black.

```
zerox(pic):=    newpic←zero(pic)
                for x∈1..cols(pic)-2
                   for y∈1..rows(pic)-2

                      int₀ ← ∑       ∑        picy1,x1
                            x1=x-1  y1=y-1

                      int₁ ← ∑       ∑        picy1,x1
                            x1=x-1  y1=y

                      int₂ ← ∑       ∑        picy1,x1
                            x1=x   y1=y-1

                      int₃ ← ∑     ∑        picy1,x1
                            x1=x  y1=y

                   maxval←max(int)
                   minval←min(int)
                   newpicy,x←255 if (maxval>0)·(minval<0)

                newpic
```

Code 4.15   Zero-crossing detector

The action of the Marr–Hildreth operator is given in Figure **4.28**, applied to the face image in Figure **4.21**(a). The output of the `LoG` operator is hard to interpret visually and is not shown here (remember that it is the zero-crossings which mark the edge points and it is hard to see them). The detected zero-crossings (for a 3×3 neighbourhood) are shown in Figures **4.28**(b) and (c) for `LoG` operators of size and variance 11×11 with $\sigma = 0.8$ and 15×15 with $\sigma = 1.8$, respectively. These show that the selection of window size and variance can be used to provide edges at differing scales. Some of the smaller regions in Figure **4.28**(b) join to form larger regions in Figure **4.28**(c). Note that one virtue of the Marr–Hildreth operator is its ability to provide *closed* edge borders which the Canny operator cannot. Another virtue is that it avoids the recursion associated with hysteresis thresholding that can require a massive stack size for large images.

The Fourier transform of a LoG operator is shown in Figure **4.29**, in relief in Figure **4.29**(a) and as a contour plot in Figure **4.29**(b). The transform is circular-symmetric, as expected. Since the transform reveals that the `LoG` operator emits low and high frequencies (those close to the origin, and those far away from the origin) it is equivalent to a *band-pass filter*. Choice of the value of σ controls the spread of the operator in the spatial domain and the 'width' of the band in the frequency domain: setting σ to a high value gives

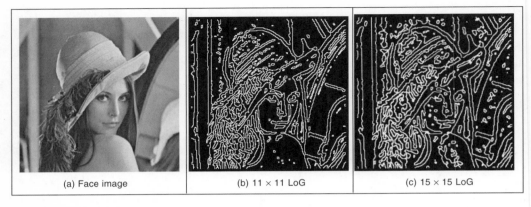

| (a) Face image | (b) 11 × 11 LoG | (c) 15 × 15 LoG |

Figure 4.28   Marr–Hildreth edge detection

low-pass filtering, as expected. This differs from first-order edge detection templates which offer a *high-pass* (differencing) filter along one axis with a *low-pass* (smoothing) action along the other axis.

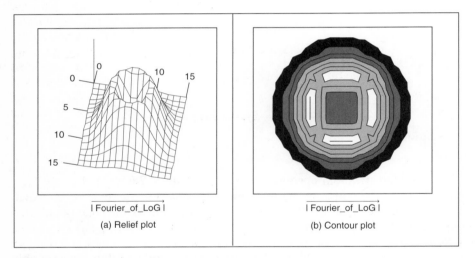

| (a) Relief plot | (b) Contour plot |

Figure 4.29   Fourier transform of LoG operator

The Marr–Hildreth operator has stimulated much attention, perhaps in part because it has an appealing relationship to human vision, and its ability for multiresolution analysis (the ability to detect edges at differing scales). In fact, it has been suggested that the original image can be reconstructed from the zero-crossings at different scales. One early study (Haralick, 1984) concluded that the Marr–Hildreth could give good performance. Unfortunately, the implementation appeared to be different from the original LoG operator (and has actually appeared in some texts in this form) as noted by one of the Marr–Hildreth study's originators (Grimson, 1985). This led to a somewhat spirited reply (Haralick, 1985) clarifying concern but also raising issues about the nature and operation of edge detection schemes which remain relevant today. Given the requirement for convolution of large templates, attention quickly focused on frequency domain implementation (Huertas, 1986), and speed improvement was later considered in some detail (Forshaw, 1988). Later, schemes were developed to refine the edges produced via the LoG approach (Ulupinar, 1990). Though speed and accuracy are major concerns with the Marr–Hildreth approach, it is also possible for zero-crossing detectors to mark as edge points ones which have no significant contrast, motivating study of their authentication (Clark, 1989). More recently, Gunn studied the relationship between mask size of the LoG operator and its error rate (Gunn, 1999). Essentially, an acceptable error rate defines a truncation error which in turn gives an appropriate mask size. Gunn also observes the paucity of studies on zero-crossing detection and offers a detector slightly more sophisticated than the one here (as it includes the case where a zero-crossing occurs at a boundary whereas the one here assumes that the zero-crossing can only occur at the centre). The similarity is not coincidental: Mark developed the one here after conversations with Steve Gunn, with whom he works!

4.4 Other edge detection operators

There have been many approaches to edge detection. This is not surprising since it is often the first stage in a vision process. The most popular operators are the Sobel, Canny and Marr–Hildreth operators. Clearly, in any implementation there is a *compromise* between (computational) cost and efficiency. In some cases, it is difficult to justify the extra complexity associated with the Canny and the Marr–Hildreth operators. This is in part due to the images: few images contain the adverse noisy situations that complex edge operators are designed to handle. Also, when finding shapes, it is often prudent to extract more than enough low-level information, and to let the more sophisticated shape detection process use, or discard, the information as appropriate. For these reasons we will study only two more edge detection approaches, and only briefly. These operators are the *Spacek* and the *Petrou* operators: both are designed to be optimal and both have different properties and a different basis (the *smoothing* functional in particular) to the Canny and Marr–Hildreth approaches. The Spacek and Petrou operators will be reviewed briefly, by virtue of their optimality. Of the other approaches, Korn developed a unifying operator for symbolic representation of grey level change (Korn, 1988).

4.4.1 Spacek operator

Canny derived an operator to satisfy performance measures describing maximum signal to noise ratio and with good localisation and chose a filter functional which maximised a composite measure of these parameters, whilst maintaining the suppression of false maxima. Spacek used a performance measure that included all three factors (Spacek, 1986). Essentially, whilst Canny maximised the ratio of the signal to noise ratio with the localisation, Spacek maximised the ratio of the product of the signal to noise ratio and the peak separation with the localisation. In Spacek's work, since the edge was again modelled as a step function, the ideal filter appeared to be of the same form as Canny's. After simplification, this resulted in a one-dimensional optimal noise smoothing filter given by:

$$f(r) = (C_1 \sin(r) + C_2 \cos(r))e^r + (C_3 \sin(r) + C_4 \cos(r))e^{-r} + 1 \qquad (4.26)$$

By numerical solution, Spacek determined optimal values for the constants as $C_1 = 13.3816$,

$C_2 = 2.7953$, $C_3 = 0.0542$ and $C_4 = -3.7953$. Spacek also showed how it was possible to derive operators which optimise filter performance for different combinations of the performance factors. In particular, an operator with the best possible noise suppression formulated by optimising the noise suppression performance alone, without the other two measures, is given by:

$$fc(r) = \frac{2\sin(\pi r)}{\pi} - \cos(\pi r) + 2r + 1 \qquad (4.27)$$

Spacek then showed how these operators could give better performance than Canny's formulation, as such challenging the optimality of the Gaussian operator for noise smoothing (in step edge detection). In application, such an advantage can be assessed only by experimentation. For example, one study (Jia, 1995) found the Spacek operator to be advantageous in automatic face recognition by its ability to retain a greater proportion of feature points to edge points than found by the Canny operator.

One difficulty with optimal smoothing functionals expressed in one-dimensional form is their extension to become a two-dimensional image operator. For the Spacek operator, one approach is to consider Equation 4.26 as a circularly symmetric functional expressed in terms of radius r and to generate the coefficients of a template-smoothing operator in this manner. For the Spacek operator, this is followed by Sobel edge detection and then by non-maximum suppression and hysteresis thresholding. The application of the Spacek operator is shown in Figure **4.30**(b) in comparison with the result achieved by the Canny operator, in Figure **4.30**(a). Clearly, there are differences between these images, the crease in the skin below the eye has appeared, as has some more detail. Clearly, the thresholds could be altered on the Canny operator to reveal different edge regions. However, some of these differences can be critical in particular applications, motivating choice of the appropriate operator.

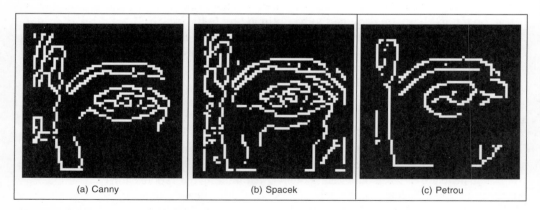

| (a) Canny | (b) Spacek | (c) Petrou |

Figure 4.30   Comparison of advanced first-order edge detection operators

4.4.2   Petrou operator

Petrou questioned the validity of the step edge model for real images (Petrou, 1991). Given that the composite performance of an image acquisition system can be considered to be that of a low-pass filter, any step-changes in the image will be smoothed to become a ramp.

As such, a more plausible model of the edge is a ramp rather than a step. For a ramp function given by:

$$u(x) = \begin{cases} 1 - 0.5e^{-ax} & x \geq 0 \\ 0.5e^{ax} & x < 0 \end{cases} \qquad (4.28)$$

where a is a positive constant depending on the image acquisition system's characteristics. A suggested range for a is between 0.5 and 3.0. The derived filter (which is optimal for these ramp edges) is:

$$f(r) = \begin{cases} e^{ar}(K_1 \sin(Ar) + K_2 \cos(Ar)) + e^{-ar}(K_3 \sin(Ar) + K_4 \cos(Ar)) + K_5 + K_6 e^{sr} \\ \qquad \qquad \qquad \qquad \qquad \qquad \qquad \qquad \qquad -w \leq r \leq 0 \quad (4.29) \\ -f(-r) \qquad \qquad \qquad \qquad \qquad \qquad \qquad \qquad 0 < r \leq w \end{cases}$$

where w is the size of the filtering operator. Optimal values for the constants K_1, K_2, K_3, K_4, K_5, K_6, A and w were determined, leading to templates which can be used to detect ramp edges. In application, the window size w is fixed first, followed by appropriate choice of a that leads to appropriate selection of the template coefficients. Since the process is based on ramp edges, and because of limits imposed by its formulation, the Petrou operator uses templates that are 12 pixels wide at minimum, in order to preserve optimal properties. As such, the operator can impose greater computational complexity but is a natural candidate for applications with the conditions for which its properties were formulated. The operator has been implemented in a similar manner to the Spacek operator. An example showing application of the Petrou operator is shown in Figure **4.30**(c). The scale of the action of the operator is clear since many small features are omitted, leaving only large-scale image features, as expected. Note that the (black) regions at the border of the picture are larger, due to the larger size of windowing operator.

4.5 Comparison of edge detection operators

Naturally, the selection of an edge operator for a particular application depends on the application itself. As has been suggested, it is not usual to require the sophistication of the advanced operators in many applications. This is reflected in analysis of the performance of the edge operators on the eye image. In order to provide a different basis for comparison, we shall consider the difficulty of low-level feature extraction in ultrasound images. As has been seen earlier (Section 3.5.4), ultrasound images are very *noisy* and require *filtering* prior to analysis. Figure **4.31**(a) is part of the ultrasound image which could have been filtered using the truncated median operator (Section 3.5.3). The image contains a feature called the pitus (it's the 'splodge' in the middle) and we shall see how different edge operators can be used to detect its perimeter, though without noise filtering. Earlier, in Section 3.5.4, we considered a comparison of statistical operators on ultrasound images. The median is actually perhaps the most popular of these processes for general (i.e. non-ultrasound) applications. Accordingly, it is of interest that one study (Bovik, 1987) has suggested that the known advantages of median filtering (the removal of noise with the preservation of edges, especially for salt and pepper noise) are shown to good effect if used as a prefilter to first- and second-order approaches, though naturally with the cost of the median filter. However, we will not consider median filtering here: its choice depends more on suitability to a particular application.

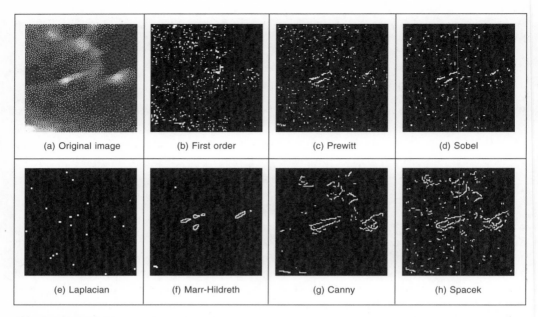

(a) Original image	(b) First order	(c) Prewitt	(d) Sobel
(e) Laplacian	(f) Marr-Hildreth	(g) Canny	(h) Spacek

Figure 4.31 Comparison of edge detection operators

The results for all edge operators have been generated using hysteresis thresholding where the thresholds were selected manually for best performance. The basic first-order operator, Figure **4.31**(b), responds rather nicely to the noise and it is difficult to select a threshold which reveals a major part of the pitus border. Some is present in the Prewitt and Sobel operators' results, Figure **4.31**(c) and Figure **4.31**(d), respectively, but there is still much noise in the processed image, though there is less in the Sobel. The Laplacian operator, Figure **4.31**(e), gives very little information indeed, which is to be expected with such noisy imagery. However, the more advanced operators can be used to good effect. The Marr–Hildreth approach improves matters, Figure **4.31**(f), but suggests that it is difficult to choose a LoG operator of appropriate size to detect a feature of these dimensions in such noisy imagery. However, the Canny and Spacek operators can be used to good effect, as shown in Figures **4.31**(g) and (h), respectively. These reveal much of the required information, together with data away* from the pitus itself. In an automated analysis system, for this application, the extra complexity of the more sophisticated operators would clearly be warranted.

4.6 Detecting image curvature

Edges are perhaps the low-level image features that are most obvious to human vision. They preserve significant features, so we can usually recognise what an image contains from its edge-detected version. However, there are *other* low-level features that can be used in computer vision. One important feature is *curvature*. Intuitively, we can consider curvature as the rate of change in edge direction. This rate of change characterises the points in a curve; points where the edge direction changes rapidly are *corners*, whereas points where there is little change in edge direction correspond to straight lines. Such extreme points are very useful for shape description and matching, since they represent significant information with reduced data.

Curvature is normally defined by considering a parametric form of a planar curve. The parametric contour $v(t) = x(t)U_x + y(t)U_y$ describes the points in a continuous curve as the end points of the position vector. Here, the values of t define an arbitrary parameterisation, the unit vectors are again $U_x = [1, 0]$ and $U_y = [0, 1]$. Changes in the position vector are given by the tangent vector function of the curve $v(t)$. That is, $\dot{v}(t) = \dot{x}(t)U_x + \dot{y}(t)U_y$. This vectorial expression has a simple intuitive meaning. If we think of the trace of the curve as the motion of a point and t is related to time, then the tangent vector defines the instantaneous motion. At any moment, the point moves with a speed given by $|\dot{v}(t)| = \sqrt{\dot{x}^2(t) + \dot{y}^2(t)}$ in the direction $\varphi(t) = \tan^{-1}(\dot{y}(t)/\dot{x}(t))$. The curvature at a point $v(t)$ describes the changes in the direction $\varphi(t)$ with respect to changes in arc length. That is,

$$\kappa(t) = \frac{d\varphi(t)}{ds} \tag{4.30}$$

where s is arc length, along the edge itself. Here φ is the angle of the tangent to the curve. That is, $\varphi = \theta \pm 90°$, where θ is the gradient direction defined in Equation 4.13. That is, if we apply an edge detector operator to an image, then we have for each pixel a gradient direction value that represents the normal direction to each point in a curve. The tangent to a curve is given by an orthogonal vector. Curvature is given with respect to arc length because a curve parameterised by arc length maintains a constant speed of motion. Thus, curvature represents changes in direction for constant displacements along the curve. By considering the chain rule, we have

$$\kappa(t) = \frac{d\varphi(t)}{dt}\frac{dt}{ds} \tag{4.31}$$

The differential ds/dt defines the change in arc length with respect to the parameter t. If we again consider the curve as the motion of a point, then this differential defines the instantaneous change in distance with respect to time. That is, the instantaneous speed. Thus,

$$ds/dt = |\dot{v}(t)| = \sqrt{\dot{x}^2(t) + \dot{y}^2(t)} \tag{4.32}$$

and

$$dt/ds = 1/\sqrt{\dot{x}^2(t) + \dot{y}^2(t)} \tag{4.33}$$

By considering that $\varphi(t) = \tan^{-1}(\dot{y}(t)/\dot{x}(t))$, then the curvature at a point $v(t)$ in Equation 4.31 is given by

$$\kappa(t) = \frac{\dot{x}(t)\ddot{y}(t) - \dot{y}(t)\ddot{x}(t)}{[\dot{x}^2(t) + \dot{y}^2(t)]^{3/2}} \tag{4.34}$$

This relationship is called the *curvature function* and it is the standard measure of curvature for *planar* curves (Apostol, 1966). An important feature of curvature is that it relates the derivative of a tangential vector to a normal vector. This can be explained by the simplified Serret–Frenet equations (Goetz, 1970) as follows. We can express the tangential vector in polar form as

$$\dot{v}(t) = |\dot{v}(t)|(\cos(\varphi(t)) + j\sin(\varphi(t))) \tag{4.35}$$

If the curve is parameterised by arc length, then $|\dot{v}(t)|$ is constant. Thus, the derivative of a tangential vector is simply given by

$$\ddot{v}(t) = |\dot{v}(t)|(-\sin(\varphi(t)) + j\cos(\varphi(t)))\,(d\varphi(t)/dt) \tag{4.36}$$

Since we are using a normalised parameterisation, then $d\varphi(t)/dt = d\varphi(t)/ds$. Thus, the tangential vector can be written as

$$\ddot{v}(t) = \kappa(t)\,\mathbf{n}(t) \tag{4.37}$$

where $\mathbf{n}(t) = |\dot{v}(t)|(-\sin(\varphi(t)) + j\cos(\varphi(t)))$ defines the direction of $\ddot{v}(t)$ whilst the curvature $\kappa(t)$ defines its modulus. The derivative of the normal vector is given by $\dot{\mathbf{n}}(t) = |\dot{v}(t)|(-\cos(\varphi(t)) - j\sin(\varphi(t)))(d\varphi(t)/ds)$ that can be written as

$$\dot{\mathbf{n}}(t) = -\kappa(t)\dot{v}(t) \tag{4.38}$$

Clearly $\mathbf{n}(t)$ is normal to $\dot{v}(t)$. Therefore, for each point in the curve, there is a pair of orthogonal vectors $\dot{v}(t)$ and $\mathbf{n}(t)$ whose moduli are proportionally related by the curvature.

Generally, the curvature of a parametric curve is computed by evaluating Equation 4.34. For a straight *line*, for example, the second derivatives $\ddot{x}(t)$ and $\ddot{y}(t)$ are *zero*, so the curvature function is *nil*. For a *circle* of radius r, we have $\dot{x}(t) = r\cos(t)$ and $\dot{y}(t) = -r\sin(t)$. Thus, $\ddot{y}(t) = -r\cos(t)$, $\ddot{x}(t) = -r\sin(t)$ and $\kappa(t) = 1/r$. However, for curves in digital images, the derivatives must be computed from discrete data. This can be done in four main ways. The most obvious approach is to calculate curvature by directly computing the difference between angular direction of successive edge pixels in a curve. A second approach is to apply the curvature function to a continuous approximation to the discrete data. In a third approach, a measure of curvature can be derived from changes in image intensity. Finally, a measure of curvature can be obtained by correlation.

4.6.1 Computing differences in edge direction

Perhaps the easier way to compute curvature in digital images is to measure the *angular change* along the curve's path. This approach was considered in early corner detection techniques (Bennett, 1975), (Groan, 1978), (Kitchen, 1982) and it merely computes the *difference* in edge *direction* between connected pixels forming a discrete curve. That is, it approximates the derivative in Equation 4.30 as the difference between neighbouring pixels. As such, curvature is simply given by

$$k(t) = \varphi_{t+1} - \varphi_{t-1} \tag{4.39}$$

where the sequence $\ldots \varphi_{t-1}, \varphi_t, \varphi_{t+1}, \varphi_{t+2} \ldots$ represents the gradient direction of a sequence of pixels defining a curve segment. Gradient direction can be obtained as the angle given by an edge detector operator. Alternatively, it can be computed by considering the position of pixels in the sequence. That is, by defining $\varphi_t = (y_{t-1} - y_{t+1})/(x_{t-1} - x_{t+1})$ where (x_t, y_t) denotes pixel t in the sequence. Since edge points are only defined at discrete points, this angle can only take eight values, so the computed curvature is very ragged. This can be smoothed out by considering the difference in mean angular direction of n pixels on the leading and trailing curve segment. That is,

$$k_n(t) = \frac{1}{n}\sum_{i=1}^{n}\varphi_{t+i} - \frac{1}{n}\sum_{i=-n}^{-1}\varphi_{t+i} \tag{4.40}$$

Averaging also gives some immunity to noise and it can be replaced by a weighted average if Gaussian smoothing is required. The number of pixels considered, the value of n, defines a compromise between accuracy and noise sensitivity. Notice that filtering techniques may also be used to reduce the quantisation effect when angles are obtained by an edge detection operator. As we have already discussed, the level of filtering is related to the size of the template (as in Section 3.4.3).

In order to compute angular differences, we need to determine connected edges. This can easily be implemented with the code already developed for hysteresis thresholding in the Canny edge operator. To compute the difference of points in a curve, the `connect` routine (Code **4.12**) only needs to be arranged to store the difference in edge direction between connected points. Code **4.16** shows an implementation for curvature detection. First, edges and magnitudes are determined. Curvature is only detected at edge points. As such, we apply maximal suppression. The function `Cont` returns a matrix containing the connected neighbour pixels of each edge. Each edge pixel is connected to one or two neighbours. The matrix `Next` stores only the direction of consecutive pixels in an edge. We use a value of −1 to indicate that there is no connected neighbour. The function `NextPixel` obtains the position of a neighbouring pixel by taking the position of a pixel and the direction of its neighbour. The curvature is computed as the difference in gradient direction of connected neighbour pixels.

```
%Curvature detection
function outputimage=Curve Connect (inputimage)

    [rows, columns]=size(inputimage);          %Image size
    outputimage=zeros(rows,columns);           %Result image
    [Mag, Ang]=Edges(inputimage);              %Edge Detection
    Mag=MaxSupr(Mag,Ang);                      Magnitude and Angle
    Next=Cont(Mag,Ang);                        %Maximal Suppression
                                               %Next connected pixels

    %Compute curvature in each pixel
    for x=1: columns-1
      for y=1: rows-1
        if Mag(y,x)~=0
          n=Next(y,x,1); m=Next(y,x,2);
            if(n~=-1 & m~=-1)
            [px,py]=NextPixel(x,y,n);
            [qx,qy]=NextPixel(x,y,m);
          outputimage(y, x)=abs(Ang(py, px)-Ang(qy, qx));
        end
      end
    end
  end
```

Code 4.16 Curvature by differences

The result of applying this form of curvature detection to an image is shown in Figure **4.32**. Here Figure **4.32**(a) contains the silhouette of an object; Figure **4.32**(b) is the curvature obtained by computing the rate of change of edge direction. In this figure, curvature is defined only at the edge points. Here, by its formulation the measurement of curvature κ gives just a thin line of differences in edge direction which can be seen to track the perimeter points of the shapes (at points where there is measured curvature). The brightest points are those with greatest curvature. In order to show the results, we have scaled the curvature values to use 256 intensity values. The estimates of corner points could be obtained by a uniformly thresholded version of Figure **4.32**(b), well in theory anyway!

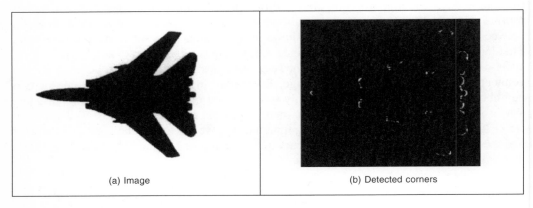

(a) Image   (b) Detected corners

Figure 4.32   Curvature detection by difference

Unfortunately, as can be seen, this approach does not provide reliable results. It is essentially a reformulation of a first-order edge detection process and presupposes that the corner information lies within the threshold data (and uses no corner structure in detection). One of the major difficulties with this approach is that measurements of angle can be severely affected by *quantisation error* and accuracy is *limited* (Bennett, 1975), a factor which will return to plague us later when we study methods for describing shapes.

4.6.2   Approximation to a continuous curve

An alternative way to obtain a measure of curvature is to evaluate Equation 4.34 for small *continuous curves* that approximate curves in discrete data (Tsai, 1994), (Lee, 1993). Continuous curves are estimated by fitting a curve to points given by the known position of image edges. A reliable value of curvature is obtained when the fitting process gives a good approximation of image segments. The main advantage of this approach is that it reduces (or at least averages) bias due to small variations between the true position of the points in the curve and the discrete position of the image pixels. That is, it reduces digitisation errors.

Small segments are generally defined by cubic polynomial functions. Cubic polynomials are a good compromise between generality of the representation and computational complexity. The fitting can be achieved by considering a parametric, or implicit, fitting equation. However, implicit forms do not provide a simple solution leading to excessive computational requirement. This is an important deterrent if we consider that it is necessary to fit a curve for each pixel forming an edge in the image. In a parametric representation, the contour $v(t)$ can be approximated by the two polynomials given by,

$$x(t) = a_x + b_x t + c_x t^2$$
$$y(t) = a_y + b_y t + c_y t^2$$

(4.41)

A simplification can be obtained by considering that $v(0)$ is the point where we want to evaluate curvature. Thus, the lower order values of the polynomial are known and are given by the pixel's co-ordinates. That is, $a_x = x(0)$ and $a_y = y(0)$. If the parameter t enumerates the points in the sequence, then this means that the pixels must be indexed by negative and positive values of t in the trailing and leading curve segments, respectively. That is, we need to index a sequence of pixels relative to the pixel where we are computing curvature.

We can obtain a definition of curvature at the point $v(0)$ by considering the derivatives of Equations 4.41 within Equation 4.34. Accordingly, the value of curvature for the pixel $v(0)$ is given by

$$\kappa(0) = 2 \frac{c_y b_x - c_x b_y}{[b_x^2 + b_y^2]^{3/2}}$$

(4.42)

In order to evaluate this expression, we need to estimate a pair of parameters for each component in Equation 4.41. These parameters can be obtained by least squares fitting (Appendix 2, Section 9.2). This fitting strategy will minimise the average error when the error in the position of the points in the digital curve has a Gaussian distribution with constant standard deviation. The main advantage of this fitting process is its simplicity and in practice even when the error assumption is not completely true, the result can provide a useful value. To estimate the four parameters of the curve it is necessary to minimise the squared error given by

$$\varepsilon_x = \sum_t w(t)(x(0) + b_x t + c_x t^2 - x(t))^2$$
$$\varepsilon_y = \sum_t w(t)(y(0) + b_y t + c_y t^2 - y(t))^2$$

(4.43)

where the weighting function $w(t)$ takes values between 0 and 1. Generally, these values are used to limit the fitting to a small rectangular area in the image (i.e. a window). That is, for a region of size $2w + 1$, the weight takes a value of one when $x(t) - x(0) \le w$ or $y(t) - y(0) \le w$ and zero otherwise. Alternatively, weights with a Gaussian distribution can also be used to increase the importance of points close to the fitting curve. By considering that the derivatives with respect to the four unknown parameters vanish at the minimum of Equation 4.43, we have that

$$\begin{bmatrix} S_{t^2} & S_{t^3} \\ S_{t^3} & S_{t^4} \end{bmatrix} \begin{bmatrix} b_x \\ c_x \end{bmatrix} = \begin{bmatrix} S_{xt} \\ S_{xt^2} \end{bmatrix} \text{ and } \begin{bmatrix} S_{t^2} & S_{t^3} \\ S_{t^3} & S_{t^4} \end{bmatrix} \begin{bmatrix} b_y \\ c_y \end{bmatrix} = \begin{bmatrix} S_{yt} \\ S_{yt^2} \end{bmatrix}$$

(4.44)

where

$$S_{t^2} = \sum_t w(t)t^2 \qquad S_{t^3} = \sum_t w(t)t^3 \qquad S_{t^4} = \sum_t w(t)t^4$$
$$S_{xt} = \sum_t w(t)(x(t) - x(0))t \qquad S_{xt^2} = \sum_t w(t)(x(t) - x(0))t^2$$
$$S_{yt} = \sum_t w(t)(y(t) - y(0))t \qquad S_{yt^2} = \sum_t w(t)(y(t) - y(0))t^2$$

(4.45)

Therefore, the solution for the best-fit model parameters is given by

$$b_x = \frac{S_{xt}S_{t^4} - S_{xt^2}S_{t^3}}{S_{t^2}S_{t^4} - S_{t^3}^2} \qquad c_x = \frac{S_{t^2}S_{xt^2} - S_{t^3}S_{xt}}{S_{t^2}S_{t^4} - S_{t^3}^2}$$

$$b_y = \frac{S_{yt}S_{t^4} - S_{yt^2}S_{t^3}}{S_{t^2}S_{t^4} - S_{t^3}^2} \qquad c_y = \frac{S_{t^2}S_{yt^2} - S_{t^3}S_{yt}}{S_{t^2}S_{t^4} - S_{t^3}^2}$$

$$(4.46)$$

Code **4.17** shows the implementation of Equation 4.41. First, we obtain the edges and the matrix Next that stores the direction of the connected pixels. For each edge pixel, we compute the leading and trailing curve segments. These segments are stored in the vectors Lchain and Rchain. These segments are obtained by following the curve until it goes out of a predefined square region. Then, we use Equations 4.44 and 4.45 to obtain the mean square fit. Finally, based on the fitted curve we compute the curvature. Figure **4.33** shows the result of the curvature obtained by this approach. Here we use a window 7 pixels wide.

```
%Curvature via fitting
function outputimage=CurvFit(inputimage)

   w=3;                                 %Parameter window size=2w+1
   [rows, columns]=size(inputimage);   %Image size
   outputimage=zeros(rows,columns);    %Result image
   [Mag,Ang]=Edges(inputimage);        %Edge Detection
   Mag=MaxSuper(Mag,Ang);              %Maximal Suppression
   Next=Cont(Mag,Ang);                 %Next connected pixels

   %compute curvature for pixel (x,y)
   for x=w+1:columns-w
     for y=w+1:rows-w
       %compute leading curve segment
       i=0;n=Next(y,x,1); p=[x,y];
       Lchain=[];
       while i<w & n~=-1
          i=i+1;
          [qx,qy]=NextPixel(p(1),p(2),n);
          p=[qx,qy];
          Lchain=[Lchain;p];
          m=rem(n+4,8);

          if(Next(p(2),p(1),1)~=-1 & Next(p(2), p(1),1)~=m)
            n=Next(p(2),p(1),1);
          elseif Next(p(2),p(1),2)~=m
            n=Next(p(2),p(1),2);
          else
            n=-1;
          end
       end

       %compute trailing curve segment
       i=0; n=Next(y,x,2); p=[x,y];
       Rchain=[];
```

```
      while i<w & n~=-1
        i=i+1;
        [qx,qy]=NextPixel(p(1),p(2),n);
        p=[qx,qy];
        Rchain=[Rchain;p];
        m=rem(n+4,8);

        if(Next(p(2),p(1),1)~=-1 & Next(p(2),p(1),1)~=m)
          n=Next(p(2),p(1),1);
        elseif Next(p(2),p(1),2)~=m
          n=Next(p(2),p(1),2);
        else
          n=-1;
        end
      end

      %Mean Squares
      st2=0; st3=0; st4=0;sxt=0; sxt2=0; syt2=0; syt2=0;
      [n,m]=size(Lchain);
      for t=1:n
        st2=st2+t*t;st3=st3+t^3; st4=st4+t^4;
        sxt=sxt+(Lchain(t,1)-x)*t; syt=syt+(Lchain(t,2)-y)*t;
        sxt2=sxt2+(Lchain(t,1)-x)*t*t; syt2=syt2+(Lchain(t,2)-y)*t*t;
      end
      [n,m]=size(Rchain);
      for t=1;n
        st2=st2+t*t; st3=st3-t^3; st4=st4+t^4;
        sxt=sxt-(Rchain(t,1)-x)*t; syt=syt-(Rchain(t,2)-y)*t;
        sxt2=sxt2+(Rchain(t,1)-x)*t*t; syt2=syt2+ (Rchain(t,2)-y)*t*t;
      end

      if((st2*st4-st3*st3)~=0)
        bx=(sxt*st4-sxt2*st3)/(st2*st4-st3*st3);
        by=(syt*st4-syt2*st3)/(st2*st4-st3*st3);
        cx=(st2*sxt2-st3*sxt)/(st2*st4-st3*st3);
        cy=(st2*syt2-st3*syt)/(st2*st4-st3*st3);
        d=sqrt((bx*bx+ by*by)^3);
        if(d~=0)
          d=abs(2*(cy*bx-cx*by)/d);
          outputimage(y,x)=d;
        end
      end
    end
  end
end
```

Code 4.17 Curvature by curve fitting

The main *problem* with this approach is that it depends on the extraction of sequences of pixels. In some cases it is very difficult to trace a digital curve in the image. This is because noise in the data can cause edges to be missed or to be found inaccurately. This problem may be handled by using a robust fitting technique. However, the implementation

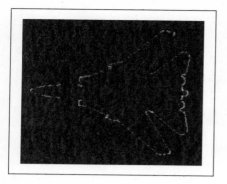

Figure 4.33 Curvature detection via curve fitting (via $\kappa(t)$)

is not evident. In the next chapters we will show how to find simple curves in a robust way. We shall show, for example, how to find circular arcs. By using this robust fitting for each image pixel, then the curvature could be computed as the inverse ratio of a circle.

4.6.3 Measuring curvature by changes in intensity

As an alternative way of measuring curvature, we can define the curvature as a function of *changes* in *image intensity*. This derivation can be based on the measure of angular changes in the discrete image. We can represent the direction at each image point as the function $\varphi(x, y)$. Thus, according to the definition of curvature, we should compute the change in these direction values along the image edge (i.e. along the curves in an image). The curve at an edge can be locally approximated by the points given by the parametric line defined by $x(t) = x + t \cos(\varphi(x, y))$ and $y(t) = y + t \sin(\varphi(x, y))$. Thus, the curvature is given by the change in the function $\varphi(x, y)$ with respect to t. That is,

$$\kappa_\varphi(x, y) = \frac{\partial \varphi(x, y)}{\partial t} = \frac{\partial \varphi(x, y)}{\partial x} \frac{\partial x(t)}{\partial t} + \frac{\partial \varphi(x, y)}{\partial y} \frac{\partial y(t)}{\partial t} \qquad (4.47)$$

where $\partial x(t)/\partial t = \cos(\varphi)$ and $\partial y(t)/\partial t = \sin(\varphi)$. By considering the definition of the gradient angle in Equation 4.13, we have that the tangent direction at a point in a line is given by $\varphi(x, y) = \tan^{-1}(Mx/(-My))$. From where we can observe that

$$\cos(\varphi) = -My/\sqrt{Mx^2 + My^2} \quad \text{and} \quad \sin(\varphi) = Mx/\sqrt{Mx^2 + My^2} \qquad (4.48)$$

By derivation of $\varphi(x, y)$ and by considering these definitions we obtain

$$\kappa_\varphi(x, y)$$

$$= \frac{1}{(Mx^2 + My^2)^{\frac{3}{2}}} \left\{ My^2 \frac{\partial Mx}{\partial x} - MxMy \frac{\partial My}{\partial x} + Mx^2 \frac{\partial My}{\partial y} - MxMy \frac{\partial Mx}{\partial y} \right\}$$

$$(4.49)$$

This defines a *forward* measure of curvature along the edge direction. We can actually use an alternative direction to measure of curvature. We can differentiate *backwards* (in the direction of $-\varphi(x, y)$) giving $\kappa_{-\varphi}(x, y)$. In this case we consider that the curve is given by $x(t) = x + t \cos(-\varphi(x, y))$ and $y(t) = y + t \sin(-\varphi(x, y))$. Thus,

$$
\kappa_{-\varphi}(x, y)
$$

$$
= \frac{1}{(Mx^2 + My^2)^{\frac{3}{2}}} \left\{ My^2 \frac{\partial Mx}{\partial x} - MxMy \frac{\partial My}{\partial x} - Mx^2 \frac{\partial My}{\partial y} + MxMy \frac{\partial Mx}{\partial y} \right\}
$$

(4.50)

Two *further* measures can be obtained by considering a forward and a backward differential along the *normal* to the edge. These differentials cannot be related to the actual definition of curvature, but can be explained intuitively. If we consider that curves are more than one pixel wide, then differentiation along the edge will measure the difference between the gradient angle between interior and exterior borders of a wide curve. In theory, the tangent angle should be the same. However, in discrete images there is a change due to the measures in a window. If the curve is a straight line, then the interior and exterior borders are the same. Thus, gradient direction normal to the edge does not change locally. As we bend a straight line, we increase the difference between the curves defining the interior and exterior borders. Thus, we expect the measure of gradient direction to change. That is, if we differentiate along the normal direction, we maximise detection of gross curvature. The value $\kappa_{\perp\varphi}(x, y)$ is obtained when $x(t) = x + t \sin(\varphi(x, y))$ and $y(t) = y + t \cos(\varphi(x, y))$. In this case,

$$
\kappa_{\perp\varphi}(x, y)
$$

$$
= \frac{1}{(Mx^2 + My^2)^{\frac{3}{2}}} \left\{ Mx^2 \frac{\partial My}{\partial x} - MxMy \frac{\partial My}{\partial x} - MxMy \frac{\partial My}{\partial y} + My^2 \frac{\partial Mx}{\partial y} \right\}
$$

(4.51)

In a *backward* formulation along a *normal* direction to the edge, we obtain:

$$
\kappa_{-\perp\varphi}(x, y)
$$

$$
= \frac{1}{(Mx^2 + My^2)^{\frac{3}{2}}} \left\{ -Mx^2 \frac{\partial My}{\partial x} + MxMy \frac{\partial Mx}{\partial x} - MxMy \frac{\partial My}{\partial y} + My^2 \frac{\partial Mx}{\partial y} \right\}
$$

(4.52)

This was originally used by Kass (1988) as a means to detect *line terminations*, as part of a feature extraction scheme called snakes (active contours) which are covered in Chapter 6. Code **4.18** shows an implementation of the four measures of curvature. The function `Gradient` is used to obtain the gradient of the image and to obtain its derivatives. The output image is obtained by applying the function according to the selection of parameter `op`.

Let us see how the four functions for estimating curvature from image intensity perform for the image given in Figure **4.32**. In general, points where the curvature is large are highlighted by each function. Different measures of curvature, Figure **4.34**, highlight differing points on the feature boundary. All measures appear to offer better performance than that derived by reformulating hysteresis thresholding, Figure **4.32**, and by fitting cubic polynomials, Figure **4.33**. Though there is little discernible performance advantage between the direction of differentiation. As the results in Figure **4.34** suggest, detecting curvature directly from

```
%Gradient Corner Detector
%op=T tangent direction
%op=TI tangent inverse
%op=N normal direction
%op=NI normal inverse

function outputimage = GradCorner(inputimage,op)

   [rows,columns]=size(inputimage); %Image size
   outputimage=zeros(rows,columns); %Result image
   [Mx,My]=Gradient(inputimage);       %Gradient images
   [M,A]=Edges(inputimage);            %Edge Suppression
    M=MaxSupr(M,A);
   [Mxx,Mxy]=Gradient(Mx);             %Derivatives of the gradient image
   [Myx,Myy]=Gradient(My);

   %compute curvature
   for x=1:columns
     for y=1:rows
       if(M(y,x)~=0)
         My2=My(y,x)^2; Mx2=Mx(y,x)^2; MxMy=Mx(y,x)*My(y,x);
         if((Mx2+My2)~=0)
           if(op=='TI')
             outputimage(y,x)=(1/(Mx2+My2)^1.5)*(My2*Mxx(y,x)-
             MxMy*Myx(y,x)-Mx2*Myy(y,x)+MxMy*Mxy(y,x));
           elseif (op=='N')
             outputimage(y,x)=(1/(Mx2+My2)^1.5)*(Mx2*Myx(y,x)-
             MxMy*Mxx(y,x)-MxMy*Myy(y,x)+My2*Mxy(y,x));
           elseif (op=='NI')
             outputimage(y,x)=(1/(Mx2+My2)^1.5)*(-Mx2*Myx(y,x)
             +MxMy*Mxx(y,x)-MxMy*Myy(y,x)+My2*Mxy(y,x));
           else % tangential as default
             outputimage(y,x)=(1/(Mx2+My2)^1.5)*(My2*Mxx(y,x)-
             MxMy*Myx(y,x)+Mx2*Myy(y,x)-MxMy*Mxy(y,x));
           end
         end
       end
     end
   end
end
```

Code 4.18 Curvature by measuring changes in intensity

an image is not a totally reliable way of determining curvature, and hence corner information. This is in part due to the higher order of the differentiation process. (Also, scale has not been included within the analysis.)

4.6.4 Autocorrelation as a measure of curvature

In the previous section, we measured curvature as the derivative of the function $\varphi(x, y)$ along a particular direction. Alternatively, a measure of curvature can be obtained by considering changes along a particular direction in the image $\mathbf{P}$ itself. This is the basic idea of *Moravec's corner* detection operator. This operator computes the average change in image intensity when a window is shifted in several directions. That is, for a pixel with co-ordinates, (x, y), and a window size of $2w + 1$ we have that

$$\mathbf{E}_{u,v}(x, y) = \sum_{i=-w}^{w} \sum_{j=-w}^{w} [\mathbf{P}_{x+i,y+j} - \mathbf{P}_{x+i+u,y+j+v}]^2 \qquad (4.53)$$

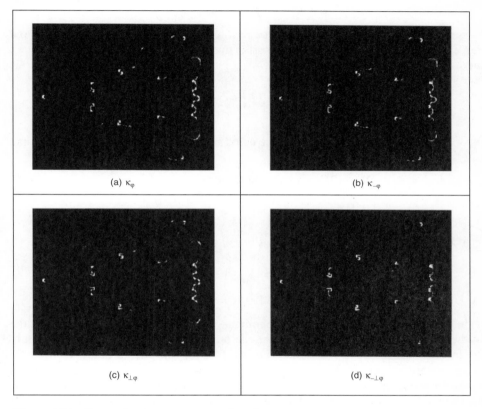

(a) κ_φ (b) $\kappa_{-\varphi}$

(c) $\kappa_{\perp\varphi}$ (d) $\kappa_{-\perp\varphi}$

Figure 4.34   Comparing image curvature detection operators

This equation approximates the *autocorrelation* function in the direction (u, v). A measure of curvature is given by the minimum value of $\mathbf{E}_{u,v}(x, y)$ obtained by considering the shifts (u, v) in the four main directions. That is, by $(1, 0)$, $(1, 1)$, $(0, 1)$ and $(-1, -1)$. The minimum is chosen because it agrees with the following two observations. First, if the pixel is in an edge defining a straight line, then $\mathbf{E}_{u,v}(x, y)$ is small for a shift along the edge and large for a shift perpendicular to the edge. In this case, we should choose the small value since the curvature of the edge is small. Secondly, if the edge defines a corner, then all the shifts produce a large value. Thus, if we also chose the minimum, then this value indicates high curvature. The main problem with this approach is that it considers only a small set of possible shifts. This problem is solved in the *Harris corner detector* (Harris, 1988) by defining an analytic expression for the autocorrelation. This expression can be obtained by considering the local approximation of intensity changes.

We can consider that the points $\mathbf{P}_{x+i,y+j}$ and $\mathbf{P}_{x+i+u,y+j+v}$ define a vector (u, v) in the image. Thus, in a similar fashion to the development given in Equation 4.53, the increment in the image function between the points can be approximated by the directional derivative $u\partial\mathbf{P}_{x+i,y+j}/\partial x + v\partial\mathbf{P}_{x+i,y+j}/\partial y$. Thus, the intensity at $\mathbf{P}_{x+i+u,y+j+v}$ can be approximated as

$$\mathbf{P}_{x+i+u,y+j+v} = \mathbf{P}_{x+i,y+j} + \frac{\partial\mathbf{P}_{x+i,y+j}}{\partial x}u + \frac{\partial\mathbf{P}_{x+i,y+j}}{\partial y}v \tag{4.54}$$

where this expression corresponds to the three first terms of the Taylor expansion around $\mathbf{P}_{x+i,y+j}$ (an expansion to first-order). If we consider this approximation in Equation 4.53 we have that

$$\mathbf{E}_{u,v}(x, y) = \sum_{i=-w}^{w}\sum_{j=-w}^{w}\left[\frac{\partial\mathbf{P}_{x+i,y+j}}{\partial x}u + \frac{\partial\mathbf{P}_{x+i,y+j}}{\partial y}v\right]^2 \tag{4.55}$$

By expansion of the squared term (and since u and v are independent of the summations), we obtain,

$$\mathbf{E}_{u,v}(x, y) = A(x, y)u^2 + 2C(x, y)uv + B(x, y)v^2 \tag{4.56}$$

where

$$A(x, y) = \sum_{i=-w}^{w}\sum_{j=-w}^{w}\left(\frac{\partial\mathbf{P}_{x+i,y+j}}{\partial x}\right)^2 \qquad B(x, y) = \sum_{i=-w}^{w}\sum_{j=-w}^{w}\left(\frac{\partial\mathbf{P}_{x+i,y+j}}{\partial y}\right)^2$$

$$C(x, y) = \sum_{i=-w}^{w}\sum_{j=-w}^{w}\left(\frac{\partial\mathbf{P}_{x+i,y+j}}{\partial x}\right)\left(\frac{\partial\mathbf{P}_{x+i,y+j}}{\partial y}\right) \tag{4.57}$$

That is, the summation of the squared components of the gradient direction for all the pixels in the window. In practice, this average can be weighted by a Gaussian function to make the measure less sensitive to noise (i.e. by filtering the image data). In order to measure the curvature at a point (x, y), it is necessary to find the vector (u, v) that minimises $\mathbf{E}_{u,v}(x, y)$ given in Equation 4.56. In a basic approach, we can recall that the minimum is obtained when the window is displaced in the direction of the edge. Thus, we can consider that $u = \cos(\varphi(x, y))$ and $v = \sin(\varphi(x, y))$. These values were defined in Equation 4.48. Accordingly, the minima values that define curvature are given by

$$\kappa_{u,v}(x, y) = \min\mathbf{E}_{u,v}(x, y) = \frac{A(x, y)M_y^2 + 2C(x, y)M_xM_y + B(x, y)M_x^2}{M_x^2 + M_y^2} \tag{4.58}$$

In a more sophisticated approach, we can consider the form of the function $\mathbf{E}_{u,v}(x, y)$. We can observe that this is a quadratic function, so it has two principal axes. We can rotate the function such that its axes have the same direction as the axes of the co-ordinate system. That is, we rotate the function $\mathbf{E}_{u,v}(x, y)$ to obtain

$$\mathbf{F}_{u,v}(x, y) = \alpha(x, y)^2u^2 + \beta(x, y)^2v^2 \tag{4.59}$$

The values of α and β are proportional to the *autocorrelation* function along the principal axes. Accordingly, if the point (x, y) is in a region of constant intensity, then we will have that both values are small. If the point defines a straight border in the image, then one value is large and the other is small. If the point defines an edge with high curvature, then both values are large. Based on these observations a measure of curvature is defined as

$$\kappa_k(x, y) = \alpha\beta - k(\alpha + \beta)^2 \tag{4.60}$$

The first term in this equation makes the measure large when the values of α and β increase. The second term is included to decrease the values in flat borders. The parameter k must be selected to control the sensitivity of the detector. The higher the value, the more sensitive to changes in the image (and therefore to noise) computed curvature will be.

In practice, in order to compute $\kappa_k(x, y)$ it is not necessary to compute explicitly the values of α and β, but the curvature can be measured from the coefficient of the quadratic expression in Equation 4.56. This can be derived by considering the matrix forms of Equations 4.56 and 4.59. That is,

$$\mathbf{E}_{u,v}(x, y) = \mathbf{P}_{x,y}^{\mathrm{T}}\mathbf{M}\mathbf{P}_{x,y} \quad \text{and} \quad \mathbf{F}_{u,v}(x, y) = \mathbf{P}_{x,y}'^{\mathrm{T}}\mathbf{Q}\mathbf{P}_{x,y}' \tag{4.61}$$

where ^{T} denotes the transpose and where

$$\mathbf{M} = \begin{bmatrix} A(x, y) & C(x, y) \\ C(x, y) & B(x, y) \end{bmatrix} \quad \text{and} \quad \mathbf{Q} = \begin{bmatrix} \alpha & 0 \\ 0 & \beta \end{bmatrix} \tag{4.62}$$

In order to relate the matrices $\mathbf{M}$ and $\mathbf{Q}$ we consider the rotation transformation

$$\mathbf{P}_{x,y}' = \mathbf{R}\mathbf{P}_{x,y} \tag{4.63}$$

Thus, the rotated system is obtained by substitution of the rotated point in $E_{u,v}(x, y)$. That is,

$$\mathbf{F}_{u,v}(x, y) = [\mathbf{R}\mathbf{P}_{x,y}']^{\mathrm{T}}\mathbf{M}\mathbf{R}\mathbf{P}_{x,y}' \tag{4.64}$$

By arranging terms, we obtain $\mathbf{F}_{u,v}(x, y) = \mathbf{P}_{x,y}'^{\mathrm{T}}\mathbf{R}^{\mathrm{T}}\mathbf{M}\mathbf{R}\mathbf{P}_{x,y}'$. By comparison with Equation 4.61, we have that

$$\mathbf{Q} = \mathbf{R}^{\mathrm{T}}\mathbf{M}\mathbf{R} \tag{4.65}$$

which means that $\mathbf{Q}$ is an orthogonal decomposition of $\mathbf{M}$. If we compute the determinant of the matrices in each side of this equation, we have that $\det(\mathbf{Q}) = \det(\mathbf{R}^{\mathrm{T}}) \det(\mathbf{M}) \det(\mathbf{R})$. Since $\det(\mathbf{R}^{\mathrm{T}}) \det(\mathbf{R}) = 1$, thus,

$$\alpha\beta = A(x, y)B(x, y) - C(x, y)^2 \tag{4.66}$$

which defines the first term in Equation 4.60. The second term can be obtained by taking the trace of the matrices in each side of this equation. Thus, we have that

$$\alpha + \beta = A(x, y) + B(x, y) \tag{4.67}$$

If we substitute these values in Equation 4.60, we have that curvature is measured by

$$\kappa_k(x, y) = A(x, y)B(x, y) - C(x, y)^2 - k(A(x, y) + B(x, y))^2 \tag{4.68}$$

Code **4.19** shows an implementation for Equations 4.57 and 4.67. The equation to be used is selected by the op parameter. Curvature is only computed at edge points. That is, at pixels whose edge magnitude is different of zero after applying maximal suppression. The first part of the code computes the coefficients of the matrix **M** according to Equation 4.56. Then, these values are used in the curvature computation.

```
%Harris Corner Detector
%op=H Harris
%op=M Minimum direction
function outputimage=Harris(inputimage, op)

  w=4;                              %Window size=2w+1
  k=100;                           %Second term constant
  [rows, columns]=size(inputimage);  %Image size
  outputimage=zeros(rows, columns);  %Result image
  [difx, dify]=Gradient(inputimage);  %Differential
  [M,A]=Edges(inputimage);          %Edge Suppression
  M=MaxSupr(M,A);

  %compute correlation
  for x=w+1: columns-w              %pixel (x,y)
    for y=w+1:rows-w
      if M(y, x)~=0
        %compute window average
        A=0;B=0;C=0;
      for i=-w:w
        for j=-w:w
          A=A+difx(y+i,x+j)^2;
          B=B+dify(y+i,x+j)^2;
          C=C+difx(y+i,x+j)*dify(y+i,x+j);
        end
      end

      if(op=='H')
          outputimage(y,x)=A*B-C^2-k*(A+B);
      else
          dx=difx(y,x);
          dy=dify(y,x);

          if dx*dx+dy*dy~=0
            outputimage(y,x)=((A*dy*Dy-
            2*C*dx*dy+B*dx*dx)/(dx*dx+dy*dy)));
          end
        end
      end
    end
  end
end
```

Code 4.19 Curvature by autocorrelation

Figure **4.35** shows the results of computing curvature using this implementation. The results are capable of showing the different curvature along the border. We can observe that $\kappa_k(x, y)$ produces more contrast between lines with low and high curvature than $\kappa_{u,v}(x, y)$.

The reason is the inclusion of the second term in Equation 4.68. In general, the measure of correlation is not only useful to compute curvature, but this technique has much wider application in finding points for matching pairs of images.

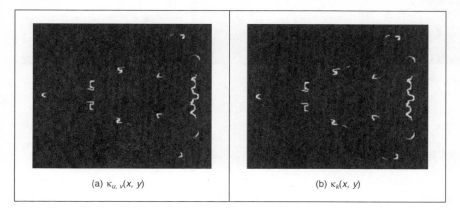

(a) $\kappa_{u,v}(x, y)$ (b) $\kappa_k(x, y)$

Figure 4.35 Curvature via the Harris operator

4.7 Describing image motion

We have looked at the main low-level features that we can extract from a single image. In the case of motion, we must consider more than one image. If we have two images obtained at different times, then the simplest way in which we can detect *motion* is by image *differencing*. That is, changes of motion can be located by subtracting the intensity values; when there is no motion, the subtraction will give a zero value and when an object in the image moves their pixel's intensity changes, so the subtraction will give a value different from zero.

In order to denote a sequence of images, we include a time index in our previous notation. That is, $\mathbf{P}(t)_{x,y}$. Thus, the image at the origin of our time is $\mathbf{P}(0)_{x,y}$ and the next image is $\mathbf{P}(1)_{x,y}$. As such the image differencing operation which delivers the difference image $\mathbf{D}$ is given by

$$\mathbf{D}(t) = \mathbf{P}(t) - \mathbf{P}(t - 1) \tag{4.69}$$

Figure **4.36** shows an example of this operation. The image in Figure **4.36**(a) is the result of subtracting the image in Figure **4.36**(b) from the one in Figure **4.36**(c). Naturally, this shows rather more than just the bits which are moving, we have not just highlighted the moving subject, we have also highlighted bits above the subject's head and around his feet. This is due mainly to change in the lighting (the shadows around the feet are to do with the subject's interaction with the lighting). However, perceived change can also be due to motion of the camera and to the motion of other objects in the field of view. In addition to these inaccuracies, perhaps the most important limitation of differencing is the lack of information about the movement itself. That is, we cannot see exactly *how* image points have moved. In order to describe the way the points in an image actually move, we should study how the pixel's position changes in each image frame.

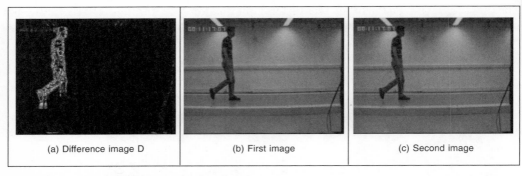

| (a) Difference image D | (b) First image | (c) Second image |

Figure 4.36   Detecting motion by differencing

4.7.1 Area-based approach

When a scene is captured at different times, 3D elements are mapped into corresponding pixels in the images. Thus, if image features are not occluded, they can be related to each other and motion can be characterised as a collection of displacements in the image plane. The displacement corresponds to the project movement of the objects in the scene and it is referred to as the *optical flow*. If you were to take an image, and its optical flow, then you should be able to construct the *next* frame in the image sequence. So optical flow is like a measurement of velocity, the movement in pixels/unit of time, more simply pixels/frame. Optical flow can be found by looking for corresponding features in images. We can consider alternative features such as points, pixels, curves or complex descriptions of objects.

The problem of finding correspondences in images has motivated the development of many techniques that can be distinguished by the features, the constraints imposed and by the optimisation or searching strategy (Dhond, 1989). When features are pixels, the correspondence can be found by observing the similarities between intensities in image regions (local neighbourhood). This approach is known as area-based matching and it is one of the most common techniques used in computer vision (Barnard, 1987). In general, pixels in non-occluded regions can be related to each other by means of a general transformation of the form by

$$\mathbf{P}(t + 1)_{x+\delta x, y+\delta y} = \mathbf{P}(t)_{x,y} + \mathbf{H}(t)_{x,y} \tag{4.70}$$

where the function $\mathbf{H}(t)_{x,y}$ compensates for intensity differences between the images, and $(\delta x, \delta y)$ defines the displacement vector of the pixel at time $t + 1$. That is, the intensity of the pixel in the frame at time $t + 1$ is equal to the intensity of the pixel in the position (x, y) in the previous frame plus some small change due to physical factors and temporal differences that induce the photometric changes in images. These factors can be due, for example, to shadows, specular reflections, differences in illumination or changes in observation angles. In a general case, it is extremely difficult to account for the photometric differences, thus the model in Equation 4.70 is generally simplified by assuming that

1.   that the *brightness* of a point in an image is *constant*; and
2.   that *neighbouring* points move with *similar* velocity.

According to the first assumption, we have that $\mathbf{H}(x) \approx 0$. Thus,

$$\mathbf{P}(t + 1)_{x+\delta x, y+\delta y} = \mathbf{P}(t)_{x,y} \tag{4.71}$$

Many techniques have used this relationship to express the matching process as an optimisation or variational problem (Jordan, 1992). The objective is to find the vector $(\delta x, \delta y)$ that minimises the error given by

$$e_{x,y} = S(\mathbf{P}(t + 1)_{x+\delta x, y+\delta y}, \mathbf{P}(t)_{x,y}) \tag{4.72}$$

where $S( )$ represents a function that measures the similarity between pixels. As such, the optimum is given by the displacement that minimises the image differences. There are alternative measures of similarity that can be used to define the matching cost (Jordan, 1992). For example, we can measure the difference by taking the absolute of the arithmetic difference. Alternatively, we can consider the correlation or the squared values of the difference or an equivalent normalised form. In practice, it is difficult to try to establish a conclusive advantage of a particular measure, since they will perform differently depending on the kind of image, the kind of noise and the nature of the motion we are observing. As such, one is free to use any measure as long as it can be justified based on particular practical or theoretical observations. The correlation and the squared difference will be explained in more detail in the next chapter when we consider how a template can be located in an image. We shall see that if we want to make the estimation problem in Equation 4.72 equivalent to maximum likelihood estimation then we should minimise the squared error. That is,

$$e_{x,y} = (\mathbf{P}(t + 1)_{x+\delta x, y+\delta y} - \mathbf{P}(t)_{x,y})^2 \tag{4.73}$$

In practice, the implementation of the minimisation is extremely prone to error since the displacement is obtained by comparing intensities of single pixels; it is very likely that the intensity changes, or that a pixel can be confused with other pixels. In order to improve performance, the optimisation includes the second assumption presented above. If neighbouring points move with similar velocity, then we can determine the displacement by considering not just a single pixel, but pixels in a neighbourhood. Thus,

$$e_{x,y} = \sum_{(x',y')\in W} (\mathbf{P}(t + 1)_{x'+\delta x, y'+\delta y} - \mathbf{P}(t)_{x',y'})^2 \tag{4.74}$$

That is, the error in the pixel at position (x, y) is measured by comparing all the pixels (x', y') in a window W. This makes the measure more stable by introducing an implicit smoothing factor. The size of the window is a compromise between noise and accuracy. Naturally, the automatic selection of the window parameter has attracted some interest (Kanade, 1994). Another important problem is the amount of computation involved in the minimisation when the displacement between frames is large. This has motivated the development of hierarchical implementations. As you can envisage, other extensions have considered more elaborate assumptions about the speed of neighbouring pixels.

A straightforward implementation of the minimisation of the squared error is presented in Code **4.20**. This function has a pair of parameters that define the maximum displacement and the window size. The optimum displacement for each pixel is obtained by comparing the error for all the potential integer displacements. In a more complex implementation, it is possible to obtain displacements with sub-pixel accuracy (Lawton, 1983). This is normally achieved by a post-processing step based on sub-pixel interpolation or by matching surfaces obtained by fitting the data at the integer positions. The effect of the selection of different window parameters can be seen in the example shown in Figure **4.37**. Figures **4.37**(a) and **4.37**(b) show an object moving up into a static background (at least for the two frames we are considering). Figures **4.37**(c), **4.37**(d) and **4.37**(e) show the displacements obtained by considering windows of increasing size. Here, we can observe that as the size of the

```
%Optical flow by correlation
%d: max displacement., w: window size 2w+1
function FlowCorr(inputimage1,inputimage2,d,w)

%Load images
L1=double(imread(inputimage 1, 'bmp'));
L2=double(imread(inputimage2,'bmp'));

%image size
[rows, columns]=size(L1); %L2 must have the same size

%result image
u=zeros(rows, columns);
v=zeros(rows, columns);

%correlation for each pixel
for x1=w+d+1:columns-w-d
  for y1=w+d+1:rows-w-d
      min=99999; dx=0; dy=0;
      %desplacement position
      for x2=x1-d:x1+d
          for y2=y1-d:y1+d
          sum=0;
          for i=-w:w% window
            for j=-w:w
                 sum=sum+(double(L1(y1+j,x1+i))-
                 double(L2(y2+j,x2+i)))^2;
              end
            end
            if (sum<min)
              min=sum;
              dx=x2-x1; dy=y2-y1;
            end
          end
      end
      u(y1,x1)=dx;
      v(y1,x1)=dy;
  end
end

%display result
quiver(u,v,.1);
```

Code 4.20 Implementation of area-based motion computation

window increases, the result is smoother, but we lose detail about the boundary of the object. We can also observe that when the window is small, they are noisy displacements near the object's border. This can be explained by considering that Equation 4.70 supposes that pixels appear in both images, but this is not true near the border since pixels appear and disappear (i.e. occlusion) from and behind the moving object. Additionally, there are problems in regions that lack intensity variation (texture). This is because the minimisation function in Equation 4.72 is almost flat and there is no clear evidence of the motion. In general, there is no effective way of handling these problems since they are due to the lack of information in the image.

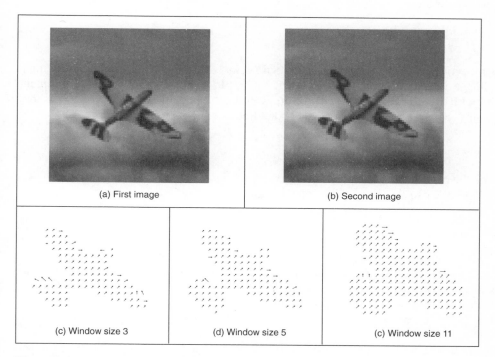

(a) First image

(b) Second image

(c) Window size 3

(d) Window size 5

(c) Window size 11

Figure 4.37   Example of area-based motion computation

4.7.2 Differential approach

Another popular way to estimate motion focuses on the observation of the differential changes in the pixel values. There are actually many ways of calculating the optical flow by this approach (Nagel, 1987; Barron, 1994). We shall discuss one of the more popular techniques (Horn, 1981). We start by considering the intensity relationship in Equation 4.71. According to this, the brightness at the point in the *new* position should be the same as the brightness at the *old* position. Like Equation 4.5, we can expand $\mathbf{P}(t + \delta t)_{x+\delta x, y+\delta y}$ by using a Taylor series as

$$\mathbf{P}(t + \delta t)_{x+\delta x, y+\delta y} = \mathbf{P}(t)_{x,y} + \delta x \frac{\partial \mathbf{P}(t)_{x,y}}{\partial x} + \delta y \frac{\partial \mathbf{P}(t)_{x,y}}{\partial y} + \delta t \frac{\partial \mathbf{P}(t)_{x,y}}{\partial t} + \xi$$

(4.75)

where ξ contains higher order terms. If we take the limit as $\delta t \to 0$ then we can ignore ξ as it also tends to zero which leaves

$$\mathbf{P}(t + \delta t)_{x+\delta x, y+\delta y} = \mathbf{P}(t)_{x,y} + \delta x \frac{\partial \mathbf{P}(t)_{x,y}}{\partial x} + \delta y \frac{\partial \mathbf{P}(t)_{x,y}}{\partial y} + \delta t \frac{\partial \mathbf{P}(t)_{x,y}}{\partial t}$$

(4.76)

Now by Equation 4.71 we can substitute for $\mathbf{P}(t + \delta t)_{x+\delta x, y+\delta y}$ to give

$$\mathbf{P}(t)_{x,y} = \mathbf{P}(t)_{x,y} + \delta x \frac{\partial \mathbf{P}(t)_{x,y}}{\partial x} + \delta y \frac{\partial \mathbf{P}(t)_{x,y}}{\partial y} + \delta t \frac{\partial \mathbf{P}(t)_{x,y}}{\partial t} \qquad (4.77)$$

which with some rearrangement gives the motion constraint equation

$$\frac{\delta x}{\delta t} \frac{\partial \mathbf{P}}{\partial x} + \frac{\delta y}{\delta t} \frac{\partial \mathbf{P}}{\partial y} = - \frac{\partial \mathbf{P}}{\partial t} \qquad (4.78)$$

We can recognise some terms in this equation. $\partial \mathbf{P}/\partial x$ and $\partial \mathbf{P}/\partial y$ are the first-order differentials of the image intensity along the two image axes. $\partial \mathbf{P}/\partial t$ is the rate of change of image intensity with time. The other two factors are the ones concerned with optical flow, as they describe movement along the two image axes. Let us call

$$u = \frac{\delta x}{\delta t} \quad \text{and} \quad v = \frac{\delta y}{\delta t}$$

These are the optical flow components: u is the *horizontal optical flow* and v is the *vertical optical flow*. We can write these into our equation to give

$$u \frac{\partial \mathbf{P}}{\partial x} + v \frac{\partial \mathbf{P}}{\partial y} = - \frac{\partial \mathbf{P}}{\partial t} \qquad (4.79)$$

This equation suggests that the optical flow and the spatial rate of intensity change together describe how an image changes with time. The equation can actually be expressed more simply in vector form in terms of the intensity change $\nabla \mathbf{P} = [\nabla x \ \nabla y] = [\partial \mathbf{P}/\partial x \ \partial \mathbf{P}/\partial y]$ and the optical flow $\mathbf{v} = [u \ v]^{\mathrm{T}}$, as the dot product

$$\nabla \mathbf{P} \cdot \mathbf{v} = - \dot{\mathbf{P}} \qquad (4.80)$$

We already have operators that can estimate the spatial intensity change, $\nabla x = \partial \mathbf{P}/\partial x$ and $\nabla y = \partial \mathbf{P}/\partial y$, by using one of the edge detection operators described earlier. We also have an operator which can estimate the rate of change of image intensity, $\nabla t = \partial \mathbf{P}/\partial t$, as given by Equation 4.69. Unfortunately, we cannot determine the optical flow components from Equation 4.79 since we have one equation in two unknowns (there are many possible pairs of values for u and v that satisfy the equation). This is actually called the *aperture problem* and makes the problem *ill-posed*. Essentially, we seek estimates of u and v that minimise error in Equation 4.86 over the entire image. By expressing Equation 4.79 as,

$$u\nabla x + v\nabla y + \nabla t = 0 \qquad (4.81)$$

we then seek estimates of u and v that minimise the error ec for all the pixels in an image

$$ec = \iint (u\nabla x + v\nabla y + \nabla t)^2 \, dx \, dy \qquad (4.82)$$

We can approach the solution (equations to determine u and v) by considering the second assumption we made earlier, namely that neighbouring points move with similar velocity. This is actually called the *smoothness constraint* as it suggests that the velocity field of the brightness varies in a smooth manner without abrupt change (or discontinuity). If we add this in to the formulation, we turn a problem that is ill-posed, without unique solution, to one that is well posed. Properly, we define the smoothness constraint as an integral over the area of interest, as in Equation 4.82. Since we want to maximise smoothness, we seek to minimise the rate of change of the optical flow. Accordingly, we seek to minimise an integral of the rate of change of flow along both axes. This is an error *es* as

$$es = \iint \left(\left(\frac{\partial u}{\partial x} \right)^2 + \left(\frac{\partial u}{\partial y} \right)^2 + \left(\frac{\partial v}{\partial x} \right)^2 + \left(\frac{\partial v}{\partial y} \right)^2 \right) dx\, dy \tag{4.83}$$

The total error is the compromise between the importance of the assumption of constant brightness and the assumption of smooth velocity. If this compromise is controlled by a *regularisation* parameter λ then the total error *e* is

$$e = \lambda \times ec + es$$

$$= \iint \left(\lambda \times \left(u \frac{\partial \mathbf{P}}{\partial x} + v \frac{\partial \mathbf{P}}{\partial y} + u \frac{\partial \mathbf{P}}{\partial t} \right)^2 + \left(\left(\frac{\partial u}{\partial x} \right)^2 + \left(\frac{\partial u}{\partial y} \right)^2 + \left(\frac{\partial v}{\partial x} \right)^2 + \left(\frac{\partial v}{\partial y} \right)^2 \right) \right) dx\, dy$$

$$\tag{4.84}$$

There is a number of ways to approach the solution (Horn, 1986), but the most appealing is perhaps also the most direct. We are concerned with providing estimates of optical flow at image points. So we are actually interested in computing the values for $u_{x,y}$ and $v_{x,y}$. We can form the error at image points, like $es_{x,y}$. Since we are concerned with image points, then we can form $es_{x,y}$ by using first-order differences, just like Equation 4.1 at the start of this chapter. Equation 4.83 can be implemented in discrete form as

$$es_{x,y} = \sum_x \sum_y \frac{1}{4} \left((u_{x+1,y} - u_{x,y})^2 + (u_{x,y+1} - u_{x,y})^2 + (v_{x+1,y} - v_{x,y})^2 + (v_{x,y+1} - v_{x,y})^2 \right)$$

$$\tag{4.85}$$

The discrete form of the smoothness constraint is then that the average rate of change of flow should be minimised. To obtain the discrete form of Equation 4.84 we then add in the discrete form of *ec* (the discrete form of Equation 4.82) to give

$$ec_{x,y} = \sum_x \sum_y (u_{x,y} \nabla x_{x,y} + v_{x,y} \nabla y_{x,y} + \nabla t_{x,y})^2 \tag{4.86}$$

where $\nabla x_{x,y} = \partial \mathbf{P}_{x,y}/\partial x$, $\nabla y_{x,y} = \partial \mathbf{P}_{x,y}/\partial y$ and $\nabla t_{x,y} = \partial \mathbf{P}_{x,y}/\partial t$ are local estimates, at the point with co-ordinates x, y, of the rate of change of the picture with horizontal direction, vertical direction and time, respectively. Accordingly, we seek values for $u_{x,y}$ and $v_{x,y}$ that minimise the total error *e* as given by

$$e_{x,y} = \sum_x \sum_y (\lambda \times ec_{x,y} + es_{x,y})$$

$$= \sum_x \sum_y \left(\begin{array}{l} \lambda \times (u_{x,y} \nabla x_{x,y} + v_{x,y} \nabla y_{x,y} + \nabla t_{x,y})^2 \\[2mm] + \frac{1}{4} \left((u_{x+1,y} - u_{x,y})^2 + (u_{x,y+1} - u_{x,y})^2 + (v_{x+1,y} - v_{x,y})^2 + (v_{x,y+1} - v_{x,y})^2 \right) \end{array} \right)$$

$$\tag{4.87}$$

Since we seek to minimise this equation with respect to $u_{x,y}$ and $v_{x,y}$ then we differentiate it separately, with respect to the two parameters of interest, and the resulting equations when equated to zero should yield the equations we seek. As such

$$\frac{\partial e_{x,y}}{\partial u_{x,y}} = (\lambda \times 2(u_{x,y}\nabla x_{x,y} + v_{x,y}\nabla y_{x,y} + \nabla t_{x,y})\,\nabla x_{x,y} + 2(u_{x,y} - \bar{u}_{x,y})) = 0$$

$$(4.88)$$

and

$$\frac{\partial e_{x,y}}{\partial v_{x,y}} = (\lambda \times 2(u_{x,y}\nabla x_{x,y} + v_{x,y}\nabla y_{x,y} + \nabla t_{x,y})\nabla y_{x,y} + 2(v_{x,y} - \bar{v}_{x,y})) = 0 \quad (4.89)$$

This gives a pair of equations in $u_{x,y}$ and $v_{x,y}$

$$(1 + \lambda(\nabla x_{x,y})^2)\,u_{x,y} + \lambda\nabla x_{x,y}\nabla y_{x,y}v_{x,y} = \bar{u}_{x,y} - \lambda\nabla x_{x,y}\nabla t_{x,y}$$

$$\lambda\nabla x_{x,y}\nabla y_{x,y}u_{x,y} + (1 + \lambda(\nabla y_{x,y})^2)\,v_{x,y} = \bar{v}_{x,y} - \lambda\nabla x_{x,y}\nabla t_{x,y}$$

$$(4.90)$$

This is a pair of equations in u and v with solution

$$(1+\lambda((\nabla x_{x,y})^2+(\nabla y_{x,y})^2))\,u_{x,y}=(1 + \lambda(\nabla y_{x,y})^2)\bar{u}_{x,y} -\lambda\nabla x_{x,y}\nabla y_{x,y}\bar{v}_{x,y}-\lambda\nabla x_{x,y}\nabla t_{x,y}$$

$$(1+\lambda((\nabla x_{x,y})^2+(\nabla y_{x,y})^2))\,v_{x,y}=-\lambda\nabla x_{x,y}\nabla y_{x,y}\,\bar{u}_{x,y}+(1+\lambda(\nabla x_{x,y})^2)\,v_{x,y}-\lambda\nabla y_{x,y}\nabla t_{x,y}$$

$$(4.91)$$

The solution to these equations is in iterative form where we shall denote the estimate of u at iteration n as $u^{<n>}$ so each iteration calculates new values for the flow at each point according to

$$u_{x,y}^{\langle n+1\rangle} = \bar{u}_{x,y}^{\langle n\rangle} - \lambda\left(\frac{\nabla x_{x,y}\bar{u}_{x,y} + \nabla y_{x,y}\bar{v}_{x,y} + \nabla t_{x,y}}{(1 + \lambda(\nabla x_{x,y}^2 + \nabla y_{x,y}^2))}\right)(\nabla x_{x,y})$$

$$v_{x,y}^{\langle n+1\rangle} = \bar{v}_{x,y}^{\langle n\rangle} - \lambda\left(\frac{\nabla x_{x,y}\bar{u}_{x,y} + \nabla y_{x,y}\bar{v}_{x,y} + \nabla t_{x,y}}{(1 + \lambda(\nabla x_{x,y}^2 + \nabla y_{x,y}^2))}\right)(\nabla y_{x,y})$$

$$(4.92)$$

Now we have it, the pair of equations gives iterative means for calculating the images of optical flow based on differentials. In order to estimate the first-order differentials, rather than use our earlier equations, we can consider neighbouring points in quadrants in successive images. This gives approximate estimates of the gradient based on the two frames. That is,

$$\nabla x_{x,y} = \frac{\begin{array}{c}(\mathbf{P}(0)_{x+1,y} + \mathbf{P}(1)_{x+1,y} + \mathbf{P}(0)_{x+1,y+1} + \mathbf{P}(1)_{x+1,y+1}) - \\ (\mathbf{P}(0)_{x,y} + \mathbf{P}(1)_{x,y} + \mathbf{P}(0)_{x,y+1} + \mathbf{P}(1)_{x,y+1})\end{array}}{8}$$

$$(4.93)$$

$$\nabla y_{x,y} = \frac{\begin{array}{c}(\mathbf{P}(0)_{x,y+1} + \mathbf{P}(1)_{x,y+1} + \mathbf{P}(0)_{x+1,y+1} + \mathbf{P}(1)_{x+1,y+1}) - \\ (\mathbf{P}(0)_{x,y} + \mathbf{P}(1)_{x,y} + \mathbf{P}(0)_{x+1,y} + \mathbf{P}(1)_{x+1,y})\end{array}}{8}$$

In fact, in a later reflection (Horn, 1993) on the earlier presentation, Horn noted with rancour that some difficulty experienced with the original technique had actually been caused by use of simpler methods of edge detection which are not appropriate here, as the simpler versions do not deliver a correctly positioned result between two images. The time differential is given by the difference between the two pixels along the two faces of the cube, as

$$\nabla t_{x,y} = \frac{\begin{aligned}(\mathbf{P}(1)_{x,y} + \mathbf{P}(1)_{x+1,y} + \mathbf{P}(1)_{x,y+1} + \mathbf{P}(1)_{x+1,y+1}) - \\ (\mathbf{P}(0)_{x,y} + \mathbf{P}(0)_{x+1,y} + \mathbf{P}(0)_{x,y+1} + \mathbf{P}(0)_{x+1,y+1})\end{aligned}}{8} \qquad (4.94)$$

Note that if the spacing between the images is other than one unit, this will change the denominator in Equations 4.93 and 4.94, but this is a constant scale factor. We also need means to calculate the averages. These can be computed as

$$\overline{u}_{x,y} = \frac{u_{x-1,y} + u_{x,y-1} + u_{x+1,y} + u_{y+1}}{2} + \frac{u_{x-1,y-1} + u_{x-1,y+1} + u_{x+1,y-1} + u_{x+1,y+1}}{4}$$

$$\overline{v}_{x,y} = \frac{v_{x-1,y} + v_{x,y-1} + v_{x+1,y} + v_{y+1}}{2} + \frac{v_{x-1,y-1} + v_{x-1,y+1} + v_{x+1,y-1} + v_{x+1,y+1}}{4}$$

$$(4.95)$$

The implementation of the computation of optical flow by the iterative solution in Equation 4.92 is presented in Code **4.21**. This function has two parameters that define the smoothing parameter and the number of iterations. In the implementation, we use the matrices u, v, uu and vv to store the old and new estimates in each iteration. The values are updated according to Equation 4.92. Derivatives and averages are computed by using Equations 4.93, 4.94 and 4.95. In a more elaborate implementation, it is convenient to include averages as we discussed in the case of single image feature operators. This will improve the accuracy and will reduce noise. Additionally, since derivatives can only be computed for small displacements, generally, gradient algorithms are implemented with a hierarchical structure. This will enable the computation of displacements larger than one pixel.

Figure **4.38** shows some examples of optical flow computation. In these examples, we used the same images as in Figure **4.37**. The first row in the figure shows three results obtained by different numbers of iterations and a fixed smoothing parameter. In this case, the estimates converged quite quickly. Note that at the start, the estimates of flow in are quite noisy, but they quickly improve; as the algorithm progresses the results are refined and a more smooth and accurate motion is obtained. The second row in Figure **4.38** shows the results for a fixed number of iterations and a variable smoothing parameter. The regularisation parameter controls the compromise between the detail and the smoothness. A *high* value of λ will enforce the *smoothness* constraint whereas a *low* value will make the *brightness* constraint dominate the result. In the results we can observe that the largest vectors point in the expected direction, upwards, whilst some of the smaller vectors are not exactly correct. This is because there is occlusion and some regions have similar textures. Clearly, we could select the brightest of these points by thresholding according to magnitude. That would leave the largest vectors (the ones which point in exactly the right direction).

Optical flow has been used in automatic gait recognition (Huang, 1999; Little, 1998), amongst other applications, partly because the displacements can be large between successive images of a walking subject, which makes the correlation approach suitable. Figure **4.39** shows the result for a walking subject where brightness depicts magnitude (direction is not shown). Figure **4.39**(a) shows the result for the differential approach, where the flow is clearly more uncertain than that produced by the correlation approach shown in Figure **4.38**(b). Another reason for using the correlation approach is that we are not concerned

```
%Optical flow by gradient method
%s=smoothing parameter
%n=number of iterations
function OpticalFlow(inputimage 1,inputimage2,s,n)

%Load images
L1=double(imread(inputimage 1,'bmp'));
L2=double(imread(inputimage2,'bmp'));

%Image size
[rows, columns]=size(l1); %l2 must have the same size

%Result flow
u=zeros(rows, columns);
v=zeros(rows, columns);

%Temporal flow
tu=zeros(rows, columns);
tv=zeros(rows, columns);

%Flow computation
for k=1:n %iterations
    for x=2:columns-1
      for y=2:rows-1
      %derivatives
        Ex=(L1(y,x+1)-L1(y,x)+L2(y,x+1)-L2(y,x)+L1(y+1,x+1)-
            L1(y+1,x)+L2(y+1,x+1)-L2(y+1,x))/4;
        Ey=(L1(y+1,x)-L1(y,x)+L2(y+1,x)-L2(y,x)+L1(y+1,x+1)-
            L1(y,x+1)+L2(y+1,x+1)-L2(y,x+1))/4;
        Et=(L2(y,x)-L1(y,x)+L2(y+1,x)-L1(y+1,x)+L2(y,x+1)L1(y,x+1)
        +L2(y+1,x+1)-L1(y+1,x+1))/4;
        %average
        AU=(u(y,x-1)+u(y,x+1)+u(y-1,x)+u(y+1,x))/4;
        AV=(v(y,x-1)+v(y,x+1)+v(y-1,x)+v(y+1,x))/4;
        %update estimates
        A=(Ex*AU+Ey*AV+Et);
        B=(1+s*(Ex*Ex+Ey*Ey));
        tu(y,x)=AU-(Ex*s*A/B);
        tv(y,x)=AV-(Ey*s*A/B);
    end %for (x,y)
end
%update
for x=2:columns-1
    for y=2:rows-1
      u(y,x)=tu(y,x); v(y,x)=tv(y,x);
    end %for (x,y)
    end
end %iterations

%display result
quiver(u,v,1);
```

Code 4.21   Implementation of gradient-based motion

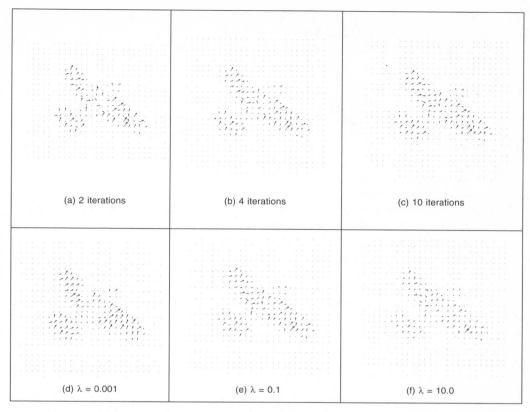

(a) 2 iterations (b) 4 iterations (c) 10 iterations

(d) $\lambda = 0.001$ (e) $\lambda = 0.1$ (f) $\lambda = 10.0$

Figure 4.38 Example of area-based motion computation

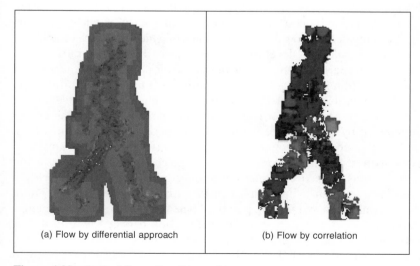

(a) Flow by differential approach (b) Flow by correlation

Figure 4.39 Optical flow of walking subject

Low-level feature extraction (including edge detection)   155

with rotation as people (generally!) walk along flat surfaces. If 360° rotation is to be considered then you have to match regions for every rotation value and this can make the correlation-based techniques computationally very demanding indeed.

4.8 Further reading

Few computer vision and image processing texts omit detail concerning edge detection operators, though few give explicit details concerning implementation. Naturally, many of the earlier texts omit the more recent techniques. (Parker, 1994) only includes C code for some of the most basic edge detection techniques. Further information can be found in journal papers; Petrou's excellent study of edge detection Petrou (1994) highlights study of the performance factors involved in the optimality of the Canny, Spacek and Petrou operators with extensive tutorial support (though we suspect Petrou junior might one day be embarrassed by the frequency with which his youthful mugshot is used – his teeth show up very well!). There have been a number of surveys of edge detection highlighting performance attributes in comparison. See, for example, Torre (1986) which gives a theoretical study of edge detection and considers some popular edge detection techniques in light of this analysis. One survey (Heath, 1997) surveys many of the more recent approaches, comparing them in particular with the Canny operator (and states where code for some of the techniques they compared can be found). This showed that best results can be achieved by tuning an edge detector for a particular application and highlighted good results by the Bergholm operator (Bergholm, 1987). Marr (1982), considers the Marr–Hildreth approach to edge detection in the light of human vision (and its influence on perception), with particular reference to scale in edge detection. Since edge detection is one of the most important vision techniques, it continues to be a focus of research interest. Accordingly, it is always worth looking at recent conference proceedings to see any new techniques, or perhaps more likely performance comparison or improvement, that might help you solve a problem.

Many of these arguments apply to corner detection as well, so the same advice applies there. There is much less attention paid by established textbooks to corner detection, though Davies (1990) devotes a chapter to the topic. Van Otterloo's fine book on shape analysis (Van Otterloo, 1991) contains a detailed analysis of measurement of (planar) curvature. Equally, determining optical flow does not get much of a mention in the established textbooks, even though it is a major low-level feature description. Rather naturally, it is to be found in depth in one of its early proponent's textbooks (Horn, 1986), but there is not a great deal elsewhere. It is often mentioned in the literature as it has led to considerable research such as computation of three-dimensional surfaces, but that is not of concern here.

There are other important issues in corner detection. It has been suggested that corner extraction can be augmented by local knowledge to improve performance (Rosin, 1996). There are actually many other corner detection schemes, each offering different attributes though with differing penalties. Important work has focused on characterising shapes using corners. In a scheme analogous to the *primal sketch* introduced earlier, there is a *curvature primal sketch* (Asada, 1986), which includes a set of primitive parameterised curvature discontinuities (such as termination and joining points). There are many other approaches: one (natural) suggestion is to define a corner as the intersection between two lines, this requires a process to find the lines; other techniques use methods that describe shape variation to find corners. We commented that filtering techniques can be included to improve the detection process; however, filtering can also be used to obtain a multiple detail representation. This representation is very useful to shape characterisation. A curvature scale space has been developed (Mokhtarian, 1986) and (Mokhtarian, 1992) to give a compact way of representing shapes, and at different scales, from coarse (low-level) to fine (detail).

Another approach to motion estimation has considered the *frequency domain* (Adelson, 1985) (yes, Fourier transforms get everywhere!). For a further overview of dense optical flow see Bulthoff (1989) and for implementation see Little (1988). The major survey (Beauchemin, 1995) of the approaches to optical flow is rather dated now, but the authors did produce freely available software (`ftp://csd.uwo.ca/pub/vision`) for the techniques that they also compared in a performance appraisal (Barron, 1994). Such an (accuracy) appraisal is particularly useful in view of the number of ways there are to estimate it. The nine techniques studied included the differential approach we have studied here, a Fourier technique and a correlation-based method. Their conclusion was that a local differential method (Lucas, 1981) and a phase-based method (Fleet, 1990) offered the most consistent performance on the datasets studied. However, there are many variables, not only in the data but also in implementation, that might lead to preference for a particular technique. Clearly, there are many impediments to the successful calculation of optical flow such as change in illumination or occlusion (and by other moving objects). In fact, there have been a number of studies on performance, e.g. of affine flow in Grossmann (1997). More recently, a thorough analysis of correlation techniques has been developed (Giachetti, 2000) with new algorithms for sub-pixel estimation. One of the more recent studies (Liu, 1998) notes how the more recent developments have been for fast or accurate techniques, without consideration of the trade-off between these two factors. The study compared the techniques mentioned previously with two newer approaches (one fast and one accurate), and also surveys real-time implementations that include implementation via parallel computers and special purpose VLSI chips.

4.9 References

Adelson, E. H. and Bergen, J. R., Spatiotemporal Energy Models for the Perception of Motion, *Journal of the Optical Society of America*, **A2**(2), pp. 284–299, 1985

Apostol, T. M., *Calculus*, 2nd Edition, **1**, Xerox College Publishing, Waltham, 1966

Asada, H. and Brady, M., The Curvature Primal Sketch, *IEEE Trans. on PAMI*, **8**(1), pp. 2–14, 1986

Barnard, S. T. and Fichler, M. A., Stereo vision, in *Encyclopedia of Artificial Intelligence*, New York: John Wiley, pp. 1083–2090, 1987

Barron, J. L., Fleet, D. J. and Beauchemin, S. S., Performance of Optical Flow Techniques, *International Journal of Computer Vision*, **12**(1), pp. 43–77, 1994

Beauchemin, S. S. and Barron, J. L., The Computation of Optical Flow, *Communications of the ACM*, pp. 433–467, 1995

Bennet, J. R. and MacDonald, J. S., On the Measurement of Curvature in a Quantised Environment, *IEEE Trans. on Computers*, **C-24**(8), pp. 803–820, 1975

Bergholm, F., Edge Focussing, *IEEE Trans. on PAMI*, **9**(6), pp. 726–741, 1987

Bovik, A. C., Huang, T. S. and Munson, D. C., The Effect of Median Filtering on Edge Estimation and Detection, *IEEE Trans. on PAMI*, **9**(2), pp. 181–194, 1987

Bulthoff, H., Little, J. and Poggio, T., A Parallel Algorithm for Real-Time Computation of Optical Flow, *Nature*, **337**(9), pp. 549–553, 1989

Canny, J., A Computational Approach to Edge Detection, *IEEE Trans. on PAMI*, **8**(6), pp. 679–698, 1986

Chen, M.-H. and Chin, R. T., Partial Smoothing Spline for Noisy +Boundaries with Corners, *IEEE Trans. on PAMI*, **15**(11), pp. 1208–1216, 1993

Clark, J. J., Authenticating Edges Produced by Zero-Crossing Algorithms, *IEEE Trans. on PAMI*, **11**(1), pp. 43–57, 1989

Davies, E. R., *Machine Vision: Theory, Algorithms and Practicalities*, Academic Press, London UK, 1990

Deriche, R., Using Canny's Criteria to Derive a Recursively Implemented Optimal Edge Detector, *International Journal of Computer Vision*, **1**, pp. 167–187, 1987

Dhond, U. R. and Aggarwal, J. K., Structure from Stereo – a Review, *IEEE Trans. on Systems, Man and Cybernetics*, **19**(6), pp. 1489–1510, 1989

Forshaw, M. R. B., Speeding Up the Marr–Hildreth Edge Operator, *CVGIP*, **41**, pp. 172–185, 1988

Giachetti, A., Matching Techniques to Compute Image Motion, *Image and Vision Computing*, **18**(3), pp. 247–260, 2000

Goetz, A., *Introduction to Differential Geometry*, Addison-Wesley, Reading, MA USA, 1970

Grimson, W. E. L. and Hildreth, E. C., Comments on 'Digital Step Edges from Zero Crossings of Second Directional Derivatives', *IEEE Trans. on PAMI*, **7**(1), pp. 121–127, 1985

Groan, F. and Verbeek, P., Freeman-Code Probabilities of Object Boundary Quantized Contours, *Computer. Vision, Graphics, Image Processing*, **7**, pp. 391–402, 1978

Grossmann, E. and Santos-Victor, J., Performance Evaluation of Optical Flow: Assessment of a New Affine Flow Method, *Robotics and Autonomous Systems*, **21**, pp. 69–82, 1997

Gunn, S. R., On the Discrete Representation of the Laplacian of Gaussian, *Pattern Recognition*, **32**(8), pp. 1463–1472, 1999

Haddon, J. F., Generalised Threshold Selection for Edge Detection, *Pattern Recognition*, **21**(3), pp. 195–203, 1988

Harris, C. and Stephens, M., A Combined Corner and Edge Detector, *Proc. Fourth Alvey Vision Conference*, pp. 147–151, 1988

Haralick, R. M., Digital Step Edges from Zero-Crossings of Second Directional Derivatives, *IEEE Trans. on PAMI*, **6**(1), pp. 58–68, 1984

Haralick, R. M., Author's Reply, *IEEE Trans. on PAMI*, **7**(1), pp. 127–129, 1985

Heath, M. D., Sarkar, S., Sanocki, T. and Bowyer, K. W., A Robust Visual Method of Assessing the Relative Performance of Edge Detection Algorithms, *IEEE Trans. on PAMI*, **19**(12), pp. 1338–1359, 1997

Horn, B. K. P. and Schunk, B. G., Determining Optical Flow, *Artificial Intelligence*, **17**, pp. 185–203, 1981

Horn, B. K. P., *Robot Vision*, MIT Press, Cambridge, MA USA 1986

Horn, B. K. P. and Schunk, B. G., 'Determining Optical Flow': a Retrospective, *Artificial Intelligence*, **59**, pp. 81–87, 1993

Huang, P. S., Harris C. J. and Nixon, M. S., Human Gait Recognition in Canonical Space using Temporal Templates, *IEE Proceedings Vision Image and Signal Processing*, **146**(2), pp. 93–100, 1999

Huertas, A. and Medioni, G., Detection of Intensity Changes with Subpixel Accuracy using Laplacian–Gaussian Masks, *IEEE Trans. on PAMI*, **8**(1), pp. 651–664, 1986

Jia, X. and Nixon, M. S., Extending the Feature Vector for Automatic Face Recognition, *IEEE Trans. on PAMI*, **17**(12), pp. 1167–1176, 1995

Jordan III, J. R. and Bovik A. C., M. S., Using Chromatic Information in Dense Stereo Correspondence, *Pattern Recognition*, **25**, pp. 367–383, 1992

Kanade, T. and Okutomi, M., A Stereo Matching Algorithm with an Adaptive Window: Theory and Experiment, *IEEE Trans. on PAMI*, **16**, pp. 920–932, 1994

Kass, M., Witkin, A. and Terzopoulos, D., Snakes: Active Contour Models, *Int. J. Comp Vis.*, **1**(4), pp. 321–331, 1988

Kitchen, L. and Rosenfeld, A., Gray-Level Corner Detection, *Pattern Recog. Lett.*, **1**(2), pp. 95–102, 1982

Korn, A. F., Toward a Symbolic Representation of Intensity Changes in Images, *IEEE Trans. on PAMI*, **10**(5), pp. 610–625, 1988

Lawton, D. T., Processing Translational Motion Sequences, *Computer Vision, Graphics and Image Processing*, **22**, pp. 116–144, 1983

Lee, C. K., Haralick, M. and Deguchi, K., Estimation of Curvature from Sampled Noisy Data, *ICVPR '93*, pp. 536–541, 1993

Little, J. J., Bulthoff, H. H. and Poggio, T., Parallel Optical Flow using Local Voting, *Proc. International Conference on Computer Vision*, pp. 454–457, 1988

Little, J. J. and Boyd, J. E., Recognizing People by their Gait: the Shape of Motion, *Videre*, **1**(2), pp. 2–32, 1998, online at http://mitpress.mit.edu/e-journals/VIDE/001/v12.html

Liu, H., Hong, T.-S., Herman, M., Camus, T. and Chellappa, R., Accuracy vs Efficiency Trade-offs in Optical Flow Algorithms, *Computer Vision and Image Understanding*, **72**(3), pp. 271–286, 1998

Marr, D. C. and Hildreth, E., Theory of Edge Detection, *Proc. Royal Society of London*, **B207**, pp. 187–217, 1980

Marr, D., *Vision*, W. H. Freeman and Co., NY USA, 1982

Mokhtarian, F. and Mackworth, A. K., Scale-Space Description and Recognition of Planar Curves and Two-Dimensional Shapes, *IEEE Trans. on PAMI*, **8**(1), pp. 34–43, 1986

Mokhtarian, F. and Mackworth, A. K., A Theory of Multi-Scale, Curvature-Based Shape Representation for Planar Curves, *IEEE Trans. on PAMI*, **14**(8), pp. 789–805, 1986

Nagel, H. H., On the Estimation of Optical Flow: Relations Between Different Approaches and Some New Results, *Artificial Intelligence*, **33**, pp. 299–324, 1987

van Otterloo, P. J., *A Contour-Oriented Approach to Shape Analysis*, Prentice Hall International (UK) Ltd, Hemel Hepstead UK, 1991

Parker, J. R., *Practical Computer Vision using C*, Wiley & Sons Inc., NY USA, 1994

Petrou, M. and Kittler, J., Optimal Edge Detectors for Ramp Edges, *IEEE Trans. on PAMI*, **13**(5), pp. 483–491, 1991

Petrou, M., The Differentiating Filter Approach to Edge Detection, *Advances in Electronics and Electron Physics*, **88**, pp. 297–345, 1994

Prewitt, J. M. S. and Mendelsohn, M. L., The Analysis of Cell Images, *Ann. N.Y. Acad. Sci.*, **128**, pp. 1035–1053, 1966

Roberts, L. G., Machine Perception of Three-Dimensional Solids, *Optical and Electro-Optical Information Processing*, MIT Press, pp. 159–197, 1965

Rosin, P. L., Augmenting Corner Descriptors, *Graphical Models and Image Processing*, **58**(3), pp. 286–294, 1996

Sobel, I.E., *Camera Models and Machine Perception*, PhD Thesis, Stanford Univ., 1970

Spacek, L. A., Edge Detection and Motion Detection, *Image and Vision Computing*, **4**(1), pp. 43–56, 1986

Torre, V. and Poggio, T. A., One Edge Detection, *IEEE Trans. on PAMI*, **8**(2), pp. 147–163, 1986

Tsai, D. M. and Chen, M. F., Curve Fitting Approach for Tangent Angle and Curvature Measurements, *Pattern Recognition*, **27**(5), pp. 699–711, 1994

Ulupinar, F. and Medioni, G., Refining Edges Detected by a LoG Operator, *CVGIP*, **51**, pp. 275–298, 1990

Venkatesh, S. and Rosin, P. L., Dynamic Threshold Determination by Local and Global Edge Evaluation, *Graphical Models and Image Processing*, **57**(2), pp. 146–160, 1995

Vliet, L. J. and Young, I. T., A Nonlinear Laplacian Operator as Edge Detector in Noisy Images, *CVGIP*, **45**, pp. 167–195, 1989

Zuniga, O. A. and Haralick, R. M., Corner Detection using the Facet Model, *Proc. IEEE Comput. Vis. and Patt. Recog. Conf.*, pp. 30–37, 1983

5
Feature extraction by shape matching

5.1 Overview

High-level *feature extraction* concerns finding shapes in computer images. To be able to recognise faces automatically, for example, one approach is to extract the component features. This requires extraction of, say, the eyes, the ears and the nose, which are the major face features. To find them, we can use their shape: the white part of the eyes is ellipsoidal; the mouth can appear as two lines, as do the eyebrows. Shape extraction implies finding their position, their orientation and their size. This feature extraction process can be viewed as similar to the way we perceive the world: many books for babies describe basic geometric shapes such as triangles, circles and squares. More complex pictures can be decomposed into a structure of simple shapes. In many applications, analysis can be guided by the way the shapes are arranged. For the example of face image analysis, we expect to find the eyes above, and either side of, the nose and we expect to find the mouth below the nose.

In feature extraction, we generally seek *invariance properties* so that the extraction process does not vary according to chosen (or specified) conditions. That is, techniques should find shapes reliably and robustly whatever the value of any parameter that can control the appearance of a shape. As a basic *invariant*, we seek immunity to changes in the *illumination* level: we seek to find a shape whether it is light or dark. In principle, as long as there is contrast between a shape and its background, the shape can be said to exist, and can then be detected. (Clearly, any computer vision technique will fail in extreme lighting conditions, you cannot see anything when it is completely dark.) Following illumination, the next most important parameter is *position*: we seek to find a shape wherever it appears. This is usually called *position-*, *location-* or *translation-invariance*. Then, we often seek to find a shape irrespective of its *rotation* (assuming that the object or the camera has an unknown orientation): this is usually called *rotation-* or *orientation-invariance*. Then, we might seek to determine the object at whatever *size* it appears, which might be due to physical change, or to how close the object has been placed to the camera. This requires *size-* or *scale-invariance*. These are the main invariance properties we shall seek from our shape extraction techniques. However, nature (as usual) tends to roll balls under our feet: there is always *noise* in images. Also since we are concerned with shapes, note that there might be more than one in the image. If one is on top of the other, it will *occlude*, or hide, the other, so not all the shape of one object will be visible.

But before we can develop image analysis techniques, we need techniques to extract the shapes. Extraction is more complex than *detection*, since extraction implies that we have

161

a description of a shape, such as its position and size, whereas detection of a shape merely implies knowledge of its existence within an image.

The techniques presented in this chapter are outlined in the table below. In order to extract a shape from an image, it is necessary to identify it from the background elements. This can be done by considering the intensity information or by comparing the pixels against a given template. In the first approach, if the brightness of the shape is known, then the pixels that form the shape can be extracted by classifying the pixels according to a fixed intensity threshold. Alternatively, if the background image is known, then this can be subtracted to obtain the pixels that define the shape of an object superimposed on the background. Template matching is a model-based approach in which the shape is extracted by searching for the best correlation between a known model and the pixels in an image. There are alternative ways to compute the correlation between the template and the image. Correlation can be implemented by considering the image or frequency domains. Additionally, the template can be defined by considering intensity values or a binary shape. The *Hough transform* defines an efficient implementation of template matching for binary templates. This technique is capable of extracting simple shapes such as lines and quadratic forms as well as arbitrary shapes. In any case, the complexity of the implementation can be reduced by considering invariant features of the shapes.

Table 5.1 Overview of Chapter 5

Shape extraction method	Technique			
Pixel brightness	Image thresholding Image subtraction			
Template matching Image and Fourier domains	Intensity template Binary templates	Hough transform	Lines Quadratic forms Arbitrary shapes	Invariance

5.2 Thresholding and subtraction

Thresholding is a simple shape extraction technique, as illustrated in Section 3.3.4 where the images could be viewed as the result of trying to separate the eye from the background. If it can be assumed that the shape to be extracted is defined by its brightness, then thresholding an image at that brightness level should find the shape. Thresholding is clearly sensitive to change in illumination: if the image illumination changes then so will the perceived brightness of the target shape. Unless the threshold level can be arranged to adapt to the change in brightness level, any thresholding technique will fail. Its attraction is *simplicity*: thresholding does not require much computational effort. If the illumination level changes in a linear fashion, then using histogram equalisation will result in an image that does not vary. Unfortunately, the result of histogram equalisation is sensitive to noise, shadows and variant illumination: noise can affect the resulting image quite dramatically and this will again render a thresholding technique useless.

Thresholding after *intensity normalisation* (Section 3.3.2) is less sensitive to noise, since the noise is stretched with the original image, and cannot affect the stretching process by much. It is, however, still sensitive to shadows and variant illumination. Again, it can only find application where the illumination can be carefully controlled. This requirement is germane to any application that uses basic thresholding. If the overall illumination level cannot be controlled, then it is possible to threshold edge magnitude data since this is insensitive to overall brightness level, by virtue of the implicit differencing process. However, edge data is rarely continuous and there can be gaps in the detected perimeter of a shape. Another major difficulty, which applies to thresholding the brightness data as well, is that there are often more shapes than one. If the shapes are on top of each other, one occludes the other and the shapes need to be separated.

An alternative approach is to *subtract* an image from a known background before thresholding (we saw how we can estimate the background in Section 3.5.2). This assumes that the background is known precisely, otherwise many more details than just the target feature will appear in the resulting image; clearly the subtraction will be unfeasible if there is *noise* on either image, and especially on both. In this approach, there is no implicit shape description, but if the thresholding process is sufficient, then it is simple to estimate basic shape parameters, such as position.

The subtraction approach is illustrated in Figure **5.1**. Here, we seek to separate or extract the walking subject from the background. We saw earlier, in Figure **3.22**, how the median filter can be used to provide an estimate of the background to the sequence of images that Figure **5.1**(a) comes from. When we subtract the background of Figure **3.22**(i) from the image of Figure **5.1**(a), we obtain most of the subject with some extra background just behind the subject's head. This is due to the effect of the moving subject on *lighting*. Also, removing the background removes some of the subject: the horizontal bars in the background have been removed from the subject by the subtraction process. These aspects are highlighted in the thresholded image, Figure **5.1**(c). It is not a particularly poor way of separating the subject from the background (we have the subject but we have chopped out his midriff) but it is not especially good either.

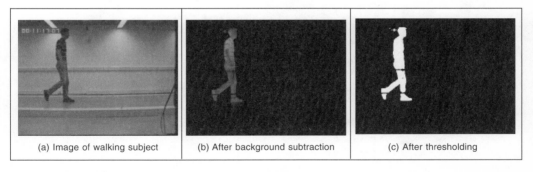

| (a) Image of walking subject | (b) After background subtraction | (c) After thresholding |

Figure 5.1   Shape extraction by subtraction and thresholding

Even though thresholding and subtraction are attractive (because of simplicity and hence their speed), the performance of both techniques is sensitive to partial shape data, to noise, variation in illumination and to occlusion of the target shape by other objects. Accordingly, many approaches to image interpretation use higher level information in shape extraction, namely how the pixels are connected within the shape. This can resolve these factors.

5.3 Template matching

5.3.1 Definition

Template matching is conceptually a simple process. We need to match a *template* to an image, where the template is a sub-image that contains the shape we are trying to find. Accordingly, we centre the template on an image point and count up how many points in the template *match* those in the image. The procedure is repeated for the entire image and the point which led to the best match, the maximum count, is deemed to be the point where the shape (given by the template) lies within the image.

Consider that we want to find the template of Figure **5.2**(b) in the image of Figure **5.2**(a). The template is first positioned at the origin and then matched with the image to give a count which reflects how well the template matched that part of the image at that position. The count of matching pixels is increased by one for each point where the brightness of the template matches the brightness of the image. This is similar to the process of template convolution, illustrated earlier in Figure **3.11**. The difference here is that points in the image are matched with those in the template, and the sum is of the number of matching points as opposed to the weighted sum of image data. The best match is when the template is placed at the position where the rectangle is matched to itself. Obviously, this process can be generalised to find, for example, templates of different *size* or *orientation*. In these cases, we have to try all the templates (at expected rotation and size) to determine the best match.

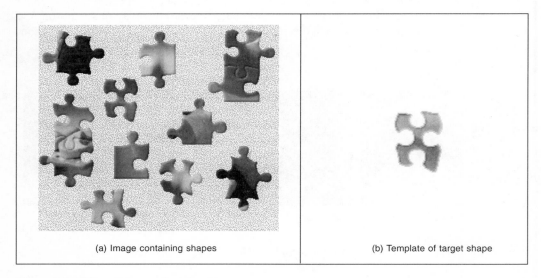

(a) Image containing shapes   (b) Template of target shape

Figure 5.2 Illustrating template matching

Formally, template matching can be defined as a method of parameter estimation. The parameters define the position (and pose) of the template. We can define a template as a discrete function $\mathbf{T}_{x,y}$. This function takes values in a window. That is, the co-ordinates of the points $(x, y) \in \mathbf{W}$. For example, for a 2×2 template we have that the set of points $\mathbf{W} = \{(0, 0), (0, 1), (1, 0), (1, 1)\}$.

Let us consider that each pixel in the image $\mathbf{I}_{x,y}$ is corrupted by additive Gaussian noise. The noise has a mean value of zero and the (unknown) standard deviation is σ. Thus the probability that a point in the template placed at coordinates (i, j) matches the corresponding pixel at position $(x, y) \in \mathbf{W}$ is given by the normal distribution

$$p_{i,j}(x, y) = \frac{1}{\sqrt{2\pi}\sigma} e^{-\frac{1}{2}\left(\frac{\mathbf{I}_{x+i,y+j} - \mathbf{T}_{x,y}}{\sigma}\right)^2} \tag{5.1}$$

Since noise affecting each pixel is independent, then the probability that the template is at the position (i, j) is the combined probability of each pixel that the template covers. That is,

$$L_{i,j} = \prod_{(x,y)\in\mathbf{W}} p_{i,j}(x, y) \tag{5.2}$$

By substitution of Equation 5.1, we have that

$$L_{i,j} = \left(\frac{1}{\sqrt{2\pi}\sigma}\right)^n e^{-\frac{1}{2}\sum_{(x,y)\in\mathbf{W}}\left(\frac{\mathbf{I}_{x+i,y+j} - \mathbf{T}_{x,y}}{\sigma}\right)^2} \tag{5.3}$$

where n is the number of pixels in the template. This function is called the *likelihood* function. Generally, it is expressed in logarithmic form to simplify the analysis. Notice that the logarithm scales the function, but it does not change the position of the maximum. Thus, by taking the logarithm the likelihood function is redefined as

$$\ln(L_{i,j}) = n \ln\left(\frac{1}{\sqrt{2\pi}\sigma}\right) - \frac{1}{2}\sum_{(x,y)\in\mathbf{W}}\left(\frac{\mathbf{I}_{x+i,y+j} - \mathbf{T}_{x,y}}{\sigma}\right)^2 \tag{5.4}$$

In *maximum likelihood estimation*, we have to choose the parameter that maximises the likelihood function. That is, the positions that minimise the rate of change of the objective function

$$\frac{\partial \ln(L_{i,j})}{\partial i} = 0 \quad \text{and} \quad \frac{\partial \ln(L_{i,j})}{\partial j} = 0 \tag{5.5}$$

That is,

$$\sum_{(x,y)\in\mathbf{W}} (\mathbf{I}_{x+i,y+j} - \mathbf{T}_{x,y})\frac{\partial \mathbf{I}_{x+i,y+j}}{\partial i} = 0$$

$$\sum_{(x,y)\in\mathbf{W}} (\mathbf{I}_{x+i,y+j} - \mathbf{T}_{x,y})\frac{\partial \mathbf{I}_{x+i,y+j}}{\partial j} = 0 \tag{5.6}$$

We can observe that these equations are also the solution of the minimisation problem given by

$$\min e = \sum_{(x,y)\in\mathbf{W}} (\mathbf{I}_{x+i,y+j} - \mathbf{T}_{x,y})^2 \tag{5.7}$$

That is, maximum likelihood estimation is equivalent to choosing the template position that minimises the squared error (the squared values of the differences between the template points and the corresponding image points). The position where the template best matches the image is the estimated position of the template within the image. Thus, if you measure the match using the squared error criterion, then you will be choosing the *maximum likelihood* solution. This implies that the result achieved by template matching is optimal for images corrupted by Gaussian noise. A more detailed examination of the method of least squares is given in Appendix 2, Section 9.2. (Note that the *central limit theorem* suggests that practically experienced noise can be assumed to be Gaussian distributed, though many images appear to contradict this assumption.) Of course you can use other error criteria such as the absolute difference rather than the squared difference or, if you feel more adventurous, then you might consider robust measures such as M-estimators.

We can derive alternative forms of the squared error criterion by considering that Equation 5.7 can be written as

$$\min e = \sum_{(x,y) \in \mathbf{W}} (\mathbf{I}^2_{x+i,y+j} - 2\mathbf{I}_{x+i,y+j} \mathbf{T}_{x,y} + \mathbf{T}^2_{x,y}) \tag{5.8}$$

The last term does not depend on the template position (i, j). As such, it is constant and cannot be minimised. Thus, the optimum in this equation can be obtained by minimising

$$\min e = \sum_{(x,y) \in \mathbf{W}} \mathbf{I}^2_{x+i,y+j} - 2 \sum_{(x,y) \in \mathbf{W}} \mathbf{I}_{x+i,y+j} \mathbf{T}_{x,y} \tag{5.9}$$

If the first term

$$\sum_{(x,y) \in \mathbf{W}} \mathbf{I}^2_{x+i,y+j} \tag{5.10}$$

is approximately constant, then the remaining term gives a measure of the similarity between the image and the template. That is, we can maximise the *cross-correlation* between the template and the image. Thus, the best position can be computed by

$$\max e = \sum_{(x,y) \in \mathbf{W}} \mathbf{I}_{x+i,y+j} \mathbf{T}_{x,y} \tag{5.11}$$

However, the squared term in Equation 5.10 can vary with position, so the match defined by Equation 5.11 can be poor. Additionally, the range of the cross-correlation function is dependent on the size of the template and it is non-invariant to changes in image lighting conditions. Thus, in an implementation it is more convenient to use either Equation 5.7 or Equation 5.9 (in spite of being computationally more demanding than the cross-correlation in Equation 5.11). Alternatively, the cross-correlation can be *normalised* as follows. We can rewrite Equation 5.8 as

$$\min e = 1 - 2 \frac{\sum_{(x,y) \in \mathbf{W}} \mathbf{I}_{x+i,y+j} \mathbf{T}_{x,y}}{\sum_{(x,y) \in \mathbf{W}} \mathbf{I}^2_{x+i,y+j}} \tag{5.12}$$

Here the first term is constant and thus the optimum value can be obtained by

$$\max e = \frac{\sum_{(x,y) \in \mathbf{W}} \mathbf{I}_{x+i,y+j} \mathbf{T}_{x,y}}{\sum_{(x,y) \in \mathbf{W}} \mathbf{I}^2_{x+i,y+j}} \tag{5.13}$$

In general, it is convenient to normalise the grey level of each image window under the template. That is,

$$\max e = \frac{\sum\limits_{(x,y)\in \mathbf{W}} (\mathbf{I}_{x+i,y+j} - \bar{\mathbf{I}}_{i,j})(\mathbf{T}_{x,y} - \bar{\mathbf{T}})}{\sum\limits_{(x,y)\in \mathbf{W}} (\mathbf{I}_{x+i,y+j} - \bar{\mathbf{I}}_{i,j})^2} \qquad (5.14)$$

where $\bar{\mathbf{I}}_{i,j}$ is the mean of the pixels $\mathbf{I}_{x+i,y+j}$ for points within the window (i.e. $(x, y) \in \mathbf{W}$) and $\bar{\mathbf{T}}$ is the mean of the pixels of the template. An alternative form to Equation 5.14 is given by *normalising* the cross-correlation. This does not change the position of the optimum and gives an interpretation as the normalisation of the cross-correlation vector. That is, the cross-correlation is divided by its modulus. Thus,

$$\max e = \frac{\sum\limits_{(x,y)\in \mathbf{W}} (\mathbf{I}_{x+i,y+j} - \bar{\mathbf{I}}_{i,j})(\mathbf{T}_{x,y} - \bar{\mathbf{T}})}{\sqrt{\sum\limits_{(x,y)\in \mathbf{W}} (\mathbf{I}_{x+i,y+j} - \bar{\mathbf{I}}_{i,j})^2 (\mathbf{T}_{x,y} - \bar{\mathbf{T}})^2}} \qquad (5.15)$$

However, this equation has a similar computational complexity to the original formulation in Equation 5.7.

A particular implementation of template matching is when the image and the template are binary. In this case, the binary image can represent regions in the image or it can contain the edges. These two cases are illustrated in the example in Figure **5.3.** The advantage of using binary images is that the amount of *computation* can be *reduced*. That is, each term in Equation 5.7 will take only two values: it will be one when $\mathbf{I}_{x+i,y+j} = \mathbf{T}_{x,y}$, and zero otherwise. Thus, Equation 5.7 can be implemented as

$$\max e = \sum\limits_{(x,y)\in \mathbf{W}} \overline{\mathbf{I}_{x+i,y+j} \oplus \mathbf{T}_{x,y}} \qquad (5.16)$$

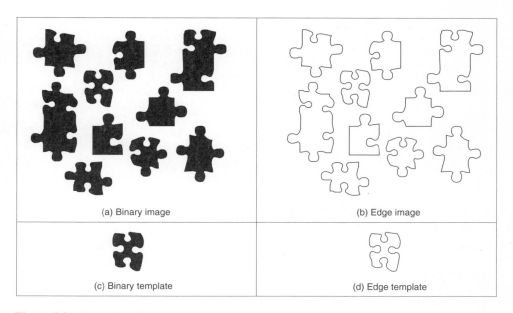

(a) Binary image | (b) Edge image

(c) Binary template | (d) Edge template

Figure 5.3 Example of binary and edge template matching

where the symbol $\overline{\oplus}$ denotes the exclusive NOR operator. This equation can be easily implemented and requires significantly fewer resources than the original matching function.

Template matching develops an *accumulator space* that stores the match of the template to the image at different locations, this corresponds to an implementation of Equation 5.7. It is called an accumulator, since the match is *accumulated* during application. Essentially, the accumulator is a two-dimensional array that holds the difference between the template and the image at different positions. The position in the image gives the same position of match in the accumulator. Alternatively, Equation 5.11 suggests that the peaks in the accumulator resulting from template correlation give the location of the template in an image: the co-ordinates of the point of best match. Accordingly, template correlation and template matching can be viewed as similar processes. The location of a template can be determined by either process. The binary implementation of template matching, Equation 5.16, usually is concerned with thresholded edge data. This equation will be reconsidered in the definition of the Hough transform, the topic of the following section.

The Matlab code to implement template matching is the function `TMatching` given in Code **5.1**. This function first clears an accumulator array, `accum`, then searches the whole picture, using pointers `i` and `j`, and then searches the whole template for matches, using pointers `x` and `y`. Notice that the position of the template is given by its centre. The accumulator elements are incremented according to Equation 5.7. The accumulator array

```
%Template Matching Implementation

function accum=TMatching(inputimage,template)

%Image size & template size
  [rows,columns]=size(inputimage);
  [rowsT,columnsT]=size(template);

  %Centre of the template
cx=floor(columnsT/2)+1;    cy=floor(rowsT/2)+1;

%Accumulator
accum=zeros(rows,columns);
%Template Position
for i=cx:columns-cx
  for j=cy:rows-cy
    %Template elements
      for x=1-cx:cx-1
        for y=1-cy:cy-1
           err=(double(inputimage(j+y,i+x))-double(template
           (y+cy,x+cx)))^2;
          accum(j,i)=accum(j,i)+err;
        end
      end
  end
end
```

Code **5.1**   Implementing template matching

is delivered as the result. The match for each position is stored in the array. After computing all the matches, the minimum element in the array defines the position where most pixels in the template matched those in the image. As such, the minimum is deemed to be the co-ordinates of the point where the template's shape is most likely to lie within the original image. It is possible to implement a version of template matching without the accumulator array, by storing the location of the minimum alone. This will give the same result though it requires little storage. However, this implementation will provide a result that cannot support later image interpretation that might require knowledge of more than just the best match.

The results of applying the template matching procedure are illustrated in Figure **5.4**. This example shows the accumulator arrays for matching the images shown in Figure **5.2**(a), **5.3**(a) and **5.3**(b) with their respective templates. The dark points in each image are at the co-ordinates of the origin of the position where the template best matched the image (the minimum). Note that there is a border where the template has not been matched to the image data. At these border points, the template extended beyond the image data, so no matching has been performed. This is the same border as experienced with template convolution, Section 3.4.1. We can observe that a better minimum is obtained, Figure **5.4**(c), from the edge images of Figure **5.3**. This is because for grey level and binary images, there is some match when the template is not exactly in the best position.

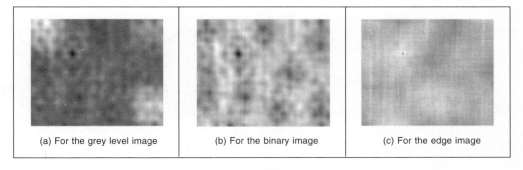

| (a) For the grey level image | (b) For the binary image | (c) For the edge image |

Figure 5.4   Accumulator arrays from template matching

Most applications require further degrees of freedom such as rotation (orientation), scale (size), or perspective deformations. Rotation can be handled by rotating the template, or by using polar co-ordinates; scale invariance can be achieved using templates of differing size. Having more parameters of interest implies that the accumulator space becomes larger; its dimensions increase by one for each extra parameter of interest. *Position*-invariant template matching, as considered here, implies a 2D parameter space, whereas the extension to *scale* and *position* invariant template matching requires a 3D parameter space.

The computational cost of template matching is *large*. If the template is square and of size $m \times m$ and is matched to an image of size $N \times N$ then since the m^2 pixels are matched at all image points (except for the border) the computational cost is $O(N^2m^2)$. This is the cost for position invariant template matching. Any further parameters of interest *increase* the computational cost in proportion to the number of values of the extra parameters. This is clearly a large penalty and so a direct digital implementation of template matching is slow. Accordingly, this guarantees interest in techniques that can deliver the same result, but faster, such as using a Fourier implementation based on fast transform calculus.

5.3.2 Fourier transform implementation

We can implement template matching via the Fourier transform by using the *duality* between convolution and multiplication. This duality establishes that a multiplication in the space domain corresponds to a convolution in the frequency domain and vice versa. This can be exploited for faster computation by using the frequency domain, given the fast Fourier transform algorithm. Thus, in order to find a shape we can compute the cross-correlation as a multiplication in the frequency domain. However, the matching process in Equation 5.11 is actually *correlation* (Section 2.3), *not* convolution. Thus, we need to express the correlation in terms of a convolution. This can be done as follows. First, we can rewrite the *correlation* in Equation 5.11 as

$$\mathbf{I} \otimes \mathbf{T} = \sum_{(x,\, y) \in W} \mathbf{I}_{x',y'} \; \mathbf{T}_{x'-i,y'-j} \tag{5.17}$$

where $x' = x + i$ and $y' = y + j$. *Convolution* is defined as

$$\mathbf{I} * \mathbf{T} = \sum_{(x,\, y) \in W} \mathbf{I}_{x',y'} \; \mathbf{T}_{i-x',j-y'} \tag{5.18}$$

Thus, in order to implement template matching in the frequency domain, we need to express Equation 5.17 in terms of Equation 5.18. This can be achieved by considering that

$$\mathbf{I} \otimes \mathbf{T} = \mathbf{I} * \mathbf{T}' = \sum_{(x,\, y) \in W} \mathbf{I}_{x',y'} \; \mathbf{T}'_{i-x',j-y'} \tag{5.19}$$

where

$$\mathbf{T}' = \mathbf{T}_{-x,-y} \tag{5.20}$$

That is, correlation is equivalent to convolution when the template is changed according to Equation 5.20. This equation reverses the co-ordinate axes and it corresponds to a horizontal and a vertical flip.

In the frequency domain, convolution corresponds to *multiplication*. As such, we have that Equation 5.19 can be implemented by

$$\mathbf{I} * \mathbf{T}' = F^{-1}(F(\mathbf{I})F(\mathbf{T}')) \tag{5.21}$$

where F denotes Fourier transformation as in Chapter 2 (and calculated by the FFT) and F^{-1} denotes the inverse FFT. This can be computationally faster than its direct implementation, given the speed advantage of the FFT. There are two ways of implementing this equation. In the first approach, we can compute $\mathbf{T}'$ by flipping the template and then computing its Fourier transform $F(\mathbf{T}')$. In the second approach, we compute the transform of $F(\mathbf{T})$ and then we compute the complex *conjugate*. That is,

$$F(\mathbf{T}') = [F(\mathbf{T})]^* \tag{5.22}$$

where [ ]* denotes the complex conjugate of the transform data (yes, we agree it's an unfortunate symbol clash with convolution, but both are standard symbols). So conjugation of the transform of the template implies that the product of the two transforms leads to correlation. That is,

$$\mathbf{I} * \mathbf{T}' = F^{-1}(F(\mathbf{I}) \, [F(\mathbf{T})]*) \qquad\qquad (5.23)$$

For both implementations, Equations 5.21 and 5.23 will evaluate the match and, more quickly for large templates than by direct implementation of template matching. Note that one assumption is that the transforms are of the same size, even though the template's shape is usually much smaller than the image. There is actually a selection of approaches; a simple solution is to include extra zero values (*zero-padding*) to make the image of the template the same size as the image.

The code to implement template matching by Fourier, FTConv, is given in Code **5.2**. The implementation takes the image and the flipped template. The template is zero-padded and then transforms are evaluated. The required convolution is obtained by multiplying the transforms and then applying the inverse. The resulting image is the magnitude of the inverse transform. This could naturally be invoked as a single function, rather than as procedure, but the implementation is less clear. This process can be formulated using brightness or edge data, as appropriate. Should we seek *scale* invariance, to find the position of a template irrespective of its size, then we need to formulate a set of templates that range in size between the maximum expected variation. Each of the templates of differing size is then matched by frequency domain multiplication. The maximum frequency domain value, for all sizes of template, indicates the position of the template and, naturally, gives a value for its size. This can of course be a rather lengthy procedure when the template ranges considerably in size.

```
%Fourier Transform Convolution

function FTConv(inputimage,template)

%image size
[rows,columns]=size(inputimage);

%FT
Fimage=fft2(inputimage,rows,columns);
Ftemplate=fft2(template,rows,columns);

%Convolution
G=Fimage.*Ftemplate;

%Modulus
Z=log(abs(fftshift(G)));

%Inverse
R=real(ifft2(G));
```

Code 5.2 Implementing convolution by the frequency domain

Figure **5.5** illustrates the results of template matching in the Fourier domain. This example uses the image and template shown in Figure **5.2.** Figure **5.5**(a) shows the flipped and padded template. The Fourier transforms of the image and of the flipped template are given in Figures **5.5**(b) and **5.5**(c), respectively. These transforms are multiplied, point by point, to achieve the image in Figure **5.5**(d). When this is inverse Fourier transformed, the result, Figure **5.5**(e), shows where the template best matched the image (the co-ordinates of the template's top left-hand corner). The resultant image contains several local maximum (in white). This can be explained by the fact that this implementation does not consider the term in Equation 5.10. Additionally, the shape can partially match several patterns in the image. Figure **5.5**(f) shows a zoom of the region where the peak is located. We can see that this peak is well defined. In contrast to template matching, the implementation in the frequency domain does not have a border. This is due to the fact that Fourier theory assumes picture replication to infinity. Note that in application, the Fourier transforms do not need to be rearranged (`fftshif`) so that the d.c. is at the centre, since this has been done here for display purposes only.

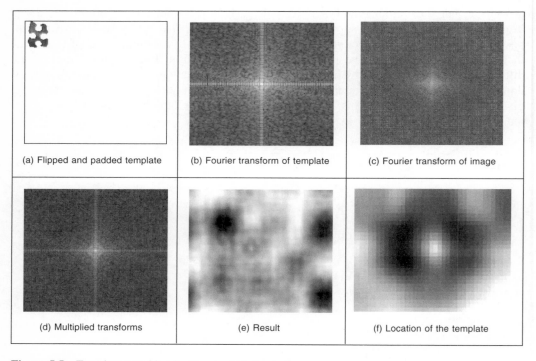

(a) Flipped and padded template	(b) Fourier transform of template	(c) Fourier transform of image
(d) Multiplied transforms	(e) Result	(f) Location of the template

Figure 5.5 Template matching by Fourier transformation

There are several further difficulties in using the transform domain for template matching in discrete images. If we seek rotation invariance, then an image can be expressed in terms of its polar co-ordinates. Discretisation gives further difficulty since the points in a rotated discrete shape can map imperfectly to the original shape. This problem is better manifest when an image is scaled in size to become larger. In such a case, the spacing between points will increase in the enlarged image. The difficulty is how to allocate values for pixels in the enlarged image which are not defined in the enlargement process. There are several interpolation approaches, but it can often appear prudent to reformulate the original approach. Further difficulties can include the influence of the image borders: Fourier theory assumes that an image replicates spatially to infinity. Such difficulty can be reduced by using window operators, such as the Hamming or the Hanning windows. These difficulties do not obtain for optical Fourier transforms and so using the Fourier transform for position-invariant template matching is often confined to optical implementations.

5.3.3 Discussion of template matching

The advantages associated with template matching are mainly theoretical since it can be very difficult to develop a template matching technique that operates satisfactorily. The results presented here have been for *position* invariance only. If invariance to *rotation* and *scale* is also required then this can cause difficulty. This is because the template is stored as a discrete set of points. When these are rotated, *gaps* can appear due to the discrete nature of the co-ordinate system. If the template is increased in size then again there will be missing points in the scaled-up version. Again, there is a frequency domain version that can handle variation in size, since scale invariant template matching can be achieved using the *Mellin transform* (Bracewell, 1986). This avoids using many templates to accommodate the variation in size by evaluating the scale-invariant match in a single pass. The Mellin transform essentially scales the spatial co-ordinates of the image using an exponential function. A point is then moved to a position given by a logarithmic function of its original co-ordinates. The transform of the scaled image is then multiplied by the transform of the template. The maximum again indicates the best match between the transform and the image. This can be considered to be equivalent to a change of variable. The logarithmic mapping ensures that scaling (multiplication) becomes addition. By the logarithmic mapping, the problem of scale invariance becomes a problem of finding the position of a match.

The Mellin transform only provides scale-invariant matching. For scale and position invariance, the Mellin transform is combined with the Fourier transform, to give the *Fourier–Mellin* transform. The Fourier–Mellin transform has many disadvantages in a digital implementation, due to the problems in spatial resolution, though there are approaches to reduce these problems (Altmann, 1984), as well as the difficulties with discrete images experienced in Fourier transform approaches.

Again, the Mellin transform appears to be much better suited to an *optical* implementation (Casasent, 1977), where *continuous* functions are available, rather than to discrete image analysis. A further difficulty with the Mellin transform is that its result is independent of the *form factor* of the template. Accordingly, a rectangle and a square appear to be the same to this transform. This implies a loss of information since the form factor can indicate that an object has been imaged from an oblique angle.

So there are innate difficulties with template matching whether it is implemented directly, or by transform calculus. For these reasons, and because many shape extraction techniques require more than just edge or brightness data, direct digital implementations of feature extraction are usually preferred. This is perhaps also influenced by the speed advantage that one popular technique can confer over template matching. This is the Hough transform, which is covered next.

5.4 Hough transform (HT)

5.4.1 Overview

The *Hough Transform* (HT) (Hough, 1962) is a technique that locates shapes in images. In particular, it has been used to extract *lines, circles* and *ellipses* (or conic sections). In the case of lines, its mathematical definition is equivalent to the Radon transform (Deans, 1981). The HT was introduced by Hough (Hough, 1962) and then used to find bubble tracks rather than shapes in images. However, Rosenfeld noted its potential advantages as an image processing algorithm (Rosenfeld, 1969). The HT was thus implemented to find lines in images (Duda, 1972) and it has been extended greatly, since it has many advantages and many potential routes for improvement. Its prime advantage is that it can deliver the *same* result as that for template matching, but *faster* (Princen, 1992), (Sklansky, 1978) (Stockman, 1977). This is achieved by a reformulation of the template matching process, based on an *evidence gathering* approach where the evidence is the *votes* cast in an accumulator array. The HT implementation defines a *mapping* from the image points into an accumulator space (Hough space). The mapping is achieved in a computationally efficient manner, based on the function that describes the target shape. This mapping requires much less computational resources than template matching. However, it still requires significant storage and high computational requirements. These problems are addressed later, since they give focus for the continuing development of the HT. However, the fact that the HT is equivalent to template matching has given sufficient impetus for the technique to be amongst the most popular of all existing shape extraction techniques.

5.4.2 Lines

We will first consider finding lines in an image. In a Cartesian parameterisation, collinear points in an image with co-ordinates (x, y) are related by their slope m and an intercept c according to:

$$y = mx + c \tag{5.24}$$

This equation can be written in homogeneous form as

$$Ay + Bx + 1 = 0 \tag{5.25}$$

where $A = -1/c$ and $B = m/c$. Thus, a line is defined by giving a pair of values (A, B). However, we can observe a symmetry in the definition in Equation 5.25. This equation is symmetric since a pair of co-ordinates (x, y) also defines a line in the space with parameters (A, B). That is, Equation 5.25 can be seen as the equation of a line for fixed co-ordinates (x, y) or as the equation of a line for fixed parameters (A, B). Thus, pairs can be used to define points and lines simultaneously (Aguado, 2000a). The HT gathers evidence of the point (A, B) by considering that all the points (x, y) define the same line in the space (A, B). That is, if the set of collinear points $\{(x_i, y_i)\}$ defines the line (A, B), then

$$Ay_i + Bx_i + 1 = 0 \tag{5.26}$$

This equation can be seen as a system of equations and it can simply be rewritten in terms of the Cartesian parameterisation as

$$c = - x_i m + y_i \tag{5.27}$$

Thus, to determine the line we must find the values of the parameters (m, c) (or (A, B) in homogeneous form) that satisfy Equation 5.27 (or 5.26, respectively). However, we must notice that the system is generally overdetermined. That is, we have more equations that unknowns. Thus, we must find the solution that comes close to satisfying all the equations simultaneously. This kind of problem can be solved, for example, using linear least squares techniques. The HT uses an *evidence gathering* approach to provide the solution.

The relationship between a point (x_i, y_i) in an image and the line given in Equation 5.27 is illustrated in Figure **5.6**. The points (x_i, y_i) and (x_j, y_j) in Figure **5.5**(a) define the lines U_i and U_j in Figure **5.6**(b), respectively. All the collinear elements in an image will define dual lines with the same concurrent point (A, B). This is independent of the line parameterisation used. The HT solves it in an efficient way by simply counting the potential solutions in an accumulator array that stores the evidence, or votes. The count is made by tracing all the dual lines for each point (x_i, y_i). Each point in the trace increments an element in the array, thus the problem of line extraction is transformed in the problem of locating a maximum in the accumulator space. This strategy is robust and has demonstrated to be able to handle noise and occlusion.

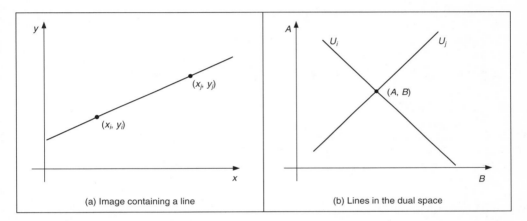

Figure 5.6 Illustrating the Hough transform for lines

The axes in the dual space represent the parameters of the line. In the case of the Cartesian parameterisation m can actually take an *infinite* range of values, since lines can vary from horizontal to vertical. Since votes are gathered in a discrete array, then this will produce *bias* errors. It is possible to consider a range of votes in the accumulator space that cover all possible values. This corresponds to techniques of antialiasing and can improve the gathering strategy (Brown, 1983), (Kiryati, 1991).

The implementation of the HT for lines, `HTLine`, is given in Code **5.3**. It is important to observe that Equation 5.27 is not suitable for implementation since the parameters can take an infinite range of values. In order to handle the infinite range for c, we use two arrays in the implementation in Code **5.3**. When the slope m is between $-45°$ and $45°$, then c does not take a large value. For other values of m the intercept c can take a very large value. Thus, we consider an accumulator for each case. In the second case, we use an array that stores the intercept with the x axis. This only solves the problem partially since we cannot guarantee that the value of c will be small when the slope m is between $-45°$ and $45°$.

Figure **5.7** shows three examples of locating lines using the HT implemented in Code **5.3**. In Figure **5.7**(a) there is a single line which generates the peak seen in Figure **5.7**(b).

```
%Hough Transform for Lines

function HTLine(inputimage)

%image size
[rows,columns]=size(inputimage);

%accumulator
acc1=zeros(rows,91);
acc2=zeros(columns,91);

%image
for x=1:columns
  for y=1:rows
     if(inputimage(y,x)==0
       for m=-45:45
          b=round(y-tan((m*pi)/180)*x);
          if(b<rows & b>0)
             acc1(b,m+45+1)=acc1(b,m+45+1)+1;
          end
       end
       for m=45:135
          b=round(x-y/tan((m*pi)/180));
          if(b<columns & b>0)
             acc2(b,m-45+1)=acc2(b,m-45+1)+1;
          end
       end
     end
  end
end
```

Code 5.3   Implementing the Hough transform for lines

The magnitude of the peak is proportional to the number of pixels in the line from which it was generated. The edges of the wrench in Figures **5.7**(b) and **5.7**(c) define two main lines. Image **5.7**(c) contains much more noise. This image was obtained by using a lower threshold value in the edge detector operator which gave rise to more noise. The accumulator results of the HT for the images in Figures **5.7**(b) and **5.7**(c) are shown in Figures **5.7**(e) and **5.7**(f), respectively. We can observe the two accumulator arrays are broadly similar in shape, and that the peak in each is at the same place. The co-ordinates of the peaks are at combinations of parameters of the lines that best fit the image. The extra number of edge points in the noisy image of the wrench gives rise to more votes in the accumulator space, as can be seen by the increased number of votes in Figure **5.7**(f) compared with Figure **5.7**(e). Since the peak is in the same place, this shows that the HT can indeed tolerate noise. The results of extraction, when superimposed on the edge image, are shown in Figures **5.7**(g) to (i). Only the two lines corresponding to significant peaks have been drawn for the image of the wrench. Here, we can see that the parameters describing the lines have been extracted well. Note that the end points of the lines are not delivered by the HT, only the parameters that describe them. You have to go back to the image to obtain line length.

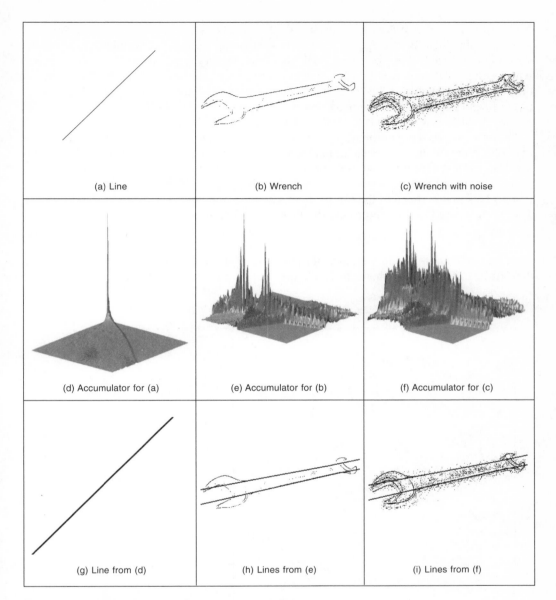

Figure 5.7 Applying the Hough transform for lines

We can see that the HT delivers a correct response, correct estimates of the parameters used to specify the line, so long as the number of collinear points along that line exceeds the number of collinear points on any other line in the image. However, the non-linearity of the parameters and the discretisation produce noisy accumulators. A major problem in implementing the basic HT for lines is the definition of an appropriate accumulator space. In application, Bresenham's line drawing algorithm (Bresenham, 1965) can be used to draw the lines of votes in the accumulator space. This ensures that lines of connected votes are drawn as opposed to use of Equation 5.27 that can lead to gaps in the drawn line. Also, *backmapping* (Gerig, 1986) can be used to determine exactly which edge points contributed to a particular peak. Backmapping is an *inverse* mapping from the accumulator space to the edge data and can allow for shape analysis of the image by removal of the edge points which contributed to particular peaks, and then by re-accumulation using the HT. Note that the computational cost of the HT depends on the number of edge points (n_e) and the length of the lines formed in the parameter space (l), giving a computational cost of $O(n_e l)$. This is considerably less than that for template matching, given earlier as $O(n^2 m^2)$.

One way to avoid the problems of the Cartesian parameterisation in the HT is to base the mapping function on an alternative parameterisation. One of the most proven techniques is called the foot-of-normal parameterisation. This parameterises a line by considering a point (x, y) as a function of an angle normal to the line, passing through the origin of the image. This gives a form of the HT for lines known as the *polar HT for lines* (Duda, 1972). The point where this line intersects the line in the image is given by

$$\rho = x \cos(\theta) + y \sin(\theta) \tag{5.28}$$

where θ is the angle of the line normal to the line in an image and ρ is the length between the origin and the point where the lines intersect, as illustrated in Figure **5.8**.

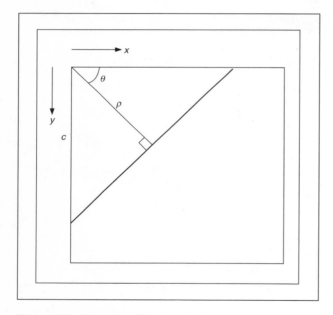

Figure 5.8   Polar consideration of a line

By recalling that two lines are perpendicular if the product of their slopes is −1, and by considering the geometry of the arrangement in Figure **5.8**, we obtain

$$c = \frac{\rho}{\sin(\theta)} \quad m = -\frac{1}{\tan(\theta)} \tag{5.29}$$

By substitution in Equation 5.24 we obtain the polar form, Equation 5.28. This provides a different mapping function: votes are now cast in a sinusoidal manner, in a 2D accumulator array in terms of θ and ρ, the parameters of interest. The advantage of this alternative mapping is that the values of the parameters θ and ρ are now bounded to lie within a specific range. The range for ρ is within 180°; the possible values of ρ are given by the image size, since the maximum length of the line is $\sqrt{2} \times N$, where N is the (square) image size. The range of possible values is now fixed, so the technique is practicable.

The implementation of the *polar HT for lines* is the function HTPLine in Code **5.4.** The accumulator array is a set of 180 bins for value of θ in the range 0 to 180°, and for values of ρ in the range 0 to $\sqrt{N^2 + M^2}$, where $N \times M$ is the picture size. Then, for image (edge) points greater than a chosen threshold, the angle relating to the bin size is evaluated (as radians in the range 0 to π) and then the value of ρ is evaluated from Equation 5.28 and the appropriate accumulator cell is incremented so long as the parameters are within range. The accumulator arrays obtained by applying this implementation to the images in Figure **5.8** is shown in Figure **5.9.** Figure **5.9**(a) shows that a single line defines a well-delineated peak. Figures **5.9**(b) and **5.9**(c) show a clearer peak compared to the implementation of the Cartesian parameterisation. This is because discretisation effects are reduced in the polar parameterisation. This feature makes the polar implementation far more practicable than the earlier, Cartesian, version.

```
%Polar Hough Transform for Lines

function HTPLine(inputimage)

%image size
[rows,columns]=size(inputimage);

%accumulator
rmax=round(sqrt(rows^2+columns^2));
acc=zeros(rmax,180);

%image
for x=1:columns
   for y=1:rows
      if(inputimage(y,x)==0)
         for m=1:180
            r=round(x*cos((m*pi)/180)+y*sin(m*pi)/180));
            if(r<rmax & r>0)  acc(r,m)=acc(r,m)+1;  end
         end
      end
   end
end
```

Code **5.4**   Implementation of the polar Hough transform for lines

5.4.3   HT for circles

The HT can be extended by replacing the equation of the curve in the detection process. The equation of the curve can be given in *explicit* or *parametric* form. In explicit form, the HT can be defined by considering the equation for a circle given by

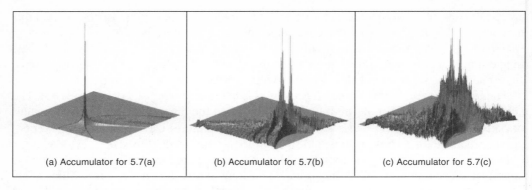

| (a) Accumulator for 5.7(a) | (b) Accumulator for 5.7(b) | (c) Accumulator for 5.7(c) |

Figure 5.9 Applying the polar Hough transform for lines

$$(x - x_0)^2 + (y - y_0)^2 = r^2 \qquad (5.30)$$

This equation defines a locus of points (x, y) centred on an origin (x_0, y_0) and with radius r. This equation can again be visualised in two dual ways: as a locus of points (x, y) in an image, or as a locus of points (x_0, y_0) centred on (x, y) with radius r.

Figure **5.10** illustrates this dual definition. Each edge point defines a set of circles in the accumulator space. These circles are defined by all possible values of the radius and they are centred on the co-ordinates of the edge point. Figure **5.10**(b) shows three circles defined by three edge points. These circles are defined for a given radius value. Actually, each edge point defines circles for the other values of the radius. This implies that the accumulator space is three dimensional (for the three parameters of interest) and that edge points map to a *cone* of votes in the accumulator space. Figure **5.10**(c) illustrates this accumulator. After gathering evidence of all the edge points, the maximum in the accumulator space again corresponds to the parameters of the circle in the original image. The procedure of evidence gathering is the same as that for the HT for lines, but votes are generated in cones, according to Equation 5.30.

Equation 5.30 can be defined in *parametric* form as

$$x = x_0 + r \cos(\theta) \quad y = y_0 + r \sin(\theta) \qquad (5.31)$$

The advantage of this representation is that it allows us to solve for the parameters. Thus, the HT mapping is defined by

$$x_0 = x - r \cos(\theta) \quad y_0 = - r \sin(\theta) \qquad (5.32)$$

These equations define the points in the accumulator space (Figure **5.10**(b)) dependent on the radius r. Note that θ is not a free parameter, but defines the trace of the curve. The trace of the curve (or surface) is commonly referred to as the *point spread function*.

The implementation of the HT for circles, `HTCircle`, is shown in Code **5.5**. This is similar to the HT for lines, except that the voting function corresponds to that in Equation 5.32 and the accumulator space is for circle data. The accumulator in the implementation is actually 2D, in terms of the centre parameters for a fixed value of the radius given as an argument to the function. This function should be called for all potential radii. A circle of votes is generated by varying `ang` (i.e. θ, but Matlab does not allow Greek symbols!) from 0° to 360°. The discretisation of `ang` controls the granularity of voting, too small an increment gives very fine coverage of the parameter space, too large a value results in very

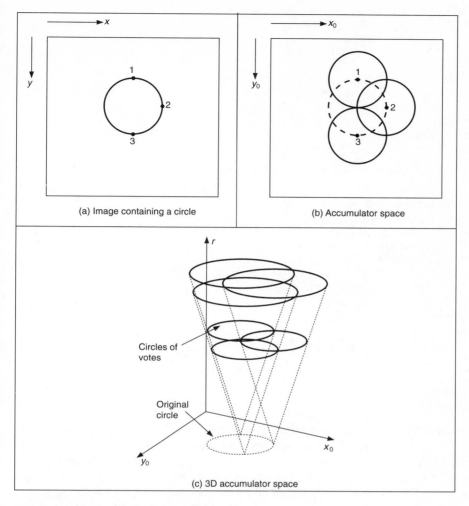

Figure 5.10 Illustrating the Hough transform for circles

sparse coverage. The accumulator space, `acc` (initially zero), is incremented only for points whose co-ordinates lie within the specified range (in this case the centre cannot lie outside the original image).

The application of the HT for circles is illustrated in Figure **5.11**. Figure **5.11**(a) shows an image with a synthetic circle. In this figure, the edges are complete and well defined. The result of the HT process is shown in Figure **5.11**(d). The peak of the accumulator space is at the centre of the circle. Note that votes exist away from the circle's centre, and rise towards the locus of the actual circle, though these background votes are much less than the actual peak. Figure **5.11**(b) shows an example of data containing occlusion and noise. The image in Figure **5.11**(c) corresponds to the same scene, but the noise level has been increased by changing the threshold value in the edge detection process. The accumulators for these two images are shown in Figures **5.11**(e) and **5.11**(f) and the circles related to the parameter space peaks are superimposed (in black) on the edge images in Figures **5.11**(g)

```
%Hough Transform for Circles

function HTCircle(inputimage,r)

%image size
[rows,columns]=size(inputimage);

%accumulator
acc=zeros(rows,columns);

%image
for x=1:columns
   for y=1:rows
      if(inputimage(y,x)==0)
         for ang=0:360
            t=(ang*pi)/180;
            x0=round(x-r*cos(t));
            y0=round(y-r*sin(t));
            if(x0<columns & x0>0 & y0<rows & y0>0)
               acc(y0,x0)=acc(y0,x0)+1;
            end
         end
      end
   end
end
```

Code 5.5   Implementation of the Hough transform for circles

to (i). We can see that the HT has the ability to tolerate occlusion and noise. Note that we do not have the earlier problem with the start and the end of the lines since the circle is a *closed* shape. In Figure **5.11**(c), there are many edge points which implies that the amount of processing time increases. The HT will detect the circle (provide the right result) as long as more points are in a circular locus described by the parameters of the target circle than there are on any other circle. This is exactly the same performance as for the HT for lines, as expected, and is consistent with the result of template matching.

In application code, *Bresenham's algorithm* for discrete circles (Bresenham, 1977) can be used to draw the circle of votes, rather than use the polar implementation of Equation 5.32. This ensures that the complete locus of points is drawn and avoids the need to choose a value for increase in the angle used to trace the circle. Bresenham's algorithm can be used to generate the points in one octant, since the remaining points can be obtained by reflection. Again, backmapping can be used to determine which points contributed to the extracted circle.

An additional example of the circle HT extraction is shown in Figure **5.12**. Figure **5.12**(a) is again a real image (albeit, one with low resolution) which was processed by Sobel edge detection and thresholded to give the points in Figure **5.12**(b). The circle detected by application of HTCircle with radius 5 pixels is shown in Figure **5.12**(c) superimposed on the edge data. The extracted circle can be seen to *match* the edge data well. This highlights the two major advantages of the HT (and of template matching): its ability to handle *noise* and *occlusion*. Note that the HT merely finds the circle with the

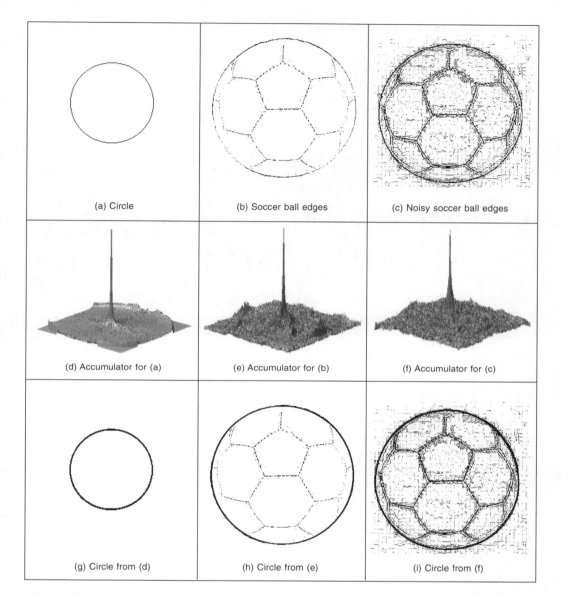

(a) Circle

(b) Soccer ball edges

(c) Noisy soccer ball edges

(d) Accumulator for (a)

(e) Accumulator for (b)

(f) Accumulator for (c)

(g) Circle from (d)

(h) Circle from (e)

(i) Circle from (f)

Figure 5.11   Applying the Hough transform for circles

maximum number of points; it is possible to include other constraints to control the circle selection process, such as gradient direction for objects with known illumination profile. In the case of the human eye, the (circular) iris is usually darker than its white surroundings.

Figure **5.12** also shows some of the difficulties with the HT, namely that it is essentially an implementation of template matching, and does not use some of the *richer* stock of information available in an image. For example, we might know constraints on *size*; the largest size and iris would be in an image like Figure **5.12**. Also, we know some of the *topology*: the eye region contains two ellipsoidal structures with a circle in the middle.

Also, we might know *brightness* information: the pupil is darker than the surrounding iris. These factors can be formulated as *constraints* on whether edge points can vote within the accumulator array. A simple modification is to make the votes proportional to edge magnitude, in this manner, points with high contrast will generate more votes and hence have more significance in the voting process. In this way, the feature extracted by the HT can be arranged to suit a particular application.

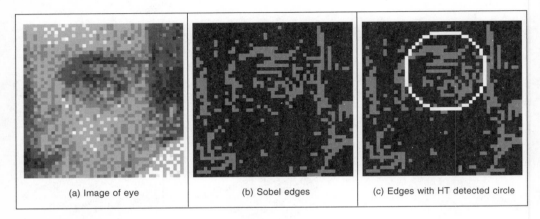

| (a) Image of eye | (b) Sobel edges | (c) Edges with HT detected circle |

Figure 5.12 Using the HT for circles

5.4.4 HT for ellipses

Circles are very important in shape detection since many objects have a circular shape. However, because of the camera's viewpoint, circles do not always look like circles in images. Images are formed by mapping a shape in 3D space into a plane (the image plane). This mapping performs a perspective transformation. In this process, a circle is deformed to look like an ellipse. We can define the mapping between the circle and an ellipse by a similarity transformation. That is,

$$\begin{bmatrix} x \\ y \end{bmatrix} = \begin{bmatrix} \cos(\rho) & \sin(\rho) \\ -\sin(\rho) & \cos(\rho) \end{bmatrix} \begin{bmatrix} S_x \\ S_y \end{bmatrix} \begin{bmatrix} x' \\ y' \end{bmatrix} + \begin{bmatrix} t_x \\ t_y \end{bmatrix} \tag{5.33}$$

where (x', y') define the co-ordinates of the circle in Equation 5.31, ρ represents the orientation, (S_x, S_y) a scale factor and (t_x, t_y) a translation. If we define

$$\begin{aligned} a_0 &= t_x \quad a_x = S_x \cos(\rho) \quad b_x = S_y \sin(\rho) \\ b_0 &= t_y \quad a_y = - S_x \sin(\rho) \quad b_y = S_y \cos(\rho) \end{aligned} \tag{5.34}$$

then we have that the circle is deformed into

$$\begin{aligned} x &= a_0 + a_x \cos(\theta) + b_x \sin(\theta) \\ y &= b_0 + a_y \cos(\theta) + b_y \sin(\theta) \end{aligned} \tag{5.35}$$

This equation corresponds to the polar representation of an ellipse. This polar form contains six parameters $(a_0, b_0, a_x, b_x, a_y, b_y)$ that characterise the shape of the ellipse. θ is not a free parameter and it only addresses a particular point in the locus of the ellipse (just as it was used to trace the circle in Equation 5.32). However, one parameter is redundant since it can be computed by considering the orthogonality (independence) of the axes of the ellipse (the product $a_x b_x + a_y b_y = 0$ which is one of the known properties of an ellipse). Thus, an ellipse is defined by its centre (a_0, b_0) and three of the axis parameters (a_x, b_x, a_y, b_y). This gives five parameters which is intuitively correct since an ellipse is defined by its centre (two parameters), it size along both axes (two more parameters) and its rotation (one parameter). In total this states that five parameters describe an ellipse, so our three axis parameters must jointly describe size and rotation. In fact, the axis parameters can be related to the orientation and the length along the axes by

$$\tan(\rho) = \frac{a_y}{a_x} \quad a = \sqrt{a_x^2 + a_y^2} \quad b = \sqrt{b_x^2 + b_y^2} \tag{5.36}$$

where (a, b) are the axes of the ellipse, as illustrated in Figure **5.13**.

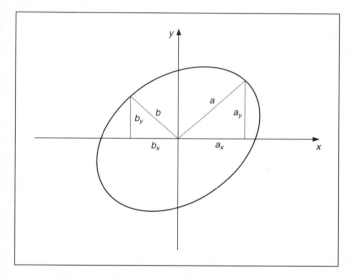

Figure 5.13 Definition of ellipse axes

In a similar way to Equation 5.31, Equation 5.35 can be used to generate the mapping function in the HT. In this case, the location of the centre of the ellipse is given by

$$a_0 = x - a_x \cos(\theta) + b_x \sin(\theta)$$
$$b_0 = y - a_y \cos(\theta) + b_y \sin(\theta) \tag{5.37}$$

The location is dependent on three parameters, thus the mapping defines the trace of a hypersurface in a 5D space. This space can be very large. For example, if there are 100 possible values for each of the five parameters, then the 5D accumulator space contains 10^{10} values. This is 10 GB of storage, which is of course tiny nowadays (at least, when someone else pays!). Accordingly there has been much interest in ellipse detection techniques which use much less space and operate much faster than direct implementation of Equation 5.37.

Code **5.6** shows the implementation of the HT mapping for ellipses. The function HTEllipse computes the centre parameters for an ellipse without rotation and with fixed axis length given as arguments. Thus, the implementation uses a 2D accumulator. In practice, in order to locate an ellipse it is necessary to try all potential values of axis length. This is computationally impossible unless we limit the computation to a few values.

```
%Hough Transform for Ellipses

function HTEllipse(inputimage,a,b)

%image size
[rows,columns]=size(inputimage);

%accumulator
acc=zeros(rows,columns);

%image
for x=1:columns
   for y=1:rows
      if(inputimage(y,x)==0)
         for ang=0:360
            t=(ang*pi)/180;
            x0=round(x-a*cos(t));
            y0=round(y-b*sin(t));
            if(x0<columns & x0>0 & y0<rows & y0>0)
               acc(y0,x0)=acc(y0,x0)+1;
            end
         end
      end
   end
end
```

Code 5.6   Implementation of the Hough transform for ellipses

Figure **5.14** shows three examples of the application of the ellipse extraction process described in Code **5.6**. The first example (Figure **5.14**(a)) illustrates the case of a perfect ellipse in a synthetic image. The array in Figure **5.14**(d) shows a prominent peak whose position corresponds to the centre of the ellipse. The examples in Figures **5.14**(b) and **5.14**(c) illustrate the use of the HT to locate a circular form when the image has an oblique view. Each example was obtained by using a different threshold in the edge detection process. Figure **5.14**(c) contains more noise data that in turn gives rise to more noise in the accumulator. We can observe that there is more than one ellipse to be located in these two figures. This gives rise to the other high values in the accumulator space. As with the earlier examples for line and circle extraction, there is again scope for interpreting the accumulator space, to discover which structures produced particular parameter combinations.

5.4.5 Parameter space decomposition

The HT gives the same (optimal) result as template matching and even though it is faster,

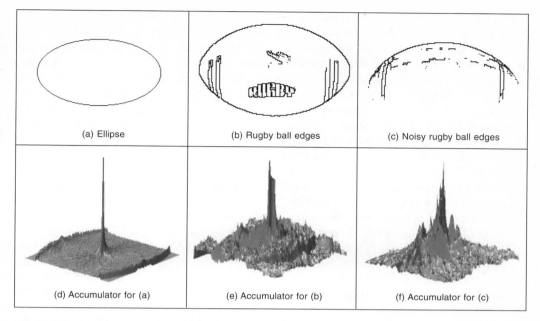

(a) Ellipse	(b) Rugby ball edges	(c) Noisy rugby ball edges
(d) Accumulator for (a)	(e) Accumulator for (b)	(f) Accumulator for (c)

Figure 5.14 Applying the Hough transform for ellipses

it still requires significant computational resources. In the previous sections, we saw that as we increase the complexity of the curve under detection, the computational requirements increase in an exponential way. Thus, the HT becomes less practical. For this reason, most of the research in the HT has focused on the development of techniques aimed to reduce its computational complexity (Illingworth, 1988), (Leavers, 1993). One important way to reduce the computation has been the use of geometric properties of shapes to decompose the parameter space. Several techniques have used different geometric properties. These geometric properties are generally defined by the relationship between points and derivatives.

5.4.5.1 Parameter space reduction for lines

For a line, the accumulator space can be reduced from 2D to 1D by considering that we can compute the slope from the information of the image. The slope can be computed either by using the *gradient direction* at a point or by considering a pair of points. That is

$$ m = \varphi \quad \text{or} \quad m = \frac{y_2 - y_1}{x_2 - x_1} \tag{5.38} $$

where φ is the gradient direction at the point. In the case of take two points, by considering Equation 5.24 we have that,

$$ c = \frac{x_2 y_1 - x_1 y_2}{x_2 - x_1} \tag{5.39} $$

Thus, according to Equation 5.29 we have that one of the parameters of the polar representation for lines, θ, is now given by

$$ \theta = -\tan^{-1}\left[\frac{1}{\varphi}\right] \quad \text{or} \quad \theta = \tan^{-1}\left[\frac{x_1 - x_2}{y_2 - y_1}\right] \tag{5.40} $$

These equations do not depend on the other parameter ρ and they provide alternative mappings to gather evidence. That is, they decompose the parametric space, such that the two parameters θ and ρ are now *independent*. The use of edge direction information constitutes the base of the line extraction method presented by O'Gorman and Clowes (O'Gorman, 1976). The use of pairs of points can be related to the definition of the randomised Hough transform (Xu, 1990). Obviously, the number of feature points considered corresponds to all the combinations of points that form pairs. By using statistical techniques, it is possible to reduce the space of points in order to consider a representative sample of the elements. That is, a subset which provides enough information to obtain the parameters with predefined and small estimation errors.

Code **5.7** shows the implementation of the parameter space decomposition for the HT for lines. The slope of the line is computed by considering a pair of points. Pairs of points are restricted to a neighbourhood of 5 by 5 pixels. The implementation of Equation 5.40 gives values between $-90°$ and $90°$. Since our accumulators only can store positive values, then we add $90°$ to all values. In order to compute ρ we use Equation 5.28 given the value of θ computed by Equation 5.40.

Figure **5.15** shows the accumulators for the two parameters θ and ρ as obtained by the implementation of Code **5.7** for the images in Figure **5.7**(a) and Figure **5.7**(b). The accumulators are now one dimensional as in Figure **5.15**(a) and show a clear peak. The peak in the first accumulator is close to $135°$. Thus, by subtracting the $90°$ introduced to make all values positive, we find that the slope of the line $\theta = -45°$. The peaks in the accumulators in Figure **5.15**(b) define two lines with similar slopes. The peak in the first accumulator represents the value of θ, whilst the two peaks in the second accumulator represent the location of the two lines. In general, when implementing parameter space decomposition it is necessary to follow a two step process. First, it is necessary to gather data in one accumulator and search for the maximum. Second, the location of the maximum value is used as a parameter value to gather data of the remaining accumulator.

5.4.5.2 *Parameter space reduction for circles*

In the case of lines the relationship between local information computed from an image and the inclusion of a group of points (pairs) is in an alternative analytical description which will be readily established. For more complex primitives, it is possible to include several geometric relationships. These relationships are not defined for an arbitrary set of points but include angular constraints that define relative positions between them. In general, we can consider different geometric properties of the circle to decompose the parameter space. This has motivated the development of many methods of parameter space decomposition (Aguado, 1996b). An important geometric relationship is given by the geometry of the second directional derivatives. This relationship can be obtained by considering that Equation 5.31 defines a position vector function. That is,

$$\omega(\theta) = x(\theta)\begin{bmatrix} 1 \\ 0 \end{bmatrix} + y(\theta)\begin{bmatrix} 0 \\ 1 \end{bmatrix} \tag{5.41}$$

where

$$x(\theta) = x_0 + r\cos(\theta) \quad y(\theta) = y_0 + r\sin(\theta) \tag{5.42}$$

In this definition, we have included the parameter of the curve as an argument in order to highlight the fact that the function defines a vector for each value of θ. The end-points of

```
%Parameter Decomposition for the Hough Transform for Lines

function HTDLine(inputimage)

%image size
[rows,columns]=size(inputimage);

%accumulator
rmax=round(sqrt(rows^2+columns^2));
accro=zeros(rmax,1);
acct=zeros(180,1);

%image
for x=1:columns
  for y=1:rows
    if(inputimage(y,x)==0)
      for Nx=x-2:x+2
        for Ny=y-2:y+2
          if(x~=Nx|y~=Ny)
            if(Nx>0 & Ny>0 &Nx<columns &Ny<rows)
              if(inputimage(Ny,Nx)==0)
                if (Ny-y~=0)
                  t=atan((x-Nx)/(Ny-y)); %Equation (5.40)
                else t=pi/2;
              end
              r=round(x*cos(t)+y*sin(t)); %Equation (5.28)

              t=round((t+pi/2)*180/pi);
              acct(t)=acct(t)+1;

              if(r<rmax & r>0)
                accro(r)=accro(r)+1;
              end
            end
          end
        end
      end
    end
  end
end
```

Code 5.7 Implementation of the parameter space reduction for the Hough transform for lines

all the vectors trace a circle. The derivatives of Equation 5.41 with respect to θ define the first and second directional derivatives. That is,

$$v'(\theta) = x'(\theta) \begin{bmatrix} 1 \\ 0 \end{bmatrix} + y'(\theta) \begin{bmatrix} 0 \\ 1 \end{bmatrix} \tag{5.43a}$$

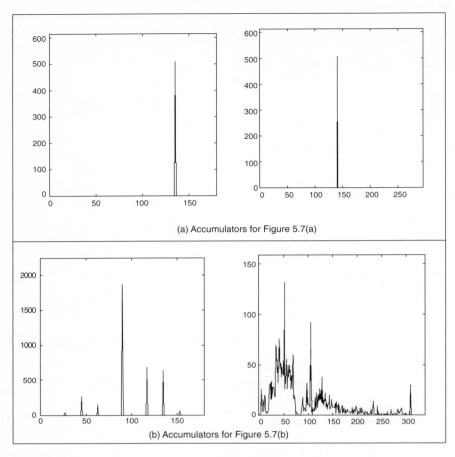

(a) Accumulators for Figure 5.7(a)

(b) Accumulators for Figure 5.7(b)

Figure 5.15 Parameter space reduction for the Hough transform for lines

$$\upsilon''(\theta) = x''(\theta) \begin{bmatrix} 1 \\ 0 \end{bmatrix} + y''(\theta) \begin{bmatrix} 0 \\ 1 \end{bmatrix} \qquad (5.43b)$$

where

$$x'(\theta) = -r \sin(\theta) \qquad y'(\theta) = r \cos(\theta)$$
$$\qquad\qquad\qquad\qquad\qquad\qquad\qquad\qquad\qquad\qquad (5.44)$$
$$x''(\theta) = -r \cos(\theta) \qquad y''(\theta) = -r \sin(\theta)$$

Figure **5.16** illustrates the definition of the first and second directional derivatives. The first derivative defines a tangential vector while the second one is similar to the vector function, but it has reverse direction. In fact, that the edge direction measured for circles can be arranged so as to point towards the centre was actually the basis of one of the early approaches to reducing the computational load of the HT for circles (Kimme, 1975).

According to Equation 5.42 and Equation 5.44, we observe that the tangent of the angle of the first directional derivative denoted as $\phi'(\theta)$ is given by

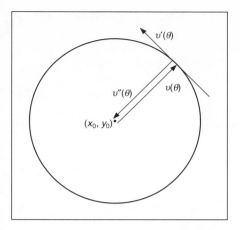

Figure 5.16 Definition of the first and second directional derivatives for a circle

$$\phi'(\theta) = \frac{y'(\theta)}{x'(\theta)} = -\frac{1}{\tan(\theta)} \qquad (5.45)$$

Angles will be denoted by using the symbol ^. That is,

$$\hat{\phi}'(\theta) = \tan^{-1}(\phi'(\theta)) \qquad (5.46)$$

Similarly, for the tangent of the second directional derivative we have that,

$$\phi''(\theta) = \frac{y''(\theta)}{x''(\theta)} = \tan(\theta) \quad \text{and} \quad \hat{\phi}''(\theta) = \tan^{-1}(\phi''(\theta)) \qquad (5.47)$$

By observing the definition of $\phi''(\theta)$, we have that

$$\phi''(\theta) = \frac{y''(\theta)}{x''(\theta)} = \frac{y(\theta) - y_0}{x(\theta) - x_0} \qquad (5.48)$$

This equation defines a straight line passing through the points $(x(\theta), y(\theta))$ and (x_0, y_0) and it is perhaps the most important relation in parameter space decomposition. The definition of the line is more evident by rearranging terms. That is,

$$y(\theta) = \phi''(\theta)(x(\theta) - x_0) + y_0 \qquad (5.49)$$

This equation is independent of the radius parameter. Thus, it can be used to gather evidence of the location of the shape in a 2D accumulator. The HT mapping is defined by the dual form given by

$$y_0 = \phi''(\theta)(x_0 - x(\theta)) + y(\theta) \qquad (5.50)$$

That is, given an image point $(x(\theta), y(\theta))$ and the value of $\phi''(\theta)$ we can generate a line of votes in the 2D accumulator (x_0, y_0). Once the centre of the circle is known, then a 1D accumulator can be used to locate the radius. The key aspect of the parameter space decomposition is the method used to obtain the value of $\phi''(\theta)$ from image data. We will consider two alternative ways. First, we will show that $\phi''(\theta)$ can be obtained by edge direction information. Second, how it can be obtained from the information of a pair of points.

In order to obtain $\phi''(\theta)$, we can use the definitions in Equation 5.46 and Equation 5.47. According to these equations, the tangents $\phi''(\theta)$ and $\phi'(\theta)$ are perpendicular. Thus,

$$\phi''(\theta) = -\frac{1}{\phi'(\theta)} \tag{5.51}$$

Thus, the HT mapping in Equation 5.50 can be written in terms of gradient direction $\phi'(\theta)$ as

$$y_0 = y(\theta) + \frac{x(\theta) - x_0}{\phi'(\theta)} \tag{5.52}$$

This equation has a simple geometric interpretation illustrated in Figure **5.17**(a). We can see that the line of votes passes through the points $(x(\theta), y(\theta))$ and (x_0, y_0). The slope of the line is perpendicular to the direction of gradient direction.

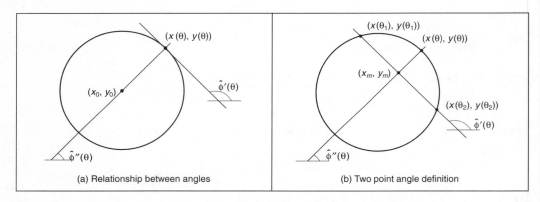

(a) Relationship between angles (b) Two point angle definition

Figure 5.17 Geometry of the angle of the first and second directional derivatives

An alternative decomposition can be obtained by considering the geometry shown in Figure **5.17**(b). In the figure we can see that if we take a pair of points (x_1, y_1) and (x_2, y_2), where $x_i = x(\theta_i)$ then the line that passes through the points has the same slope as the line at a point $(x(\theta), y(\theta))$. Accordingly,

$$\phi'(\theta) = \frac{y_2 - y_1}{x_2 - x_1} \tag{5.53}$$

where $\theta = \frac{1}{2}(\theta_1 + \theta_2)$ \hfill (5.54)

Based on Equation 5.53 we have that

$$\phi''(\theta) = -\frac{x_2 - x_1}{y_2 - y_1} \tag{5.55}$$

The problem with using a pair of points is that by Equation 5.53 we cannot determine the location of the point $(x(\theta), y(\theta))$. Fortunately, the voting line also passes through the midpoint of the line between the two selected points. Let us define this point as

$$x_m = \tfrac{1}{2}(x_1 + x_2) \quad y_m = \tfrac{1}{2}(y_1 + y_2) \tag{5.56}$$

Thus, by substitution of Equation 5.53 in 5.52 and by replacing the point $(x(\theta), y(\theta))$ by (x_m, y_m), we have that the HT mapping can be expressed as

$$y_0 = y_m + \frac{(x_m - x_0)(x_2 - x_1)}{(y_2 - y_1)} \tag{5.57}$$

This equation does not use gradient direction information, but is based on pairs of points. This is analogous to the parameter space decomposition of the line presented in Equation 5.40. In that case, the slope can be computed by using gradient direction or, alternatively, by taking a pair of points. In the case of the circle, the tangent (and therefore the angle of the second directional derivative) can be computed by the gradient direction (i.e. Equation 5.51) or by a pair of points (i.e. Equation 5.55). However, it is important to notice that there are some other combinations of parameter space decomposition (Aguado, 1996a).

Code **5.8** shows the implementation of the parameter space decomposition for the HT for circles. The implementation only detects the position of the circle and it gathers evidence by using the mapping in Equation 5.57. Pairs of points are restricted to a neighbourhood between 10×10 pixels and 12×12 pixels. We avoid using pixels that are close to each other since they do not produce accurate votes. We also avoid using pixels that are far away from each other, since by distance it is probable that they do not belong to the same circle and would only increase the noise in the accumulator. In order to trace the line, we use two equations that are selected according to the slope.

Figure **5.18** shows the accumulators obtained by the implementation of Code **5.8** for the images in Figure **5.11**(a) and Figure **5.11**(b). Both accumulators show a clear peak that represents the location of the circle. Small peaks in the background of the accumulator in Figure **5.11**(b) corresponds to circles with only a few points. In general, there is a compromise between the *spread* of the peak and the *noise* in the accumulator. The peak can be made narrower by considering pairs of points that are more widely spaced. However, this can also increases the level of background noise. Background noise can be reduced by taking points that are closer together, but this makes the peak wider.

5.4.5.3 *Parameter space reduction for ellipses*

Part of the simplicity in the parameter decomposition for circles comes from the fact that circles are (naturally) isotropic. Ellipses have more free parameters and are geometrically more complex. Thus, geometrical properties involve more complex relationships between points, tangents and angles. However, they maintain the geometric relationship defined by the angle of the second derivative. According to Equation 5.41 and Equation 5.43, the vector position and directional derivatives of an ellipse in Equation (5.35) have the components

$$\begin{aligned} x'(\theta) = -a_x \sin(\theta) + b_x \cos(\theta) & \qquad y'(\theta) = -a_y \sin(\theta) + b_y \cos(\theta) \\ x''(\theta) = -a_x \cos(\theta) - b_x \sin(\theta) & \qquad y''(\theta) = -a_y \cos(\theta) - b_y \sin(\theta) \end{aligned} \tag{5.58}$$

The tangent of angle of the first and second directional derivatives is given by

$$\phi'(\theta) = \frac{y'(\theta)}{x'(\theta)} = \frac{-a_y \cos(\theta) + b_y \sin(\theta)}{-a_x \cos(\theta) + b_x \sin(\theta)}$$

$$\phi''(\theta) = \frac{y''(\theta)}{x''(\theta)} = \frac{-a_y \cos(\theta) - b_y \sin(\theta)}{-a_x \cos(\theta) - b_x \sin(\theta)} \tag{5.59}$$

```
%Parameter Decomposition for the Hough Transform for Circles

function HTDCircle(inputimage)

%image size
[rows,columns]=size(inputimage);

%accumulator
acc=zeros(rows,columns);

%gather evidence
for x1=1:columns
   for y1=1:rows
     if(inputimage(y1,x1)==0)
        for x2=x1-12:x1+12
           for y2=y1-12:y1+12
              if(abs(x2-x1)>10|abs(y2-y1)>10)
                 if(x2>0 & y2>0 & x2<columns & y2<rows)
                    if(inputimage(y2,x2)==0)
                       xm=(x1+x2)/2;    ym=(y1+y2)/2;
                         if(y2-y1~=0)    m=((x2-x1)/(y2-y1));
                          else      m=99999999;
                         end
                      if(m>-1 & m<1)
                         for x0=1:columns
                            y0=round(ym+m*(xm-x0));
                            if(y0>0 & y0<rows)
                               acc(y0,x0)=acc(y0,x0)+1;
                            end
                         end
                      else
                         for y0=1:rows
                            x0=round(xm+(ym-y0)/m);
                            if(x0>0 & x0<columns)
                               acc(y0,x0)=acc(y0,x0)+1;
                            end
                         end
                      end
                    end
                 end
              end
           end
        end
     end
   end
end
```

Code 5.8   Parameter space reduction for the Hough transform for circles

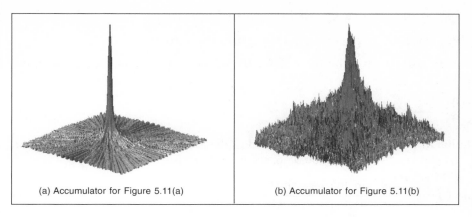

(a) Accumulator for Figure 5.11(a)

(b) Accumulator for Figure 5.11(b)

Figure 5.18 Parameter space reduction for the Hough transform for circles

By considering Equation 5.58 we have that Equation 5.48 is also valid for an ellipse. That is,

$$\frac{y(\theta) - y_0}{x(\theta) - x_0} = \phi''(\theta) \tag{5.60}$$

The geometry of the definition in this equation is illustrated in Figure **5.19**(a). As in the case of circles, this equation defines a line that passes through the points $(x(\theta), y(\theta))$ and (x_0, y_0). However, in the case of the ellipse the angles $\hat{\phi}'(\theta)$ and $\hat{\phi}''(\theta)$ are not orthogonal. This makes the computation of $\phi''(\theta)$ more complex. In order to obtain $\phi''(\theta)$ we can extend the geometry presented in Figure **5.17**(b). That is, we take a pair of points to define a line whose slope defines the value of $\phi'(\theta)$ at another point. This is illustrated in Figure **5.19**(b). The line in Equation 5.60 passes through the middle point (x_m, y_m). However, it is not orthogonal to the tangent line. In order to obtain an expression of the HT mapping, we will first show that the relationship in Equation 5.54 is also valid for ellipses. Then we will use this equation to obtain $\phi''(\theta)$.

The relationships in Figure **5.19**(b) do not depend on the orientation or position of the ellipse. Thus, we have that three points can be defined by

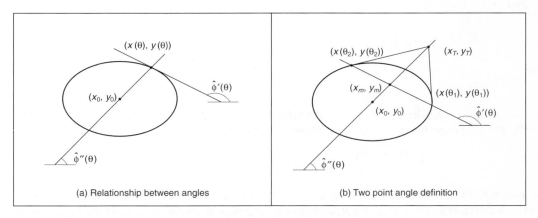

(a) Relationship between angles

(b) Two point angle definition

Figure 5.19 Geometry of the angle of the first and second directional derivative

$$x_1 = a_x \cos(\theta_1) \qquad x_2 = a_x \cos(\theta_2) \qquad x(\theta) = a_x \cos(\theta)$$

$$y_1 = b_x \sin(\theta_1) \qquad y_2 = b_x \sin(\theta_2) \qquad y(\theta) = b_x \sin(\theta) \tag{5.61}$$

The point $(x(\theta), y(\theta))$ is given by the intersection of the line in Equation 5.60 with the ellipse. That is,

$$\frac{y(\theta) - y_0}{x(\theta) - x_0} = \frac{a_x}{b_y} \cdot \frac{y_m}{x_m} \tag{5.62}$$

By substitution of the values of (x_m, y_m) defined as the average of the co-ordinates of the points (x_1, y_1) and (x_2, y_2) in Equation 5.56, we have that

$$\tan(\theta) = \frac{a_x}{b_y} \cdot \frac{b_y \sin(\theta_1) + b_y \sin(\theta_2)}{a_x \cos(\theta_1) + a_x \cos(\theta_2)} \tag{5.63}$$

Thus, $\quad \tan(\theta) = \tan(\tfrac{1}{2}(\theta_1 + \theta_2)) \tag{5.64}$

From this equation it is evident that the relationship in Equation 5.54 is also valid for ellipses. Based on this result, the tangent angle of the second directional derivative can be defined as

$$\phi''(\theta) = \frac{b_y}{a_x} \tan(\theta) \tag{5.65}$$

By substitution in Equation 5.62 we have that

$$\phi''(\theta) = \frac{y_m}{x_m} \tag{5.66}$$

This equation is valid when the ellipse is not translated. If the ellipse is translated then the tangent of the angle can be written in terms of the points (x_m, y_m) and (x_T, y_T) as

$$\phi''(\theta) = \frac{y_T - y_m}{x_T - x_m} \tag{5.67}$$

By considering that the point (x_T, y_T) is the intersection point of the tangent lines at (x_1, y_1) and (x_2, y_2) we obtain

$$\phi''(\theta) = \frac{AC + 2BD}{2A + BC} \tag{5.68}$$

where
$$A = y_1 - y_2 \quad B = x_1 - x_2$$
$$C = \phi_1 + \phi_2 \quad D = \phi_1 \cdot \phi_2 \tag{5.69}$$

and ϕ_1, ϕ_2 are the slope of the tangent to the points. Finally, by considering Equation 5.60, the HT mapping for the centre parameter is defined as

$$y_0 = y_m + \frac{AC + 2BD}{2A + BC}(x_0 - x_m) \tag{5.70}$$

This equation can be used to gather evidence that is independent of rotation or scale. Once the location is known, a 3D parameter space is needed to obtain the remaining parameters. However, these parameters can also be computed independently using two 2D parameter spaces (Aguado, 1996b). Of course you can avoid using the gradient direction in Equation 5.68 by including more points. In fact, the tangent $\phi''(\theta)$ can be computed by taking four points (Aguado, 1996a). However, the inclusion of more points generally leads to more background noise in the accumulator.

Code **5.9** shows the implementation of the ellipse location mapping in Equation 5.57. As in the case of the circle, pairs of points need to be restricted to a neighbourhood. In the implementation, we consider pairs at a fixed distance given by the variable i. Since we are including gradient direction information, the resulting peak is generally quite wide. Again, the selection of the distance between points is a compromise between the level of background noise and the width of the peak.

```
%Parameter Decomposition for Ellipses
function HTDEllipse(inputimage)

%image size
[rows,columns]=size(inputimage);

%edges
[M,Ang]=Edges(inputimage);
M=MaxSupr(M,Ang);

%accumulator
acc=zeros(rows,columns);

%gather evidence
for x1=1:columns
   for y1=1:1:rows
     if(M(y1,x1)~=0)
        for i=60:60
          x2=x1-i; y2=y1-I;
          incx=1; incy=0;
          for k=0: 8*i-1
             if(x2>0 & y2>0 & x2<columns & y2<rows)
             if M(y2,x2)~=0

               m1=Ang(y1,x1); m2=Ang(y2,x2);

               if(abs(m1-m2)>.2)

                  xm=(x1+x2)/2; ym=(y1+y2)/2;
                  m1=tan(m1);    m2=tan(m2);

                  A=y1-y2; B=x2-x1;
                  C=m1+m2; D=m1*m2
                  N=(2*A+B*C)
                  if N~=0
                    m=(A*C+2*B*D)/N;
                  else
                    m=99999999;
                  end
```

```
                if(m>-1 & m<1)
                    for x0=1:columns
                        y0=round(ym+m*(x0-xm));
                        if(y0>0 & y0<rows)
                            acc(y0,x0)=acc(y0,x0)+1;
                        end
                    end
                else
                    for y0=1:rows
                        x0=round(xm+(y0-ym)/m).
                        if(x0>0 & x0<columns)
                            acc(y0,x0)=acc(y0,x0)+1
                        end
                    end
                end %if abs
            end   %if M
            end

            x2=x2=incx;y2=y2+incy;

            if x2>x1+I
                x2=x1+i;
                incx=0;         incy=1;
                y2=y2+incy;
            end

            if y2>y1+i
                y2=y1+i;
                incx=-1;            incy=0;
                x2=x2+incx;
            end

            if x2<x1-i
                x2=x1-i;
                incx=0      incy=-1;
                y2=y2+incy;
            end
        end %for k
      end %for I
    end %if(x1,y1)
  end %y1
end %x1
```

Code 5.9 Implementation of the parameter space reduction for the Hough transform for ellipses

Figure **5.20** shows the accumulators obtained by the implementation of Code **5.9** for the images in Figure **5.14**(a) and Figure **5.14**(b). The peak represents the location of the ellipses. In general, there is noise and the accumulator is wide. This is for two main reasons. First, when the gradient direction is not accurate, then the line of votes does not pass exactly over the centre of the ellipse. This forces the peak to become wider with less height. Second, in order to avoid numerical instabilities we need to select points that are well separated. However, this increases the probability that the points do not belong to the same ellipse, thus generating background noise in the accumulator.

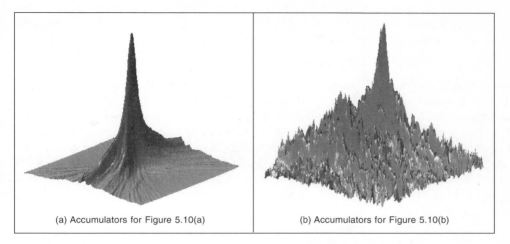

(a) Accumulators for Figure 5.10(a)   (b) Accumulators for Figure 5.10(b)

Figure 5.20   Parameter space reduction for the Hough transform for ellipses

5.5   Generalised Hough transform (GHT)

Many shapes are far more complex than lines, circles or ellipses. It is often possible to partition a complex shape into several geometric primitives, but this can lead to a highly complex data structure. In general it is more convenient to extract the whole shape. This has motivated the development of techniques that can find *arbitrary* shapes using the evidence-gathering procedure of the HT. These techniques again give results equivalent to those delivered by matched template filtering, but with the computational advantage of the evidence gathering approach. An early approach offered only limited capability for arbitrary shapes (Merlin, 1975). The full mapping is called the *Generalised HT* (GHT) (Ballard, 1981) and can be used to locate arbitrary shapes with unknown *position*, *size* and *orientation*. The GHT can be formally defined by considering the duality of a curve. One possible implementation can be based on the discrete representation given by tabular functions. These two aspects are explained in the following two sections.

5.5.1   Formal definition of the GHT

The formal analysis of the HT provides the route for generalising it to arbitrary shapes. We can start by generalising the definitions in Equation 5.41. In this way a model shape can be defined by a curve

$$v(\theta) = x(\theta)\begin{bmatrix} 1 \\ 0 \end{bmatrix} + y(\theta)\begin{bmatrix} 0 \\ 1 \end{bmatrix} \tag{5.71}$$

For a circle, for example, we have that $x(\theta) = r\cos(\theta)$ and $y(\theta) = r\sin(\theta)$. Any shape can be represented by following a more complex definition of $x(\theta)$ and $y(\theta)$.

In general, we are interested in matching the model shape against a shape in an image. However, the shape in the image has a different location, orientation and scale. Originally the GHT defines a scale parameter in the x and y directions, but due to computational complexity and practical relevance the use of a single scale has become much more popular. Analogous to Equation 5.33, we can define the image shape by considering translation, rotation and change of scale. Thus, the shape in the image can be defined as

$$\omega(\theta, b, \lambda, \rho) = b + \lambda \mathbf{R}(\rho)\upsilon(\theta) \tag{5.72}$$

where $b = (x_0, y_0)$ is the translation vector λ is a scale factor and $\mathbf{R}(\rho)$ is a rotation matrix (as in Equation 5.31). Here we have included explicitly the parameters of the transformation as arguments, but to simplify the notation they will be omitted later. The shape of $\omega(\theta, b, \lambda, \rho)$ depends on four parameters. Two parameters define the location b, plus the rotation and scale. It is important to notice that s does not define a free parameter, but only traces the curve.

In order to define a mapping for the HT we can follow the approach used to obtain Equation 5.35. Thus, the location of the shape is given by

$$b = \omega(\theta) - \lambda \mathbf{R}(\rho)\upsilon(\theta) \tag{5.73}$$

Given a shape $\omega(\theta)$ and a set of parameters b, λ and ρ, this equation defines the location of the shape. However, we do not know the shape $\omega(\theta)$ (since it depends on the parameters that we are looking for), but we only have a point in the curve. If we call $\omega_i = (\omega_{xi}, \omega_{yi})$ the point in the image, then

$$b = \omega_i - \lambda \mathbf{R}(\rho)\upsilon(\theta) \tag{5.74}$$

defines a system with four unknowns and with as many equations as points in the image. In order to find the solution we can gather evidence by using a four-dimensional accumulator space. For each potential value of b, λ and ρ, we trace a point spread function by considering all the values of θ. That is, all the points in the curve $\upsilon(\theta)$.

In the GHT the gathering process is performed by adding an extra constraint to the system that allows us to match points in the image with points in the model shape. This constraint is based on gradient direction information and can be explained as follows. We said that ideally we would like to use Equation 5.73 to gather evidence. For that we need to know the shape $\omega(\theta)$ and the model $\upsilon(\theta)$, but we only know the discrete points ω_i and we have supposed that these are the same as the shape, i.e. that $\omega(\theta) = \omega_i$. Based on this assumption, we then consider all the potential points in the model shape, $\upsilon(\theta)$. However, this is not necessary since we only need the point in the model, $\upsilon(\theta)$, that corresponds to the point in the shape, $\omega(\theta)$. We cannot know the point in the shape, $\upsilon(\theta)$, but we can compute some properties from the model and from the image. Then, we can check whether these properties are similar at the point in the model and at a point in the image. If they are indeed *similar*, then the points might *correspond*: if they do we can gather evidence of the parameters of the shape. The GHT considers as feature the gradient direction at the point. We can generalise Equation 5.45 and Equation 5.46 to define the gradient direction at a point in the arbitrary model. Thus,

$$\phi'(\theta) = \frac{y'(\theta)}{x'(\theta)} \quad \text{and} \quad \hat{\phi}'(\theta) = \tan^{-1}(\phi'(\theta)) \tag{5.75}$$

Thus Equation 5.73 is true only if the gradient direction at a point in the image matches the rotated gradient direction at a point in the (rotated) model, that is

$$\phi_i' = \hat{\phi}'(\theta) - \rho \tag{5.76}$$

where $\hat{\phi}_i'$ is the angle at the point ω_i. Note that according to this equation, gradient direction is independent of scale (in theory at least) and it changes in the same ratio as rotation. We can constrain Equation 5.74 to consider only the points $\upsilon(\theta)$ for which

$$\phi_i' - \hat{\phi}'(\theta) + \rho = 0 \tag{5.77}$$

That is, a point spread function for a given edge point ω_i is obtained by selecting a subset of points in $\upsilon(\theta)$ such that the edge direction at the image point rotated by ρ equals the gradient direction at the model point. For each point ω_i and selected point in $\upsilon(\theta)$ the point spread function is defined by the HT mapping in Equation 5.74.

5.5.2 Polar definition

Equation 5.74 defines the mapping of the HT in Cartesian form. That is, it defines the votes in the parameter space as a pair of co-ordinates (x, y). There is an alternative definition in polar form. The polar implementation is more common than the Cartesian form Hecker (1994) and Sonka (1994). The advantage of the polar form is that it is easy to implement since changes in rotation and scale correspond to addition in the angle-magnitude representation. However, ensuring that the polar vector has the correct direction incurs more complexity.

Equation 5.74 can be written in a form that combines rotation and scale as

$$b = \omega(\theta) - \gamma(\lambda, \rho) \tag{5.78}$$

where $\gamma^T(\lambda, \rho) = [\gamma_x(\lambda, \rho) \; \gamma_y(\lambda, \rho)]$ and where the combined rotation and scale is

$$\begin{aligned}
\gamma_x(\lambda, \rho) &= \lambda(x(\theta) \cos(\rho) - y(\theta) \sin(\rho)) \\
\gamma_y(\lambda, \rho) &= \lambda(x(\theta) \sin(\rho) + y(\theta) \cos(\rho))
\end{aligned} \tag{5.79}$$

This combination of rotation and scale defines a vector, $\gamma(\lambda, \rho)$, whose tangent angle and magnitude are given by

$$\tan(\alpha) = \frac{\gamma_y(\lambda, \rho)}{\gamma_x(\lambda, \rho)} \quad r = \sqrt{\gamma_x^2(\lambda, \rho) + \gamma_y^2(\lambda, \rho)} \tag{5.80}$$

The main idea here is that if we know the values for α and r, then we can gather evidence by considering Equation 5.78 in polar form. That is,

$$b = \omega(\theta) - re^\alpha \tag{5.81}$$

Thus, we should focus on computing values for α and r. After some algebraic manipulation, we have that

$$\alpha = \phi(\theta) + \rho \quad r = \lambda\Gamma(\theta) \tag{5.82}$$

where

$$\phi(\theta) = \tan^{-1}\left(\frac{y(\theta)}{x(\theta)}\right) \Gamma(\theta) = \sqrt{x^2(\theta) + y^2(\theta)} \tag{5.83}$$

In this definition, we must include the constraint defined in Equation 5.77. That is, we gather evidence only when the gradient direction is the *same*. Notice that the square root in the definition of the magnitude in Equation 5.83 can have positive and negative values. The sign must be selected in a way that the vector has the correct direction.

5.5.3 The GHT technique

Equations 5.74 and 5.81 define an HT mapping function for arbitrary shapes. The geometry of these equations is shown in Figure **5.21**. Given an image point ω_i we have to find a displacement vector $\gamma(\lambda, \rho)$. When the vector is placed at ω_i, then its end is at the point b. In the GHT jargon, this point is called the reference point. The vector $\gamma(\lambda, \rho)$ can be easily obtained as $\lambda R(\rho) \upsilon(\theta)$ or alternatively as re^{α}. However, in order to evaluate these equations, we need to know the point $\upsilon(\theta)$. This is the crucial step in the evidence gathering process. Notice the remarkable similarity between Figures **5.17**(a), **5.19**(a) and Figure **5.21**(a). This is not a coincidence, but Equation 5.60 is a particular case of Equation 5.73.

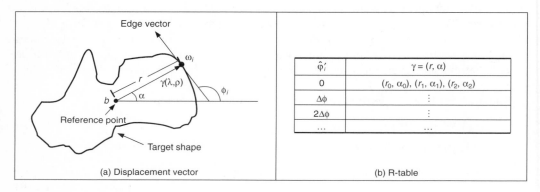

Figure 5.21 Geometry of the GHT

The process of determining $\upsilon(\theta)$ centres on solving Equation 5.76. According to this equation, since we know $\hat{\phi}_i'$, then we need to find the point $\upsilon(\theta)$ whose gradient direction is $\hat{\phi}_i' + \rho = 0$. Then we must use $\upsilon(\theta)$ to obtain the displacement vector $\gamma(\lambda, \rho)$. The GHT pre-computes the solution of this problem and stores it an array called the *R-table*. The R-table stores for each value of $\hat{\phi}_i'$ the vector $\gamma(\lambda, \rho)$ for $\rho = 0$ and $\lambda = 1$. In polar form, the vectors are stored as a magnitude direction pair and in Cartesian form as a co-ordinate pair.

The possible range for $\hat{\phi}_i'$ is between $-\pi/2$ and $\pi/2$ radians. This range is split into N equispaced slots, or bins. These slots become rows of data in the R-table. The edge direction at each border point determines the appropriate row in the R-table. The length, r, and direction, α, from the reference point is entered into a new column element, at that row, for each border point in the shape. In this manner, the N rows of the R-table have elements related to the border information, elements for which there is no information contain null vectors. The length of each row is given by the number of edge points that have the edge direction corresponding to that row; the total number of elements in the R-table equals the number of edge points above a chosen threshold. The *structure* of the R-table for N edge direction bins and m template border points is illustrated in Figure **5.21**(b).

The process of *building* the R-table is illustrated in Code **5.10**. In this code, we implement

```
%R-Table
function T=RTable(entries,inputimage)
%image size
[rows,columns]=size(inputimage);
%edges
[M,Ang]=Edges(inputimage);
M=MaxSupr(M,Ang);
%compute reference point
xr=0; yr=0; p=0;
for x=1:columns
  for y=1:rows
    if(M(y,x)~=0)
      xr=xr+x;
      yr=yr+y;
      p=p+1;
    end
  end
end
xr=round(xr/p);
yr=round(yr/p);
%accumulator
D=pi/entries;
s=0;      %number of entries in the table
t=[];
F=zeros(entries,1); %number of entries in the row
%for each edge point
for x=1:columns
  for y=1:rows
    if(M(y,x)~=0)

      phi=Ang(y,x);
      i=round((phi+(pi/2))/D);
      if(i==0) i=1; end;

      V=F(i)+1;

      if(V>s)
        s=s+1;
        T(:,:,s)=zeros(entries,2);
      end;

      T(i,1,V)=x-xr;
      T(i,2,V)=y-yr;
      F(i)=F(I)+1;


    end %if
  end %y
end %x
```

Code 5.10 Implementation of the construction of the R-table

the Cartesian definition given in Equation 5.74. According to this equation the displacement vector is given by

$$\gamma(1, 0) = \omega(\theta) - b \qquad (5.84)$$

The matrix **T** stores the co-ordinates of $\gamma(1, 0)$. This matrix is expanded to accommodate all the computed entries.

Code **5.11** shows the implementation of the gathering process of the GHT. In this case we use the Cartesian definition in Equation 5.74. The co-ordinates of points given by

```
%Generalised Hough Transform

function GHT(inputimage,RTable)

%image size
[rows,columns]=size(inputimage);

%table size
[rowsT,h,columnsT]=size(RTable);
D=pi/rowsT;

%edges
[M,Ang]=Edges(inputimage);
M=MaxSupr(M,Ang);

%accumulator
acc=zeros(rows,columns);

%for each edge point
for x=1:columns
  for y=1:rows
    if(M(y,x)~=0)

       phi=Ang(y,x);
       i=round((phi+(pi/2))/D);
       if(i==0) i=1; end;

       for j=1:columnsT
         if(RTable(i,1,j)==0 & RTable(i,2,j)==0)
           j=columnsT; %no more entries
         else
           a0=x-RTable(i,1,j); b0=y-RTable (1, 2, j);
           if(a0>0 & a0<columns & b0>0 & b0<rows)
             acc(b0,a0)=acc(b0,a0)+1;
           end
         end
       end
    end %if
  end %y
end %x
```

Code **5.11** Implementing the GHT

evaluation of all R-table points for the particular row indexed by the gradient magnitude are used to increment cells in the accumulator array. The maximum number of votes occurs at the location of the original reference point. After all edge points have been inspected, the location of the shape is given by the maximum of an accumulator array.

Note that if we want to try other values for rotation and scale, then it is necessary to compute a table $\gamma(\lambda, \rho)$ for all potential values. However, this can be avoided by considering that $\gamma(\lambda, \rho)$ can be computed from $\gamma(1, 0)$. That is, if we want to accumulate evidence for $\gamma(\lambda, \rho)$, then we use the entry indexed by $\hat{\phi}'_i + \rho$ and we rotate and scale the vector $\gamma(1, 0)$. That is,

$$\gamma_x(\lambda, \rho) = \lambda(\gamma_x(1, 0) \cos(\rho) - \gamma_y(1, 0) \sin(\rho))$$

$$\gamma_y(\lambda, \rho) = \lambda \, (\gamma_x(1, 0) \sin(\rho) + \gamma_y(1, 0) \cos(\rho))$$

(5.85)

In the case of the polar form, the angle and magnitude need to be defined according to Equation 5.82.

The application of the GHT to detect an arbitrary shape with unknown translation is illustrated in Figure **5.22**. We constructed an R-table from the template shown in Figure **5.2**(a). The table contains 30 rows. The accumulator in Figure **5.22**(c) was obtained by applying the GHT to the image in Figure **5.22**(b). Since the table was obtained from a shape with the same scale and rotation as the primitive in the image, then the GHT produces an accumulator with a clear peak at the centre of mass of the shape.

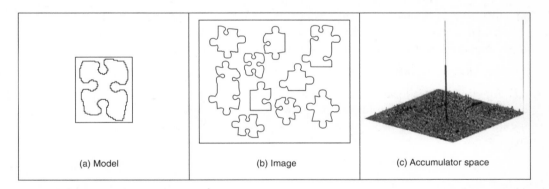

| (a) Model | (b) Image | (c) Accumulator space |

Figure 5.22   Example of the GHT

Although the example in Figure **5.22** shows that the GHT is an effective method for shape extraction, there are several inherent difficulties in its formulation (Grimson, 1990), (Aguado, 2000). The most evident problem is that the table does not provide an accurate representation when objects are scaled and translated. This is because the table implicitly assumes that the curve is represented in discrete form. Thus, the GHT maps a discrete form into a discrete parameter space. Additionally, the transformation of scale and rotation can induce other discretisation errors. This is because when discrete images are mapped to be larger, or when they are rotated, loci which are unbroken sets of points rarely map to unbroken sets in the new image. Another important problem is the excessive computation required by the four-dimensional parameter space. This makes the technique impractical. Also, the GHT is clearly dependent on the accuracy of directional information. By these factors, the results provided by the GHT can become less reliable. A solution is to use an analytic form instead of a table (Aguado, 1998). This avoids discretisation errors and makes the technique more reliable. This also allows the extension to affine or other transformations. However, this technique requires solving for the point $\upsilon(\theta)$ in an analytic way, increasing the computational load. A solution is to reduce the number of points by considering characteristic points defined as points of high curvature. However, this still requires the use of a four-dimensional accumulator. An alternative to reduce this computational load is to include the concept of invariance in the GHT mapping.

5.5.4 Invariant GHT

The problem with the GHT (and other extensions of the HT) is that they are very general. That is, the HT gathers evidence for a single point in the image. However, a point on its own provides little information. Thus, it is necessary to consider a large parameter space to cover all the potential shapes defined by a given image point. The GHT improves evidence gathering by considering a point and its gradient direction. However, since gradient direction changes with rotation, then the evidence gathering is improved in terms of noise handling, but little is done about computational complexity.

In order to reduce computational complexity of the GHT, we can consider replacing the gradient direction by another feature. That is, by a feature that is not affected by *rotation*. Let us explain this idea in more detail. The main aim of the constraint in Equation (5.77), is to include gradient direction to reduce the number of votes in the accumulator by identifying a point $\upsilon(\theta)$. Once this point is known, then we obtain the displacement vector $\gamma(\lambda, \rho)$. However, for each value of rotation, we have a different point in $\upsilon(\theta)$. Now let us replace that constraint in Equation 5.76 by a constraint of the form

$$Q(\omega_i) = Q(\upsilon(\theta)) \tag{5.86}$$

The function Q is said to be invariant and it computes a feature at the point. This feature can be, for example, the colour of the point, or any other property that does not change in the model and in the image. By considering Equation 5.86, we have that Equation 5.77 is redefined as

$$Q(\omega_i) - Q(\upsilon(\theta)) = 0 \tag{5.87}$$

That is, instead of searching for a point with the same gradient direction, we will search for the point with the same invariant feature. The advantage is that this feature will not change with rotation or scale, so we only require a 2D space to locate the shape. The definition of Q depends on the application and the type of transformation. The most general invariant properties can be obtained by considering geometric definitions. In the case of rotation and scale changes (i.e. similarity transformations) the fundamental invariant property is given by the concept of angle. An angle is defined by three points and its value remains unchanged when it is rotated and scaled. Thus, if we associate to each edge point ω_i a set of other two points $\{\omega_j, \omega_T\}$ then we can compute a geometric feature that is invariant to similarity transformations. That is,

$$Q(\omega_i) = \frac{X_j Y_i - X_i Y_j}{X_i X_j + Y_i Y_j} \tag{5.88}$$

where $X_k = \omega_k - \omega_T$, $Y_k = \omega_k - \omega_T$. Equation 5.88 defines the tangent of the angle at the point

ω_T. In general, we can define the points $[\omega_j, \omega_T]$ in different ways. An alternative geometric arrangement is shown in Figure **5.23**(a). Given the points ω_i and a fixed angle ϑ, then we determine the point ω_j such that the angle between the tangent line at ω_j and the line that joins the points is ϑ. The third point is defined by the intersection of the tangent lines at ω_i and ω_j. The tangent of the angle β is defined by Equation 5.88. This can be expressed in terms of the points and its gradient directions as

$$Q(\omega_i) = \frac{\phi_i' - \phi_j'}{1 + \phi_i' \phi_j'} \tag{5.89}$$

We can replace the gradient angle in the R-table by the angle β. The form of the new invariant table is shown in Figure **5.23**(c). Since the angle β does not change with rotation or change of scale, then we do not need to change the index for each potential rotation and scale. However, the displacement vector changes according to rotation and scale (i.e. Equation 5.85). Thus, if we want an invariant formulation, then we must also change the definition of the position vector.

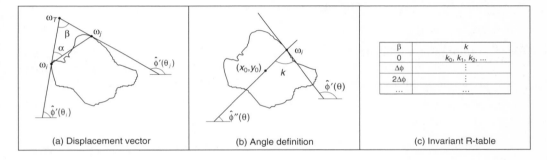

β	k
0	$k_0, k_1, k_2, \ldots$
$\Delta\phi$	:
$2\Delta\phi$	:
...	...

(a) Displacement vector   (b) Angle definition   (c) Invariant R-table

Figure 5.23 Geometry of the invariant GHT

In order to locate the point b we can generalise the ideas presented in Figure **5.17**(a) and Figure **5.19**(a). Figure **5.23**(b) shows this generalisation. As in the case of the circle and ellipse, we can locate the shape by considering a line of votes that passes through the point b. This line is determined by the value of ϕ_i''. We will do two things. First, we will find an invariant definition of this value. Second, we will include it on the GHT table.

We can develop Equation 5.73 as

$$\begin{bmatrix} x_0 \\ y_0 \end{bmatrix} = \begin{bmatrix} \omega_{xi} \\ \omega_{yi} \end{bmatrix} + \lambda \begin{bmatrix} \cos(\rho) & \sin(\rho) \\ -\sin(\rho) & \cos(\rho) \end{bmatrix} \begin{bmatrix} x(\theta) \\ y(\theta) \end{bmatrix} \tag{5.90}$$

Thus, Equation 5.60 generalises to

$$\phi_i'' = \frac{\omega_{yi} - y_0}{\omega_{xi} - x_0} = \frac{[-\sin(\rho) \quad \cos(\rho)] y(\theta)}{[\cos(\rho) \quad \sin(\rho)] x(\theta)} \tag{5.91}$$

By some algebraic manipulation, we have that

$$\phi_i'' = \tan(\xi - \rho) \tag{5.92}$$

where

$$\xi = \frac{y(\theta)}{x(\theta)} \tag{5.93}$$

In order to define ϕ_i'' we can consider the tangent angle at the point ω_i. By considering the derivative of Equation 5.72 we have that

$$\phi_i' = \frac{[-\sin(\rho) \quad \cos(\rho)]\, y'(\theta)}{[\cos(\rho) \quad \sin(\rho)]\, x'(\theta)} \tag{5.94}$$

Thus,

$$\phi_i' = \tan(\phi - \rho) \tag{5.95}$$

where

$$\phi = \frac{y'(\theta)}{x'(\theta)} \tag{5.96}$$

By considering Equation 5.92 and Equation 5.95 we define

$$\hat{\phi}_i'' = k + \hat{\phi}_i' \tag{5.97}$$

The important point in this definition is that the value of k is invariant to rotation. Thus, if we use this value in combination with the tangent at a point we can have an invariant characterisation. In order to see that k is invariant, we solve it for Equation 5.97. That is,

$$k = \hat{\phi}_i' - \hat{\phi}_i'' \tag{5.98}$$

Thus,

$$k = \xi - \rho - (\phi - \rho) \tag{5.99}$$

That is,

$$k = \xi - \phi \tag{5.100}$$

That is, independent of rotation. The definition of k has a simple geometric interpretation illustrated in Figure **5.23**(b).

In order to obtain an invariant GHT, it is necessary to know for each point ω_i, the corresponding point $\upsilon(\theta)$ and then compute the value of ϕ_i''. Then evidence can be gathered by the line in Equation 5.91. That is,

$$y_0 = \phi_i''(x_0 - \omega_{xi}) + \omega_{yi} \tag{5.101}$$

In order to compute ϕ_i'' we can obtain k and then use Equation 5.100. In the standard tabular form the value of k can be precomputed and stored as function of the angle β.

Code **5.12** illustrates the implementation to obtain the invariant R-table. This code is based on Code **5.10**. The value of α is set to $\pi/4$ and each element of the table stores a single value computed according to Equation 5.98. The more cumbersome part of the code is to search for the point ω_j. We search in two directions from ω_i and we stop once an edge point has been located. This search is performed by tracing a line. The trace is dependent on the slope. When the slope is between -1 and $+1$ we then determine a value of y for each value of x, otherwise we determine a value of x for each value of y.

Code **5.13** illustrates the evidence gathering process according to Equation 5.101. This

```
%Invariant R-Table

function T=RTableInv(entries,inputimage)

%image size
[rows,columns]=size(inputimage);

%edges
[M,Ang]=Edges(inputimage);
M=MaxSupr(M,Ang);

alfa=pi/4;
D=pi/entries;
s=0;      %number of entries in the table
t=0;
F=zeros(entries,1);   %number of entries in the row

%compute reference point
xr=0; yr=0; p=0;
for x=1:columns
  for y=1:rows
    if(M(y,x)~=0)
      xr=xr+x;
      yr=yr+y;
      p=p+1;
    end
  end
end
xr=round(xr/p);
yr=round(yr/p);

%for each edge point
for x=1:columns
  for y=1:rows
    if(M(y,x)~=0)
      %search for the second point
      x1=-1; y1=-1;
      phi=Ang(y,x);
      m=tan(phi-alfa);

      if(m>-1 & m<1)
        for i=3:columns
          c=x+i;
          j=round(m*(c-x)+y);
          if(j>0 & j<rows & c>0 & c<columns & M(j,c)~=0)
            x1=c;  y1=j;
            i=columns;
          end

          c=x-i;
          j=round(m*(c-x)+y);
          if(j>0 & j<rows & c>0 & c<columns & M(j,c)~=0)
            x1=c;  y1=j;
            i=columns;
          end
        end
```

```
      else
        for j=3:rows
          c=y+j;
          i=round(x+(c-y)/m);
          if(c>0 & c<rows & i>0 & i<columns & M(c,i)~=0)
            x1=i ;  y1=c;
            i=rows;
          end
          c=y-j;
          i=round(x+(c-y)/m);
          if(c>0 & c<rows & i>0 & i<columns & M(c,i)~=0)
            x1=i;  y1=c;
            i=rows;
          end
        end
      end

    if(x1~=-1)
      %compute beta
        phi=tan(Ang(y,x));
        phj=tan(Ang(y1,x1));
        if((1+phi*phj)~=0)
          beta=atan((phi-phj)/(1+phi*phj));
        else
          beta=1.57;
        end

        %compute k
        if((x-xr)~=0)
          ph=atan((y-yr)/(x-xr));
        else
          ph=1.57:
        end
        k=ph-Ang(y,x);

        %insert in the table
        i=round((beta+(pi/2))/D);
        if (i==0)i=1;  end;

        V=F(i)+1;

    if(V>s)
      s=s+1;
      T(:,s)=zeros(entries, 1);
        end;

        T(i,V)=k;
        F(i)=F(i)+1;
      end

    end %if
  end %y
end %x
```

Code 5.12 Constructing of the invariant R-table

```
%Invariant Generalised Hough Transform

function GHTInv(inputimage,RTable)

%image size
[rows,columns]=size(inputimage);

%table size
[rowsT,h,columnsT]=size(RTable);
D=pi/rowsT;

% edges
[M,Ang]=Edges(inputimage);
M=MaxSupr(M,Ang);

alfa=pi/4;

%accumulator
acc=zeros(rows,columns);

%for each edge point
for x=1:columns
  for y=1:rows
    if(M(y,x)~=0)
       %search for the second point
       x1=-1; y1=-1;
       phi=Ang(y,x);
       m=tan(phi-alfa);

       if(m>-1 & m<1)
          for i=3:columns
             c=x+i;
             j=round(m*(c-x)+y);
             if(j>0 & j<rows & c>0 & c<columns & M(j,c)~=0)
                x1=c; y1=j;
                i=columns;
             end
             c=x-i;
             j=round(m*(c-x)+y);
             if(j>0 & j<rows & c>0 & c<columns & M(j,c)~=0)
                x1=c; y1=j;
                i=columns;
             end
          end
       else
          for j=3:rows
             c=y+j;
             i=round(x+(c-y)/m);
             if(c>0 & c<rows & i>0 & i<columns & M(c,i)~=0)
                x1=i; y1=c;
                i=rows;
             end
```

```
                    c=y-j;
                    i=round(x+(c-y)/m);
                    if(c>0 & c<rows & i>0 & i<columns & M(c,i)~=0)
                       x1=i; y1=c;
                       i=rows;
                    end
                end
            end

            if(x1~=-1)
                %compute beta
                  phi=tan(Ang(y,x));
                  phj=tan(Ang(y1,x1));
                  if((1+phi*phj)~=0)
                     beta=atan((phi-phj)/(1+phi*phj));
                  else
                     beta=1.57;
                  end

                  i=round((beta+(pi/2))/D);
                  if(i==0)  i=1;  end;

                  %search for k
                  for j=1:columnsT
                     if(RTable(i,j)==0)
                        j=columnsT; % no more entries
                     else
                        k=RTable(i,j);
                        %lines of votes
                        m=tan(k+Ang(y,x));
                     if(m>-1 & m<1)
                        for x0=1:columns
                           y0=round(y+m*(x0-x));
                           if(y0>0 & y0<rows)
                              acc(y0,x0)=acc(y0,x0)+1;
                           end
                        end
                     else
                        for y0=1:rows
                           x0=round(x+(y0-y)/m);
                           if(x0>0 & x0<columns)
                              acc(y0,x0)=acc(y0,x0)+1;
                           end
                        end
                     end
                  end
               end
            end
         end %if
      end %y
end %x
```

Code 5.13   Implementation of the invariant GHT

code is based in the implementation presented in Code **5.11**. We use the value of β defined in Equation 5.89 to index the table passed as a parameter to the function `GHTInv`. The data k recovered from the table is used to compute the slope of the angle defined in Equation 5.97. This is the slope of the line of votes traced in the accumulators.

Figure **5.24** shows the accumulator obtained by the implementation of Code **5.13**. Figure **5.24**(a) shows the template used in this example. This template was used to construct the R-Table in Code **5.12.** The R-table was used to accumulate evidence when searching for the piece of the puzzle in the image in Figure **5.24**(b). Figure **5.24**(c) shows the result of the evidence gathering process. We can observe a peak at the location of the object. However, this accumulator contains significant noise. The noise is produced since rotation and scale change the value of the computed gradient. Thus, the line of votes is only an approximation. Another problem is that pairs of points ω_i and ω_j might not be found in an image, thus the technique is more sensitive to occlusion and noise than the GHT.

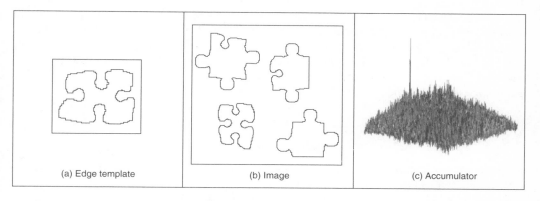

| (a) Edge template | (b) Image | (c) Accumulator |

Figure 5.24   Applying the invariant GHT

5.6   Other extensions to the HT

The motivation for extending the HT is clear: *keep* the *performance*, but *improve* the *speed*. There are other approaches to reduce the computational load of the HT. These approaches aim to improve speed and reduce memory by focusing on smaller regions of the accumulator space. These approaches have included: the *Fast HT* (Li, 1986) which successively splits the accumulator space into quadrants and continues to study the quadrant with most evidence; the *Adaptive HT* (Illingworth, 1987) which uses a fixed accumulator size to iteratively focus onto potential maxima in the accumulator space; and the *Randomised HT* (Xu, 1990) which uses a random search of the accumulator space; and pyramidal techniques. One main problem with techniques which do not search the full accumulator space, but a reduced version to save speed, is that the wrong shape can be extracted (Princen, 1989), a problem known as *phantom shape location*. These approaches can also be used (with some variation) to improve speed of performance in template matching. There have been many approaches aimed to improve performance of the HT and of the GHT.

Alternative approaches to the GHT include two *Fuzzy* HTs: (Philip, 1991) which (Sonka, 1994) includes uncertainty of the perimeter points within a GHT structure and (Han, 1994) which approximately fits a shape but which requires application-specific specification of a fuzzy membership function. There have been two major reviews of the state of research in the HT (Illingworth, 1988), (Leavers, 1993) and a textbook (Leavers, 1992) which cover many of these topics. The analytic approaches to improving the HTs performance use mathematical analysis to reduce size, and more importantly dimensionality, of the accumulator space. This concurrently improves speed. A review of HT-based techniques for circle extraction (Yuen, 1990) covered some of the most popular techniques available at the time.

5.7 Further reading

The majority of further reading in finding shapes concerns papers, many of which have already been referenced. An excellent survey of the techniques used for feature extraction (including template matching, deformable templates etc.) can be found in (Trier, 1996). Few of the textbooks devote much space to shape extraction. One text alone is dedicated to shape analysis (Van Otterloo, 1991) and contains many discussions on symmetry. For implementation, (Parker, 1994) only includes C code for template matching and for the HT for lines, but no more. Other techniques use a similar evidence gathering process to the HT. These techniques are referred to as Geometric Hashing and Clustering Techniques (Lamdan, 1988), (Stockman, 1987). In contrast with the HT, these techniques do not define an analytic mapping, but they gather evidence by grouping a set of features computed from the image and from the model.

5.8 References

Aguado, A. S., *Primitive Extraction via Gathering Evidence of Global Parameterised Models*, PhD Thesis, University of Southampton, 1996

Aguado, A. S., Montiel, E. and Nixon, M. S., On Using Directional Information for Parameter Space Decomposition in Ellipse Detection, *Pattern Recognition*, **28**(3), pp. 369–381, 1996

Aguado, A. S., Nixon, M. S. and Montiel, M. E., Parameterising Arbitrary Shapes via Fourier Descriptors for Evidence-Gathering Extraction, *Computer Vision and Image Understanding*, **69**(2), pp. 202–221, 1998

Aguado, A. S., Montiel, E. and Nixon, M. S., On the Intimate Relationship Between the Principle of Duality and the Hough Transform, *Proceedings of the Royal Society A*, **456**, pp. 503–526, 2000

Aguado, A. S., Montiel, E. and Nixon, M. S., Bias Error Analysis of the Generalised Hough Transform, *Journal of Mathematical Imaging and Vision*, **12**, pp. 25–42, 2000

Altman, J. and Reitbock, H. J. P., A Fast Correlation Method for Scale- and Translation-Invariant Pattern Recognition, *IEEE Trans. on PAMI*, **6**(1), pp. 46–57, 1984

Ballard, D. H., Generalising the Hough Transform to Find Arbitrary Shapes, *CVGIP*, **13**, pp. 111–122, 1981

Bracewell, R. N., *The Fourier Transform and its Applications*, 2nd Edition, McGraw-Hill Book Co., Singapore, 1986

Bresenham, J. E., Algorithm for Computer Control of a Digital Plotter, *IBM Systems Journal*, **4**(1), pp. 25–30, 1965

Bresenham, J. E., A Linear Algorithm for Incremental Digital Display of Circular Arcs, *Comms. of the ACM*, **20**(2), pp. 750–752, 1977

Brown, C. M., Inherent bias and noise in the Hough transform, *IEEE Trans. on PAMI*, **5**, pp. 493–505, 1983

Casasent, D. and Psaltis, D., New Optical Transforms for Pattern Recognition, *Proceedings of the IEEE*, **65**(1), pp. 77–83, 1977

Deans, S. R., Hough Transform from the Radon Transform, *IEEE Trans. on PAMI*, **13**, pp. 185–188, 1981

Duda, R. O. and Hart, P. E., Use of the Hough Transform to Detect Lines and Curves in Pictures, *Comms. of the ACM*, **15**, pp. 11–15, 1972

Gerig, G. and Klein, F., Fast Contour Identification through Efficient Hough Transform and Simplified Interpretation Strategy, *Proc. 8th Int. Conf. Pattern Recog.*, pp. 498–500, 1986

Grimson, W. E. L. and Huttenglocher, D. P., On the Sensitivity of the Hough Transform for Object Recognition, *IEEE Trans. on PAMI*, **12**, pp. 255–275, 1990

Han, J. H., Koczy, L. T. and Poston, T., Fuzzy Hough Transform, *Pattern Recog. Lett.*, **15**, pp. 649–659, 1994

Hecker, Y. C. and Bolle, R. M., On Geometric Hashing and the Generalized Hough Transform, *IEEE Trans. On Systems, Man and Cybernetics*, **24**, pp. 1328–1338, 1994

Hough, P. V. C., Method and Means for Recognising Complex Patterns, *US Patent 3969654*, 1962

Illingworth, J. and Kittler, J., The Adaptive Hough Transform, *IEEE Trans. on PAMI*, **9**(5), pp. 690–697, 1987

Illingworth, J. and Kittler, J., A Survey of the Hough Transform, *CVGIP*, **48**, pp. 87–116, 1988

Kimme, C., Ballard, D. and Sklansky, J., Finding Circles by an Array of Accumulators, *Comms. ACM*, **18**(2), pp. 120–1222, 1975

Kiryati, N. and Bruckstein, A. M., Antialiasing the Hough Transform, *CVGIP: Graphical Models and Image Processing*, **53**, pp. 213–222, 1991

Lamdan, Y., Schawatz, J. and Wolfon, H., Object Recognition by Affine Invariant Matching, *Proc. IEEE Conf. on Computer Vision and Pattern Recognition*, pp. 335–344, 1988

Leavers, V., *Shape Detection in Computer Vision using the Hough Transform*, London: Springer-Verlag, 1992

Leavers, V., Which Hough Transform, *CVGIP: Image Understanding*, **58**, pp. 250–264, 1993

Li, H. and Lavin, M. A., Fast Hough Transform: a Hierarchical Approach, *CVGIP*, **36**, pp. 139–161, 1986

Merlin, P. M. and Farber, D. J., A Parallel Mechanism for Detecting Curves in Pictures, *IEEE Trans. on Computers*, **24**, pp. 96–98, 1975

O'Gorman F. and Clowes M. B., Finding Picture Edges through Collinearity of Feature Points, *IEEE Trans. On Computers*, **25**(4), pp. 449–456, 1976

Parker, J. R., *Practical Computer Vision using C*, Wiley & Sons Inc., NY USA, 1994

Philip, K. P., *Automatic Detection of Myocardial Contours in Cine Computed Tomographic Images*, PhD Thesis, Univ. Iowa USA, 1991

Princen, J., Yuen, H. K., Illingworth, J. and Kittler, J., Properties of the Adaptive Hough Transform, *Proc. 6th Scandinavian Conf. on Image Analysis*, Oulu Finland, June 1992

Princen, J., Illingworth, J. and Kittler, J., A Formal Definition of the Hough Transform: Properties and Relationships, *J. Mathematical Imaging and Vision*, **1**, pp. 153–168, 1992

Rosenfeld, A., *Picture Processing by Computer*, Academic Press, London UK, 1969

Sklansky, J., On the Hough Technique for Curve Detection, *IEEE Trans. on Computers*, **27**, pp. 923–926, 1978

Sonka, M., Hllavac, V. and Boyle, R., *Image Processing, Analysis and Computer Vision*, Chapman Hall, London UK, 1994

Stockman, G. C. and Agrawala, A. K., Equivalence of Hough Curve Detection to Template Matching, *Comms. of the ACM*, **20**, pp. 820–822, 1977

Stockman, G., Object Recognition and Localization via Pose Clustering, *CVGIP*, **40**, pp. 361–387, 1987

Trier, O. D., Jain, A. K. and Taxt, T., Feature Extraction Methods for Character Recognition – a Survey, *Pattern Recognition*, **29**(4), pp. 641–662, 1996

Van Otterloo, P. J., *A Contour-Oriented Approach to Shape Analysis*, Prentice Hall International (UK) Ltd, Hemel Hempstead, 1991

Yuen, H. K., Princen, J., Illingworth, J. and Kittler, J., Comparative Study of Hough Transform Methods for Circle Finding, *Image and Vision Computing*, **8**(1), pp. 71–77, 1990

Xu, L., Oja, E. and Kultanen, P., A New Curve Detection Method: Randomised Hough Transform, *Pattern Recog. Lett.*, **11**, pp. 331–338, 1990

6

Flexible shape extraction (snakes and other techniques)

6.1 Overview

The previous chapter covered finding shapes by matching. This implies knowledge of a model (mathematical or template) of the target shape (feature). The shape is *fixed* in that it is flexible only in terms of the parameters that define the shape, or the parameters that define a template's appearance. Sometimes, however, it is not possible to model a shape with sufficient accuracy, or to provide a template of the target as needed for the GHT. It might be that the exact shape is *unknown* or it might be that the perturbation of that shape is *impossible* to parameterise. In this case, we seek techniques that can *evolve* to the target solution, or adapt their result to the data. This implies the use of flexible shape formulations. This chapter presents four techniques that can be used to find flexible shapes in images. These are summarised in Table 6.1 and can be distinguished by the matching functional used to indicate the extent of match between image data and a shape. If the shape is flexible or *deformable*, so as to match the image data, we have a *deformable template*. This is where we shall start. Later, we shall move to techniques that are called *snakes*, because of their movement. We shall explain two different implementations of the snake model. The first one is based on discrete minimisation and the second one on finite element analysis. We shall also look at finding shapes by the *symmetry* of their appearance. This technique finds any symmetric shape by gathering evidence by considering features between pairs of points. Finally, we shall consider approaches that use the *statistics* of a shape's possible appearance to control selection of the final shape, called *active shape models*.

Table 6.1 Overview of Chapter 6

	Deformable templates	
	Snakes	Discrete minimisation
Flexible shape extraction		Finite elements
	Symmetry operations	
	Active shape models	

6.2 Deformable templates

One of the earlier approaches to deformable template analysis (Yuille, 1991) was aimed to find facial features for purposes of recognition. The approach considered an eye to be comprised of an iris which sits within the sclera (the white bit) and which can be modelled as a combination of a circle that lies within a parabola. Clearly, the circle and a version of the parabola can be extracted by using Hough transform techniques, but this cannot be achieved in combination. When we combine the two shapes and allow them to change in size and orientation, whilst retaining their spatial relationship (that the iris or circle should reside within the sclera or parabola), then we have a deformable template.

The parabola is a shape described by a set of points (x, y) related by

$$y = a - \frac{a}{b^2}x^2 \qquad (6.1)$$

where, as illustrated in Figure **6.1**(a), a is the height of the parabola and b is its radius. As such, the maximum height is a and the minimum height is zero. A similar equation describes the lower parabola, it terms of b and c. The 'centre' of both parabolae is $\mathbf{c}_p$. The circle is as defined earlier, with centre co-ordinates $\mathbf{c}_c$ and radius r. We then seek values of the parameters which give a best match of this template to the image data. Clearly, one match we would like to make concerns matching the edge data to that of the template, like in the Hough transform. The set of values for the parameters which give a template matches the most edge points (since edge points are found at the boundaries of features) could then be deemed to be the best set of parameters describing the eye in an image. We then seek values of parameters that maximise

$$\{\mathbf{c}_p, a, b, c, \mathbf{c}_c, r\} = \max \left(\sum_{x,y \in \text{circle.perimeter,parabolae.perimeter}} \mathbf{E}_{x,y} \right) \qquad (6.2)$$

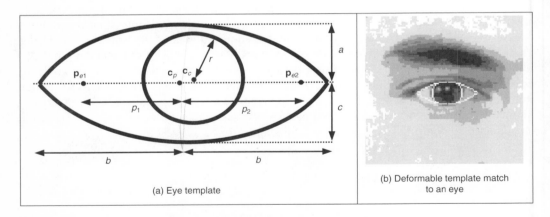

(a) Eye template

(b) Deformable template match to an eye

Figure 6.1   Finding an eye with a deformable template

Naturally, this would prefer the larger shape to the smaller ones, so we could divide the contribution of the circle and the parabolae by their perimeter to give an edge energy contribution E_e

$$E_e = \frac{\sum\limits_{x,y\in\text{circle.perimeter}} \mathbf{E}_{x,y}}{\text{circle.perimeter}} + \frac{\sum\limits_{x,y\in\text{parabolae.perimeter}} \mathbf{E}_{x,y}}{\text{parabolae.perimeter}} \tag{6.3}$$

and we seek a combination of values for the parameters $\{\mathbf{c}_p, a, b, c, \mathbf{c}_c, r\}$ which maximise this energy. This, however, implies little knowledge of the *structure* of the eye. Since we know that the sclera is white (usually) and the iris is darker than it, then we could build this information into the process. We can form an energy E_v for the circular region which averages the brightness over the circle area as

$$E_v = -\sum_{x,y\in\text{circle}} \mathbf{P}_{x,y} \Big/ \text{circle.area} \tag{6.4}$$

This is formed in the negative, since maximising its value gives the best set of parameters. Similarly, we can form an energy functional for the light regions where the eye is white as E_p

$$E_p = \sum_{x,y\in\text{parabolae-circle}} \mathbf{P}_{x,y} \Big/ \text{parabolae-circle.area} \tag{6.5}$$

where parabolae-circle implies points within the parabolae but not within the circle. We can then choose a set of parameters which maximise the combined energy functional formed by adding each energy when weighted by some chosen factors as

$$E = c_e \cdot E_e + c_v \cdot E_v + c_p \cdot E_p \tag{6.6}$$

where c_e, c_v and c_p are the weighting factors. In this way, we are choosing values for the parameters which simultaneously maximise the chance that the edges of the circle and the perimeter coincide with the image edges, that the inside of the circle is dark and that the inside of the parabolae are light. The value chosen for each of the weighting factors controls the influence of that factor on the eventual result.

The energy fields are shown in Figure **6.2** when computed over the entire image. Naturally, the valley image shows up regions with low image intensity and the peak image shows regions of high image intensity, like the whites of the eyes. In its original formulation, this approach actually had five energy terms and the extra two are associated with the points $\mathbf{P}_{e1}$ and $\mathbf{P}_{e2}$ either side of the iris in Figure **6.1**(a).

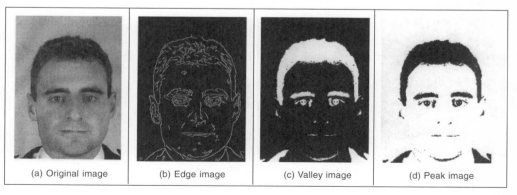

Figure 6.2 Energy fields over whole face image

This is where the problem starts, as we now have 11 parameters (eight for the shapes and three for the weighting coefficients). We could of course simply cycle through every possible value. Given, say, 100 possible values for each parameter, we then have to search 10^{22} combinations of parameters which would be no problem given multithread computers with Terrahertz processing speed achieved via optical interconnect, but that is not now. Naturally, we can reduce the number of combinations by introducing constraints on the relative size and position of the shapes, e.g. the circle should lie wholly within the parabolae, but this will not reduce the number of combinations much. We can seek two alternatives: one is to use *optimisation* techniques. The original approach (Yuille, 1991) favoured the use of gradient descent techniques; currently, the *genetic algorithm* approach (Goldberg, 1988) seems to be most favoured and this has been shown to good effect for deformable template eye extraction on a database of 1000 faces (Benn, 1999) (this is the source of the images shown here). The alternative is to seek a different technique that uses fewer parameters. This is where we move to *snakes* that are a much more popular approach. These snakes evolve a set of *points* (a contour) to match the image data, rather than evolving a shape.

6.3 Active contours (snakes)

6.3.1 Basics

Active contours or *snakes* (Kass, 1988) are a completely different approach to feature extraction. An active contour is a set of points which aims to enclose a target feature, the feature to be extracted. It is a bit like using a balloon to 'find' a shape: the balloon is placed outside the shape, enclosing it. Then by taking air out of the balloon, making it smaller, the shape is found when the balloon stops shrinking, when it fits the target shape. By this manner, active contours arrange a set of points so as to describe a target feature by enclosing it. Snakes are actually quite recent and their original formulation was as an interactive extraction process, though they are now usually deployed for automatic feature extraction.

An initial contour is placed outside the target feature, and is then evolved so as to enclose it. The process is illustrated in Figure **6.3** where the target feature is the perimeter of the iris. First, an initial contour is placed outside the iris, Figure **6.3**(a). The contour is then minimised to find a new contour which shrinks so as to be closer to the iris, Figure **6.3**(b). After seven iterations, the contour points can be seen to match the iris perimeter well, Figure **6.3**(d).

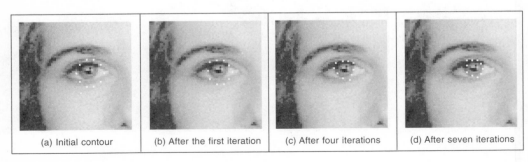

| (a) Initial contour | (b) After the first iteration | (c) After four iterations | (d) After seven iterations |

Figure 6.3 Using a snake to find an eye's iris

Active contours are actually expressed as an *energy minimisation* process. The target feature is a minimum of a suitably formulated energy functional. This energy functional includes more than just edge information: it includes properties that control the way the contour can stretch and curve. In this way, a snake represents a *compromise* between its *own* properties (like its ability to bend and stretch) and *image* properties (like the edge magnitude). Accordingly, the energy functional is the addition of a function of the contour's internal energy, its constraint energy, and the image energy: these are denoted E_{int}, E_{image}, and E_{con}, respectively. These are functions of the set of points which make up a snake, $\mathbf{v}(s)$, which is the set of x and y co-ordinates of the points in the snake. The energy functional is the integral of these functions of the snake, given $s \in [0, 1]$ is the normalised length around the snake. The energy functional E_{snake} is then:

$$E_{snake} = \int_{s=0}^{1} E_{int}(\mathbf{v}(s)) + E_{image}(\mathbf{v}(s)) + E_{con}(\mathbf{v}(s))\, ds \qquad (6.7)$$

In this equation: the internal energy, E_{int}, controls the natural behaviour of the snake and hence the arrangement of the snake points; the image energy, E_{image}, attracts the snake to chosen low-level features (such as *edge* points); and the constraint energy, E_{con}, allows higher level information to control the snake's evolution. The aim of the snake is to evolve by *minimising* Equation 6.7. New snake contours are those with lower energy and are a better match to the target feature (according to the values of E_{int}, E_{image}, and E_{con}) than the original set of points from which the active contour has evolved. In this manner, we seek to choose a set of points $\mathbf{v}(s)$ such that

$$\frac{dE_{snake}}{d\mathbf{v}} = 0 \qquad (6.8)$$

This can of course select a maximum rather than a minimum, and a second-order derivative can be used to discriminate between a maximum and a minimum. However, this is not usually necessary as a minimum is usually the only stable solution (on reaching a maximum, it would then be likely to pass over the top to then minimise the energy). Prior to investigating how we can minimise Equation 6.7, let us first consider the parameters which can control a snake's behaviour.

The energy functionals are expressed in terms of functions of the snake, and of the image. These functions contribute to the snake energy according to values chosen for respective weighting coefficients. In this manner, the internal image energy is defined to be a weighted summation of first- and second-order derivatives around the contour

$$E_{int} = \alpha(s)\left|\frac{d\mathbf{v}(s)}{ds}\right|^2 + \beta(s)\left|\frac{d^2\mathbf{v}(s)}{ds^2}\right|^2 \qquad (6.9)$$

The first-order differential, $d\mathbf{v}(s)/ds$, measures the energy due to *stretching* which is the *elastic* energy since high values of this differential imply a high rate of change in that region of the contour. The second-order differential, $d^2\mathbf{v}(s)/ds^2$, measures the energy due to *bending*, the *curvature* energy. The first-order differential is weighted by $\alpha(s)$ which controls the contribution of the elastic energy due to point spacing; the second-order differential is weighted by $\beta(s)$ which controls the contribution of the curvature energy due to point variation. Choice of the values of α and β controls the shape the snake aims to attain. Low values for α imply the points can change in spacing greatly, whereas higher values imply that the snake aims to attain evenly spaced contour points. Low values for β imply that curvature is not minimised and the contour can form corners in its perimeter whereas high values predispose the snake to smooth contours. These are the properties of the contour itself, which is just part of a snake's compromise between its own properties and measured features in an image.

The image energy attracts the snake to low-level features, such as brightness or edge data. The original formulation suggested that lines, edges and terminations could contribute to the energy function. Their energy is denoted E_{line}, E_{edge} and E_{term}, respectively, and are controlled by weighting coefficients w_{line}, w_{edge} and w_{term}, respectively. The image energy is then:

$$E_{image} = w_{line} E_{line} + w_{edge} E_{edge} + w_{term} E_{term} \qquad (6.10)$$

The *line* energy can be set to the image intensity at a particular point. If black has a lower value than white, then the snake will be extracted to dark features. Altering the sign of w_{line} will attract the snake to brighter features. The *edge* energy can be that computed by application of an edge detection operator, the magnitude, say, of the output of the Sobel edge detection operator. The *termination* energy, E_{term} as measured by Equation 4.52, can include the curvature of level image contours (as opposed to the curvature of the snake, controlled by $β(s)$), but this is rarely used. It is most common to use the edge energy, though the line energy can find application.

6.3.2 The Greedy algorithm for snakes

The implementation of a snake, to evolve a set of points to minimise Equation 6.7, can use finite elements, or finite differences, which is complicated and follows later. It is easier to start with the *Greedy algorithm* (Williams, 1992) which implements the energy minimisation process as a purely discrete algorithm, illustrated in Figure **6.4**. The process starts by specifying an initial contour. Earlier, Figure **6.3**(a) used a circle of 16 points along the perimeter of a circle. Alternatively, these can be specified manually. The Greedy algorithm then evolves the snake in an iterative manner by local neighbourhood search around contour points to select new ones which have lower snake energy. The process is called Greedy by virtue of the way the search propagates around the contour. At each iteration, all contour points are evolved and the process is actually repeated for the first contour point. The index to snake points is computed modulo S (the number of snake points).

For a set of snake points $\mathbf{v}_s$, $\forall s \in 0, S - 1$, the energy functional minimised for each snake point is:

$$E_{snake}(s) = E_{int}(\mathbf{v}_s) + E_{image}(\mathbf{v}_s) \qquad (6.11)$$

This is expressed as

$$E_{snake}(s) = \alpha(s)\left|\frac{d\mathbf{v}_s}{ds}\right|^2 + \beta(s)\left|\frac{d^2\mathbf{v}_s}{ds^2}\right|^2 + \gamma(s)E_{edge} \qquad (6.12)$$

where the first-order and second-order differentials are approximated for each point searched in the local neighbourhood of the currently selected contour point. The weighting parameters, α, β and γ, are all functions of the contour. Accordingly, each contour point has associated values for α, β and γ. An implementation of the specification of an initial contour by a function `point` is given in Code **6.1**. In this implementation, the contour is stored as a

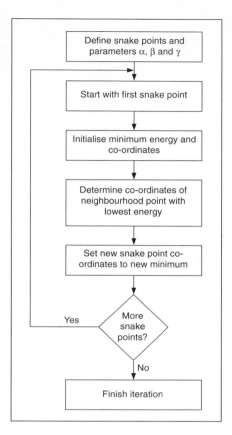

Figure 6.4 Operation of the Greedy algorithm

matrix of vectors. Each vector has five elements: two are the x and y co-ordinates of the contour point, the remaining three parameters are the values of α, β and γ for that contour point, set here to be 0.5, 0.5 and 1.0, respectively. The `no` contour points are arranged to be in a circle, radius `rad` and centre (`xc`, `yc`). As such, a vector is returned for each snake point, `point`$_s$, where (`point`$_s$)$_0$, (`point`$_s$)$_1$, (`point`$_s$)$_2$, (`point`$_s$)$_3$, (`point`$_s$)$_4$ are the x co-ordinate, the y co-ordinate and α, β and γ for the particular snake point s: $\mathbf{x}_s$, $\mathbf{y}_s$, α_s, β_s, and γ_s, respectively.

The first-order differential is approximated as the modulus of the difference between the average spacing of contour points (evaluated as the Euclidean distance between them), and the Euclidean distance between the currently selected image point $\mathbf{v}_s$ and the next contour point. By selection of an appropriate value of $\alpha(s)$ for each contour point $\mathbf{v}_s$, this can control the spacing between the contour points.

$$\left|\frac{d\mathbf{v}_s}{ds}\right|^2 = \left|\sum_{i=0}^{S-1} \frac{\|\mathbf{v}_i - \mathbf{v}_{i+1}\|}{S} - \|\mathbf{v}_s - \mathbf{v}_{s+1}\|\right|$$

$$= \left|\sum_{i=0}^{S-1} \frac{\sqrt{(\mathbf{x}_i - \mathbf{x}_{i+1})^2 + (\mathbf{y}_i - \mathbf{y}_{i+1})^2}}{S} - \sqrt{(\mathbf{x}_s - \mathbf{x}_{s+1})^2 + (\mathbf{y}_s - \mathbf{y}_{s+1})^2}\right| \quad (6.13)$$

```
points(rad,no,xc,yc):=  for s∈0..no-1

                          x_s ←xc+floor( rad·cos ( (s·2·π)/no ) +0.5 )

                          y_s ←yc+floor( rad·sin ( (s·2·π)/no ) +0.5 )

                          α_s←0.5
                          β_s←0.5
                          γ_s←1

                                      ⎡ x_s ⎤
                                      ⎢ y_s ⎥
                          point_s ←   ⎢ α_s ⎥
                                      ⎢ β_s ⎥
                                      ⎣ γ_s ⎦

                          point
```

Code 6.1   Specifying in initial contour

as evaluated from the x and y co-ordinates of the adjacent snake point $(\mathbf{x}_{s+1}, \mathbf{y}_{s+1})$ and the co-ordinates of the point currently inspected $(\mathbf{x}_s, \mathbf{y}_s)$. Clearly, the first-order differential, as evaluated from Equation 6.13, drops to zero when the contour is evenly spaced, as required. This is implemented by the function `Econt` in Code **6.2** which uses a function `diff` to evaluate the average spacing and a function `diff2` to evaluate the Euclidean distance between the currently searched point $(\mathbf{v}_s)$ and the next contour point $(\mathbf{v}_{s+1})$. The arguments to E_{cont} are the x and y co-ordinates of the point currently being inspected, `x` and `y`, the index of the contour point currently under consideration, `s`, and the contour itself, `cont`.

```
dist(s,contour):=
          s1←mod(s,rows(contour))
          s2←mod(s+1,rows(contour))
          √[ (contour_s1 )_0 -(contour_s2 )_0 ]^2 +[ (contour_s1 )_1 -(contour_s2 )_1 ]^2

dist2(x,y,s,contour):=  s2←mod(s+1,rows(contour))
                        √[ (contour_s2 )_0 -x]^2 +[ (contour_s2 )_1 -y]^2

                                                    rows(cont)-1
Econt(x,y,s,cont) :=   D← ───1───  ·      Σ        dist(s1,cont)
                          rows(cont)      s1=0
                       |D-dist2(x,y,s,cont)|
```

Code 6.2   Evaluating the contour energy

The second-order differential can be implemented as an estimate of the curvature between the next and previous contour points, $\mathbf{v}_{s+1}$ and $\mathbf{v}_{s-1}$, respectively, and the point in the local neighbourhood of the currently inspected snake point $\mathbf{v}_s$:

$$\left| \frac{d^2\mathbf{v}_s}{ds^2} \right|^2 = |(\mathbf{v}_{s+1} - 2\mathbf{v}_s + \mathbf{v}_{s-1})|^2$$

$$= (\mathbf{x}_{s+1} - 2\mathbf{x}_s + \mathbf{x}_{s-1})^2 + (\mathbf{y}_{s+1} - 2\mathbf{y}_s + \mathbf{y}_{s-1})^2$$

(6.14)

This is implemented by a function `Ecur` in Code **6.3**, whose arguments again are the x and y co-ordinates of the point currently being inspected, `x` and `y`, the index of the contour point currently under consideration, `s`, and the contour itself, `cont`.

```
Ecur(x,y,s,con)  :=| s1←mod(s-1+rows(con),rows(con))
                   | s3←mod(s+1,rows(con))
                   | [(con_s1)_0 - 2·x+(con_s3)_0]^2 +[(con_s1)_1 - 2·y+(con_s3)_1]^2
```

Code 6.3   Evaluating the contour curvature

E_{edge} can be implemented as the magnitude of the Sobel edge operator at point x, y. This is normalised to ensure that its value lies between zero and unity. This is also performed for the elastic and curvature energies in the current region of interest and is achieved by normalisation using Equation 3.2 arranged to provide an output ranging between 0 and 1. The edge image could also be normalised within the current window of interest, but this makes it more possible that the result is influenced by noise. Since the snake is arranged to be a minimisation process, the edge image is inverted so that the points with highest edge strength are given the lowest edge value (0) whereas the areas where the image is constant are given a high value (1). Accordingly, the snake will be attracted to the edge points with greatest magnitude. The normalisation process ensures that the contour energy and curvature and the edge strength are balanced forces and eases appropriate selection of values for α, β and γ.

The Greedy algorithm then uses these energy functionals to minimise the composite energy functional, Equation 6.12, given in the function `grdy` in Code **6.4**. This gives a single iteration in the evolution of a contour wherein all snake points are searched. The energy for each snake point is first determined and is stored as the point with minimum energy. This ensures that if any other point is found to have equally small energy, then the contour point will remain in the same position. Then, the local 3×3 neighbourhood is searched to determine whether any other point has a lower energy than the current contour point. If it does, then that point is returned as the new contour point.

A verbatim implementation of the Greedy algorithm would include three thresholds. One is a threshold on tangential direction and another on edge magnitude. If an edge point were adjudged to be of direction above the chosen threshold, and with magnitude above its corresponding threshold, then β can be set to zero for that point to allow corners to form. This has not been included in Code **6.4**, in part because there is mutual dependence between α and β. Also, the original presentation of the Greedy algorithm proposed to

```
grdy(edg,con)  :=  | for s1∈0..rows(con)
                   |   s←mod(s1,rows(con))
                   |   xmin←(con_s)_0
                   |   ymin←(con_s)_1
                   |   forces←balance[(con_s)_0,(con_s)_1,edg,s,con]
                   |   Emin←(con_s)_2.Econt(xmin,ymin,s,con)
                   |   Emin←Emin+(con_s)_3·Ecur(xmin,ymin,s,con)
                   |   Emin←Emin+(con_s)_4·(edg_0)_((con_s)_1,(con_s)_0)
                   |   for x∈(con_s)_0-1..(con_s)_0+1
                   |     for y∈(con_s)_1-1..(con_s)_1+1
                   |       if check(x,y,edg_0)
                   |         | xx←x-(con_s)_0+1
                   |         | yy←y-(con_s)_1+1
                   |         | Ej←(con_s)_2·(forces_(0,0))_yy,xx
                   |         | Ej←Ej+(con_s)_3·(forces_(0,1))_yy,xx
                   |         | Ej←Ej+(con_s)_4·(edg_0)_y,x
                   |         | if Ej<Emin
                   |         |   | Emin←Ej
                   |         |   | xmin←x
                   |         |   | ymin←y
                   |                    ⎡  xmin    ⎤
                   |                    ⎢  ymin    ⎥
                   |   con_s ←          ⎢ (con_s)_2 ⎥
                   |                    ⎢ (con_s)_3 ⎥
                   |                    ⎣ (con_s)_4 ⎦
                   | con
```

Code 6.4   The Greedy algorithm

continue evolving the snake until it becomes static, when the number of contour points moved in a single iteration are below the third threshold value. This can lead to instability since it can lead to a situation where contour points merely oscillate between two solutions and the process would appear not to converge. Again, this has not been implemented here.

The effect of varying α and β is shown in Figure **6.5** and Figure **6.6**. Setting α to zero removes influence of *spacing* on the contour points' arrangement. In this manner, the points will become unevenly spaced, Figure **6.5**(b), and eventually can be placed on top of each other. Reducing the control by spacing can be desirable for features that have high localised curvature. Low values of α can allow for bunching of points in such regions, giving a better feature description.

Setting β to zero removes influence of *curvature* on the contour points' arrangement, allowing corners to form in the contour, as illustrated in Figure **6.6**. This is manifest in the first iteration, Figure **6.6**(b), and since with β set to zero for the whole contour, each contour point can become a corner with high curvature, Figure **6.6**(c), leading to the rather ridiculous result in Figure **6.6**(d). Reducing the control by curvature can clearly be desirable for features that have high localised curvature. This illustrates the mutual dependence between α and β, since low values of α can accompany low values of β in regions of high

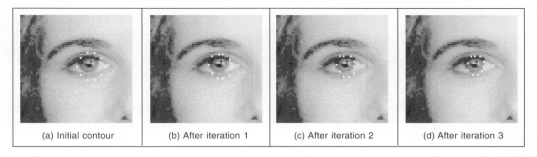

| (a) Initial contour | (b) After iteration 1 | (c) After iteration 2 | (d) After iteration 3 |

Figure 6.5 Effect of removing control by spacing

localised curvature. Setting γ to zero would force the snake to ignore image data and evolve under its own forces. This would be rather farcical. The influence of γ is reduced in applications where the image data used is known to be noisy. Note that one fundamental problem with a discrete version is that the final solution can oscillate when it swaps between two sets of points which are both with equally low energy. This can be prevented by detecting the occurrence of oscillation. A further difficulty is that as the contour becomes smaller, the number of contour points actually constrains the result as they cannot be compressed into too small a space. The only solution to this is to resample the contour.

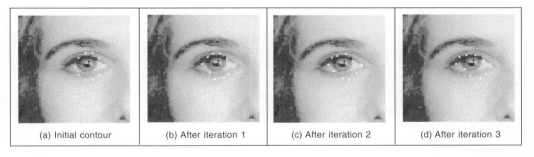

| (a) Initial contour | (b) After iteration 1 | (c) After iteration 2 | (d) After iteration 3 |

Figure 6.6 Effect of removing low curvature control

6.3.3 Complete (Kass) snake implementation

The Greedy method iterates around the snake to find local minimum energy at snake points. This is an *approximation*, since it does not necessarily determine the 'best' local minimum in the region of the snake points, by virtue of iteration. A *complete snake implementation*, or *Kass snake*, solves for all snake points in one step to ensure that the snake moves to the best local energy minimum. We seek to choose snake points ($\mathbf{v}(s) = (\mathbf{x}(s), \mathbf{y}(s))$) in such a manner that the energy is minimised, Equation 6.8. Calculus of variations shows how the solution to Equation 6.7 reduces to a pair of differential equations that can be solved by finite difference analysis (Waite, 1990). This results in a set of equations that iteratively provide new sets of contour points. By calculus of variations, we shall consider an admissible solution $\hat{\mathbf{v}}(s)$ perturbed by a small amount, $\varepsilon\delta\mathbf{v}(s)$, which achieves minimum energy, as:

$$\frac{dE_{\text{snake}}(\hat{\mathbf{v}}(s) + \varepsilon\delta\mathbf{v}(s))}{d\varepsilon} = 0 \tag{6.15}$$

where the perturbation is spatial, affecting the x and y co-ordinates of a snake point:

$$\delta \mathbf{v}(s) = (\delta_x(s), \, \delta_y(s)) \qquad (6.16)$$

This gives the perturbed snake solution as

$$\hat{\mathbf{v}}(s) + \varepsilon \delta \mathbf{v}(s) = (\hat{x}(s) + \varepsilon \delta_x(s), \hat{y}(s) + \varepsilon \delta_y(s)) \qquad (6.17)$$

where $\hat{x}(s)$ and $\hat{y}(s)$ are the x and y co-ordinates, respectively, of the snake points at the solution $(\hat{\mathbf{v}}(s) = (\hat{x}(s), \hat{y}(s))$. By setting the constraint energy E_{con} to zero, the snake energy, Equation 6.7, becomes:

$$E_{\text{snake}}(\mathbf{v}(s)) = \int_{s=0}^{1} \{E_{\text{int}}(\mathbf{v}(s)) + E_{\text{image}}(\mathbf{v}(s))\} \, ds \qquad (6.18)$$

Edge magnitude information is often used (so that snakes are attracted to edges found by an edge detection operator) so we shall replace E_{image} by E_{edge}. By substitution for the perturbed snake points, we obtain

$$E_{\text{snake}}(\hat{\mathbf{v}}(s) + \varepsilon \delta \mathbf{v}(s)) = \int_{s=0}^{1} \{E_{\text{int}}(\hat{\mathbf{v}}(s) + \varepsilon \delta \mathbf{v}(s)) + E_{\text{edge}}(\hat{\mathbf{v}}(s) + \varepsilon \delta \mathbf{v}(s))\} \, ds$$

$$(6.19)$$

By substitution from Equation 6.9, we obtain

$$E_{\text{snake}}(\hat{\mathbf{v}}(s) + \varepsilon \delta \mathbf{v}(s))$$

$$= \int_{s=0}^{s=1} \left\{ \alpha(s) \left| \frac{d(\hat{\mathbf{v}}(s) + \varepsilon \delta \mathbf{v}(s)}{ds} \right|^2 + \beta(s) \left| \frac{d^2(\hat{\mathbf{v}}(s) + \varepsilon \delta \mathbf{v}(s)}{ds^2} \right|^2 + E_{\text{edge}}(\hat{\mathbf{v}}(s) + \varepsilon \delta \mathbf{v}(s)) \right\} ds$$

$$(6.20)$$

By substitution from Equation 6.17,

$$E_{\text{snake}}(\hat{\mathbf{v}}(s) + \varepsilon \delta \mathbf{v}(s))$$

$$= \int_{s=0}^{s=1} \left[\begin{array}{l} \alpha(s) \left\{ \begin{array}{l} \left(\dfrac{d\hat{x}(s)}{ds} \right)^2 + 2\varepsilon \dfrac{d\hat{x}(s)}{ds} \dfrac{d\delta_x(s)}{ds} + \left(\varepsilon \dfrac{d\delta_x(s)}{ds} \right)^2 \\[3mm] + \left(\dfrac{d\hat{y}(s)}{ds} \right)^2 + 2\varepsilon \dfrac{d\hat{y}(s)}{ds} \dfrac{d\delta_y(s)}{ds} + \left(\varepsilon \dfrac{d\delta_y(s)}{ds} \right)^2 \end{array} \right\} \\[10mm] + \beta(s) \left\{ \begin{array}{l} \left(\dfrac{d^2\hat{x}(s)}{ds^2} \right)^2 + 2\varepsilon \dfrac{d^2\hat{x}(s)}{ds^2} \dfrac{d^2\delta_x(s)}{ds^2} + \left(\varepsilon \dfrac{d^2\delta_x(s)}{ds^2} \right)^2 \\[3mm] + \left(\dfrac{d^2\hat{y}(s)}{ds^2} \right)^2 + 2\varepsilon \dfrac{d^2\hat{y}(s)}{ds^2} \dfrac{d^2\delta_y(s)}{ds^2} + \left(\varepsilon \dfrac{d^2\delta_y(s)}{ds^2} \right)^2 \end{array} \right\} \\[10mm] + E_{\text{edge}}(\hat{\mathbf{v}}(s) + \varepsilon \delta \mathbf{v}(s)) \end{array} \right] ds \qquad (6.21)$$

By expanding E_{edge} at the perturbed solution by Taylor series, we obtain

$$E_{edge}(\hat{\mathbf{v}}(s) + \varepsilon\delta\mathbf{v}(s)) = E_{edge}\left(\hat{x}(s) + \varepsilon\delta_x(s), \hat{y}(s) + \varepsilon\delta_y(s)\right)$$

$$= E_{edge}\left(\hat{x}(s), \hat{y}(s)\right) + \varepsilon\delta_x(s)\left.\frac{\partial E_{edge}}{\partial x}\right|_{\hat{x},\hat{y}} + \varepsilon\delta_y(s)\left.\frac{\partial E_{edge}}{\partial y}\right|_{\hat{x},\hat{y}} + O(\varepsilon^2) \quad (6.22)$$

This implies that the image information must be twice differentiable which holds for edge information, but not for some other forms of image energy. Ignoring higher order terms in ε (since ε is small), by reformulation Equation 6.21 becomes

$$E_{snake}(\hat{\mathbf{v}}(s) + \varepsilon\delta\mathbf{v}(s)) = E_{snake}(\hat{\mathbf{v}}(s))$$

$$+ 2\varepsilon\int_{s=0}^{s=1}\alpha(s)\frac{d\hat{x}(s)}{ds}\frac{d\delta_x(s)}{ds} + \beta(s)\frac{d^2\hat{x}(s)}{ds^2}\frac{d^2\delta_x(s)}{ds^2} + \left.\frac{\delta_x(s)}{2}\frac{\partial E_{edge}}{\partial x}\right|_{\hat{x},\hat{y}} ds$$

$$+ 2\varepsilon\int_{s=0}^{s=1}\alpha(s)\frac{d\hat{y}(s)}{ds}\frac{d\delta_y(s)}{ds} + \beta(s)\frac{d^2\hat{y}(s)}{ds^2}\frac{d^2\delta_y(s)}{ds^2} + \left.\frac{\delta_y(s)}{2}\frac{\partial E_{edge}}{\partial y}\right|_{\hat{x},\hat{y}} ds$$

$$(6.23)$$

Since the perturbed solution is at a minimum, the integration terms in Equation 6.23 must be identically zero:

$$\int_{s=0}^{s=1}\alpha(s)\frac{d\hat{x}(s)}{ds}\frac{d\delta_x(s)}{ds} + \beta(s)\frac{d^2\hat{x}(s)}{ds^2}\frac{d^2\delta_x(s)}{ds^2} + \left.\frac{\delta_x(s)}{2}\frac{\partial E_{edge}}{\partial x}\right|_{\hat{x},\hat{y}} ds = 0$$

$$(6.24)$$

$$\int_{s=0}^{s=1}\alpha(s)\frac{d\hat{y}(s)}{ds}\frac{d\delta_y(s)}{ds} + \beta(s)\frac{d^2\hat{y}(s)}{ds^2}\frac{d^2\delta_y(s)}{ds^2} + \left.\frac{\delta_y(s)}{2}\frac{\partial E_{edge}}{\partial y}\right|_{\hat{x},\hat{y}} ds = 0$$

$$(6.25)$$

By integration we obtain

$$\left[\alpha(s)\frac{d\hat{x}(s)}{ds}\delta_x(s)\right]_{s=0}^{1} - \int_{s=0}^{s=1}\frac{d}{ds}\left\{\alpha(s)\frac{d\hat{x}(s)}{ds}\right\}\delta_x(s)ds +$$

$$\left[\beta(s)\frac{d^2\hat{x}(s)}{ds^2}\frac{d\delta_x(s)}{ds}\right]_{s=0}^{1} - \left[\frac{d}{ds}\left\{\beta(s)\frac{d^2\hat{x}(s)}{ds^2}\right\}\delta_x(s)\right]_{s=0}^{1}$$

$$+ \int_{s=0}^{s=1}\frac{d^2}{ds^2}\left\{\beta(s)\frac{d^2\hat{x}(s)}{ds^2}\right\}\delta_x(s)ds + \frac{1}{2}\int_{s=0}^{1}\left.\frac{\partial E_{edge}}{\partial x}\right|_{\hat{x},\hat{y}}\delta_x(s)ds = 0 \quad (6.26)$$

Since the first, third and fourth terms are zero (since for a closed contour, $\delta_x(1) - \delta_x(0) = 0$ and $\delta_y(1) - \delta_y(0) = 0$), this reduces to

$$\int_{s=0}^{s=1} \left[-\frac{d}{ds}\left\{\alpha(s)\frac{d\hat{x}(s)}{ds}\right\} + \frac{d^2}{ds^2}\left\{\beta(s)\frac{d^2\hat{x}(s)}{ds^2}\right\} + \frac{1}{2}\frac{\partial E_{\text{edge}}}{\partial x}\bigg|_{\hat{x},\hat{y}} \right] \delta_x(s)ds = 0$$

(6.27)

Since this equation holds for all $\delta_x(s)$ then,

$$-\frac{d}{ds}\left\{\alpha(s)\frac{d\hat{x}(s)}{ds}\right\} + \frac{d^2}{ds^2}\left\{\beta(s)\frac{d^2\hat{x}(s)}{ds^2}\right\} + \frac{1}{2}\frac{\partial E_{\text{edge}}}{\partial x}\bigg|_{\hat{x},\hat{y}} = 0 \qquad (6.28)$$

Similarly, by a similar development of Equation 6.25 we obtain

$$-\frac{d}{ds}\left\{\alpha(s)\frac{d\hat{y}(s)}{ds}\right\} + \frac{d^2}{ds^2}\left\{\beta(s)\frac{d^2\hat{y}(s)}{ds^2}\right\} + \frac{1}{2}\frac{\partial E_{\text{edge}}}{\partial y}\bigg|_{\hat{x},\hat{y}} = 0 \qquad (6.29)$$

This has reformulated the original energy minimisation framework, Equation 6.7, into a pair of differential equations. To implement a complete snake, we seek the solution to Equation 6.28 and Equation 6.29. By the method of finite differences, we substitute for $dx(s)/ds \cong \mathbf{x}_{s+1} - \mathbf{x}_s$, the first-order difference, and the second-order difference is $d^2\mathbf{x}(s)/ds^2 \cong \mathbf{x}_{s+1} - 2\mathbf{x}_s + \mathbf{x}_{s-1}$ (as in Equation 6.12), which by substitution into Equation 6.28, for a contour discretised into S points equally spaced by an arc length h (remembering that the indices $s \in [1, S)$ to snake points are computed modulo S), gives

$$-\frac{1}{h}\left\{\alpha_{s+1}\frac{(\mathbf{x}_{s+1} - \mathbf{x}_s)}{h} - \alpha_s\frac{(\mathbf{x}_s - \mathbf{x}_{s-1})}{h}\right\}$$

$$+\frac{1}{h^2}\left\{\beta_{s+1}\frac{\mathbf{x}_{s+2} - 2\mathbf{x}_{s+1} + \mathbf{x}_s)}{h^2} - 2\beta_s\frac{(\mathbf{x}_{s+1} - 2\mathbf{x}_s + \mathbf{x}_{s-1})}{h^2} + \beta_{s-1}\frac{(\mathbf{x}_s - 2\mathbf{x}_{s-1} + \mathbf{x}_{s-2})}{h^2}\right\}$$

$$+\frac{1}{2}\frac{\partial E_{\text{edge}}}{\partial x}\bigg|_{x_s,y_s} = 0 \qquad (6.30)$$

By collecting the coefficients of different points, Equation 6.30 can be expressed as

$$f_s = a_s\mathbf{x}_{s-2} + b_s\mathbf{x}_{s-1} + c_s\mathbf{x}_s + d_s\mathbf{x}_{s+1} + e_s\mathbf{x}_{s+2} \qquad (6.31)$$

where

$$f_s = -\frac{1}{2}\frac{\partial E_{\text{edge}}}{\partial x}\bigg|_{\mathbf{x}_s,\mathbf{y}_s} \qquad a_s = \frac{\beta_{s-1}}{h^4} \qquad b_s = -\frac{2(\beta_s + \beta_{s-1})}{h^4} - \frac{\alpha_s}{h^2}$$

$$c_s = \frac{\beta_{s+1} + 4\beta_s + \beta_{s-1}}{h^4} + \frac{\alpha_{s+1} + \alpha_s}{h^2} \qquad d_s = -\frac{2(\beta_{s+1} + \beta_s)}{h^4} - \frac{\alpha_{s+1}}{h^2} \qquad e_s = \frac{\beta_{s+1}}{h^4}$$

This is now in the form of a linear (matrix) equation:

$$\mathbf{Ax} = fx(\mathbf{x}, \mathbf{y}) \qquad (6.32)$$

where $fx(\mathbf{x}, \mathbf{y})$ is the first-order differential of the edge magnitude along the x axis and where

$$\mathbf{A} = \begin{bmatrix} c_1 & d_1 & e_1 & 0 & . \, . & a_1 & b_1 \\ b_2 & c_2 & d_2 & e_2 & 0 & . \, . & a_2 \\ a_3 & b_3 & c_3 & d_3 & e_3 & 0 & \\ \vdots & \vdots & \vdots & \vdots & \vdots & & \\ e_{s-1} & 0 & . \, . & a_{s-1} & b_{s-1} & c_{s-1} & d_{s-1} \\ d_s & e_s & 0 & . \, . & a_s & b_s & c_s \end{bmatrix}$$

Similarly, by analysis of Equation 6.29 we obtain:

$$\mathbf{Ay} = fy(\mathbf{x}, \mathbf{y}) \tag{6.33}$$

where $fy(\mathbf{x}, \mathbf{y})$ is the first-order difference of the edge magnitude along the y axis. These equations can be solved iteratively to provide a new vector $\mathbf{v}^{\langle i+1 \rangle}$ from an initial vector $\mathbf{v}^{\langle i \rangle}$ where i is an evolution index. The iterative solution is

$$\frac{(\mathbf{x}^{\langle i+1 \rangle} - \mathbf{x}^{\langle i \rangle})}{\Delta} + \mathbf{Ax}^{\langle i+1 \rangle} = fx(\mathbf{x}^{\langle i \rangle}, \mathbf{y}^{\langle i \rangle}) \tag{6.34}$$

where the control factor Δ is a scalar chosen to control convergence. The control factor, Δ, actually controls the rate of evolution of the snake: large values make the snake move quickly, small values make for slow movement. As usual, fast movement implies that the snake can pass over features of interest without noticing them, whereas slow movement can be rather tedious. So the appropriate choice for Δ is again a compromise, this time between selectivity and time. The formulation for the vector of y co-ordinates is:

$$\frac{(\mathbf{y}^{\langle i+1 \rangle} - \mathbf{y}^{\langle i \rangle})}{\Delta} + \mathbf{Ay}^{\langle i+1 \rangle} = fy(\mathbf{x}^{\langle i \rangle}, \mathbf{y}^{\langle i \rangle}) \tag{6.35}$$

By rearrangement, this gives the final pair of equations that can be used iteratively to evolve a contour; the complete snake solution is then:

$$\mathbf{x}^{\langle i+1 \rangle} = \left(\mathbf{A} + \frac{1}{\Delta} \mathbf{I} \right)^{-1} \left(\frac{1}{\Delta} \mathbf{x}^{\langle i \rangle} + fx(\mathbf{x}^{\langle i \rangle}, \mathbf{y}^{\langle i \rangle}) \right) \tag{6.36}$$

where $\mathbf{I}$ is the identity matrix. This implies that the new set of x co-ordinates is a weighted sum of the initial set of contour points and the image information. The fraction is calculated according to specified snake properties, the values chosen for α and β. For the y co-ordinates we have

$$\mathbf{y}^{\langle i+1 \rangle} = \left(\mathbf{A} + \frac{1}{\Delta} \mathbf{I} \right)^{-1} \left(\frac{1}{\Delta} \mathbf{y}^{\langle i \rangle} + fy(\mathbf{x}^{\langle i \rangle}, \mathbf{y}^{\langle i \rangle}) \right) \tag{6.37}$$

The new set of contour points then becomes the starting set for the *next* iteration. Note that this is a continuous formulation, as opposed to the discrete (Greedy) implementation. One *penalty* is the need for matrix inversion, affecting speed. Clearly, the benefits are that co-ordinates are calculated as *real* functions and the *complete* set of new contour points is provided at each iteration. The result of implementing the complete solution is illustrated in Figure **6.7**. The initialisation, Figure **6.7**(a), is the same as for the Greedy algorithm, but with 32 contour points. At the first iteration, Figure **6.7**(b), the contour begins to shrink and moves towards the eye's iris. By the sixth iteration, Figure **6.7**(c) some of the contour points have snagged on strong edge data, particularly in the upper part of the contour. At this point, however, the excessive curvature becomes inadmissible, and the contour releases these points to achieve a smooth contour again, one which is better matched to the edge data and the chosen snake features. Finally, Figure **6.7**(e) is where the contour ceases to move. Part of the contour has been snagged on strong edge data in the eyebrow whereas the remainder of the contour matches the chosen feature well.

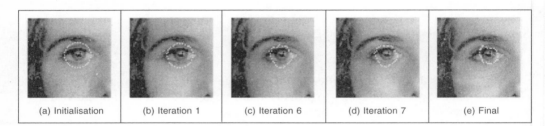

| (a) Initialisation | (b) Iteration 1 | (c) Iteration 6 | (d) Iteration 7 | (e) Final |

Figure 6.7 Illustrating the evolution of a complete snake

Clearly, a different solution could be obtained by using different values for the snake parameters; in application the choice of values for α, β and Δ must be made very carefully. In fact, this is part of the difficulty in using snakes for practical feature extraction; a further difficulty is that the result depends on where the initial contour is placed. These difficulties are called *parameterisation* and *initialisation*, respectively. These problems have motivated much research and development.

6.3.4 Other snake approaches

There are many further considerations to implementing snakes and there is a great wealth of material. One consideration is that we have only considered *closed* contours. There are, naturally, *open contours*. These require slight difference in formulation for the Kass snake (Waite, 1990) and only minor modification for implementation in the Greedy algorithm. One difficulty with the Greedy algorithm is its sensitivity to noise due to its local neighbourhood action. Also, the Greedy algorithm can end up in an oscillatory position where the final contour simply jumps between two equally attractive energy minima. One solution (Lai, 1994) resolved this difficulty by increasing the size of the snake neighbourhood, but this incurs much greater complexity. In order to allow snakes to *expand*, as opposed to contract a *normal force* can be included which inflates a snake and pushes it over unattractive features (Cohen, 1991; Cohen, 1993). The force is implemented by addition of

$$F_{\text{normal}} = \rho \mathbf{n}(s) \tag{6.38}$$

to the evolution equation, where $\mathbf{n}(s)$ is the normal force and ρ weights its effect. This is inherently sensitive to the magnitude of the normal force that, if too large, can force the contour to pass over features of interest. Another way to allow expansion is to modify the elasticity constraint (Berger, 1991) so that the internal energy becomes

$$E_{\text{int}} = \alpha(s) \left(\left| \frac{d\mathbf{v}(s)}{ds} \right|^2 - (L + \varepsilon) \right)^2 + \beta(s) \left| \frac{d^2\mathbf{v}(s)}{ds^2} \right|^2 \tag{6.39}$$

where the length adjustment ε when positive, $\varepsilon > 0$, and added to the contour length L causes the contour to expand. When negative, $\varepsilon < 0$, this causes the length to reduce and so the contour contracts. To avoid imbalance due to the contraction force, the technique can be modified to remove it (by changing the continuity and curvature constraints) without losing the controlling properties of the internal forces (Xu, 1994) (and which, incidentally, allowed corners to form in the snake). This gives a contour no prejudice to expansion or contraction as required. The technique allowed for integration of prior shape knowledge; methods have also been developed to allow *local shape* to influence contour evolution (Williams, 1992; Berger, 1991).

Some snake approaches have included factors that attract contours to regions using statistical models (Ronfard, 1994) or texture (Ivins, 1995), to complement operators that combine edge detection with region-growing. Also, the snake model can be generalised to higher dimensions and there are 3D snake *surfaces* (Wang, 1992; Cohen, 1992). Finally, an approach has introduced snakes for moving objects, by including velocity (Peterfreund, 1999).

6.3.5 Further snake developments

Snakes have been formulated not only to include local shape, but also phrased in terms of *regularisation* (Lai, 1995) where a single parameter controls snake evolution, emphasising a snake's natural compromise between its own forces and the image forces. Regularisation involves using a single parameter to control the balance between the external and the internal forces. Given a regularisation parameter λ, the snake energy of Equation 6.7 can be given as

$$E_{\text{snake}}(\mathbf{v}(s)) = \int_{s=0}^{1} \{ \lambda E_{\text{int}}(\mathbf{v}(s)) + (1 - \lambda) E_{\text{image}}(\mathbf{v}(s)) \} \, ds \tag{6.40}$$

Clearly, if $\lambda = 1$ then the snake will use the internal energy only whereas if $\lambda = 0$, then the snake will be attracted to the selected image function only. Usually, regularisation concerns selecting a value in between zero and one guided, say, by knowledge of the likely confidence in the edge information. In fact, Lai's approach calculates the regularisation parameter at contour points as

$$\lambda_i = \frac{\sigma_\eta^2}{\sigma_i^2 + \sigma_\eta^2} \tag{6.41}$$

where σ_i^2 appears to be the variance of the point i and σ_η^2 is the variance of the noise at the point (even digging into Lai's PhD thesis provided no explicit clues here, save that 'these parameters may be learned from training samples' – if this is impossible a procedure can be invoked). As before, λ_i lies between zero and one, and where the variances are bounded as

$$\frac{1}{\sigma_i^2} + \frac{1}{\sigma_\eta^2} = 1 \tag{6.42}$$

This does actually link these *generalised* active contour models to an approach we shall meet later, where the target shape is extracted conditional upon its expected variation. Lai's approach also addressed *initialisation*, and showed how a GHT could be used to initialise an active contour and built into the extraction process. There is, however, natural limitation on using a single contour for extraction, since it is never known precisely where to stop.

In fact, many of the problems with initialisation with active contours can be resolved by using a *dual contour* approach (Gunn, 1997) that also includes local shape and regularisation. This approach aims to enclose the target shape within an inner and an outer contour. The outer contour *contracts* whilst the inner contour *expands*. A balance is struck between the two contours to allow them to allow the target shape to be extracted. Gunn showed how shapes could be extracted successfully, even when the target contour was far from the two initial contours. Further, the technique was shown to provide better immunity to initialisation, in comparison with the results of a Kass snake, and Xu's approach.

Later, the dual approach was extended to a discrete space (Gunn, 1998), using an established search algorithm. The search used dynamic programming which has already been used within active contours to find a global solution (Lai, 1995) and in matching and tracking contours (Geiger, 1995). Although only relatively recent, Gunn's approach has already been used within an enormous study (using a database of over 20 000 images no less) on automated cell segmentation for cervical cancer screening (Bamford, 1998), achieving more than 99% accurate segmentation. The approach is formulated as a discrete search using a dual contour approach, illustrated in Figure **6.8**. The inner and the outer contour aim to be inside and outside the target shape, respectively. The space between the inner and the outer contour is divided into lines (like the spokes on the wheel of a bicycle) and M points are taken along each of the N lines. We then have a grid of $M \times N$ points, in which the target contour (shape) is expected to lie. The full lattice of points is shown in Figure **6.9**(a). Should we need higher resolution, then we can choose large values of M and N, but this in turn implies more computational effort. One can envisage strategies which allow for

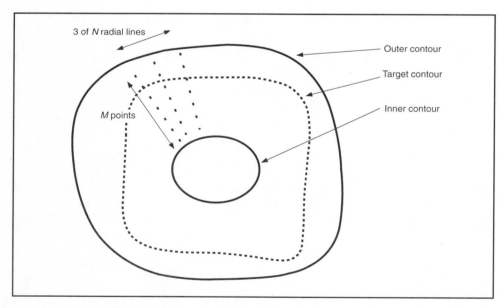

Figure 6.8 Discrete dual contour point space

linearisation of the coverage of the space in between the two contours, but these can make implementation much more complex.

The approach again uses *regularisation*, where the snake energy is a discrete form to Equation 6.40 so the energy at a snake point (unlike earlier formulations, e.g. Equation 6.11) is

$$E(\mathbf{v}_i) = \lambda E_{\text{int}}(\mathbf{v}_i) + (1 - \lambda)E_{\text{ext}}(\mathbf{v}_i) \tag{6.43}$$

where the internal energy is formulated as

$$E_{\text{int}}(\mathbf{v}_i) = \left(\frac{|\mathbf{v}_{i+1} - 2\mathbf{v}_i + \mathbf{v}_{i-1}|}{|\mathbf{v}_{i+1} - \mathbf{v}_{i-1}|}\right)^2 \tag{6.44}$$

The numerator expresses the curvature, seen earlier in the Greedy formulation. It is scaled by a factor that ensures the contour is *scale invariant* with no *prejudice* as to the *size* of the contour. If there is no prejudice, the contour will be attracted to smooth contours, given appropriate choice of the regularisation parameter. As such, the formulation is simply a more sophisticated version of the Greedy algorithm, dispensing with several factors of limited value (such as the need to choose values for three weighting parameters: one only now need be chosen; the elasticity constraint has also been removed, and that is perhaps more debatable). The interest here is that the search for the optimal contour is constrained to be between two contours, as in Figure **6.8**. By way of a snake's formulation, we seek the contour with minimum energy. When this is applied to a contour which is bounded, then we seek a minimum cost path. This is a natural target for the well-known Viterbi (dynamic programming) algorithm (for its application in vision, see, for example, Geiger (1995)). This is designed precisely to do this: to find a minimum cost path within specified bounds. In order to formulate it by dynamic programming we seek a cost function to be minimised. When we formulate a cost function C between one snake element and the next as

$$C_i(\mathbf{v}_{i+1}, \mathbf{v}_i) = \min[C_{i-1}(\mathbf{v}_i, \mathbf{v}_{i-1}) + \lambda E_{\text{int}}(\mathbf{v}_i) + (1 - \lambda)E_{\text{ext}}(\mathbf{v}_i)] \tag{6.45}$$

In this way, we should be able to choose a path through a set of snakes that minimises the total energy, formed by the compromise between internal and external energy at that point, together with the path that led to the point. As such, we will need to store the energies at points within the matrix, which corresponds directly to the earlier tessellation. We also require a position matrix to store for each stage (i) the position ($\mathbf{v}_{i-1}$) that minimises the cost function at that stage ($C_i(\mathbf{v}_{i+1}, \mathbf{v}_i)$). This also needs initialisation to set the first point, $C_1(\mathbf{v}_1, \mathbf{v}_0) = 0$. Given a *closed* contour (one which is completely joined together) then for an arbitrary start point, we separate the optimisation routine to determine the best starting and end points for the contour. The full search space is illustrated in Figure **6.9**(a). Ideally, this should be searched for a closed contour, the target contour of Figure **6.8**. It is computationally less demanding to consider an *open* contour, where the ends do not join. We can approximate a closed contour by considering it to be an open contour in *two* stages. In the first stage, Figure **6.9**(b), the mid-points of the two lines at the start and end are taken as the starting conditions. In the second stage, Figure **6.9**(c), the points determined by dynamic programming half way round the contour (i.e. for two lines at $N/2$) are taken as the start and the end points for a new open-contour dynamic programming search, which then optimises the contour from these points. The premise is that the points half way round the contour will be at, or close to, their optimal position after the first stage and it is the points at, or near, the starting points in the first stage that require refinement. This reduces the computational requirement by a factor of M^2.

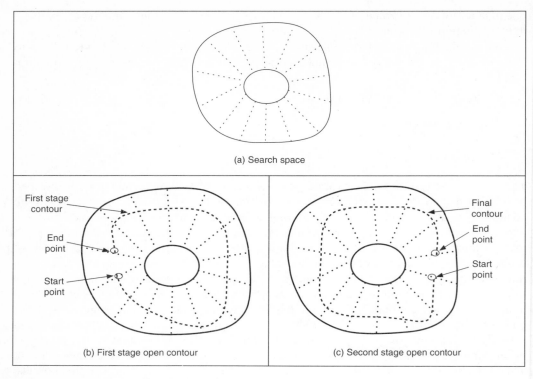

Figure 6.9 Discrete dual contour point space

The technique was originally demonstrated to extract the face boundary, for feature extraction within automatic face recognition, as illustrated in Figure **6.10**. The outer boundary (Figure **6.10**(a)) was extracted using a convex hull which in turn initialised an inner and an outer contour (Figure **6.10**(b)). The final extraction by the dual discrete contour is the boundary of facial skin, Figure **6.10**(c). The number of points in the mesh naturally limits the accuracy with which the final contour is extracted, but application could naturally be followed by use of a continuous Kass snake to improve final resolution. In fact, it was shown that human faces could be discriminated by the contour extracted by this technique, though the study highlighted potential difficulty with facial organs and illumination. As already mentioned, it was later deployed in cell analysis where the inner and the outer contours were derived by analysis of the stained-cell image.

Snakes, or evolutionary approaches to shape extraction, remain an attractive and stimulating area of research, so as ever it is well worth studying the literature to find new, accurate, techniques with high performance and low computational cost. We shall now move to determining *symmetry* which, though more a low-level operation, actually uses evidence gathering in some implementations thus motivating its later inclusion.

6.4 Discrete symmetry operator

The *discrete symmetry operator* (Reisfeld, 1995) uses a totally different basis to find

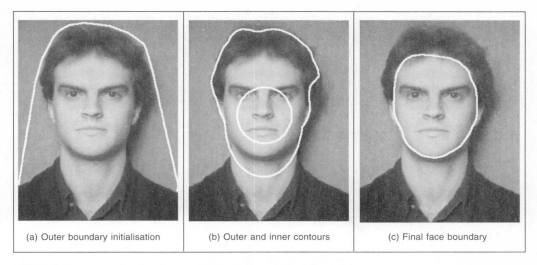

| (a) Outer boundary initialisation | (b) Outer and inner contours | (c) Final face boundary |

Figure 6.10   Extracting the face outline by a discrete dual contour

shapes. Rather than rely on finding the border of a shape, or its shape, it locates features according to their *symmetrical properties*. The operator essentially forms an *accumulator* of points that are measures of symmetry between image points. Pairs of image points are attributed symmetry values that are derived from a *distance* weighting function, a *phase* weighting function and the *edge* magnitude at each of the pair of points. The distance weighting function controls the scope of the function, to control whether points which are more distant contribute in a similar manner to those which are close together. The phase weighting function shows when edge vectors at the pair of points point to each other. The symmetry accumulation is at the centre of each pair of points. In this way the accumulator measures the degree of symmetry between image points, controlled by the edge strength. The distance weighting function D is

$$D(i, j, \sigma) = \frac{1}{\sqrt{2\pi\sigma}} e^{-\frac{|\mathbf{P}_i - \mathbf{P}_j|}{2\sigma}} \tag{6.46}$$

where i and j are the indices to two image points $\mathbf{P}_i$ and $\mathbf{P}_j$ and the deviation σ controls the scope of the function, by scaling the contribution of the distance between the points in the exponential function. A small value for the deviation σ implies local operation and detection of local symmetry. Larger values of σ imply that points that are further apart contribute to the accumulation process, as well as ones that are close together. In, say, application to the image of a face, large and small values of σ will aim for the whole face or the eyes, respectively.

The effect of the value of σ on the distance weighting function is illustrated in Figure **6.11**. Figure **6.11**(a) shows the effect of a small value for the deviation, $\sigma = 0.6$, and shows that the weighting is greatest for closely spaced points and drops rapidly for points with larger spacing. Larger values of σ imply that the distance weight drops less rapidly for points that are more widely spaced, as in Figure **6.11**(b) where $\sigma = 5$, allowing points which are spaced further apart to contribute to the measured symmetry. The phase weighting function P is

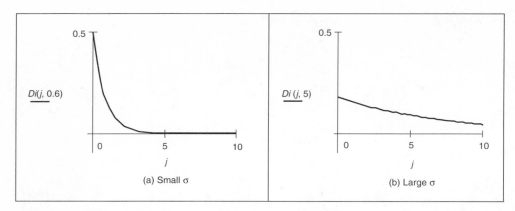

Figure 6.11 Effect of σ on distance weighting

$$P(i, j) = (1 - \cos(\theta_i + \theta_j - 2\alpha_{ij})) \times (1 - \cos(\theta_i - \theta_j)) \qquad (6.47)$$

where θ is the edge direction at the two points and where α_{ij} measures the direction of a line joining the two points:

$$\alpha_{ij} = \tan^{-1}\left(\frac{y(\mathbf{P}_j) - y(\mathbf{P}_i)}{x(\mathbf{P}_j) - x(\mathbf{P}_i)}\right) \qquad (6.48)$$

where $x(\mathbf{P}_i)$ and $y(\mathbf{P}_i)$ are the x and y co-ordinates of the point $\mathbf{P}_i$, respectively. This function is minimum when the edge direction at two points is in the same direction ($\theta_j = \theta_i$), and is a maximum when the edge direction is away from each other ($\theta_i = \theta_j + \pi$), along the line joining the two points, ($\theta_j = \alpha_{ij}$).

The effect of relative edge direction on phase weighting is illustrated in Figure **6.12** where Figure **6.12**(a) concerns two edge points that point towards each other and describes the effect on the phase weighting function by varying α_{ij}. This shows how the phase weight is maximum when the edge direction at the two points is along the line joining them, in this case when $\alpha_{ij} = 0$ and $\theta_i = 0$. Figure **6.12**(b) concerns one point with edge direction along the line joining two points, where the edge direction at the second point is varied. The phase weighting function is maximum when the edge direction at each point is towards each other, in this case when $| \theta_j | = \pi$.

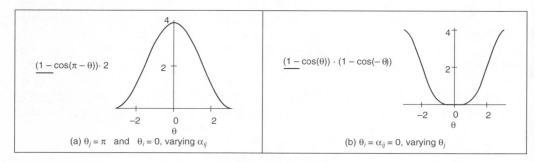

Figure 6.12 Effect of relative edge direction on phase weighting

The symmetry relation between two points is then defined as

$$C(i, j, \sigma) = D(i, j, \sigma) \times P(i, j) \times E(i) \times E(j) \tag{6.49}$$

where E is the edge magnitude expressed in logarithmic form as

$$E(i) = \log(1 + M(i)) \tag{6.50}$$

where M is the edge magnitude derived by application of an edge detection operator. The symmetry contribution of two points is accumulated at the mid-point of the line joining the two points. The total symmetry $S_{\mathbf{P}_m}$ at point $\mathbf{P}_m$ is the sum of the measured symmetry for all pairs of points which have their mid-point at $\mathbf{P}_m$, i.e. those points $\Gamma(\mathbf{P}_m)$ given by

$$\Gamma(\mathbf{P}_m) = \left[(i, j) \middle| \frac{\mathbf{P}_i + \mathbf{P}_j}{2} = \mathbf{P}_m \wedge i \neq j \right] \tag{6.51}$$

and the accumulated symmetry is then

$$S_{\mathbf{P}_m}(\sigma) = \sum_{i,j \in \Gamma(\mathbf{P}_m)} C(i, j, \sigma) \tag{6.52}$$

The result of applying the symmetry operator to two images is shown in Figure **6.13**, for small and large values of σ. Figures **6.13**(a) and (d) show the image of a square and the edge image of a heart, respectively, to which the symmetry operator was applied; Figures **6.13**(b) and (e) are for the symmetry operator with a *low* value for the deviation parameter,

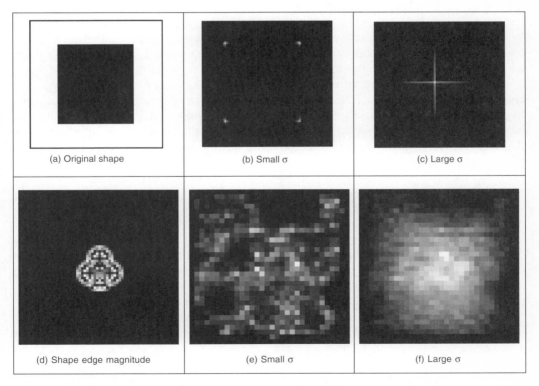

| (a) Original shape | (b) Small σ | (c) Large σ |

| (d) Shape edge magnitude | (e) Small σ | (f) Large σ |

Figure 6.13 Applying the symmetry operator for feature extraction

showing detection of areas with high localised symmetry; Figures **6.13**(c) and (e) are for a *large* value of the deviation parameter which detects overall symmetry and places a peak near the centre of the target shape. In Figures **6.13**(c) and (e) the symmetry operator acts as a corner detector where the edge direction is discontinuous. In Figure **6.13**(e), the discrete symmetry operator provides a peak close to the position of the accumulator space peak in the GHT. Note that if the reference point specified in the GHT is the centre of symmetry, the results of the discrete symmetry operator and the GHT would be the same for large values of deviation.

This is a discrete operator, recently a continuous version has been developed (Zabrodsky, 1995), and a later clarification (Kanatani, 1997) was aimed to address potential practical difficulty associated with hierarchy of symmetry (namely that symmetrical shapes have subsets of regions, also with symmetry). There have also been a number of sophisticated approaches to detection of skewed symmetry (Gross, 1994) and (Cham, 1995), with later extension to detection in orthographic projection (Vangool, 1995). Another generalisation addresses the problem of scale (Reisfeld, 1996) and extracts points of symmetry, together with scale. Recently (Parsons, 1999) a focusing ability has been added to the discrete symmetry operator by reformulating the distance weighting function. None as yet has alleviated the computational burden associated with the discrete symmetry operator. (Neither Matlab nor Mathcad is particularly advantageous here, the associated worksheets read in bitmaps of the results rather than calculate them!)

6.5 Flexible shape models

So far, our approaches to analysing shape have concerned a match to image data. This has concerned usually a match between a model (either a template that can deform, or a shape that can evolve) and a single image. An active contour is flexible, but its evolution is essentially controlled by local properties, such as the local curvature or edge strength. The chosen value for, or the likely range of, the parameters to weight these functionals may have been learnt by extensive testing on a database of images of similar type to the one used in application, or selected by experience. A completely different approach is to consider that if the database contains all possible *variations* of a shape, like its appearance or pose, then the database can form a model of the likely variation of that shape. As such, if we can incorporate this as a global constraint, whilst also guiding the match to the most likely version of a shape, then we have a deformable approach which is guided by the *statistics* of the likely variation in a shape. These approaches are termed *flexible templates* and use *global* shape constraints formulated from exemplars in training data.

This major new approach is called *active shape modelling*. The essence of this approach concerns a point model of a shape: the variation in these points is called the *point distribution model*. The chosen *landmark* points are labelled on the training images. The set of training images aims to capture all possible variations of the shape. Each point describes a particular point on the boundary, so order is important in the labelling process. Example choices for these points include where the curvature is high (e.g. the corner of an eye) or at the apex of an arch where the contrast is high (e.g. the top of an eyebrow). The statistics of the variations in position of these points describe the ways in which a shape can appear.

Naturally, there is a lot of data. If we choose lots of points and we have lots of training images, then we shall end up with an enormous number of points. That is where *principal components analysis* comes in as it can compress data into the most significant items.

Principal components analysis is an established mathematical tool unfortunately beyond the scope of this text, but help is available in *Numerical Recipes* (Press, 1992). Essentially, it rotates a co-ordinate system so as to achieve maximal discriminatory capability: we might not be able to see something if we view it from two distinct points, but if we view it from some point in between then it is quite clear. That is what is done here: the co-ordinate system is rotated so as to work out the most significant variations in the morass of data. Given a set of N training examples where each example is a set of n points, for the ith training example $\mathbf{x}_i$ we have

$$\mathbf{x}_i = (x_{1i}, x_{2i}, \ldots x_{ni}) \quad i \in 1, N \tag{6.53}$$

where x_{ki} is the kth variable in the ith training example. When this is applied to shapes, each element is the two co-ordinates of each point. The average is then computed over the whole set of training examples as

$$\overline{\mathbf{x}} = \frac{1}{N} \sum_{i=1}^{N} \mathbf{x}_i \tag{6.54}$$

The deviation of each example from the mean $\delta\mathbf{x}_i$ is then

$$\delta\mathbf{x}_i = \mathbf{x}_i - \overline{\mathbf{x}} \tag{6.55}$$

This difference reflects how far each example is from the mean at a point. The $2n \times 2n$ covariance matrix $\mathbf{S}$ shows how far all the differences are from the mean as

$$\mathbf{S} = \frac{1}{N} \sum_{i=1}^{N} \delta\mathbf{x}_i \delta\mathbf{x}_i^{\mathrm{T}} \tag{6.56}$$

Principal components analysis of this covariance matrix shows how much these examples, and hence a shape, can change. In fact, any of the exemplars of the shape can be approximated as

$$\mathbf{x}_i = \overline{\mathbf{x}} + \mathbf{P}\mathbf{w} \tag{6.57}$$

where $\mathbf{P} = (\mathbf{p}_1, \mathbf{p}_2, \ldots \mathbf{p}_t)$ is a matrix of the first t eigenvectors, and $\mathbf{w} = (w_1, w_2, \ldots w_t)^T$ is a corresponding vector of weights where each weight value controls the contribution of a particular eigenvector. Different values in $\mathbf{w}$ give different occurrences of the model, or shape. Given that these changes are within specified limits, then the new model or shape will be similar to the basic (mean) shape. This is because the modes of variation are described by the (unit) eigenvectors of $\mathbf{S}$, as

$$\mathbf{S}\mathbf{p}_k = \lambda_k \mathbf{p}_k \tag{6.58}$$

where λ_k denotes the eigenvalues and the eigenvectors obey orthogonality such that

$$\mathbf{p}_k \mathbf{p}_k^T = 1 \tag{6.59}$$

and where the eigenvalues are rank ordered such that $\lambda_k \geq \lambda_{k+1}$. Here, the largest eigenvalues correspond to the most significant modes of variation in the data. The proportion of the variance in the training data, corresponding to each eigenvector, is proportional to the corresponding eigenvalue. As such, a limited number of eigenvalues (and eigenvectors) can be used to encompass the majority of the data. The remaining eigenvalues (and eigenvectors) correspond to modes of variation that are hardly present in the data (like the proportion of very high frequency contribution of an image; we can reconstruct an image mainly from the low frequency components, as used in image coding). Note that in order to examine the statistics of the labelled landmark points over the training set applied to a new shape, the points need to be aligned and established procedures are available (Cootes, 1995).

The process of application (to find instances of the modelled shape) involves an iterative approach to bring about an increasing match between the points in the model and the image. This is achieved by examining regions around model points to determine the best nearby match. This provides estimates of the appropriate translation, scale rotation and eigenvectors to best fit the model to the data, and is repeated until the model converges to the data, when there is little change to the parameters. Since the models only change to better fit the data, and are controlled by the expected appearance of the shape, they were called active shape models. The application of an active shape model to find the brain stem in a magnetic Resonance image is shown in Figure **6.14** where the initial position is shown at the top left and the final extraction, after 14 iterations, is at the bottom right, with the results at four and eight iterations in between.

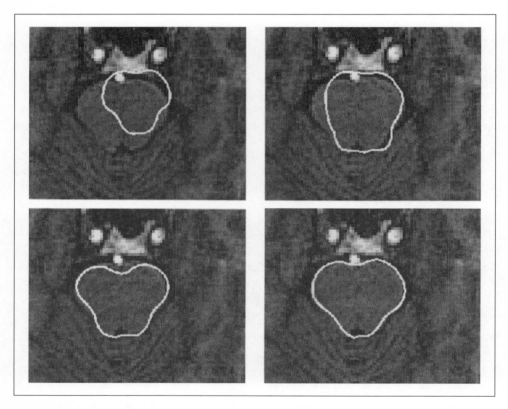

Figure 6.14 Finding the brain stem using an active shape model (© *BMVA Press 1997*)

Active shape models have been applied in face recognition (Lanitis, 1997), medical image analysis (Cootes, 1994) (including 3D analysis (Hill, 1994), and in industrial inspection (Cootes, 1995). Recently, a similar theory has been used to develop a new approach that incorporates texture, called *active appearance models* (AAMs) (Cootes, 1998). This approach again represents a shape as a set of landmark points and uses a set of training data to establish the potential range of variation in the shape. One major difference is that AAMs explicitly include texture and updates model parameters to move landmark points closer to image points by matching texture in an iterative search process. The essential differences between ASMs and AAMs include:

1. that ASMs use texture information local to a point, whereas AAMs use texture information in a whole region;
2. that ASMs seek to minimise the distance between model points and the corresponding image points, whereas AAMs seek to minimise distance between a synthesised model and a target image;
3. that AAMs search around the current position – typically along profiles normal to the boundary, whereas AAMs consider the image only at the current position.

A recent comparison (Cootes, 1999) has shown that although ASMs can be faster in implementation than AAMs, the AAMs can require fewer landmark points and can converge to a better result, especially in terms of texture (wherein the AAM was formulated). We await with interest further developments in these approaches to flexible shape modelling.

6.6 Further reading

The majority of further reading in finding shapes concerns papers, many of which have already been referenced. An excellent survey of the techniques used for *feature extraction* (including template matching, deformable templates etc.) can be found in Trier (1996) whilst a broader view was taken later (Jain, 1998). A comprehensive survey of flexible extractions from *medical* imagery (McInerney, 1996) reinforces the dominance of snakes in medical image analysis, to which they are particularly suited given a target of smooth shapes. (An excellent survey of history and progress of medical image analysis has appeared recently (Duncan, 2000).) Few of the textbooks devote much space to shape extraction and snakes are too recent a development to be included in many textbooks. One text alone is dedicated to shape analysis (Otterloo, 1991) and contains many discussions on symmetry. For implementation, Parker (1994) only includes C code for template matching and for the HT for lines, but no more. A visit to Dr Cootes' website suggests that a text might be on the way on flexible shape modelling, so we can await that with interest.

6.7 References

Bamford, P. and Lovell, B., Unsupervised Cell Nucleus Segmentation with Active Contours, *Signal Processing*, **71**, pp. 203–213, 1998

Berger, M. O., Towards Dynamic Adaption of Snake Contours, *Proc. 6th Int. Conf. on Image Analysis and Processing*, Como, Italy, pp. 47–54, 1991

Cham, T. J. and Cipolla, R., Symmetry Detection Through Local Skewed Symmetries, *Image and Vision Computing*, **13**(5), pp. 439–450, 1995

Cohen, L. D., NOTE: On Active Contour Models and Balloons, *CVGIP: Image Understanding*, **53**(2), pp. 211–218, 1991

Cohen, I., Cohen, L. D. and Ayache, N., Using Deformable Surfaces to Segment 3D

Images and Inter Differential Structures, *CVGIP: Image Understanding*, **56**(2), pp. 242–263, 1992

Cohen, L. D. and Cohen, I., Finite-Element Methods for Active Contour Models and Balloons for 2D and 3D Images, *IEEE Trans. on PAMI*, **15**(11), pp. 1131–1147, 1993

Cootes, T. F., Hill, A., Taylor, C. J. and Haslam, J., The Use of Active Shape Models for Locating Structures in Medical Images, *Image and Vision Computing*, **12**(6), pp. 355–366, 1994

Cootes, T. F., Taylor, C. J., Cooper, D. H. and Graham, J., Active Shape Models – their Training and Application, *CVIU*, **61**(1), pp. 38–59, 1995

Cootes, T., Edwards, G. J. and Taylor, C. J., A Comparative Evaluation of Active Appearance Model Algorithms, in: Lewis, P. J. and Nixon, M. S. (eds) *Proc. British Machine Vision Conference 1998 BMVC98*, **2,** pp. 680–689, 1998

Cootes, T. F., Edwards, G. J. and Taylor, C. J., Active Appearance Models, in*:* Burkhardt, H. and Neumann, B. (eds), *Proc. ECCV 98*, **2**, pp. 484–498, 1998

Cootes, T. F., Edwards, G. J. and Taylor, C. J., Comparing Active Shape Models with Active Appearance Models, in: Pridmore, T. and Elliman, D. (eds), *Proc. British Machine Vision Conference 1999 BMVC99*, **1**, pp. 173–182, 1998

Duncan, J. S. and Ayache, N., Medical Image Analysis: Progress Over Two Decades and the Challenges Ahead, *IEEE Trans. on PAMI*, **22**(1), pp. 85–106, 2000

Geiger, D., Gupta, A., Costa, L. A. and Vlontsos, J., Dynamical Programming for Detecting, Tracking and Matching Deformable Contours, *IEEE Trans. on PAMI*, **17**(3), pp. 294–302, 1995

Goldberg, D., *Genetic Algorithms in Search, Optimisation and Machine Learning*, Addison-Wesley, 1988

Gross, A. D. and Boult, T. E., Analysing Skewed Symmetries, *International Journal of Computer Vision*, **13**(1), pp. 91–111, 1994

Gunn, S. R. and Nixon, M. S., A Robust Snake Implementation: a Dual Active Contour, *IEEE Trans. on PAMI*, **19**(1), pp. 63–68, 1997

Gunn, S. R. and Nixon, M. S., Global and Local Active Contours for Head Boundary Extraction, *Int. J. Comp. Vis.*, **30**(1), pp. 43–54, 1998

Hill, A., Cootes, T. F., Taylor, C. J. and Lindley, K., Medical Image Interpretation: a Generic Approach using Deformable Templates, *Journal of Medical Informatics*, **19**(1), pp. 47–59, 1994

Jain, A. K., Zhong, Y. and Dubuisson-Jolly, M-P., Deformable Template Models: a Review, *Signal Processing*, **71**, pp. 109–129, 1998

Ivins, J. and Porrill, J., Active Region Models for Segmenting Textures and Colours, *Image and Vision Computing*, **13**(5), pp. 431–437, 1995

Kanatani, K., Comments on 'Symmetry as a Continuous Feature', *IEEE Trans. on PAMI*, **19**(3), pp. 246–247, 1997

Kass, M., Witkin, A. and Terzopoulos, D., Snakes: Active Contour Models, *Int. J. Comp Vis.*, **1**(4), pp. 321–331, 1988

Lai, K. F. and Chin, R. T., On Regularisation, Extraction and Initialisation of the Active Contour Model (Snakes), *Proc. 1st Asian Conference on Computer Vision*, pp. 542–545, 1994

Lai, K. F. and Chin, R. T., Deformable Contours – Modelling and Extraction, *IEEE Trans. on PAMI*, **17**(11), pp. 1084–1090, 1995

Lanitis, A., Taylor, C. J. and Cootes, T., Automatic Interpretation and Coding of Face Images using Flexible Models, *IEEE Trans. on PAMI*, **19**(7), pp. 743–755, 1997

McInerney, T. and Terzopolous, D., Deformable Models in Medical Image Analysis, a Survey, *Medical Image Analysis*, **1**(2), pp. 91–108, 1996

Parker, J. R., *Practical Computer Vision using C*, Wiley & Sons Inc., NY USA, 1994

Parsons, C. J. and Nixon, M. S., Introducing Focus in the Generalised Symmetry Operator, *IEEE Signal Processing Letters*, **6**(1), 1999

Peterfreund, N., Robust Tracking of Position and Velocity, *IEEE Trans. on PAMI*, **21**(6), pp. 564–569, 1999

Press, W. H., Teukolsky, S. A., Vettering, W. T. and Flannery, B. P., *Numerical Recipes in C – The Art of Scientific Computing*, 2nd Edition, Cambridge University Press, Cambridge UK, 1992

Reisfeld, D., Wolfson, H. and Yeshurun, Y., Context-Free Attentional Operators: the Generalised Symmetry Transform, *Int. J. Comp. Vis.*, **14**, pp. 119–130, 1995

Reisfeld, D., The Constrained Phase Congruency Feature Detector: Simultaneous Localization, Classification and Scale Determination, *Pattern Recognition Letters*, **17**(11), pp. 1161–1169, 1996

Ronfard, R., Region-based Strategies for Active Contour Models, *Int. J. Comp. Vision*, **13**(2), pp. 229–251, 1994

Vangool, L., Moons, T., Ungureanu, D. and Oosterlinck, A. The Characterisation and Detection of Skewed Symmetry, *Computer Vision and Image Understanding*, **61**(1), pp.138–150, 1995

Sonka, M., Hllavac, V. and Boyle, R., *Image Processing, Analysis and Computer Vision*, Chapman Hall, London UK, 1993

Trier, O. D., Jain, A. K. and Taxt, T., Feature Extraction Methods for Character Recognition – a Survey, *Pattern Recognition*, **29**(4), pp. 641–662, 1996

Wang, Y. F. and Wang, J. F., Surface Reconstruction using Deformable Models with Interior and Boundary Constraints, *IEEE Trans. on PAMI*, **14**(5), pp. 572–579, 1992

Waite, J. B. and Welsh, W. J., Head Boundary Location Using Snakes, *Br. Telecom Journal*, **8**(3), pp. 127–136, 1990

Williams, D. J. and Shah, M., A Fast Algorithm for Active Contours and Curvature Estimation, *CVGIP: Image Understanding*, **55**(1), pp. 14–26, 1992

Xu, G., Segawa, E. and Tsuji, S., Robust Active Contours with Insensitive Parameters, *Pattern Recognition* **27**(7), pp. 879–884, 1994

Yuille, A. L., Deformable Templates for Face Recognition, *Journal of Cognitive Neuroscience*, **3**(1), pp. 59–70, 1991

Zabrodsky, H., Peleg, S. and Avnir, D., Symmetry as a Continuous Feature, *IEEE Trans. on PAMI*, **17**(12), pp. 1154–1166, 1995

7

Object description

7.1 Overview

Objects are represented as a collection of pixels in an image. Thus, for purposes of recognition we need to describe the properties of groups of pixels. The description is often just a set of numbers – the object's *descriptors*. From these, we can compare and recognise objects by simply matching the descriptors of objects in an image against the descriptors of known objects. However, in order to be useful for recognition, descriptors should have four important properties. First, they should define a *complete set*. That is, two objects must have the same descriptors if and only if they have the same shape. Secondly, they should be *congruent*. As such, we should be able to recognise *similar* objects when they have *similar* descriptors. Thirdly, it is convenient that they have *invariant* properties. For example, *rotation* invariant descriptors will be useful for recognising objects whatever their *orientation*. Other important invariance properties naturally include scale and position and also invariance to affine and perspective changes. These last two properties are very important when recognising objects observed from different viewpoints. In addition to these three properties, the descriptors should be a *compact* set. Namely, a descriptor should represent the essence of an object in an efficient way. That is, it should only contain information about what makes an object unique, or different from the other objects. The quantity of information used to describe this characterisation should be less than the information necessary to have a complete description of the object itself. Unfortunately, there is no set of complete and compact descriptors to characterise general objects. Thus, the best recognition performance is obtained by carefully selected properties. As such, the process of recognition is strongly related to each particular application with a particular type of object.

In this chapter, we present the characterisation of objects by two forms of descriptors. These descriptors are summarised in Table **7.1**. *Region* and *shape* descriptors characterise

Table 7.1 Overview of Chapter 7

Object description	Shape boundary	Chain codes	
		Fourier descriptors	Cumulative angular function
			Elliptic descriptors
	Region	Basic	Area Perimeter Compactness Dispersion
		Moments	First order Centralised Zernike

an arrangement of pixels within the *area* and the arrangement of pixels in the *perimeter* or *boundary*, respectively. This region versus perimeter kind of representation is common in image analysis. For example, edges can be located by *region growing* (to label area) or by *differentiation* (to label perimeter), as covered in Chapter 4. There are actually many techniques that can be used to obtain descriptors of an object's boundary. Here, we shall just concentrate on three forms of descriptors: *chain codes* and two forms based on *Fourier characterisation*. For region descriptors we shall distinguish between basic descriptors and statistical descriptors defined by moments.

7.2 Boundary descriptions

7.2.1 Boundary and region

A region usually describes *contents* (or interior points) which are surrounded by a *boundary* (or perimeter) which is often called the region's *contour*. The form of the contour is generally referred to as its *shape*. A point can be defined to be on the boundary (contour) if it is part of the region and there is at least one pixel in its neighbourhood that is not part of the region. The boundary itself is usually found by contour following: we first find one point on the contour and then progress round the contour either in a clockwise direction, or anti-clockwise, finding the nearest (or next) contour point.

In order to define the interior points in a region and the points in the boundary, we need to consider neighbouring relationships between pixels. These relationships are described by means of *connectivity* rules. There are two common ways of defining connectivity: *4-way* (or 4-neighbourhood) where only immediate *neighbours* are analysed for connectivity; or *8-way* (or 8-neighbourhood) where all the eight pixels surrounding a chosen pixel are analysed for connectivity. These two types of connectivity are illustrated in Figure **7.1**. In this figure, the pixel is shown in light grey and its neighbours in dark grey. In 4-way connectivity, Figure **7.1**(a), a pixel has four neighbours in the directions north, east, south and west, its immediate neighbours. The four extra neighbours in 8-way connectivity, Figure **7.1**(b), are those in the directions north east, south east, south west and north west, the points at the *corners*.

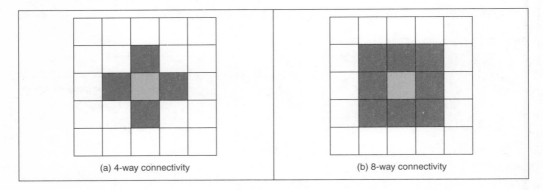

(a) 4-way connectivity   (b) 8-way connectivity

Figure 7.1   Main types of connectivity analysis

A boundary and a region can be defined using both types of connectivity and they are always *complementary*. That is, if the boundary pixels are connected in 4-way, then the region pixels will be connected in 8-way and vice versa. This relationship can be seen in the example shown in Figure **7.2**. In the example in this figure, the boundary is shown in dark grey and the region in light grey. We can observe that for a diagonal boundary, the 4-way connectivity gives a staircase boundary whereas 8-way connectivity gives a diagonal line formed from the points at the corners of the neighbourhood. Notice that all the pixels that form the region in Figure **7.2**(b) have 8-way connectivity, whilst the pixels in Figure **7.2**(c) have 4-way connectivity. This is complementary to the pixels in the border.

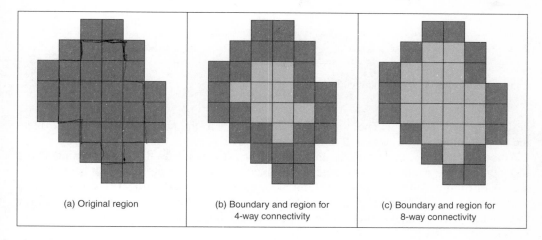

| (a) Original region | (b) Boundary and region for 4-way connectivity | (c) Boundary and region for 8-way connectivity |

Figure 7.2   Boundaries and regions

7.2.2   Chain codes

In order to obtain a representation of a contour, we can simply store the co-ordinates of a sequence of pixels in the image. Alternatively, we can just store the relative position between consecutive pixels. This is the basic idea behind *chain codes*. Chain codes are actually one of the oldest techniques in computer vision originally introduced in the 1960s (Freeman, 1961) (an excellent review came later (Freeman, 1974). Essentially, the set of pixels in the border of a shape is translated into a set of connections between them. Given a complete border, one that is a set of connected points, then starting from one pixel we need to be able to determine the direction in which the next pixel is to be found. Namely, the next pixel is one of the adjacent points in one of the major compass directions. Thus, the chain code is formed by concatenating the number that designates the direction of the next pixel. That is, given a pixel, the successive direction from one pixel to the next pixel becomes an element in the final code. This is repeated for each point until the start point is reached when the (closed) shape is completely analysed.

Directions in 4-way and 8-way connectivity can be assigned as shown in Figure **7.3**. The chain codes for the example region in Figure **7.2**(a) are shown in Figure **7.4**. Figure **7.4**(a) shows the chain code for the 4-way connectivity. In this case, we have that the direction from the start point to the next is south (i.e. code 2), so the first element of the chain code

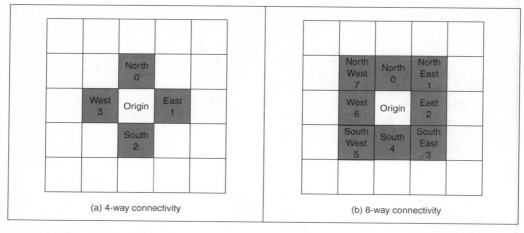

Figure 7.3 Connectivity in chain codes

describing the shape is 2. The direction from point P1 to the next, P2, is east (code 1) so the next element of the code is 1. The next point after P2 is P3 that is south giving a code 2. This coding is repeated until P23 that is connected eastwards to the starting point, so the last element (the twenty-fourth element) of the code is 1. The code for 8-way connectivity shown in Figure **7.4**(b) is obtained in an analogous way, but the directions are assigned according to the definition in Figure **7.3**(b). Notice that the length of the code is shorter for this connectivity, given that the number of boundary points is smaller for 8-way connectivity than it is for 4-way.

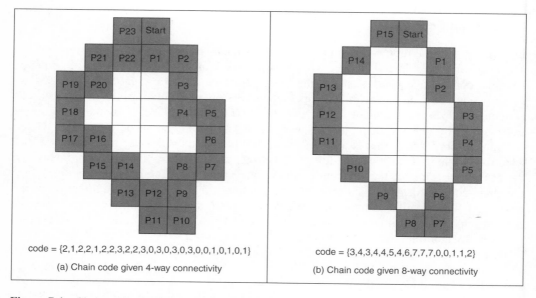

Figure 7.4 Chain codes by different connectivity

Clearly this code will be different when the start point changes. Accordingly, we need *start point invariance*. This can be achieved by considering the elements of the code to constitute the digits in an integer. Then, we can shift the digits *cyclically* (replacing the least significant digit with the most significant one, and shifting all other digits left one place). The smallest integer is returned as the *start point invariant chain code description*. This is illustrated in Figure **7.5** where the original chain code is that from the shape in Figure **7.4**. Here, the result of the first shift is given in Figure **7.5**(b) – this is equivalent to the code that would have been derived by using point P1 as the starting point. The result of two shifts, in Figure **7.5**(c) is the chain code equivalent to starting at point P2, but this is not a code corresponding to the minimum integer. The minimum integer code, as in Figure **7.5**(d), is the minimum of all the possible shifts and is actually the chain code which would have been derived by starting at point P8. That fact could not be used in application since we would need to find P8, naturally, it is much easier to shift to achieve a minimum integer.

In addition to starting point invariance, we can also obtain a code that does not change with *rotation*. This can be achieved by expressing the code as a difference of chain code: relative descriptions remove rotation dependence. Change of *scale* can complicate matters greatly, since we can end up with a set of points which is of different size to the original set. As such, the boundary needs to be *resampled* before coding. This is a tricky issue. Furthermore, *noise* can have drastic effects. If salt and pepper *noise* were to remove or add some points then the code would change. Clearly, such problems can lead to great difficulty with chain codes. However, their main virtue is their *simplicity* and as such they remain a popular technique for shape description. Further developments of chain codes have found application with *corner detectors* (Seeger, 1994; Liu, 1990). However, the need to be able to handle noise, the requirement of connectedness, and the local nature of description naturally motivates alternative approaches. Noise can be reduced by *filtering*, which naturally leads back to the *Fourier transform*, with the added advantage of a *global* description.

code = {3,4,3,4,4,5,4,6,7,7,7,0,0,1,1,2}	code = {4,3,4,4,5,4,6,7,7,7,0,0,1,1,2,3}
(a) Initial chain code	(b) Result of one shift
code = {3,4,4,5,4,6,7,7,7,0,0,1,1,2,3,4}	code = {0,0,1,1,2,3,4,3,4,4,5,4,6,7,7,7}
(c) Result of two shifts	(d) Minimum integer chain code

Figure 7.5   Start point invariance in chain codes

7.2.3   Fourier descriptors

Fourier descriptors, often attributed to early work by Cosgriff (1960), allow us to bring the power of Fourier theory to shape description. The main idea is to characterise a contour by a set of numbers that represent the frequency content of a whole shape. Based on frequency analysis we can select a *small* set of numbers (the Fourier coefficients) that describe a shape rather than any noise (i.e. the noise affecting the spatial position of the boundary pixels). The general recipe to obtain a Fourier description of the curve involves two main steps. First, we have to define a representation of a curve. Secondly, we expand it using Fourier theory. We can obtain alternative flavours by combining different curve representations and different Fourier expansions. Here, we shall consider Fourier descriptors of angular and complex contour representations. However, Fourier expansions can be developed for other curve representations (Van Otterloo, 1991).

In addition to the curve's definition, a factor that influences the development and properties of the description is the choice of Fourier expansion. If we consider that the trace of a curve defines a periodic function, then we can opt to use a Fourier series expansion. However, we could also consider that the description is not periodic. Thus, we could develop a representation based on the Fourier transform. In this case, we could use alternative Fourier integral definitions. Here, we will develop the presentation based on expansion in Fourier series. This is the common way used to describe shapes in pattern recognition.

It is important to notice that although a curve in an image is composed of discrete pixels, Fourier descriptors are developed for continuous curves. This is convenient since it leads to a discrete set of Fourier descriptors. Additionally, we should remember that the pixels in the image are actually the sampled points of a continuous curve in the scene. However, the formulation leads to the definition of the integral of a continuous curve. In practice, we do not have a continuous curve, but a sampled version. Thus, the expansion is actually approximated by means of numerical integration.

7.2.3.1 Basis of Fourier descriptors

In the most basic form, the co-ordinates of boundary pixels are x and y point co-ordinates. A Fourier description of these essentially gives the set of spatial frequencies that fit the boundary points. The *first* element of the Fourier components (the d.c. component) is simply the average value of the x and y co-ordinates, giving the co-ordinates of the centre point of the boundary, expressed in complex form. The *second* component essentially gives the radius of the circle that best fits the points. Accordingly, a circle can be described by its zero- and first-order components (the d.c. component and first harmonic). The *higher* order components increasingly describe detail, as they are associated with higher frequencies.

This is illustrated in Figure **7.6**. Here, the Fourier description of the ellipse in Figure **7.6**(a) is the frequency components in Figure **7.6**(b), depicted in logarithmic form for purposes of display. The Fourier description has been obtained by using the ellipse boundary points' co-ordinates. Here we can see that the low order components dominate the description,

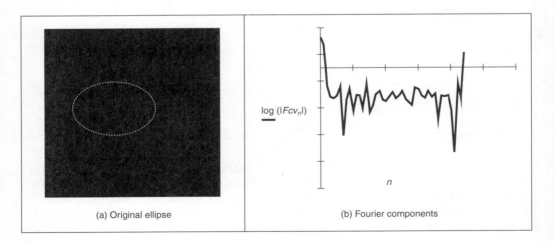

(a) Original ellipse   (b) Fourier components

Figure 7.6 An ellipse and its Fourier description

as to be expected for such a smooth shape. In this way, we can derive a set numbers that can be used to *recognise* the boundary of a shape: a similar ellipse should give a similar set of numbers whereas a completely different shape will result in a completely different set of numbers.

We do, however, need to check the result. One way is to take the descriptors of a circle, since the first harmonic should be the circle's radius. A better way though is to *reconstruct* the shape from its descriptors, if the reconstruction matches the original shape then the description would appear correct. Naturally, we can reconstruct a shape from this Fourier description since the descriptors are *regenerative*. The zero-order component gives the position (or origin) of a shape. The ellipse can be reconstructed by adding in all spatial components, to extend and compact the shape along the *x* and *y* axes, respectively. By this inversion, we return to the original ellipse. When we include the zero and first descriptor, then we reconstruct a circle, as expected, shown in Figure **7.7**(b). When we include all Fourier descriptors the reconstruction, Figure **7.7**(c), is very close to the original, Figure **7.7**(a), with slight difference due to discretisation effects.

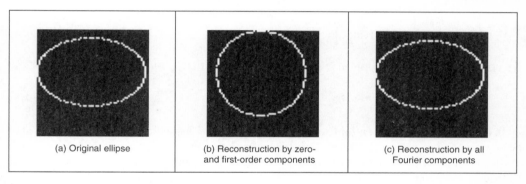

(a) Original ellipse	(b) Reconstruction by zero- and first-order components	(c) Reconstruction by all Fourier components

Figure 7.7 Reconstructing an ellipse from a Fourier description

But this is only an outline of the basis to Fourier descriptors, since we have yet to consider descriptors which give the same description whatever an object's position, scale and rotation. Here we have just considered an object's description that is achieved in a manner that allows for reconstruction. In order to develop practically useful descriptors, we shall need to consider more basic properties. As such, we first turn to the use of Fourier theory for shape description.

7.2.3.2 Fourier expansion

In order to define a Fourier expansion, we can start by considering that a continuous curve $c(t)$ can be expressed as a summation of the form

$$c(t) = \sum_k c_k f_k(t) \tag{7.1}$$

where c_k define the coefficients of the expansion and the collection of functions and $f_k(t)$ define the basis functions. The expansion problem centres on finding the coefficients given a set of basis functions. This equation is very general and different basis functions can also be used. For example, $f_k(t)$ can be chosen such that the expansion defines a polynomial. Other bases define splines, Lagrange and Newton interpolant functions. A Fourier expansion represents periodic functions by a basis defined as a set of infinite complex exponentials. That is,

$$c(t) = \sum_{k=-\infty}^{\infty} c_k e^{jk\omega t} \tag{7.2}$$

Here, ω defines the fundamental frequency and it is equal to $T/2\pi$ where T is the period of the function. The main feature of the Fourier expansion is that it defines an orthogonal basis. This simply means that

$$\int_0^T f_k(t)f_j(t)\,dt = 0 \tag{7.3}$$

for $k \neq j$. This property is important for two main reasons. First, it ensures that the expansion does not contain redundant information (each coefficient is *unique* and contains no information about the other components). Secondly, it simplifies the computation of the coefficients. That is, in order to solve for c_k in Equation 7.1, we can simply multiply both sides by $f_k(t)$ and perform integration. Thus, the coefficients are given by

$$c_k = \int_0^T c(t)f_k(t)\,dt \bigg/ \int_0^T f_k^2(t)\,dt \tag{7.4}$$

By considering the definition in Equation 7.2 we have that

$$c_k = \frac{1}{T} \int_0^T c(t)e^{-jk\omega t}\,dt \tag{7.5}$$

In addition to the exponential form given in Equation 7.2, the Fourier expansion can also be expressed in trigonometric form. This form shows that the Fourier expansion corresponds to the summation of trigonometric functions that increase in frequency. It can be obtained by considering that

$$c(t) = c_0 + \sum_{k=1}^{\infty} (c_k e^{jk\omega t} + c_{-k} e^{-jk\omega t}) \tag{7.6}$$

In this equation the values of $e^{jk\omega t}$ and $e^{-jk\omega t}$ define pairs of complex conjugate vectors. Thus c_k and c_{-k} describe a complex number and its conjugate. Let us define these numbers as

$$c_k = c_{k,1} - jc_{k,2} \quad \text{and} \quad c_{-k} = c_{k,1} + jc_{k,2} \tag{7.7}$$

By substitution of this definition in Equation 7.6 we obtain

$$c(t) = c_0 + 2\sum_{k=1}^{\infty} \left(c_{k,1}\left(\frac{e^{jk\omega t} + e^{-jk\omega t}}{2}\right) + jc_{k,2}\left(\frac{-e^{jk\omega t} + e^{-jk\omega t}}{2}\right) \right) \tag{7.8}$$

That is,

$$c(t) = c_0 + 2\sum_{k=1}^{\infty} (c_{k,1}\cos(k\omega t) + c_{k,2}\sin(k\omega t)) \tag{7.9}$$

If we define

$$a_k = 2c_{k,1} \quad \text{and} \quad b_k = 2c_{k,2} \tag{7.10}$$

then we obtain the standard trigonometric form given by

$$c(t) = \frac{a_0}{2} + \sum_{k=1}^{\infty} (a_k \cos(k\omega t) + b_k \sin(k\omega t)) \tag{7.11}$$

The coefficients of this expansion, a_k and b_k, are known as the *Fourier descriptors*. These control the amount of each frequency that contributes to make up the curve. Accordingly, these descriptors can be said to *describe* the curve since they do not have the same values for different curves. Notice that according to Equations 7.7 and 7.10 the coefficients of the trigonometric and exponential form are related to by

$$c_k = \frac{a_k - jb_k}{2} \quad \text{and} \quad c_{-k} = \frac{a_k + jb_k}{2} \tag{7.12}$$

The coefficients in Equation 7.11 can be obtained by considering the orthogonal property in Equation 7.3. Thus, one way to compute values for the descriptors is

$$a_k = \frac{2}{T} \int_0^T c(t) \cos(k\omega t)\, dt \quad \text{and} \quad b_k = \frac{2}{T} \int_0^T c(t) \sin(k\omega t)\, dt \tag{7.13}$$

In order to obtain the Fourier descriptors, a curve can be represented by the complex exponential form of Equation 7.2 or by the sin/cos relationship of Equation 7.11. The descriptors obtained by using either of the two definitions are equivalent, and they can be related by the definitions of Equation 7.12. Generally, Equation 7.13 is used to compute the coefficients since it has a more intuitive form. However, some works have considered the complex form (e.g. Granlund (1972)). The complex form provides an elegant development of rotation analysis.

7.2.3.3 Shift invariance

Chain codes required special attention to give start point invariance. Let us see if that is required here. The main question is whether the descriptors will change when the curve is shifted. In addition to Equations 7.2 and 7.11, a Fourier expansion can be written in another sinusoidal form. If we consider that

$$|c_k| = \sqrt{a_k^2 + b_k^2} \quad \text{and} \quad \varphi_k = \tan^{-1}(b_k / a_k) \tag{7.14}$$

then the Fourier expansion can be written as

$$c(t) = \frac{a_0}{2} + \sum_{k=0}^{\infty} |c_k| \cos(k\omega t + \varphi_k) \tag{7.15}$$

Here $|c_k|$ is the *amplitude* and φ_k is the *phase* of the Fourier coefficient. An important property of the Fourier expansion is that $|c_k|$ does not change when the function $c(t)$ is shifted (i.e. translated), as in Section 2.6.1. This can be observed by considering the definition of Equation 7.13 for a shifted curve $c(t + \alpha)$. Here, α represents the shift value. Thus,

$$a'_k = \frac{2}{T} \int_0^T c(t' + \alpha) \cos(k\omega t')\, dt \quad \text{and} \quad b'_k = \frac{2}{T} \int_0^T c(t' + \alpha) \sin(k\omega t')\, dt \tag{7.16}$$

By defining a change of variable by $t = t' + \alpha$, we have

$$a'_k = \frac{2}{T} \int_0^T c(t) \cos(k\omega t - k\omega\alpha)\, dt \quad \text{and} \quad b'_k = \frac{2}{T} \int_0^T c(t) \sin(k\omega t - k\omega\alpha)\, dt \tag{7.17}$$

After some algebraic manipulation we obtain

$$a'_k = a_k \cos(k\omega\alpha) + b_k \sin(k\omega\alpha) \quad \text{and} \quad b'_k = b_k \cos(k\omega\alpha) - a_k \sin(k\omega\alpha)$$

(7.18)

The amplitude $|c'_k|$ is given by

$$|c'_k| = \sqrt{(a_k \cos(k\omega\alpha) + b_k \sin(k\omega\alpha))^2 + (b_k \cos(k\omega\alpha) - a_k \sin(k\omega\alpha))^2}$$

(7.19)

That is,

$$|c'_k| = \sqrt{a_k^2 + b_k^2}$$

(7.20)

Thus, the amplitude is independent of the shift α. Although shift invariance could be incorrectly related to translation invariance, actually, as we shall see, this property is related to rotation invariance in shape description.

7.2.3.4 *Discrete computation*

Before defining Fourier descriptors, we must consider the numerical procedure necessary to obtain the Fourier coefficients of a curve. The problem is that Equations 7.11 and 7.13 are defined for a *continuous* curve. However, given the discrete nature of the image, the curve $c(t)$ will be described by a collection of *points*. This discretisation has two important effects. First, it limits the number of frequencies in the expansion. Secondly, it forces numerical approximation to the integral defining the coefficients.

Figure **7.8** shows an example of a discrete approximation of a curve. Figure **7.8**(a) shows a continuous curve in a period, or interval, T. Figure **7.8**(b) shows the approximation of the curve by a set of discrete points. If we try to obtain the curve from the sampled points, we will find that the sampling process reduces the amount of detail. According to the Nyquist theorem, the maximum frequency f_c in a function is related to the sample period τ by

$$\tau = \frac{1}{2 f_c}$$

(7.21)

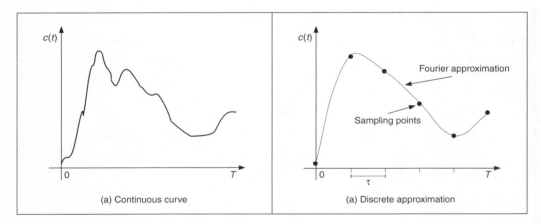

(a) Continuous curve

(a) Discrete approximation

Figure 7.8   Example of a discrete approximation

Thus, if we have m sampling points, then the sampling period is equal to $\tau = T/m$. Accordingly, the maximum frequency in the approximation is given by

$$f_c = \frac{m}{2T} \qquad (7.22)$$

Each term in Equation 7.11 defines a trigonometric function at frequency $f_k = k/T$. By comparing this frequency with the relationship in Equation 7.15, we have that the maximum frequency is obtained when

$$k = \frac{m}{2} \qquad (7.23)$$

Thus, in order to define a smooth curve that passes through the m regularly-sampled points, we need to consider only $m/2$ coefficients. The other coefficients define frequencies higher than the maximum frequency. Accordingly, the Fourier expansion can be redefined as

$$c(t) = \frac{a_0}{2} + \sum_{k=1}^{m/2} (a_k \cos(k\omega t) + b_k \sin(k\omega t)) \qquad (7.24)$$

In practice, Fourier descriptors are computed for fewer coefficients than the limit of $m/2$. This is because the low frequency components provide most of the features of a shape. High frequencies are easily affected by noise and only represent detail that is of little value to recognition. We can interpret Equation 7.22 the other way around: if we know the maximum frequency in the curve, then we can determine the appropriate number of samples. However, the fact that we consider $c(t)$ to define a continuous curve implies that in order to obtain the coefficients in Equation 7.13, we need to evaluate an integral of a continuous curve. The approximation of the integral is improved by increasing the sampling points. Thus, as a practical rule, in order to improve accuracy, we must try to have a large number of samples even if it is theoretically limited by the Nyquist theorem.

Our curve is only a set of discrete points. We want to maintain a continuous curve analysis in order to obtain a set of discrete coefficients. Thus, the only alternative is to approximate the coefficients by approximating the value of the integrals in Equation 7.13. We can approximate the value of the integral in several ways. The most straightforward approach is to use a Riemann sum. Figure **7.9** illustrates this approach. In Figure **7.9**(b), the integral is approximated as the summation of the rectangular areas. The middle point of each rectangle corresponds to each sampling point. Sampling points are defined at the points whose parameter is $t = i\tau$ where i is an integer between 1 and m. We consider that c_i defines the value of the function at the sampling point i. That is,

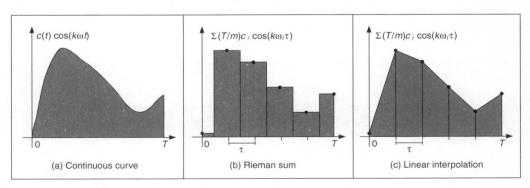

Figure 7.9   Integral approximation

$$c_i = c(i\tau) \tag{7.25}$$

Thus, the height of the rectangle for each pair of coefficients is given by $c_i \cos(k\omega i\tau)$ and $c_i \sin(k\omega i\tau)$. Each interval has a length $\tau = T/m$. Thus,

$$\int_0^T c(t) \cos(k\omega t)dt \approx \sum_{i=1}^{m} \frac{T}{m} c_i \cos(k\omega i\tau)$$

and $\quad \displaystyle\int_0^T c(t) \sin(k\omega t)dt \approx \sum_{i=1}^{m} \frac{T}{m} c_i \sin(k\omega i\tau) \tag{7.26}$

Accordingly, the Fourier coefficients are given by

$$a_k = \frac{2}{m} \sum_{i=1}^{m} c_i \cos(k\omega i\tau) \quad \text{and} \quad b_k = \frac{2}{m} \sum_{i=1}^{m} c_i \sin(k\omega i\tau) \tag{7.27}$$

Here, the error due to the discrete computation will be reduced with increase in the number of points used to approximate the curve. These equations actually correspond to a linear approximation to the integral. This approximation is shown in Figure **7.9**(c). In this case, the integral is given by the summation of the trapezoidal areas. The sum of these areas leads to Equation 7.26. Notice that b_0 is zero and a_0 is twice the average of the c_i values. Thus, the first term in Equation 7.24 is the average (or centre of gravity) of the curve.

7.2.3.5 Cumulative angular function

Fourier descriptors can be obtained by using many boundary representations. In a straightforward approach we could consider, for example, that t and $c(t)$ define the angle and modulus of a polar parameterisation of the boundary. However, this representation is not very general. For some curves, the polar form does not define a single valued curve, and thus we cannot apply Fourier expansions. A more general description of curves can be obtained by using the angular function parameterisation. This function was already defined in Chapter 4 in the discussion about curvature.

The angular function $\varphi(s)$ measures the angular direction of the tangent line as a function of arc length. Figure 7.10 illustrates the angular direction at a point in a curve. In Cosgriff (1960) this angular function was used to obtain a set of Fourier descriptors. However, this first approach to Fourier characterisation has some undesirable properties. The main problem is that the angular function has discontinuities even for smooth curves. This is because the angular direction is bounded from zero to 2π. Thus, the function has *discontinuities* when the angular direction increases to a value of more than 2π or decreases to be less than zero (since it will change abruptly to remain within bounds). In Zahn and Roskies' approach (Zahn, 1972), this problem is eliminated by considering a normalised form of the cumulative angular function.

The *cumulative angular function* at a point in the curve is defined as the amount of angular change from the starting point. It is called *cumulative*, since it represents the summation of the angular change to each point. Angular change is given by the derivative of the angular function $\varphi(s)$. We discussed in Chapter 4 that this derivative corresponds to the curvature $\kappa(s)$. Thus, the cumulative angular function at the point given by s can be defined as

$$\gamma(s) = \int_0^s \kappa(r)dr - \kappa(0) \tag{7.28}$$

Here, the parameter s takes values from zero to L (i.e. the length of the curve). Thus, the initial and final values of the function are $\gamma(0) = 0$ and $\gamma(L) = -2\pi$, respectively. It is important to notice that in order to obtain the final value of -2π, the curve must be traced in a clockwise direction. Figure **7.10** illustrates the relation between the angular function and the cumulative angular function. In the figure, $z(0)$ defines the initial point in the curve. The value of $\gamma(s)$ is given by the angle formed by the inclination of the tangent to $z(0)$ and that of the tangent to the point $z(s)$. If we move the point $z(s)$ along the curve, this angle will change until it reaches the value of -2π. In Equation 7.28, the cumulative angle is obtained by adding the small angular increments for each point.

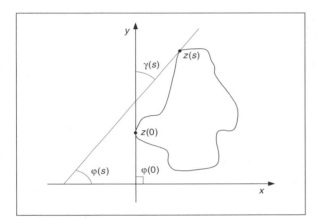

Figure 7.10 Angular direction

The cumulative angular function avoids the discontinuities of the angular function. However, it still has two problems. First, it has a discontinuity at the end. Secondly, its value depends on the length of curve analysed. These problems can be solved by defining the normalised function $\gamma^*(t)$ where

$$\gamma^*(t) = \gamma\left(\frac{L}{2\pi}t\right) + t \tag{7.29}$$

Here t takes values from 0 to 2π. The factor $L/2\pi$ normalises the angular function such that it does not change when the curve is scaled. That is, when $t = 2\pi$, the function evaluates the final point of the function $\gamma(s)$. The term t is included to avoid discontinuities at the end of the function (remember that the function is periodic). That is, it enforces $\gamma^*(0) = \gamma^*(2\pi) = 0$. Additionally, it causes the cumulative angle for a circle to be zero. This is consistent as a circle is generally considered the simplest curve and, intuitively, simple curves will have simple representations.

Figure **7.11** illustrates the definitions of the cumulative angular function with two examples. Figures **7.11**(b) to (d) define the angular functions for a circle in Figure **7.11**(a). Figures **7.11**(f) to (h) define the angular functions for the rose in Figure **7.11**(e). Figures **7.11**(b)

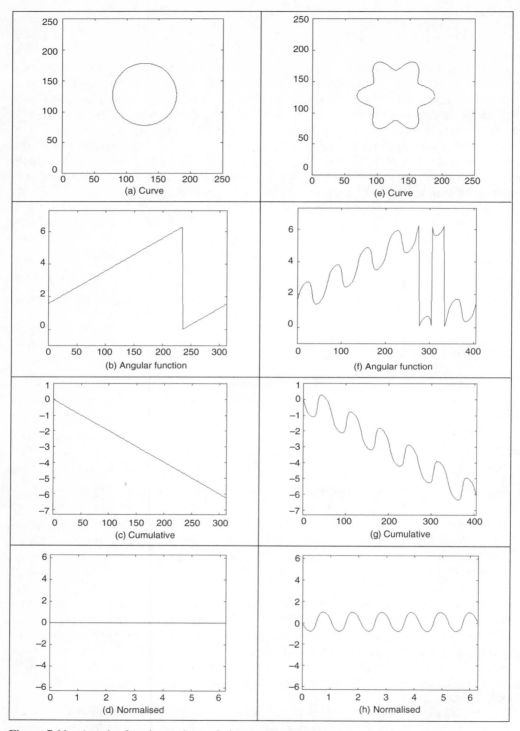

Figure 7.11   Angular function and cumulative angular function

and (f) define the angular function $\varphi(s)$. We can observe the typical toroidal form. Once the curve is greater than 2π there is a discontinuity whilst its value returns to zero. The position of the discontinuity actually depends on the selection of the starting point. The cumulative function $\gamma(s)$ shown in Figures **7.11**(c) and (g) inverts the function and eliminates discontinuities. However, the start and end points are not the same. If we consider that this function is periodic, then there is a discontinuity at the end of each period. The normalised form $\gamma^*(t)$ shown in Figures **7.11**(d) and (h) has no discontinuity and the period is normalised to 2π.

The normalised cumulative functions are very nice indeed. However, it is tricky to compute them from images. Additionally, since they are based on measures of changes in angle, they are very sensitive to noise and difficult to compute at inflexion points (e.g. corners). Code **7.1** illustrates the computation of the angular functions for a curve given by a sequence of pixels. The matrices X and Y store the co-ordinates of each pixel. The code has two important steps. First, the computation of the angular function stored in the matrix A. Generally, if we use only the neighbouring points to compute the angular function, then the resulting function is useless due to noise and discretisation errors. Thus, it is necessary to include a procedure that can obtain accurate measures. For purposes of illustration, in the presented code we average the position of pixels in order to filter out noise; however, other techniques such as the fitting process discussed in Section 4.7.2 can provide a suitable alternative. The second important step is the computation of the cumulative function. In this case, the increment in the angle cannot be computed as the simple difference between the current and precedent angular values. This will produce a discontinuous function. Thus, we need to consider the periodicity of the angles. In the code, this is achieved by checking the increment in the angle. If it is greater than a threshold, then we consider that the angle has exceeded the limits of zero or 2π.

Figure **7.12** shows an example of the angular functions computed using Code **7.1**, for a discrete curve. These are similar to those in Figures **7.11**(a) to (d), but show noise due to discretisation which produces a ragged effect on the computed values. The effects of noise will be reduced if we use more points to compute the average in the angular function. However, this reduces the level of detail in the curve. Additionally, it makes it more difficult to detect when the angle exceeds the limits of zero or 2π. In a Fourier expansion, noise will affect the coefficients of the high frequency components, as seen in Figure **7.12**(d).

In order to obtain a description of the curve we need to expand $\gamma^*(t)$ in Fourier series. In a straightforward approach we can obtain $\gamma^*(t)$ from an image and apply the definition in Equation 7.27 for $c(t) = \gamma^*(t)$. However, we can obtain a computationally more attractive development with some algebraic simplifications. By considering the form of the integral in Equation 7.13 we have that

$$a_k^* = \frac{1}{\pi} \int_0^{2\pi} \gamma^*(t) \cos(kt)\,dt \quad \text{and} \quad b_k^* = \frac{1}{\pi} \int_0^{2\pi} \gamma^*(t) \sin(kt)\,dt \tag{7.30}$$

By substitution of Equation 7.29 we obtain

$$a_0^* = \frac{1}{\pi} \int_0^{2\pi} \gamma((L/2\pi)t)\,dt + \frac{1}{\pi} \int_0^{2\pi} t\,dt$$

$$a_k^* = \frac{1}{\pi} \int_0^{2\pi} \gamma((L/2\pi)t) \cos(kt)\,dt + \frac{1}{\pi} \int_0^{2\pi} t \cos(kt)\,dt \tag{7.31}$$

```
%Angular function
function AngFuncDescrp(curve)

%Function
 X=curve(1,:);Y=curve(2,:);
 M=size(X,2);%number points

%Arc length
 S=zeros(1,m);
 S(1)=sqrt((X(1)-X(m))^2+(Y(1)-Y(m))^2);
 for i=2:m
    S(i)=S(i-1)+sqrt((X(i)-X(i-1))^2+(Y(i)-Y(i-1))^2);
 End
 L=S(m);

%Normalised Parameter
 t=(2*pi*S)/L;

%Graph of the curve
 subplot(3,3,1);
 plot(X,Y);
 mx=max(max(X),max(Y))+10;
 axis([0,mx,0,mx]); axis square;      %Aspect ratio

%Graph of the angular function y'/x'
 avrg=10;
 A=zeros(1,m);
 for i=1:m
    x1=0; x2=0; y1=0; y2=0;
    for j=1:avrg
       pa=i-j; pb=i+j;
       if(pa<1) pa=m+pa; end
       if(pb>m) pb=pb-m; end
       x1=x1+X(pa); y1=y1+Y(pa);
       x2=x2+X(pb); y2=y2+Y(pb);
    end
x1=x1/avrg; y1=y1/avrg;
x2=x2/avrg; y2=y2/avrg;
dx=x2-x1;    dy=y2-y1;

if(dx==0) dx=.00001; end
    if dx>0 & dy>0
    A(i)=atan(dy/dx);
    elseif dx>0 & dy<0
      A(i)=atan(dy/dx)+2*pi;
    else
      A(i)=atan(dy/dx)+pi;
    end
end

subplot(3,3,2);
```

```
    plot(S,A);
    axis([0,S(m),-1,2*pi+1]);

%Cumulative angular G(s)=-2pi
    G=zeros(1,m);
    for i=2:m
        d=min(abs(A(i)-A(i-1)),abs(abs(A(i)-A(i-1))-2*pi));

        if d>.5
          G(i)=G(i-1);
        elseif (A(i)-A(i-1))<-pi
          G(i)=G(i-1)-(A(i)-A(i-1)+2*pi);
        elseif (A(i)-A(i-1))>pi
          G(i)=G(i-1)-(A(i)-A(i-1)-2*pi);
        else
          G(i)=G(i-1)-(A(i)-A(i-1));
        end
    end

    subplot(3,3,3);

    plot(S,G);
    axis([0,S(m),-2*pi-1,1]);

%Cumulative angular Normalised
    F=G+t;

    subplot(3,3,4);
    plot(t,F);
    axis([0,2*pi,-2*pi,2*pi]);
```

Code 7.1 Angular functions

$$b_k^* = \frac{1}{\pi} \int_0^{2\pi} \gamma((L/2\pi)t) \sin(kt)\,dt + \frac{1}{\pi} \int_0^{2\pi} t \sin(kt)\,dt$$

By computing the second integrals of each coefficient, we obtain a simpler form as

$$a_0^* = 2\pi + \frac{1}{\pi} \int_0^{2\pi} \gamma((L/2\pi)t)\,dt$$

$$a_k^* = \frac{1}{\pi} \int_0^{2\pi} \gamma((L/2\pi)t) \cos(kt)\,dt \qquad (7.32)$$

$$b_k^* = -\frac{2}{k} + \frac{1}{\pi} \int_0^{2\pi} \gamma((L/2\pi)t) \sin(kt)\,dt$$

In an image, we measure distances, thus it is better to express these equations in arc-length form. For that, we know that $s = (L/2\pi)t$. Thus,

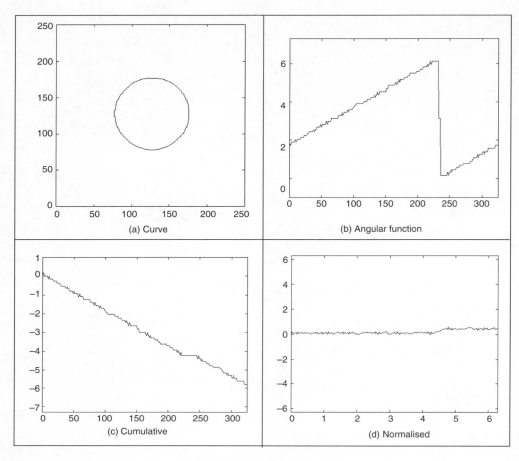

Figure 7.12 Discrete computation of the angular functions

$$dt = \frac{2\pi}{L} ds \tag{7.33}$$

Accordingly, the coefficients in Equation 7.32 can be rewritten as,

$$a_0^* = 2\pi + \frac{2}{L} \int_0^L \gamma(s)\,ds$$

$$a_k^* = \frac{2}{L} \int_0^L \gamma(s) \cos\left(\frac{2\pi k}{L} s\right) ds \tag{7.34}$$

$$b_k^* = -\frac{2}{k} + \frac{2}{L} \int_0^L \gamma(s) \sin\left(\frac{2\pi k}{L} s\right) ds$$

In a similar way to Equation 7.26, the Fourier descriptors can be computed by approximating the integral as a summation of rectangular areas. This is illustrated in Figure **7.13**. Here, the discrete approximation is formed by rectangles of length τ_i and height γ_i. Thus,

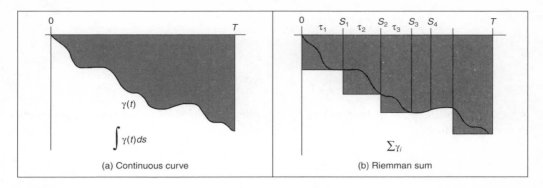

Figure 7.13 Integral approximations

$$a_0^* = 2\pi + \frac{2}{L} \sum_{i=1}^{m} \gamma_i \tau_i$$

$$a_k^* = \frac{2}{L} \sum_{i=1}^{m} \gamma_i \tau_i \cos\left(\frac{2\pi k}{L} s_i\right)$$ (7.35)

$$b_k^* = -\frac{2}{k} + \frac{2}{L} \sum_{i=1}^{m} \gamma_i \tau_i \sin\left(\frac{2\pi k}{L} s_i\right)$$

where s_i is the arc length at the ith point. Note that

$$s_i = \sum_{r=1}^{i} \tau_r$$ (7.36)

It is important to observe that although the definitions in Equation 7.35 only use the discrete values of $\gamma(t)$, they obtain a Fourier expansion of $\gamma^*(t)$. In the original formulation (Zahn, 1972), an alternative form of the summations is obtained by rewriting the coefficients in terms of the increments of the angular function. In this case, the integrals in Equation 7.34 are evaluated for each interval. Thus, the coefficients are represented as a summation of integrals of constant values as,

$$a_0^* = 2\pi + \frac{2}{L} \sum_{i=1}^{m} \int_{s_{i-1}}^{s_i} \gamma_i \, ds$$

$$a_k^* = \frac{2}{L} \sum_{i=1}^{m} \int_{s_{i-1}}^{s_i} \gamma_i \cos\left(\frac{2\pi k}{L} s\right) ds$$ (7.37)

$$b_k^* = -\frac{2}{k} + \frac{2}{L} \sum_{i=1}^{m} \int_{s_{i-1}}^{s_i} \gamma_i \sin\left(\frac{2\pi k}{L} s\right) ds$$

By evaluating the integral we obtain

$$a_0^* = 2\pi + \frac{2}{L} \sum_{i=1}^{m} \gamma_i (s_i - s_{i-1})$$

$$a_k^* = \frac{1}{\pi k} \sum_{i=1}^{m} \gamma_i \left(\sin\left(\frac{2\pi k}{L} s_i \right) - \sin\left(\frac{2\pi k}{L} s_{i-1} \right) \right) \tag{7.38}$$

$$b_k^* = -\frac{2}{k} + \frac{1}{\pi k} \sum_{i=1}^{m} \gamma_i \left(\cos\left(\frac{2\pi k}{L} s_i \right) - \cos\left(\frac{2\pi k}{L} s_{i-1} \right) \right)$$

A further simplification can be obtained by considering that Equation 7.28 can be expressed in discrete form as

$$\gamma_i = \sum_{r=1}^{i} \kappa_r \tau_r - \kappa_0 \tag{7.39}$$

where κ_r is the curvature (i.e. the difference of the angular function) at the rth point. Thus,

$$a_0^* = -2\pi - \frac{2}{L} \sum_{i=1}^{m} \kappa_i s_{i-1}$$

$$a_k^* = -\frac{1}{\pi k} \sum_{i=1}^{m} \kappa_i \tau_i \sin\left(\frac{2\pi k}{L} s_{i-1} \right) \tag{7.40}$$

$$b_k^* = -\frac{2}{k} - \frac{1}{\pi k} \sum_{i=1}^{m} \kappa_i \tau_i \cos\left(\frac{2\pi k}{L} s_{i-1} \right) + \frac{1}{\pi k} \sum_{i=1}^{m} \kappa_i \tau_i$$

Since

$$\sum_{i=1}^{m} \kappa_i \tau_i = 2\pi \tag{7.41}$$

thus,

$$a_0^* = -2\pi - \frac{2}{L} \sum_{i=1}^{m} \kappa_i s_{i-1}$$

$$a_k^* = -\frac{1}{\pi k} \sum_{i=1}^{m} \kappa_i \tau_i \sin\left(\frac{2\pi k}{L} s_{i-1} \right) \tag{7.42}$$

$$b_k^* = -\frac{1}{\pi k} \sum_{i=1}^{m} \kappa_i \tau_i \cos\left(\frac{2\pi k}{L} s_{i-1} \right)$$

These equations were originally presented in Zahn (1972) and are algebraically equivalent to Equation 7.35. However, they express the Fourier coefficients in terms of increments in the angular function rather than in terms of the cumulative angular function. In practice, both implementations (Equations 7.35 and 7.40) produce equivalent Fourier descriptors.

It is important to notice that the parameterisation in Equation 7.21 does not depend on the position of the pixels, but only on the change in angular information. That is, shapes in different position and with different scale will be represented by the same curve $\gamma^*(t)$. Thus, the Fourier descriptors obtained are *scale* and *translation* invariant. *Rotation* invariant descriptors can be obtained by considering the shift invariant property of the coefficients' amplitude. Rotating a curve in an image produces a shift in the angular function. This is because the rotation changes the starting point in the curve description. Thus, according to Section 7.2.3.2, the values

$$|c_k^*| = \sqrt{(a_k^*)^2 + (b_k^*)^2} \qquad\qquad (7.43)$$

provide a rotation, scale and translation invariant description. The function Ang FourierDescrp in Code **7.2** computes the Fourier descriptors in this equation by using the definitions in Equation 7.35. This code uses the angular functions in Code **7.1**.

```
%Fourier descriptors based on the Angular function
function AngFuncDescrp(curve,n,scale)
            %n=number coefficients
            %if n=0 then n=m/2
            %Scale amplitude output
%Angular functions
 AngFuncDescrp(curve);

%Fourier Descriptors
 if(n==0) n=floor(m/2); end;     %number of coefficients

 a=zeros(1,n); b=zeros(1,n);     %Fourier coefficients

for k=1:n
    a(k)=a(k)+G(1)*(S(1))*cos(2*pi*k*S(1)/L);
    b(k)=b(k)+G(1)*(S(1))*sin(2*pi*k*S(1)/L);
        for i=2:m
          a(k)=a(k)+G(i)*(S(i)-S(i-1))*cos(2*pi*k*S(i)/L);
          b(k)=b(k)+G(i)*(S(i)-S(i-1))*sin(2*pi*k*S(i)/L);
        end
    a(k)=a(k)*(2/L);
    b(k)=b(k)*(2/L)-2/k;
end
 %Graphs
 subplot(3,3,7);
 bar(a);
 axis([0,n,-scale,scale]);

 subplot(3,3,8);
 bar(b);
 axis([0,n,-scale,scale]);

%Rotation invariant Fourier descriptors
    CA=zeros(1,n);
    for k=1:n
      CA(k)=sqrt(a(k)^2+b(k)^2);
    end

%Graph of the angular coefficients
 subplot(3,3,9);
 bar(CA);
 axis([0,n,-scale,scale]);
```

Code 7.2 Angular Fourier descriptors

Figure **7.14** shows three examples of the results obtained using Code **7.2**. In each example, we show the curve, the angular function, the cumulative normalised angular

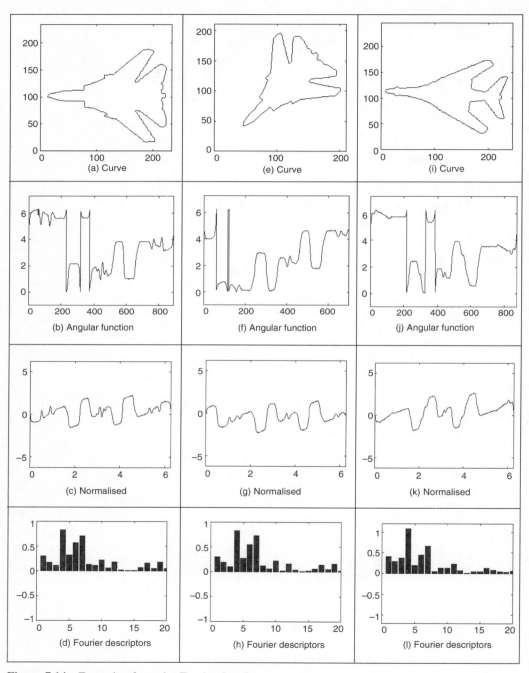

Figure 7.14 Example of angular Fourier descriptors

function and the Fourier descriptors. The curves in Figures **7.14**(a) and (e) represent the same object (the contour of an F-14 fighter), but the curve in Figure **7.14**(e) was scaled and rotated. We can see that the angular function changes significantly, whilst the normalised function is very similar but with a shift due to the rotation. The Fourier descriptors shown in Figures **7.14**(d) and (h) are quite similar since they characterise the same object. We can see a clear difference between the normalised angular function for the object presented in Figure **7.14**(i) (the contour of a different plane, a B1 bomber). These examples show that Fourier coefficients are indeed invariant to scale and rotation, and that they can be used to characterise different objects.

7.2.3.6 Elliptic Fourier descriptors

The cumulative angular function transforms the two-dimensional description of a curve into a one-dimensional periodic function suitable for Fourier analysis. In contrast, *elliptic Fourier descriptors* maintain the description of the curve in a two-dimensional space (Granlund, 1972). This is achieved by considering that the image space defines the complex plane. That is, each pixel is represented by a complex number. The first co-ordinate represents the real part whilst the second co-ordinate represents the imaginary part. Thus, a curve is defined as

$$c(t) = x(t) + jy(t) \tag{7.44}$$

Here we will consider that the parameter t is given by the arc-length parameterisation. Figure **7.15** shows an example of the complex representation of a curve. This example

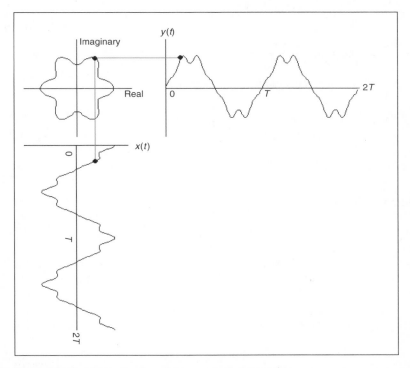

Figure 7.15 Example of complex curve representation

illustrates two periods of each component of the curve. Generally, $T = 2\pi$, thus the fundamental frequency is $\omega = 1$. It is important to notice that this representation can be used to describe open curves. In this case, the curve is traced twice in opposite directions. In fact, this representation is very general and can be extended to obtain the elliptic Fourier description of irregular curves (i.e. those without derivative information) (Montiel, 1996), (Montiel, 1997).

In order to obtain the elliptic Fourier descriptors of a curve, we need to obtain the Fourier expansion of the curve in Equation 7.44. The Fourier expansion can be performed by using the complex or trigonometric form. In the original work (Granlund, 1972), the expansion is expressed in the complex form. However, other works have used the trigonometric representation (Kuhl, 1982). Here, we will pass from the complex form to the trigonometric representation. The trigonometric representation is more intuitive and easier to implement.

According to Equation 7.5 we have that the elliptic coefficients are defined by

$$c_k = c_{xk} + jc_{yk} \tag{7.45}$$

where

$$c_{xk} = \frac{1}{T} \int_0^T x(t)e^{-jk\omega t} dt \quad \text{and} \quad c_{yk} = \frac{1}{T} \int_0^T y(t)e^{-jk\omega t} dt \tag{7.46}$$

By following Equation 7.12, we notice that each term in this expression can be defined by a pair of coefficients. That is,

$$c_{xk} = \frac{a_{xk} - jb_{xk}}{2} \qquad c_{yk} = \frac{a_{yk} - jb_{yk}}{2}$$

$$c_{x-k} = \frac{a_{xk} + jb_{xk}}{2} \qquad c_{y-k} = \frac{a_{yk} + jb_{yk}}{2} \tag{7.47}$$

Based on Equation 7.13 the trigonometric coefficients are defined as

$$a_{xk} = \frac{2}{T} \int_0^T x(t)\cos(k\omega t) dt \quad \text{and} \quad b_{xk} = \frac{2}{T} \int_0^T x(t)\sin(k\omega t) dt$$

$$a_{yk} = \frac{2}{T} \int_0^T y(t)\cos(k\omega t) dt \quad \text{and} \quad b_{yk} = \frac{2}{T} \int_0^T y(t)\sin(k\omega t) dt \tag{7.48}$$

That according to Equation 7.27 can be computed by the discrete approximation given by

$$a_{xk} = \frac{2}{m} \sum_{i=1}^{m} x_i \cos(k\omega i\tau) \quad \text{and} \quad b_{xk} = \frac{2}{m} \sum_{i=1}^{m} x_i \sin(k\omega i\tau)$$

$$a_{yk} = \frac{2}{m} \sum_{i=1}^{m} y_i \cos(k\omega i\tau) \quad \text{and} \quad b_{yk} = \frac{2}{m} \sum_{i=1}^{m} y_i \sin(k\omega i\tau) \tag{7.49}$$

where x_i and y_i define the value of the functions $x(t)$ and $y(t)$ at the sampling point i. By considering Equations 7.45 and 7.47 we can express c_k as the sum of a pair of complex numbers. That is,

$$c_k = A_k - jB_k \quad \text{and} \quad c_{-k} = A_k + jB_k \tag{7.50}$$

where

$$A_k = \frac{a_{xk} + ja_{yk}}{2} \quad \text{and} \quad B_k = \frac{b_{xk} + jb_{yk}}{2} \tag{7.51}$$

Based on the definition in Equation 7.45, the curve can be expressed in the exponential form given in Equation 7.6 as

$$c(t) = c_0 + \sum_{k=1}^{\infty} (A_k - jB_k)e^{jk\omega t} + \sum_{k=-\infty}^{-1} (A_k + jB_k)e^{jk\omega t} \tag{7.52}$$

Alternatively, according to Equation 7.11 the curve can be expressed in trigonometric form as

$$c(t) = \frac{a_{x0}}{2} + \sum_{k=1}^{\infty} \left(a_{xk} \cos(k\omega t) + b_{xk} \sin(k\omega t) \right)$$
$$+ j\left(\frac{a_{y0}}{2} + \sum_{k=1}^{\infty} \left(a_{yk} \cos(k\omega t) + b_{yk} \sin(k\omega t) \right) \right) \tag{7.53}$$

Generally, this equation is expressed in matrix form as

$$\begin{bmatrix} x(t) \\ y(t) \end{bmatrix} = \frac{1}{2} \begin{bmatrix} a_{x0} \\ a_{y0} \end{bmatrix} + \sum_{k=1}^{\infty} \begin{bmatrix} a_{xk} & b_{xk} \\ a_{yk} & b_{yk} \end{bmatrix} \begin{bmatrix} \cos(k\omega t) \\ \sin(k\omega t) \end{bmatrix} \tag{7.54}$$

Each term in this equation has an interesting geometric interpretation as an elliptic phasor (a rotating vector). That is, for a fixed value of k, the trigonometric summation defines the locus of an ellipse in the complex plane. We can imagine that as we change the parameter t the point traces ellipses moving at a speed proportional to the harmonic number k. This number indicates how many cycles (i.e. turns) give the point in the time interval from zero to T. Figure **7.16**(a) illustrates this concept. Here, a point in the curve is given as the summation of three vectors that define three terms in Equation 7.54. As the parameter t changes, each vector defines an elliptic curve. In this interpretation, the values of $a_{x0}/2$ and $a_{y0}/2$ define the start point of the first vector (i.e. the location of the curve). The major axes of each ellipse are given by the values of $|A_k|$ and $|B_k|$. The definition of the ellipse locus for a frequency is determined by the coefficients as shown in Figure **7.16**(b).

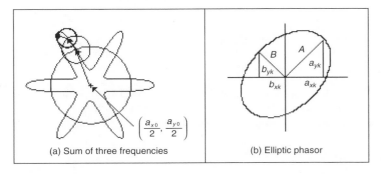

(a) Sum of three frequencies   (b) Elliptic phasor

Figure 7.16 Example of a contour defined by elliptic Fourier descriptors

7.2.3.7 Invariance

As in the case of angular Fourier descriptors, elliptic Fourier descriptors can be defined such that they remain invariant to geometric transformations. In order to show these definitions we must first study how geometric changes in a shape modify the form of the Fourier coefficients. Transformations can be formulated by using both the exponential or trigonometric form. We will consider changes in translation, rotation and scale using the trigonometric definition in Equation 7.54.

Let us denote $c'(t) = x'(t) + jy'(t)$ as the transformed contour. This contour is defined as

$$\begin{bmatrix} x'(t) \\ y'(t) \end{bmatrix} = \frac{1}{2} \begin{bmatrix} a'_{x0} \\ a'_{y0} \end{bmatrix} + \sum_{k=1}^{\infty} \begin{bmatrix} a'_{xk} & b'_{xk} \\ a'_{yk} & b'_{yk} \end{bmatrix} \begin{bmatrix} \cos(k\omega t) \\ \sin(k\omega t) \end{bmatrix} \tag{7.55}$$

If the contour is translated by t_x and t_y along the real and the imaginary axes, respectively, we have that

$$\begin{bmatrix} x'(t) \\ y'(t) \end{bmatrix} = \frac{1}{2} \begin{bmatrix} a_{x0} \\ a_{y0} \end{bmatrix} + \sum_{k=1}^{\infty} \begin{bmatrix} a_{xk} & b_{xk} \\ a_{yk} & b_{yk} \end{bmatrix} \begin{bmatrix} \cos(k\omega t) \\ \sin(k\omega t) \end{bmatrix} + \begin{bmatrix} t_x \\ t_y \end{bmatrix} \tag{7.56}$$

That is,

$$\begin{bmatrix} x'(t) \\ y'(t) \end{bmatrix} = \frac{1}{2} \begin{bmatrix} a_{x0} + 2t_x \\ a_{y0} + 2t_y \end{bmatrix} + \sum_{k=1}^{\infty} \begin{bmatrix} a_{xk} & b_{xk} \\ a_{yk} & b_{yk} \end{bmatrix} \begin{bmatrix} \cos(k\omega t) \\ \sin(k\omega t) \end{bmatrix} \tag{7.57}$$

Thus, by comparing Equation 7.55 and Equation 7.57, we have that the relationship between the coefficients of the transformed and original curves is given by

$$a'_{xk} = a_{xk} \quad b'_{xk} = b_{xk} \quad a'_{yk} = a_{yk} \quad b'_{yk} = b_{yk} \quad \text{for } k \neq 0$$

$$a'_{x0} = a_{x0} + 2t_x \quad a'_{y0} = a_{y0} + 2t_y \tag{7.58}$$

Accordingly, all the coefficients remain invariant under translation except a_{x0} and a_{y0}. This result can be intuitively derived by considering that these two coefficients represent the position of the centre of gravity of the contour of the shape and translation changes only the position of the curve.

The change in scale of a contour $c(t)$ can be modelled as the dilation from its centre of gravity. That is, we need to translate the curve to the origin, scale it and then return it to its original location. If s represents the scale factor, then these transformations define the curve as,

$$\begin{bmatrix} x'(t) \\ y'(t) \end{bmatrix} = \frac{1}{2} \begin{bmatrix} a_{x0} \\ a_{y0} \end{bmatrix} + s \sum_{k=1}^{\infty} \begin{bmatrix} a_{xk} & b_{xk} \\ a_{yk} & b_{yk} \end{bmatrix} \begin{bmatrix} \cos(k\omega t) \\ \sin(k\omega t) \end{bmatrix} \tag{7.59}$$

Notice that in this equation the scale factor does not modify the coefficients a_{x0} and a_{y0} since the curve is expanded with respect to its centre. In order to define the relationships between the curve and its scaled version, we compare Equation 7.55 and Equation 7.59. Thus,

$$a'_{xk} = sa_{xk} \quad b'_{xk} = sb_{xk} \quad a'_{yk} = sa_{yk} \quad b'_{yk} = sb_{yk} \quad \text{for } k \neq 0$$

$$a'_{x0} = a_{x0} \quad a'_{y0} = a_{y0} \tag{7.60}$$

That is, under dilation, all the coefficients are multiplied by the scale factor except a_{x0} and a_{y0} which remain invariant.

Rotation can be defined in a similar way to Equation 7.59. If ρ represents the rotation angle, then we have that

$$\begin{bmatrix} x'(t) \\ y'(t) \end{bmatrix} = \frac{1}{2} \begin{bmatrix} a_{x0} \\ a_{y0} \end{bmatrix} + \begin{bmatrix} \cos(\rho) & \sin(\rho) \\ -\sin(\rho) & \cos(\rho) \end{bmatrix} \sum_{k=1}^{\infty} \begin{bmatrix} a_{xk} & b_{xk} \\ a_{yk} & b_{yk} \end{bmatrix} \begin{bmatrix} \cos(k\omega t) \\ \sin(k\omega t) \end{bmatrix} \quad (7.61)$$

This equation can be obtained by translating the curve to the origin, rotating it and then returning it to its original location. By comparing Equation 7.55 and Equation 7.61, we have that

$$a'_{xk} = a_{xk} \cos(\rho) + a_{yk} \sin(\rho) \qquad b'_{xk} = b_{xk} \cos(\rho) + b_{yk} \sin(\rho)$$

$$a'_{yk} = -a_{xk} \sin(\rho) + a_{yk} \cos(\rho) \qquad b'_{yk} = -b_{xk} \sin(\rho) + b_{yk} \cos(\rho) \quad (7.62)$$

$$a'_{x0} = a_{x0} \qquad a'_{y0} = a_{y0}$$

That is, under translation, the coefficients are defined by a linear combination dependent on the rotation angle, except for a_{x0} and a_{y0} which remain invariant. It is important to notice that rotation relationships are also applied for a change in the starting point of the curve.

Equations 7.58, 7.60 and 7.62 define how the elliptic Fourier coefficients change when the curve is translated, scaled or rotated, respectively. We can combine these results to define the changes when the curve undergoes the three transformations. In this case, transformations are applied in succession. Thus,

$$a'_{xk} = s(a_{xk} \cos(\rho) + a_{yk} \sin(\rho)) \qquad b'_{xk} = s(b_{xk} \cos(\rho) + b_{yk} \sin(\rho))$$

$$a'_{yk} = s(-a_{xk} \sin(\rho) + a_{yk} \cos(\rho)) \qquad b'_{yk} = s(-b_{xk} \sin(\rho) + b_{yk} \cos(\rho)) \quad (7.63)$$

$$a'_{x0} = a_{x0} + 2t_x \qquad a'_{y0} = a_{y0} + 2t_y$$

Based on this result we can define alternative invariant descriptors. In order to achieve invariance to translation, when defining the descriptors the coefficient for $k = 0$ is not used. In Granlund (1972) invariant descriptors are defined based on the complex form of the coefficients. Alternatively, invariant descriptors can be simply defined as

$$\frac{|A_k|}{|A_1|} + \frac{|B_k|}{|B_1|} \quad (7.64)$$

The advantage of these descriptors with respect to the definition in Granlund (1972) is that they do not involve negative frequencies and that we avoid multiplication by higher frequencies that are more prone to noise. By considering the definitions in Equations 7.51 and 7.63 we can prove that,

$$\frac{|A'_k|}{|A'_1|} = \frac{\sqrt{a_{xk}^2 + a_{yk}^2}}{\sqrt{a_{x1}^2 + a_{y1}^2}} \quad \text{and} \quad \frac{|B'_k|}{|B'_1|} = \frac{\sqrt{b_{xk}^2 + b_{yk}^2}}{\sqrt{b_{x1}^2 + b_{y1}^2}} \quad (7.65)$$

These equations contain neither the *scale* factor, s, nor the *rotation*, ρ. Thus, they are *invariant*. Notice that if the square roots are removed then invariance properties are still maintained. However, high-order frequencies can have undesirable effects.

The function `EllipticDescrp` in Code **7.3** computes the elliptic Fourier descriptors

```
%Elliptic Fourier Descriptors
function EllipticDescrp(curve,n,scale)
            %n=num coefficients
            %if n=0 then n=m/2
            %Scale amplitude output
%Function from image
X=curve(1,:);
Y=curve(2,:);
m=size(X,2);

%Graph of the curve
        subplot(3,3,1);
        plot(X,Y);
        mx=max(max(X),max(Y))+10;
        axis([0,mx,0,mx]); %Axis of the graph pf the curve
        axis square;    %Aspect ratio

%Graph of X
        p=0:2*pi/m:2*pi-pi/m;    %Parameter
        subplot(3,3,2);
        plot(p,X);
        axis([0,2*pi,0,mx]); %Axis of the graph pf the curve

%Graph of Y
        subplot(3,3,3);
        plot(p,Y);
        axis([0,2*pi,0,mx]); %Axis of the graph pf the curve
%Elliptic Fourier Descriptors
 if(n==0) n=floor(m/2); end; %number of coefficients

  %Fourier Coefficients
  ax=zeros(1,n); bx=zeros(1,n);
  ay=zeros(1,n); by=zeros(1,n);

  t=2*pi/m;

  for k=1:n
    for i=1:m
      ax(k)=ax(k)+X(i)*cos(k*t*(i-1));
      bx(k)=bx(k)+X(i)*sin(k*t*(i-1));
      ay(k)=ay(k)+Y(i)*cos(k*t*(i-1));
      by(k)=by(k)+Y(i)*sin(k*t*(i-1));
    end

  ax(k)=ax(k)*(2/m);
  bx(k)=bx(k)*(2/m);
  ay(k)=ay(k)*(2/m);
  by(k)=by(k)*(2/m);
end

%Graph coefficient ax
subplot(3,3,4);
```

```
bar(ax);
axis([0,n,-scale,scale]);

%Graph coefficient ay
subplot(3,3,5);
bar(ay);
axis([0,n,-scale,scale]);

%Graph coefficient bx
subplot(3,3,6);
bar(bx);
axis([0,n,-scale,scale]);

%Graph coefficient by
subplot(3,3,7);
bar(by);
axis([0,n,-scale,scale]);

%Invariant
 CE=zeros(1,n);
 for k=1:n
    CE(k)=sqrt((ax(k)^2+ay(k)^2)/(ax(1)^2+ay(1)^2))
       +sqrt((bx(k)^2+by(k)^2)/(bx(1)^2+by(1)^2));
end

%Graph of Elliptic descriptors
   subplot(3,3,8);
   bar(CE);
   axis([0,n,0,2.2]);
```

Code 7.3 Elliptic Fourier descriptors

of a curve. The code implements Equations 7.49 and 7.64 in a straightforward way. By default, the number of coefficients is half of the number of points that define the curve. However, the number of coefficients can be specified by the parameter n. The number of coefficients used defines the level of detail of the characterisation. In order to illustrate this idea, we can consider the different curves that are obtained by using a different number of coefficients. Figure **7.17** shows an example of the reconstruction of a contour. In Figure **7.17**(a) we can observe that the first coefficient represents an ellipse. When the second coefficient is considered (Figure **7.17**(b)), then the ellipse changes into a triangular shape. When adding more coefficients the contour is refined until the curve represents an accurate approximation of the original contour. In this example, the contour is represented by 100 points. Thus, the maximum number of coefficients is 50.

Figure **7.18** shows three examples of the results obtained using Code **7.3**. Each example shows the original curve, the x and y co-ordinate functions and the Fourier descriptors defined in Equation 7.64. The maximum in Equation 7.64 is equal to two and is obtained when $k = 1$. In the figure we have scaled the Fourier descriptors to show the differences between higher order coefficients. In this example, we can see that the Fourier descriptors for the curves in Figures **7.18**(a) and (e) (F-14 fighter) are very similar. Small differences

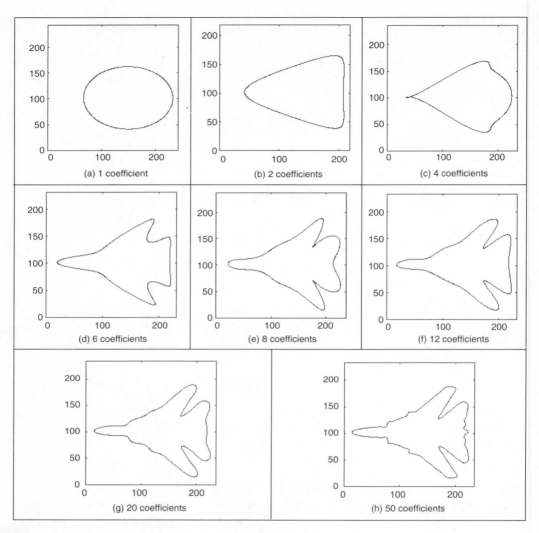

Figure 7.17 Fourier approximation

can be explained by discretisation errors. However, the coefficients remain the same after changing its location, orientation and scale. The descriptors of the curve in Figure **7.18**(i) (B1 bomber) are clearly different, showing that elliptic Fourier descriptors truly characterise the shape of an object.

Fourier descriptors are one of the most popular boundary descriptions. As such, they have attracted considerable attention and there are many further aspects. Naturally, we can use the descriptions for shape recognition (Aguado, 1998). It is important to mention that some work has suggested that there is some ambiguity in the Fourier characterisation. Thus, an alternative set of descriptors has been designed specifically to reduce ambiguities (Crimmins, 1982). However, it is well known that Fourier expansions are unique. Thus, Fourier characterisation should uniquely represent a curve. Additionally, the mathematical opacity of the technique in Crimmins (1982) does not lend itself to tutorial type presentation.

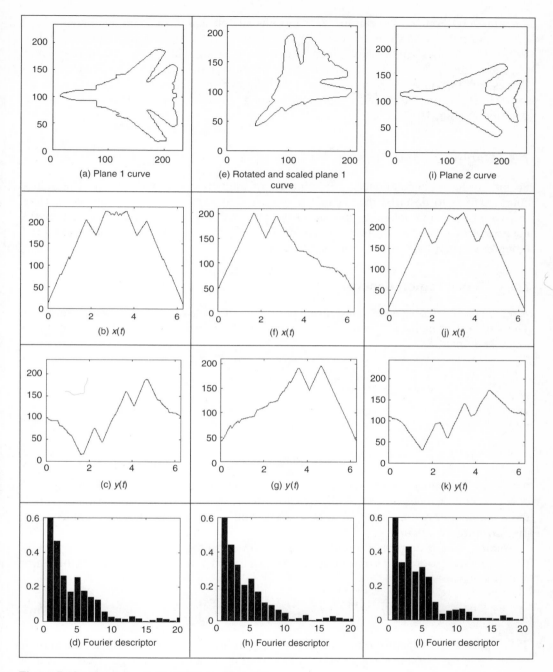

Figure 7.18 Example of elliptic Fourier descriptors

Interestingly, there has not been much study on alternative decompositions to Fourier, though Walsh functions have been suggested for shape representation (Searle, 1970) and recently wavelets have been used (Kashi, 1996) (though these are not an orthonormal basis function). 3D Fourier descriptors were introduced for analysis of simple shapes (Staib, 1992) and have recently been found to give good performance in application (Undrill, 1997). Fourier descriptors have been also used to model shapes in computer graphics (Aguado, 2000). Naturally, Fourier descriptors cannot be used for occluded or mixed shapes, relying on extraction techniques with known indifference to occlusion (the HT, say). However, there have been approaches aimed to classify partial shapes using Fourier descriptors (Lin, 1987).

7.3 Region descriptors

So far, we have concentrated on descriptions of the perimeter, or boundary. The natural counterpart is to describe the *region*, or the *area*, by *regional shape descriptors*. Here, there are two main contenders that differ in focus: basic regional descriptors characterise the geometric properties of the region; moments concentrate on density of the region. First, though, we shall look at the simpler descriptors.

7.3.1 Basic region descriptors

A region can be described by considering scalar measures based on its geometric properties. The simplest property is given by its size or area. In general, the area of a region in the plane is defined as

$$A(S) = \int_x \int_y I(x, y) \, dy \, dx \qquad (7.66)$$

where $I(x, y) = 1$ if the pixel is within a shape, $(x, y) \in S$, and 0 otherwise. In practice, integrals are approximated by summations. That is,

$$A(S) = \sum_x \sum_y I(x, y) \Delta A \qquad (7.67)$$

where ΔA is the area of one pixel. Thus, if $\Delta A = 1$, then the area is measured in pixels. Area changes with changes in scale. However, it is invariant to image rotation. Small errors in the computation of the area will appear when applying a rotation transformation due to discretisation of the image.

Another simple property is defined by the perimeter of the region. If $x(t)$ and $y(t)$ denote the parametric co-ordinates of a curve enclosing a region S, then the perimeter of the region is defined as

$$P(S) = \int_t \sqrt{x^2(t) + y^2(t)} \, dt \qquad (7.68)$$

This equation corresponds to the sums of all the infinitesimal arcs that define the curve. In the discrete case, $x(t)$ and $y(t)$ are defined by a set of pixels in the image. Thus, Equation 7.68 is approximated by

$$P(S) = \sum_i \sqrt{(x_i - x_{i-1})^2 + (y_i - y_{i-1})^2} \qquad (7.69)$$

where x_i and y_i represent the co-ordinates of the ith pixel forming the curve. Since pixels are organised in a square grid, then the terms in the summation can only take two values.

When the pixels (x_i, y_i) and (x_{i-1}, y_{i-1}) are 4-neighbours (as shown in Figure **7.1**(a)), the summation term is unity. Otherwise, the summation term is equal to $\sqrt{2}$. Notice that the discrete approximation in Equation 7.69 produces small errors in the measured perimeter. As such, it is unlikely that an exact value of $2\pi r$ will be achieved for the perimeter of a circular region of radius r.

Based on the perimeter and area it is possible to characterise the compactness of a region. *Compactness* is an oft-expressed measure of shape given by the ratio of perimeter to area. That is,

$$C(S) = \frac{4\pi A(s)}{P^2(s)} \tag{7.70}$$

In order to show the meaning of this equation, we can rewrite it as

$$C(S) = \frac{A(s)}{P^2(s)/4\pi} \tag{7.71}$$

Here, the denominator represents the area of a circle whose perimeter is $P(S)$. Thus, compactness measures the ratio between the area of the shape and the circle that can be traced with the same perimeter. That is, compactness measures the efficiency with which a boundary encloses an area. For a circular region (Figure **7.19**(a)) we have that $C(S) \simeq 1$ (Figure **7.20**). This represents the maximum compactness value. Figures **7.19**(b) and (c) show two examples in which compactness is reduced. If we take the perimeter of these regions and draw a circle with the same perimeter, then we can observe that the circle contains more area. This means that the shapes are not compact. A shape becomes more compact if we move region pixels far away from the centre of gravity of the shape to fill empty spaces closer to the centre of gravity. Note that compactness alone is not a good discriminator of a region; low values of C are associated with involuted regions such as the one in Figure **7.19**(b) and also with simple though highly elongated shapes. This ambiguity can be resolved by employing additional shape measures.

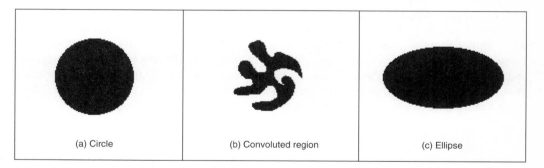

| (a) Circle | (b) Convoluted region | (c) Ellipse |

Figure 7.19 Examples of compactness

Another measure that can be used to characterise regions is dispersion. Dispersion (irregularity) has been measured as the ratio of major chord length to area (Chen, 1995). A simple version of this measure can be defined as

$$I(S) = \frac{\pi \max((x_i - \bar{x})^2 + (y_i - \bar{y})^2)}{A(S)} \qquad (7.72)$$

where $(\bar{x}, \bar{y})$ represent the co-ordinates of the centre of mass of the region. Notice that the numerator defines the area of the maximum circle enclosing the region. Thus, this measure describes the density of the region. An alternative measure of dispersion can actually also be expressed as the ratio of the maximum to the minimum radius. That is,

$$IR(S) = \frac{\max\left(\sqrt{(x_i - \bar{x})^2 + (y_i - \bar{y})^2}\right)}{\min\left(\sqrt{(x_i - \bar{x})^2 + (y_i - \bar{y})^2}\right)} \qquad (7.73)$$

This measure defines the ratio between the radius of the maximum circle enclosing the region and the maximum circle that can be contained in the region. Thus, the measure will increase as the region spreads. One *disadvantage* of the irregularity measures is that they are insensitive to slight *discontinuity* in the shape, such as a thin crack in a disk. On the other hand, these discontinuities will be registered by the earlier measures of compactness since the perimeter will increase disproportionately with the area.

Code **7.4** shows the implementation for the region descriptors. The code is a straightforward implementation of Equations 7.67, 7.69, 7.70, 7.72 and 7.73. A comparison of these measures for the three regions shown in Figure **7.19** is shown in Figure **7.20**. Clearly, for the circle the compactness and dispersion measures are close to unity. For the ellipse the compactness decreases whilst the dispersion increases. The convoluted region has the lowest compactness measure and the highest dispersion values. Clearly, these measurements can be used to characterise and hence discriminate between areas of differing shape.

Other measures, rather than focus on the geometric properties, characterise the structure of a region. This is the case of the *Poincarré measure* and the *Euler number*. The Poincarré measure concerns the number of holes within a region. Alternatively, the Euler number is the difference between the number of connected regions and the number of holes in them. There are many more potential measures for shape description in terms of structure and geometry. We could evaluate global or local *curvature* (convexity and concavity) as a further measure of geometry; we could investigate *proximity* and *disposition* as a further measure of structure. However, these do not have the advantages of a unified structure. We are simply suggesting measures with descriptive ability but this ability is reduced by the correlation between different measures. We have already seen the link between the Poincarré measure and the Euler number. There is a natural link between circularity and irregularity. As such we shall now look at a unified basis for shape description which aims to reduce this correlation and provides a unified theoretical basis for region description.

7.3.2 Moments

Moments describe a shape's *layout* (the arrangement of its pixels), a bit like combining area, compactness, irregularity and higher order descriptions together. Moments are a *global* description of a shape, accruing this same advantage as Fourier descriptors since there is an in-built ability to discern, and filter, noise. Further, in image analysis, they are *statistical moments*, as opposed to *mechanical* ones, but the two are analogous. For example, the mechanical moment of inertia describes the rate of change in momentum; the statistical second-order moment describes the rate of change in a shape's area. In this way, statistical

```
%Region descriptors (compactness)

function RegionDescrp(inputimage)

%Image size
[rows,columns]=size(inputimage);

%area
A=0;
  for x=1:columns
    for y=1:rows
       if inputimage(y,x)==0 A=A+1; end
  end
end

%Obtain Contour
C=Contour(inputimage);

%Perimeter & mean
X=C(1,:); Y=C(2,:); m=size(X,2);

mx=X(1); my=Y(1);
P=sqrt((X(1)-X(m))^2+(Y(1)-Y(m))^2);
for i=2:m
  P=P+sqrt((X(i)-X(i-1))^2+(Y(i)-Y(i-1))^2);
  mx=mx+X(i); my=my+Y(i);
end

mx=mx/m; my=my/m;

%Compactness
Cp=4*pi*A/P^2;

%Dispersion
 max=0; min=99999;

  for i=1:m
    d=((X(i)-mx)^2+(Y(i)-my)^2);
    if (d>max) max=d; end
    if (d<min) min=d; end
  end

  I=pi*max/A;
  IR=sqrt(max/min);

%Results
disp('perimeter=');      disp(P);
disp('area=');           disp(A);
disp('Compactness=');    disp(Cp);
disp('Dispersion=');     disp(I);
disp('DispersionR=');    disp(IR);
```

Code 7.4   Evaluating basic region descriptors

A(S) = 4917	A(S) = 2316	A(S) = 6104
P(S) = 259.27	P(S) = 498.63	P(S) = 310.93
C(S) = 0.91	C(S) = 0.11	C(S) = 0.79
I(S) = 1.00	I(S) = 2.24	I(S) = 1.85
IR(S) = 1.03	IR(S) = 6.67	IR(S) = 1.91
(a) Descriptors for the circle	(b) Descriptors for the convoluted region	(c) Descriptors for the ellipse

Figure 7.20 Basic region descriptors

moments can be considered as a global region description. Moments for image analysis were again originally introduced in the 1960s (Hu, 1962) (an exciting time for computer vision researchers too!) and an excellent and fairly up-to-date review is available (Prokop, 1992).

Moments are actually often associated more with *statistical* pattern recognition than with *model-based* vision since a major assumption is that there is an *unoccluded* view of the target shape. Target images are often derived by thresholding, usually one of the optimal forms that can require a single object in the field of view. More complex applications, including handling occlusion, could presuppose *feature extraction* by some means, with a model to in-fill for the missing parts. However, moments do provide a global description with invariance properties and with the advantages of a compact description aimed to avoid the effects of noise. As such, they have proved popular and successful in many applications.

The *two-dimensional Cartesian moment* is actually associated with an order that starts from low (where the lowest is zero) up to higher orders. The moment of order p and q, m_{pq} of a function $I(x, y)$, is defined as

$$m_{pq} = \int_{-\infty}^{\infty} \int_{-\infty}^{\infty} x^p y^q I(x, y) \, dx \, dy \tag{7.74}$$

For discrete images, Equation 7.74 is usually approximated by

$$m_{pq} = \sum_x \sum_y x^p y^q I(x, y) \Delta A \tag{7.75}$$

These descriptors have a *uniqueness* property in that if the function satisfies certain conditions, then moments of all orders exist. Also, and conversely, the set of descriptors uniquely determines the original function, in a manner similar to reconstruction via the inverse Fourier transform. However, these moments are descriptors, rather than a specification which can be used to reconstruct a shape. The *zero-order moment*, m_{00}, is

$$m_{00} = \sum_x \sum_y I(x, y) \Delta A \tag{7.76}$$

which represents the total mass of a function. Notice that this equation is equal to Equation 7.67 when $I(x, y)$ takes values of zero and one. However, Equation 7.76 is more general since the function $I(x, y)$ can take a range of values. In the definition of moments, these values are generally related to density. The two *first-order moments*, m_{01} and m_{10}, are given by

$$m_{10} = \sum_x \sum_y x I(x, y) \Delta A \quad m_{01} = \sum_x \sum_y y I(x, y) \Delta A \tag{7.77}$$

For binary images, these values are proportional to the shape's centre co-ordinates (the values merely require division by the shape's area). In general, the *centre of mass* $(\bar{x}, \bar{y})$ can be calculated from the ratio of the first-order to the zero-order components as

$$\bar{x} = \frac{m_{10}}{m_{00}} \qquad \bar{y} = \frac{m_{01}}{m_{00}} \tag{7.78}$$

The first ten x-axis moments of a smooth shape are shown in Figure **7.21**. The moments rise exponentially so are plotted in logarithmic form. Evidently, the moments provide a set of descriptions of the shape: measures that can be collected together to differentiate between different shapes.

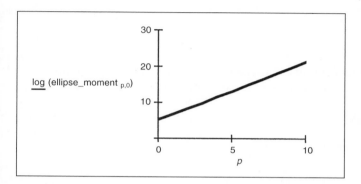

Figure 7.21   Horizontal axis ellipse moments

Should there be an intensity transformation that *scales* brightness by a particular factor, say α, such that a new image $I'(x, y)$ is a transformed version of the original one $I(x, y)$ given by

$$I'(x, y) = \alpha I(x, y) \tag{7.79}$$

Then the transformed moment values m'_{pq} are related to those of the original shape m_{pq} by

$$m'_{pq} = \alpha m_{pq} \tag{7.80}$$

Should it be required to distinguish *mirror symmetry* (reflection of a shape about a chosen axis), then the rotation of a shape about the, say, x axis gives a new shape $I'(x, y)$ which is the reflection of the shape $I(x, y)$ given by

$$I'(x, y) = I(-x, y) \tag{7.81}$$

The transformed moment values can be given in terms of the original shape's moments as

$$m'_{pq} = (-1)^p m_{pq} \tag{7.82}$$

However, we are usually concerned with more basic invariants than mirror images, namely invariance to *position*, *size* and *rotation*. Given that we now have an estimate of a shape's centre (in fact, a reference point for that shape), the *centralised moments*, μ_{pq}, which are invariant to *translation*, can be defined as

$$\mu_{pq} = \sum_x \sum_y (x - \bar{x})^p (y - \bar{y})^q I(x, y) \Delta A \tag{7.83}$$

Clearly, the zero-order *centralised* moment is again the shape's area. However, the first-order centralised moment μ_{01} is given by

$$\mu_{01} = \sum_x \sum_y (y - \bar{y})^1 I(x, y) \Delta A$$

$$= \sum_x \sum_y yI(x, y)\Delta A - \sum_x \sum_y \bar{y}I(x, y)\Delta A$$

$$= m_{01} - \bar{y} \sum_x \sum_y I(x, y)\Delta A \qquad (7.84)$$

$$= m_{01} - \frac{m_{01}}{m_{00}} m_{00}$$

$$= 0$$

$$= \mu_{10}$$

Clearly, neither of the first-order centralised moments has any description capability since they are both zero. Going to higher order, one of the second-order moments, μ_{20}, is

$$\mu_{20} = \sum_x \sum_y (x - \bar{x})^2 I(x, y) \Delta A$$

$$= \sum_x \sum_y (x^2 - 2x\bar{x} + \bar{x}^2)I(x, y)\Delta A$$

$$= m_{20} - 2m_{10}\frac{m_{10}}{m_{00}} + \left(\frac{m_{10}}{m_{00}}\right)^2 m_{00} \qquad (7.85)$$

$$= m_{20} - \left(\frac{m_{10}}{m_{00}}\right)^2$$

and this has descriptive capability.

The use of moments to describe an ellipse is shown in Figure **7.22**. Here, an original

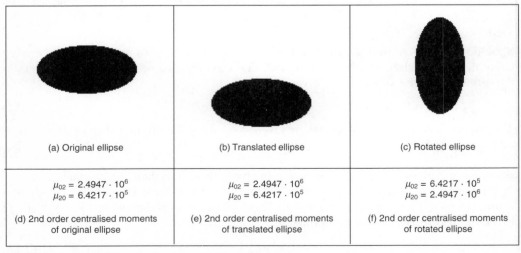

(a) Original ellipse

(b) Translated ellipse

(c) Rotated ellipse

$\mu_{02} = 2.4947 \cdot 10^6$ $\mu_{20} = 6.4217 \cdot 10^5$	$\mu_{02} = 2.4947 \cdot 10^6$ $\mu_{20} = 6.4217 \cdot 10^5$	$\mu_{02} = 6.4217 \cdot 10^5$ $\mu_{20} = 2.4947 \cdot 10^6$
(d) 2nd order centralised moments of original ellipse	(e) 2nd order centralised moments of translated ellipse	(f) 2nd order centralised moments of rotated ellipse

Figure 7.22   Describing a shape by centralised moments

ellipse, Figure **7.22**(a), gives the second-order moments in Figure **7.22**(d). In all cases, the first-order moments are zero, as expected. The moments, Figure **7.22**(e), of the translated ellipse, Figure **7.22**(b), are the same as those of the original ellipse. In fact, these moments show that the greatest rate of change in mass is around the horizontal axis, as consistent with the ellipse. The second-order moments, Figure **7.22**(f), of the ellipse when rotated by 90°, Figure **7.22**(c), are simply swapped around, as expected: the rate of change of mass is now greatest around the vertical axis. This illustrates how centralised moments are invariant to translation, but not to rotation.

However, centralised moments are as yet only *translation* invariant. In order to accrue invariance to scale, we require *normalised central moments*, η_{pq}, defined as (Hu, 1962).

$$\eta_{pq} = \frac{\mu_{pq}}{\mu_{00}^{\gamma}} \tag{7.86}$$

where

$$\gamma = \frac{p+q}{2} + 1 \quad \forall p + q \geq 2 \tag{7.87}$$

Seven rotation *invariant moments* can be computed from these given by

$$M1 = \eta_{20} + \eta_{02}$$
$$M2 = (\eta_{20} - \eta_{02})^2 + 4\eta_{11}^2$$
$$M3 = (\eta_{30} - 3\eta_{12})^2 + (3\eta_{21} - \eta_{03})^2$$
$$M4 = (\eta_{30} + \eta_{12})^2 + (\eta_{21} + \eta_{03})^2$$
$$M5 = (\eta_{30} - 3\eta_{12})(\eta_{30} + \eta_{12}) + ((\eta_{30} + \eta_{12})^2 - 3(\eta_{21} - \eta_{03})^2)$$
$$\quad + (3\eta_{21} - \eta_{03})(\eta_{21} + \eta_{03})(3(\eta_{30} + \eta_{12})^2 - (\eta_{21} + \eta_{03})^2) \tag{7.88}$$
$$M6 = (\eta_{20} - \eta_{02})((\eta_{30} + \eta_{12})^2 - (\eta_{21} + \eta_{03})^2) + 4\eta_{11}(\eta_{30} + \eta_{12})(\eta_{21} + \eta_{03})$$
$$M7 = (3\eta_{21} - \eta_{03})(\eta_{30} + \eta_{12})((\eta_{30} + \eta_{12})^2 - 3(\eta_{21} + \eta_{03})^2)$$
$$\quad + (3\eta_{12} - \eta_{30})(\eta_{21} + \eta_{03})(3(\eta_{12} + \eta_{30})^2 - (\eta_{21} + \eta_{03})^2)$$

The first of these, $M1$ and $M2$, are second-order moments, those for which $p + q = 2$. Those remaining are third-order moments, since $p + q = 3$. (The first-order moments are of no consequence since they are zero.) The last moment $M7$ is introduced as a skew invariant designed to distinguish mirror images.

Code **7.5** shows the Mathcad implementation that computes the invariant moments $M1$, $M2$ and $M3$. The code computes the moments by straight implementation of Equations 7.81 and 7.86. The use of these invariant moments to describe three shapes is illustrated in Figure **7.23**. Figure **7.23**(b) corresponds to the same plane in Figure **7.23**(a) but with a change of scale and a rotation. Thus, the invariant moments for these two shapes are very similar. In contrast, the invariant moments for the plane in Figure **7.23**(c) differ.

These invariant moments have the most important invariance properties. However, these moments are not orthogonal, as such there is potential for reducing the size of the set of moments required to describe a shape accurately. This can be achieved by using *Zernike moments* (Teague, 1980) that give an orthogonal set of rotation-invariant moments. *Rotation* invariance is achieved by using polar representation, as opposed to the Cartesian

```
μ(p,q,shape):=   cmom←0

                 xc←  ──────────── · Σ     (shape_i)_0
                      rows(shape)   i=0

                 yc←  ──────────── · Σ     (shape_i)_1
                      rows(shape)   i=0

                 for s∈0..rows(shape)-1
                     cmom←cmom+[(shape_s)_0-xc]^p·[(shape_s)_1-yc]^q·(shape_s)_2
                 cmom
```

$$\eta(p,q,im) := \frac{\mu(p,q,im)}{\mu(0,0,im)^{\frac{p+q}{2}+1}}$$

```
M1(im):=η(2,0,im)+η(0,2,im)
M2(im):=(η(2,0,im)-η(0,2,im))^2+4·η(1,1,im)^2
M3(im):=(η(3,0,im)-3·η(1,2,im))^2+(3·η(2,1,im)-η(0,3,im))^2
```

Code 7.5 Computing **M1**, **M2** and **M3**

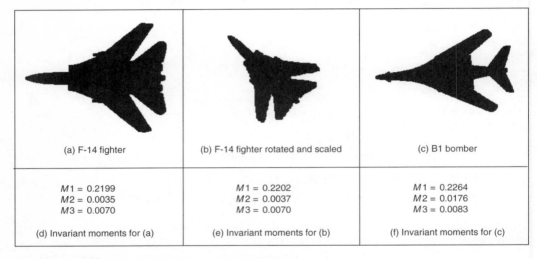

(a) F-14 fighter	(b) F-14 fighter rotated and scaled	(c) B1 bomber
$M1 = 0.2199$ $M2 = 0.0035$ $M3 = 0.0070$	$M1 = 0.2202$ $M2 = 0.0037$ $M3 = 0.0070$	$M1 = 0.2264$ $M2 = 0.0176$ $M3 = 0.0083$
(d) Invariant moments for (a)	(e) Invariant moments for (b)	(f) Invariant moments for (c)

Figure 7.23 Describing a shape by invariant moments

parameterisation for centralised moments. The *complex* Zernike moment, Z_{pq}, is

$$Z_{pq} = \frac{p+1}{\pi} \int_0^{2\pi} \int_0^{\infty} V_{pq}(r,\theta)^* f(r,\theta) r \, dr \, d\theta \qquad (7.89)$$

where p is now the radial magnitude and q is the radial direction and where * denotes the complex conjugate of a *Zernike polynomial*, V_{pq}, given by

$$V_{pq}(r,\theta) = R_{pq}(r)e^{jq\theta} \quad \text{where} \quad p-q \text{ is } even \text{ and } 0 \leq q \leq p \qquad (7.90)$$

where R_{pq} is a real-valued polynomial given by

$$R_{pq}(r) = \sum_{m=0}^{\frac{p-q}{2}} (-1)^m \frac{(p-m)!}{m! \left(\dfrac{p-2m+q}{2} \right)! \left(\dfrac{p-2m-q}{2} \right)!} r^{p-2m} \qquad (7.91)$$

These polynomials are orthogonal within the unit circle, so an analysed shape has to be re-mapped to be of this size before calculation of its moments. The *orthogonality* of these polynomials assures the *reduction* in the set of numbers used to describe a shape. More simply, the radial polynomials can be expressed as

$$R_{pq}(r) = \sum_{k=q}^{p} B_{pqk} r^k \qquad (7.92)$$

where the Zernike coefficients are

$$B_{pqk} = (-1)^{\frac{p-k}{2}} \frac{((p+k)/2)!}{((p-k)/2)!((k+q)/2)!((k-q)/2)!} \qquad (7.93)$$

for $p - k =$ even. The Zernike moments can actually be calculated from centralised moments as

$$Z_{pq} = \frac{p+1}{\pi} \sum_{k=q}^{p} \sum_{l=0}^{t} \sum_{m=0}^{q} (-j)^m \binom{t}{l}\binom{q}{m} B_{pqk} \mu_{(k-2l-q+m)(q+2l-m)} \qquad (7.94)$$

where $t = (k - q)/2$ and where

$$\binom{t}{l} = \frac{t!}{l!(t-l)!} \qquad (7.95)$$

Analysis (and by using Equation 7.83, assuming x, y are constrained to the interval $[-1, 1]$) gives

$$Z_{00} = \frac{\mu_{00}}{\pi}$$

$$Z_{11} = \frac{2}{\pi} (\mu_{01} - j\mu_{10}) = 0 \qquad (7.96)$$

$$Z_{22} = \frac{3}{\pi} (\mu_{02} - j2\mu_{11} - \mu_{20})$$

which can be extended further (Teague, 1980), and with remarkable similarity to the Hu invariant moments (Equation 7.88).

The magnitude of these Zernike moments remains invariant to rotation which affects only the phase; the Zernike moments can be made *scale* invariant by normalisation. An additional advantage is that there is a reconstruction theorem. For Nm moments, the original shape f can be reconstructed from its moments and the Zernike polynomials as

$$f(x, y) \approx \sum_{p=0}^{Nm} \sum_{q} Z_{pq} V_{pq}(x, y) \qquad (7.97)$$

These descriptors have been shown to good effect in application by reconstructing a good approximation to a shape with only few descriptors (Boyce, 1983) and in recognition (Khotanzad, 1990). There are *pseudo Zernike moments* (Teh, 1988) aimed to relieve the restriction on normalisation to the unit circle, as well as *complex moments* (Abu-Mostafa, 1985), again aimed to provide a simpler moment description with invariance properties. Finally, there are *affine invariant moments* which do not change with position, rotation and different scales along the co-ordinate axes, as a result, say, of a camera not being normal to the object plane. Here, the earliest approach appears to be by Flusser and Suk (Flusser, 1993). One of the reviews (Teh, 1988) concentrates on information content (redundancy), noise sensitivity and on representation ability, comparing the performance of several of the more popular moments in these respects.

7.4 Further reading

This chapter has essentially been based on unified techniques for border and region description. There is actually much more to contour and region analysis than indicated at the start of the chapter, for this is one the start points of morphological analysis. The neighbourhood can be extended to be larger (Marchand, 1997) and there is consideration of appropriate distance metrics for this (Das, 1988). A much more detailed study of boundary-based representation and application can be found in Van Otterloo's fine text (Van Otterloo, 1991). Naturally, there are many other ways to describe features, though few have the unique attributes of moments and Fourier descriptors. Naturally, there is an inter-relation between boundary and region description: *curvature* can be computed from a chain code (Rosenfeld, 1974); Fourier descriptors can also be used to calculate region descriptions (Kiryati, 1989). There have been many approaches to boundary approximation by fitting curves to the data. Some of these use polynomial approximation, or there are many *spline-based* techniques. A spline is a local function used to model a feature in sections. There are *quadratic* and *cubic* forms (for a good review of spline theory, try Ahlberg *et al.* (1967) or Dierckx (1995)), of interest, *snakes* are actually energy minimising splines. There are many methods for polygonal approximations to curves, and recently a new measure has been applied to compare performance on a suitable curve of techniques based on dominant point analysis (Rosin, 1997). To go with the earlier-mentioned review (Prokop and Reeves, 1992) there is a book available on moment theory (Mukundan and Ramakrishnan, 1998) showing the whole moment picture and even how to calculate moments from Fourier and Hartley transforms. The skeleton of a shape can be derived by the *medial axis transform* (Blum, 1967) and then used for recognition. This is a natural target for *thinning* techniques that have not been covered here. An excellent survey of these techniques, as used in character description following extraction, can be found in Trier *et al.* (1996) – describing use of moments and Fourier descriptors.

7.5 References

Abu-Mostafa, Y. S. and Psaltis, D., Image Normalisation by Complex Moments, *IEEE Trans. on PAMI*, **7**, pp. 46–55, 1985

Aguado, A. S., Nixon, M. S. and Montiel, E., Parameterising Arbitrary Shapes via Fourier Descriptors for Evidence-Gathering Extraction, *CVIU: Computer Vision and Image Understanding*, **69**(2), pp. 202–221, 1998

Aguado, A. S., Montiel, E. and Zaluska, E., Modelling Generalised Cylinders via Fourier Morphing, in press *ACM Transactions on Graphics*, 2000

Ahlberg, J. H., Nilson, E. N. and Walsh, J. L., *The Theory of Splines and Their Applications*, Academic Press, NY, USA, 1967

Bennet, J. R. and MacDonald, J. S., On the Measurement of Curvature in a Quantised Environment, *IEEE Trans. on Computers*, **C-24**(8), pp. 803–820, 1975

Blum, H., A Transformation for Extracting New Descriptors of Shape, in Wathen-Dunn, W. (ed), *Models for the Perception of Speech and Visual Form*, MIT Press, Cambridge, Mass USA, 1967

Boyce, J. F. and Hossack, W. J., Moment Invariants for Pattern Recognition, *Pattern Recog. Lett.*, **1**, pp. 451–456, 1983

Chen, Y. Q., Nixon, M. S. and Thomas, D. W., Texture Classification using Statistical Geometric Features, *Pattern Recog.*, **28**(4), pp. 537–552, 1995

Cosgriff, R. L., Identification of Shape, Rep. 820-11, ASTIA AD 254792, Ohio State Univ. Research Foundation, Columbus, Ohio USA, 1960

Crimmins, T. R., A Complete Set of Fourier Descriptors for Two-Dimensional Shapes, *IEEE Transaction Systems, Man and Cybernetics*, **12**(6), pp. 848–855, 1982

Das, P. P. and Chatterji, B. N., Knight's Distances in Digital Geometry, *Pattern Recog. Lett.*, **7**, pp. 215–226, 1988

Dierckx, P., *Curve and Surface Fitting with Splines*, Oxford University Press, Oxford UK, 1995

Flusser, J. and Suk, T., Pattern-Recognition by Affine Moment Invariants, *Pattern Recog.*, **26**(1), pp. 167–174, 1993

Freeman, H., On the Encoding of Arbitrary Geometric Configurations, *IRE Trans.*, **EC-10**(2), pp. 260–268, 1961

Freeman, H., Computer Processing of Line Drawing Images, *Computing Surveys*, **6**(1), pp. 57–95, 1974

Granlund, G. H., Fourier Preprocessing for Hand Print Character Recognition, *IEEE Trans. on Comp.*, **21**, pp. 195–201, 1972

Hu, M. K., Visual Pattern Recognition by Moment Invariants, *IRE Trans. Information Theory*, **IT-8**, pp. 179–187, 1962

Kashi, R. S., Bhoj-Kavde, P., Nowakowski, R. S. and Papathomas, T. V., 2-D Shape Representation and Averaging using Normalised Wavelet Descriptors, *Simulation*, **66**(3), pp. 164–178, 1996

Khotanzad, A. and Hong, Y. H., Invariant Image Recognition by Zernike Moments, *IEEE Trans. on PAMI*, **12**, pp. 489–498, 1990

Kiryati, N. and Maydan, D., Calculating Geometric Properties from Fourier Representation, *Pattern Recog.*, **22**(5), pp. 469–475, 1989

Kuhl, F. P. and Giardina, C. R., Elliptic Fourier Descriptors of a Closed Contour, *CVGIP*, **18**, pp. 236–258, 1982

Lin, C. C. and Chellappa, R., Classification of Partial 2D Shapes using Fourier Descriptors, *IEEE Trans. on PAMI*, **9**(5), pp. 686–690, 1987

Liu, H. C. and Srinath, M. D., Corner Detection from Chain-Coded Curves, *Pattern Recog.*, **23**(1), pp. 51–68, 1990

Marchand, S. and Sharaiha, Y. M., Discrete Convexity, Straightness and the 16-Neighbourhood, *Computer Vision and Image Understanding*, **66**(3), pp. 416–429, 1997

Montiel, E., Aguado, A. S. and Zaluska, E., Topology in Fractals, *Chaos, Solitons and Fractals*, **7**(8), pp. 1187–1207, 1996

Montiel, E., Aguado, A. S. and Zaluska, E., Fourier Series Expansion of Irregular Curves, *Fractals*, **5**(1), pp. 105–199, 1997

Mukundan, R. and Ramakrishnan, K.R., *Moment Functions in Image Analysis: Theory and Applications,* World Scientific Pte. Ltd., Singapore, 1998.

Persoon, E. and Fu, K.-S., Shape Description Using Fourier Descriptors, *IEEE Trans. SMC*, **3**, pp. 170–179, 1977

Prokop, R. J. and Reeves, A. P., A Survey of Moment-Based Techniques for Unoccluded Object Representation and Recognition, *CVGIP: Graphical Models and Image Processing*, **54**(5), pp. 438–460, 1992

Rosenfeld, A., Digital Straight Line Segments, *IEEE Trans. on Computers*, **23**, pp. 1264–1269, 1974

Rosin, P. and Venkatesh, S., Extracting Natural Scales Using Fourier Descriptors, *Pattern Recog.*, **26(9)**, pp. 1383–1393, 1993

Rosin, P., Techniques for Assessing Polygonal Approximations to Curves, *IEEE Trans. on PAMI*, **19**(6), pp. 659–666, 1997

Searle, N. H., Shape Analysis by use of Walsh Functions, in: *Machine Intelligence 5*, B. Meltzer and D. Mitchie (eds), Edinburgh University Press, 1970

Seeger, U. and Seeger, R., Fast Corner Detection in Gray-Level Images, *Patt. Recog. Lett.*, **15**, pp. 669–675, 1994

Staib, L. and Duncan, J., Boundary Finding with Parametrically Deformable Models, *IEEE Trans. on PAMI*, **14**, pp. 1061–1075, 1992

Teague, M. R., Image Analysis by the General Theory of Moments, *J. Opt. Soc. Am.,* **70**, pp. 920–930, 1980

Teh, C. H. and Chin, R. T., On Image Analysis by the Method of Moments, *IEEE Trans. on PAMI*, **10**, pp. 496–513, 1988

Trier, O. D., Jain, A. K. and Taxt, T., Feature Extraction Methods for Character Recognition – a Survey, *Pattern Recognition*, **29**(4), pp. 641–662, 1996

Undrill, P. E., Delibasis, K. and Cameron, G. G., An Application of Genetic Algorithms to Geometric Model-Guided Interpretation of Brain Anatomy, *Pattern Recog.*, **30**(2), pp. 217–227, 1997

Van Otterloo, P. J., *A Contour-Oriented Approach to Shape Analysis*, Prentice Hall International (UK) Ltd, Hemel Hempstead, 1991

Zahn, C. T. and Roskies, R. Z., Fourier Descriptors for Plane Closed Curves, *IEEE Trans. on Computers*, **C-21**(3), pp. 269–281, 1972

8
Introduction to texture description, segmentation and classification

8.1 Overview

This chapter is concerned with how we can use many of the feature extraction and description techniques presented earlier to characterise regions in an image. The aim here is to describe how we can collect measurements for purposes of recognition, using texture.

We shall first look at what is meant by texture and then how we can use Fourier transform techniques, statistics and region measures to describe it. We shall then look at how the measurements provided by these techniques, the description of the texture, can be collected together to recognise it. Finally, we shall label an image according to the texture found within it, to give a segmentation into classes known to exist within the image. Since we could be recognising shapes described by Fourier descriptors, or by region measures, the material is actually general and could be applied for purposes of recognition to measures other than texture.

Table 8.1 Overview of Chapter 8

Texture description	Fourier Transform	Energy
	Co-occurrence	Entropy
	Regions	Inertia
Texture classification	k nearest neighbour rule	
Texture segmentation	Convolution	
	Tiling	
	Thresholding	

8.2 What is texture?

Texture is actually a very nebulous concept, often attributed to human perception, as either the feel or the appearance of (woven) fabric. Everyone has their own interpretation as to the nature of texture; there is no mathematical definition for texture, it simply exists. By way of reference, let us consider one of the dictionary definitions Oxford (1996):

> **texture** *n.*, & *v.t.* **1.** *n.* arrangement of threads etc. in textile fabric. characteristic feel due to this; arrangement of small constituent parts, perceived structure, (*of* skin, rock, soil, organic tissue, literary work, etc.); representation of structure and detail of objects in art; . . .

That covers quite a lot. If we change 'threads' for 'pixels' then the definition could apply to images (except for the bit about artwork). Essentially, texture can be what we define it to be. Why might we want to do this? By way of example, analysis of remotely sensed images is now a major application of image processing techniques. In such analysis, pixels are labelled according to the categories of a required application, such as whether the ground is farmed or urban in land-use analysis, or water for estimation of surface analysis. An example of a remotely sensed image is given in Figure **8.1**(a) which is of an urban area (in the top left) and some farmland. Here, the image resolution is low and each pixel corresponds to a large area of the ground. Square groups of pixels have then been labelled either as urban, or as farmland, according to their texture properties as shown in Figure **8.1**(b) where black represents the area classified as urban and white is for the farmland. In this way we can assess the amount of area that urban areas occupy. As such, we have used *real* textures to label pixels, the perceived textures of the urban and farming areas.

As an alternative definition of texture, we can consider it as a database of images that researchers use to test their algorithms. Many texture researchers have used a database of

(a) Remotely sensed image	(b) Classification result

Figure 8.1 Example of texture analysis

pictures of textures (Brodatz, 1968), produced for artists and designers, rather than for digital image analysis. Parts of three of the Brodatz texture images are given in Figure **8.2**. Here, the French canvas (Brodatz index D20) in Figure **8.2**(a) is a detail of Figure **8.2**(b) (Brodatz index D21) taken at four times the magnification. The beach sand in Figure **8.2**(c), (Brodatz index D29) is clearly of a different texture to that of cloth. Given the diversity of texture, there are now many databases available on the Web, at the sites given in Chapter 1 or at this book's website. Alternatively, we can define texture as a quantity for which texture extraction algorithms provide meaningful results. One study (Karru, 1996) suggests

> The answer to the question 'is there any texture in the image?' depends not only on the input image, but also on the goal for which the image texture is used and the textural features that are extracted from the image.

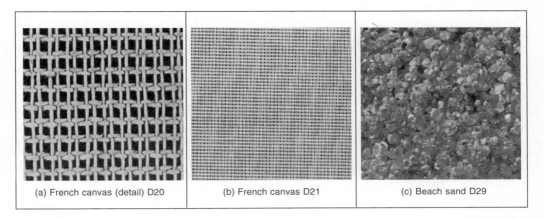

| (a) French canvas (detail) D20 | (b) French canvas D21 | (c) Beach sand D29 |

Figure 8.2 Three Brodatz textures

Essentially, there is no unique definition of texture. There is no unique mathematical model to synthesise texture; there are many ways to describe and extract it. It is a very large and exciting field of research and there continue to be many new developments.

Clearly, images will usually contain samples of more than one texture. Accordingly, we would like to be able to *describe* texture (*texture descriptions* are measurements which characterise a texture) and then to *classify* it (classification is attributing the correct class label to a set of measurements) and then perhaps to segment an image according to its texture content. We have used similar classification approaches to characterise the shape descriptions in the previous chapter. Actually these are massive fields of research that move on to the broad subject of pattern recognition. We shall look at an introduction here, later references will point you to topics of particular interest and to some of the more recent developments. The main purpose of this introduction is to show how the measurements can be collected together to recognise objects. Texture is used as the vehicle for this since it is a region-based property that has not as yet been covered. Since texture itself is an enormous subject, you will find plenty of references to established approaches and to surveys of the field. First, we shall look at approaches to deriving the features (measurements) which can be used to describe textures. Broadly, these can be split into *structural* (transform-based), *statistical* and *combination* approaches. Clearly the frequency content of an image will reflect its texture; we shall start with Fourier. First though we shall consider some of the required properties of the descriptions.

8.3 Texture description

8.3.1 Performance requirements

The purpose of texture description is to derive some measurements that can be used to classify a particular texture. As such, there are *invariance* requirements on the measurements, as there were for shape description. Actually, the invariance requirements for feature extraction, namely invariance to position, scale and rotation, can apply equally to texture extraction. After all texture is a feature, albeit a rather nebulous one as opposed to the definition of a shape. Clearly we require *position* invariance: the measurements describing a texture should not vary with the position of the analysed section (of a larger image). Also, we require *rotation* invariance but this is not as strong a requirement as position invariance; the definition of texture does not imply knowledge of orientation, but could be presumed to. The least strong requirement is that of *scale*, for this depends primarily on application. Consider using texture to analyse forests in remotely sensed images. Scale invariance would imply that closely spaced young trees should give the same measure as widely spaced mature trees. This should be satisfactory if the purpose is only to analyse foliage cover. It would be unsatisfactory if the purpose was to measure age for purposes of replenishment, since a scale-invariant measure would be of little use as it could not, in principle, distinguish between young trees and old ones.

Unlike feature extraction, texture description rarely depends on edge extraction since one main purpose of edge extraction is to remove reliance on overall *illumination* level. The higher order invariants, such as perspective invariance, are rarely applied to texture description. This is perhaps because many applications are like remotely sensed imagery, or are in constrained industrial application where the camera geometry can be controlled.

8.3.2 Structural approaches

The most basic approach to texture description is to generate the Fourier transform of the image and then to group the transform data in some way so as to obtain a set of measurements. Naturally, the size of the set of measurements is smaller than the size of the image's transform. In Chapter 2 we saw how the transform of a set of horizontal lines was a set of vertical spatial frequencies (since the point spacing varies along the vertical axis). Here, we must remember that for display we rearrange the Fourier transform so that the d.c. component is at the centre of the presented image.

The transforms of the three Brodatz textures of Figure **8.2** are shown in Figure **8.3**. Figure **8.3**(a) shows a collection of frequency components which are then replicated with the same structure (consistent with the Fourier transform) in Figure **8.3**(b). (Figures **8.3**(a) and (b) also show the frequency scaling property of the Fourier transform: greater magnification reduces the high frequency content.) Figure **8.3**(c) is clearly different in that the structure of the transform data is spread in a different manner to that of Figures **8.3**(a) and (b). Naturally, these images have been derived by application of the FFT which we shall denote as

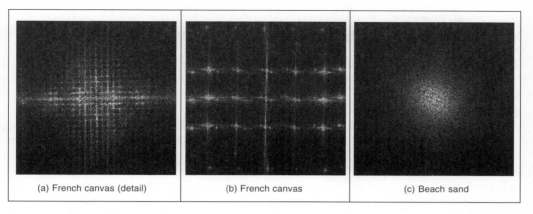

| (a) French canvas (detail) | (b) French canvas | (c) Beach sand |

Figure 8.3 Fourier transforms of the three Brodatz textures

$$\mathbf{FP} = \mathrm{FFT}(\mathbf{P}) \tag{8.1}$$

where $\mathbf{FP}_{u,v}$ and $\mathbf{P}_{x,y}$ are the transform and pixel data, respectively. One clear advantage of the Fourier transform is that it possesses shift invariance (Section 2.6.1): the transform of a bit of (large and uniform) cloth will be the same, whatever segment we inspect. This is consistent with the observation that phase is of little use in Fourier-based texture systems (Pratt, 1992), so the modulus of the transform (its magnitude) is usually used. The transform is of the same size as the image, even though conjugate symmetry of the transform implies that we do not need to use all its components as measurements. As such we can *filter* the Fourier transform (Section 2.8) so as to select those frequency components deemed to be of interest to a particular application. Alternatively, it is convenient to collect the magnitude transform data in different ways to achieve a reduced set of measurements. First though the transform data can be normalised by the sum of the squared values of each magnitude component (excepting the zero-frequency components, those for $u = 0$ and $v = 0$), so that the magnitude data is invariant to linear shifts in illumination to obtain normalised Fourier coefficients **NFP** as

$$\mathbf{NFP}_{u,v} = \frac{|\mathbf{FP}_{u,v}|}{\sqrt{\sum_{(u\neq0)\wedge(v\neq0)} |\mathbf{FP}_{u,v}|^2}} \tag{8.2}$$

Alternatively, histogram equalisation (Section 3.3.3) can provide such invariance but is more complicated than using Equation 8.2. The spectral data can then be described by the *entropy*, h, as

$$h = \sum_{u=1}^{N} \sum_{v=1}^{N} \mathbf{NFP}_{u,v} \log(\mathbf{NFP}_{u,v}) \tag{8.3}$$

or by their *energy*, e, as

$$e = \sum_{u=1}^{N} \sum_{v=1}^{N} (\mathbf{NFP}_{u,v})^2 \tag{8.4}$$

Another measure is their *inertia*, i, defined as

Introduction to texture description, segmentation and classification   295

$$i = \sum_{u=1}^{N} \sum_{v=1}^{N} (u - v)^2 \mathbf{NFP}_{u,v} \qquad (8.5)$$

These measures are shown for the three Brodatz textures in Code **8.1**. In a way, they are like the shape descriptions in the previous chapter: the measures should be the same for the same object and should differ for a different one. Here, the texture measures are actually different for each of the textures. Perhaps the detail in the French canvas, Code **8.1**(a), could be made to give a closer measure to that of the full resolution, Code **8.1**(b), by using the frequency scaling property of the Fourier transform, discussed in Section 2.6.3. The beach sand clearly gives a different set of measures from the other two, Code **8.1**(c). In fact, the beach sand in Code **8.1**(c) would appear to be more similar to the French canvas in Code **8.1**(b), since the inertia and energy measures are much closer than those for Code **8.1**(a) (only the entropy measure in Code **8.1**(a) is closest to Code **8.1**(b)). This is consistent with the images: each of the beach sand and French canvas has a large proportion of higher frequency information, since each is a finer texture than that of the detail in the French canvas.

entropy(FD20)=-253.11	entropy(FD21)=-196.84	entropy(FD29)=-310.61
inertia(FD20)=5.55·10^5	inertia(FD21)=6.86·10^5	inertia(FD29)=6.38·10^5
energy(FD20)=5.41	energy(FD21)=7.49	energy(FD29)=12.37
(a) French canvas (detail)	(b) French canvas	(c) Beach sand

Code 8.1 Measures of the Fourier transforms of the three Brodatz textures

By Fourier analysis, the measures are inherently *position*-invariant. Clearly, the entropy, inertia and energy are relatively immune to *rotation*, since order is not important in their calculation. Also, the measures can be made *scale* invariant, as a consequence of the frequency scaling property of the Fourier transform. Finally, the measurements (by virtue of the normalisation process) are inherently invariant to linear changes in *illumination*. Naturally, the descriptions will be subject to noise. In order to handle large data sets we need a larger set of measurements (larger than the three given here) in order to better discriminate between different textures. Other measures can include:

1. the energy in the major peak;
2. the Laplacian of the major peak;
3. the largest horizontal frequency;
4. the largest vertical frequency.

Amongst others, these are elements of Liu's features (Liu, 1990) chosen in a way aimed to give Fourier transform-based measurements good performance in noisy conditions.

Naturally, there are many other transforms and these can confer different attributes in analysis. The wavelet transform is very popular since it allows for localisation in time and frequency (Laine, 1993) and (Lu, 1997). Other approaches use the Gabor wavelet (Bovik, 1990), (Jain, 1991) and (Daugman, 1993), as introduced in Section 2.7.3. One comparison between Gabor wavelets and tree- and pyramidal-structured wavelets suggested that Gabor has the greater descriptional ability, but a penalty of greater computational complexity (Pichler, 1996). There has also been renewed resurgence of interest in Markov random fields (Gimmel' farb, 1996) and (Wu, 1996). Others, such as the Walsh transform (where the basis functions are 1s and 0s) appear yet to await application in texture description, no doubt due to basic properties. In fact, a recent survey (Randen, 2000) includes use of Fourier, wavelet and discrete cosine transforms (Section 2.7.1) for texture characterisation. These approaches are structural in nature: an image is viewed in terms of a transform applied to a whole image as such exposing its *structure*. This is like the dictionary definition of an arrangement of parts. Another part of the dictionary definition concerned *detail*: this can of course be exposed by analysis of the high frequency components but these can be prone to noise. An alternative way to analyse the detail is to consider the *statistics* of an image.

8.3.3 Statistical approaches

The most famous statistical approach is the *co-occurrence matrix*. This was the result of the first approach to describe, and then classify, image texture (Haralick, 1973). It remains popular today, by virtue of good performance. The co-occurrence matrix contains elements that are counts of the number of pixel pairs for specific brightness levels, when separated by some distance and at some relative inclination. For brightness levels $b1$ and $b2$ the co-occurrence matrix $\mathbf{C}$ is

$$\mathbf{C}_{b1,b2} = \sum_{x=1}^{N} \sum_{y=1}^{N} (\mathbf{P}_{x,y} = b1) \wedge (\mathbf{P}_{x',y'} = b2) \tag{8.6}$$

where the x co-ordinate x' is the offset given by the specified distance d and inclination θ by

$$x' = x + d \cos(\theta) \quad \forall \ (d \in 1, \max(d)) \wedge (\theta \in 0, 2\pi) \tag{8.7}$$

and the y co-ordinate y' is

$$y' = y + d \sin(\theta) \quad \forall \ (d \in 1, \max(d)) \wedge (\theta \in 0, 2\pi) \tag{8.8}$$

When Equation 8.6 is applied to an image, we obtain a square, symmetric, matrix whose dimensions equal the number of grey levels in the picture. The co-occurrence matrices for the three Brodatz textures of Figure **8.2** are shown in Figure **8.4**. In the co-occurrence matrix generation, the maximum distance was 1 pixel and the directions were set to select the four nearest neighbours of each point. Now the result for the two samples of French canvas, Figures **8.4**(a) and (b), appear to be much more similar and quite different to the co-occurrence matrix for sand, Figure **8.4**(c). As such, the co-occurrence matrix looks like it can better expose the underlying nature of texture than can the Fourier description. This is because the co-occurrence measures spatial relationships between brightness, as opposed to frequency content. This clearly gives alternative results. To generate results faster, the number of grey levels can be reduced by brightness scaling of the whole image, reducing the dimensions of the co-occurrence matrix, but this reduces discriminatory ability.

These matrices have been achieved by the implementation in Code **8.2**. The subroutine `tex_cc` generates the co-occurrence matrix of an image `im` given a maximum distance `d` and a number of directions `dirs`. If `d` and `dirs` are set to 1 and 4, respectively (as was

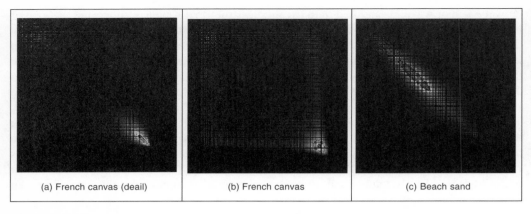

(a) French canvas (deail)	(b) French canvas	(c) Beach sand

Figure 8.4 Co-occurrence matrices of the three Brodatz textures

used to generate the results in Figure **8.4**), then the co-occurrence will be evaluated from a point and its four nearest neighbours. First, the co-occurrence matrix is cleared. Then, for each point in the image and for each value of distance and relative inclination (and so long as the two points are within the image), then the element of the co-occurrence matrix indexed by the brightnesses of the two points is incremented. Finally, the completed co-occurrence matrix is returned. Note that even though the co-occurrence matrix is symmetric, this factor cannot be used to speed its production.

```
tex_cc(im,dist,dirs):=
              for x∈0..maxbri
                 for y∈0..maxbri
                     cocc_y,x←0
              for x∈0..cols(im)-1
                 for y∈0..rows(im)-1
                    for r∈1..dist

                       for θ∈0,(2·π)/dirs..2.π
                       xc←floor(x+r·cos(θ))
                       yc←floor(y+r·sin(θ))
                       if (0≤yc)·(yc<rows(im))·(0≤xc)·(xc<cols(im))
                          cocc_imy,x,imyc,xc ←cocc_imy,x,imyc,xc +1

              cocc
```

Code 8.2 Co-occurrence matrix generation

Again, we need measurements that describe these matrices. We shall use the measures of entropy, inertia and energy defined earlier. The results are shown in Code **8.3**. Unlike visual analysis of the co-occurrence matrices, the difference between the measures of the three textures is less clear: classification from them will be discussed later. Clearly, the co-occurrence matrices have been reduced to only three different measures. In principle, these measurements are again invariant to linear shift in illumination (by virtue of brightness comparison) and to rotation (since order is of no consequence in their description and rotation only affects co-occurrence by discretisation effects). As with Fourier, scale can affect the structure of the co-occurrence matrix, but the description can be made scale invariant.

entropy(CCD20)=7.052·10^5	entropy(CCD21)=5.339·10^5	entropy(CCD29)=6.445·10^5
inertia(CCD20)=5.166·10^8	inertia(CCD21)=1.528·10^9	inertia(CCD29)=1.139·10^8
energy(CCD20)=5.16·10^8	energy(CCD21)=3.333·10^7	energy(CCD29)=5.315·10^7
(a) French canvas (detail)	(b) French canvas	(c) Beach sand

Code 8.3 Measures of co-occurrence matrices of the three Brodatz textures

Grey level difference statistics (a first-order measure) were later added to improve descriptional capability (Weszka, 1976). Other statistical approaches include the statistical feature matrix (Wu, 1992) with the advantage of faster generation.

8.3.4 Combination approaches

The previous approaches have assumed that we can represent textures by purely structural, or purely statistical description, combined in some appropriate manner. Since texture is not an exact quantity, and is more a nebulous one, there are naturally many alternative descriptions. One approach (Chen, 1995) suggested that texture combines geometrical structures (as, say, in patterned cloth) with statistical ones (as, say, in carpet) and has been shown to give good performance in comparison with other techniques, and using the *whole* Brodatz data set. The technique is called Statistical Geometric Features (SGF), reflecting the basis of its texture description. This is not a dominant texture characterisation: the interest here is that we shall now see the earlier *shape measures* in action, describing texture. Essentially, geometric features are derived from images, and then described by using statistics. The geometric quantities are actually derived from $NB - 1$ binary images **B** which are derived from the original image **P** (which has NB brightness levels). These binary images are given by

$$\mathbf{B}(\alpha)_{x,y} = \begin{vmatrix} 1 & \text{if } P_{x,y} = \alpha \\ 0 & \text{otherwise} \end{vmatrix} \quad \forall \alpha \in 1, NB \tag{8.9}$$

Then, the points in each binary region are connected into regions of 1s and 0s. Four geometrical measures are made on these data. First, in each binary plane, the number of regions of 1s and 0s (the number of connected sets of 1s and 0s) is counted to give $NOC1$ and $NOC0$. Then, in each plane, each of the connected regions is described by its *irregularity* which is a local shape measure of a region **R** of connected 1s giving irregularity $I1$ defined by

$$I1(\mathbf{R}) = \frac{1 + \sqrt{\pi} \max_{i \in \mathbf{R}} \sqrt{(x_i - \bar{x})^2 + (y_i - \bar{y})^2}}{\sqrt{N(\mathbf{R})}} - 1 \tag{8.10}$$

where x_i and y_i are co-ordinates of points within the region, $\bar{x}$ and $\bar{y}$ are the region's centroid (its mean x and y co-ordinates), and N is the number of points within (i.e. the area of) the region. The irregularity of the connected 0s, $I0(\mathbf{R})$, is similarly defined. When this is applied to the regions of 1s and 0s it gives two further geometric measures, $IRGL1(i)$ and $IRGL0(i)$, respectively. To balance the contributions from different regions, the irregularity of the regions of 1s in a particular plane is formed as a weighted sum $WI1(\alpha)$ as

$$WI1(\alpha) = \frac{\sum_{\mathbf{R} \in \mathbf{B}(\alpha)} N(\mathbf{R})I(\mathbf{R})}{\sum_{\mathbf{R} \in \mathbf{P}} N(\mathbf{R})} \tag{8.11}$$

giving a single irregularity measure for each plane. Similarly, the weighted irregularity of the connected 0s is $WI0$. Together with the two counts of connected regions, $NOC1$ and $NOC0$, the weighted irregularities give the four geometric measures in SGF. The statistics are derived from these four measures. The derived statistics are the maximum value of each measure across all binary planes, M. Using $m(\alpha)$ to denote any of the four measures, the maximum is

$$M = \max_{\alpha i \in 1, NB} (m(\alpha)) \tag{8.12}$$

the average $\bar{m}$ is

$$\bar{m} = \frac{1}{255} \sum_{\alpha=1}^{NB} m(\alpha) \tag{8.13}$$

the sample mean $\bar{s}$ is

$$\bar{s} = \frac{1}{\sum_{\alpha=1}^{NB} m(\alpha)} \sum_{\alpha=1}^{NB} \alpha m(\alpha) \tag{8.14}$$

and the final statistic is the sample standard deviation ssd as

$$ssd = \sqrt{\frac{1}{\sum_{\alpha=1}^{NB} m(\alpha)} \sum_{\alpha=1}^{NB} (\alpha - \bar{s})^2 m(\alpha)} \tag{8.15}$$

The irregularity measure can be replaced by *compactness* (Section 7.3.1) but compactness varies with rotation, though this was not found to influence results much (Chen, 1995).

In order to implement these measures, we need to derive the sets of connected 1s and 0s in each of the binary planes. This can be achieved by using a version of the `connect` routine in hysteresis thresholding (Section 4.2.5). The reformulation is necessary because the `connect` routine just labels connected points whereas the irregularity measures require a list of points in the connected region so that the centroid (and hence the maximum distance of a point from the centroid) can be calculated. The results for four of the measures (for the region of 1s, the maximum and average values of the number of connected regions and of the weighted irregularity) are shown in Code **8.4**. Again, the set of measures is different for each texture. Of note, the last measure, $\overline{m}(WI1)$, does not appear to offer much discriminatory capability here whereas the measure $M(WI1)$ appears to be a much more potent descriptor. Classification, or *discrimination*, is to select which class the measures refer to.

M(NOC1)=52.0	M(NOC1)=178	M(NOC1)=81
$\overline{m}$(NOC1)=8.75	$\overline{m}$(NOC1)=11.52	$\overline{m}$(NOC1)=22.14
M(WI1)=1.50	M(WI1)=1.42	M(WI1)=1.00
$\overline{m}$(WI1)=0.40	$\overline{m}$(WI1)=0.35	$\overline{m}$(WI1)=0.37
(a) French canvas (detail)	(b) French canvas	(c) Beach sand

Code 8.4 Four of the SGF measures of the three Brodatz textures

8.4 Classification

8.4.1 The *k*-nearest neighbour rule

In application, usually we have a description of a texture *sample* and we want to find which element of a database best matches that sample. Thus is *classification*: to associate the appropriate *class label* (type of texture) with the test sample by using the measurements that describe it. One way to make the association is by finding the member of the class (the sample of a known texture) with measurements which differ by the least amount from the test sample's measurements. In terms of *Euclidean* distance, the difference d between the M descriptions of a sample, $\mathbf{s}$, and the description of a known texture, $\mathbf{k}$, is

$$d = \sqrt{\sum_{i=1}^{M} (\mathbf{s}_i - \mathbf{k}_i)^2} \tag{8.16}$$

which is also called the L_2 *norm*. Alternative distance metrics include: the L_1 *norm* which is the sum of the modulus of the differences between the measurements

$$L_1 = \sum_{i=1}^{M} |\mathbf{s}_i - \mathbf{k}_i| \tag{8.17}$$

and the Bhattacharyya distance B

$$B = -\ln \sum_{i=1}^{M} \sqrt{\mathbf{s}_i \times \mathbf{k}_i} \tag{8.18}$$

but this appears to be used less, like other metrics such as the Matusita difference.

If we have M measurements of N known samples of textures and we have O samples of each, then we have an M-dimensional *feature space* that contains the $N \times O$ points. If we select the point, in the feature space, which is closest to the current sample, then we have selected the sample's *nearest neighbour*. This is illustrated in Figure **8.5** where we have a two-dimensional feature space produced by the two measures made on each sample, measure 1 and measure 2. Each sample gives different values for these measures but the samples of different classes give rise to clusters in the feature space where each cluster is associated with a single class. In Figure **8.5** we have seven samples of two known textures: Class A and Class B depicted by ✕ and ◯, respectively. We want to classify a test sample, depicted by **+**, as belonging either to Class A or to Class B (i.e. we assume that the training data contains representatives of all possible classes). Its nearest neighbour, the sample with least distance, is one of the samples of Class A so we could then say that our test appears to be another sample of Class A (i.e. the class label associated with it is Class A). Clearly, the clusters will be far apart for measures that have good discriminatory ability whereas the clusters will overlap for measures that have poor discriminatory ability. That is how we can choose measures for particular tasks. Before that, let us look at how best to associate a class label with our test sample.

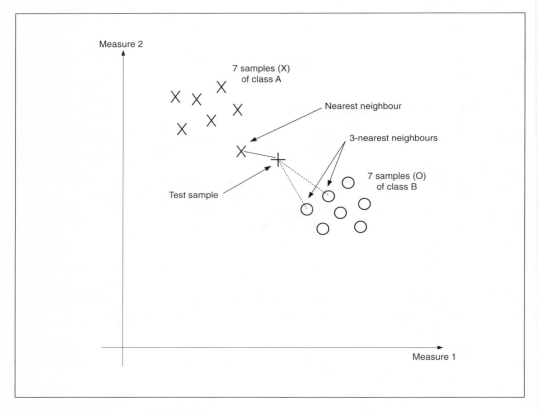

Figure 8.5 Feature space and classification

Classifying a test sample as the training sample it is closest to in feature space is actually a specific case of a general classification rule known as the *k-nearest neighbour rule*. In this rule, the class selected is the *mode* of the sample's nearest k neighbours. By the k-nearest neighbour rule, for $k = 3$, we select the nearest three neighbours (those three with the least distance) and their mode, the maximally represented **class**, is attributed to the sample. In Figure **8.5**, the 3-nearest neighbour is actually Class B since the three nearest samples contain one from Class A (its nearest neighbour) and two from Class B. Since there are two elements of Class B, then the sample is attributed to this class by the 3-nearest neighbour rule. As such, selection from more than one point introduces a form of feature space smoothing and allows the classification decision not to be affected by noisy *outlier* points. Clearly, this smoothing has greater effect for larger values of k. (Further details concerning a more modern view of the k-nearest neighbour rule can be found in Michie et al. (1994).

A Mathcad implementation of the k-nearest neighbour rule is given in Code **8.5**. The arguments are `test` (the vector of measurements of the test sample), `data` (the list of vectors of measurements of all samples), `size` (the value of k) and `no`. The final parameter `no` dictates the structure of the presented data and is the number of classes within that data. The training data is presumed to have been arranged so that samples of each class are all stored together. For two classes in the training data, `no = 2`, where each occupies one-half (the same situation as in Figure **8.5**). If `no = 3` then there are three classes, each occupying one-third of the complete data set and the first third contains the first class, the second third contains samples of another class whilst the remaining third contains samples of the final class. In application, first the distances between the current sample, `test`, and all other samples are evaluated by using the function `distance`. Then the k nearest neighbours are selected to form a vector of distances `min`, these are the k neighbours which are closest (in the feature space) to the sample test. The number of feature space splits `fsp` is the spacing between the classes in the `data`. The class which occurs the most number of times in the set of `size` nearest neighbours is then returned as the k-nearest neighbour, by incrementing the class number to which each of the k neighbours is associated. (If no such decision is possible, i.e. there is no maximally represented class, then the technique can be arranged to return the class of the nearest neighbour, by default.)

```
k_nn(test,data,size,no):=
            for i∈0..rows(data)-1
              │ dist_i←0
              │ for j∈0..cols(date)-1
              │   dist_i←distance(test,data,i)
            for i∈0..size-1
              │ posmin←coord(min(dist),dist)
              │ dis_posmin←max(dist)+1
              │ min_i←posmin
            fsp← rows(data)
                  ─────────
                     no
            for j∈1..no
              class_j←0
            for i∈0..size-1
              for j∈1..no
                class_j←class_j+1 if [min_i≥(j-1)·fsp]·(min_i<j·fsp)
            test_class←coord(max(class),class)
            test_class
```

Code 8.5   Implementing the k-nearest neighbour rule

The result of testing the *k*-nearest neighbour routine is illustrated on synthetic data in Code **8.6**. Here there are two different data sets. The first, Code **8.6**(a), has three classes of which there are three samples (each sample is a row of data, so this totals nine rows) and each sample is made up of three measurements (the three columns). As this is synthetic data, it can be seen that each class is quite distinct: the first class is for measurements around [1, 2, 3]; the second class is around [4, 6, 8]; and the third is around [8, 6, 3]. A small amount of noise has been added to the measurements. We then want to see the class associated with a test sample with measurements [4, 6, 8], Code **8.6**(b). The result is either class 1, class 2 or class 3. Naturally, the 1-nearest nearest neighbour, Code **8.6**(c), associates the test sample with the class with the closest measurements which is class 2 as the test sample's nearest neighbour is the fourth row of data. The 3-nearest neighbour, Code **8.6**(d), is again class 2 as the nearest three neighbours are the fourth, fifth and sixth rows and each of these is from class 2.

$$\text{population1} := \begin{bmatrix} 1 & 2 & 3 \\ 1.1 & 2 & 3.1 \\ 1 & 2.1 & 3 \\ 4 & 6 & 8 \\ 3.9 & 6.1 & 8.1 \\ 4.1 & 5.9 & 8.2 \\ 8.8 & 6.1 & 2.8 \\ 7.8 & 5.9 & 3.3 \\ 8.8 & 6.4 & 3.1 \end{bmatrix}$$

(a) 3 classes, 3 samples, 3 features

$$\text{population2} := \begin{bmatrix} 2 & 4 & 6 & 8 \\ 2.1 & 3.9 & 6.2 & 7.8 \\ 2.3 & 3.6 & 5.8 & 8.3 \\ 2.5 & 4.5 & 6.5 & 8.5 \\ 3.4 & 4.4 & 6.6 & 8.6 \\ 2.3 & 4.6 & 6.4 & 8.5 \end{bmatrix}$$

(e) 2 classes, 3 samples, 4 features

```
test_point1:=(4 6 8)
```
(b) First test sample

```
test_point2:=(2.5 3.8 6.4 8.3)
```
(f) Second test sample

```
k_nn(test_point1,population1,1,3)=2
```
(c) 1-nearest neighbour

```
k_nn(test_point2,population2,1,2)=1
```
(g) 1-nearest neighbour

```
k_nn(test_point1,population1,3,3)=2
```
(d) 3-nearest neighbour

```
k_nn(test_point2,population2,3,2)=2
```
(h) 3-nearest neighbour

Code 8.6   Applying the *k*-nearest neighbour rule to synthetic data

The second data set, Code **8.6**(e), is two classes with three samples each made up of four measures. The test sample, Code **8.6**(f), is actually associated with class 1 by the 1-nearest neighbour, Code **8.6**(g), but with class 2 for the 3-nearest neighbour, Code **8.6**(h). This is because the test sample is actually closest to the sample in the third row. After the third row, the next two closest samples are in the fourth and sixth rows. As the nearest neighbour is in a different class (class 1) to that of the next two nearest neighbours (class 2); a different result has occurred when there is more *smoothing* in the feature space (when the value of k is increased).

The Brodatz database actually contains 112 textures, but few descriptions have been evaluated on the whole database, usually concentrating on a subset. It has been shown that the SGF description can afford better classification capability than the co-occurrence matrix and the Fourier transform features (described by Liu's features) (Chen, 1995). For experimental procedure, the Brodatz pictures were scanned into 256×256 images which were split into 16 64×64 sub-images. Nine of the sub-images were selected at random and results were classified using *leave-one-out cross-validation* (Lachenbruch, 1968). *Leave-one-out* refers to a procedure where one of the samples is selected as the test sample, the others form the training data (this is the leave-one-out rule). *Cross-validation* is where the test is repeated for all samples: each sample becomes the test data once. In the comparison, the eight optimal Fourier transform features were used (Liu, 1990), and the five most popular measures from the co-occurrence matrix. The correct classification rate, the number of samples attributed to the correct class, showed better performance by the combination of statistical and geometric features (86%), as opposed to use of single measures. The enduring capability of the co-occurrence approach was reflected by their (65%) performance in comparison with Fourier (33% – whose poor performance is rather surprising). An independent study (Walker, 1996) has confirmed the experimental advantage of SGF over the co-occurrence matrix, based on a (larger) database of 117 cervical cell specimen images. Another study (Ohanian, 1992) concerned the features which optimised classification rate and compared co-occurrence, fractal-based, Markov random field and Gabor-derived features. By analysis on synthetic and real imagery, via the k-nearest neighbour rule, the results suggested that co-occurrence offered the best overall performance. More recently (Porter, 1996), wavelets, Gabor wavelets and Gaussian Markov random fields have been compared (on a limited subset of the Brodatz database) to show that the wavelet-based approach had the best overall classification performance (in noise as well) together with the smallest computational demand.

8.4.2 Other classification approaches

Classification is the process by which we attribute a class label to a set of measurements. Essentially, this is the heart of pattern recognition: intuitively, there must be many approaches. These include *statistical* and *structural* approaches: a review can be found in Shalkoff (1992) and a more modern view in Cherkassky and Mulier (1998). One major approach is to use a *neural network* which is a common alternative to using a classification rule. Essentially, modern approaches centre around using *multi-layer perceptrons* with *artificial neural networks* in which the computing elements aim to mimic properties of neurons in the human brain. These networks require *training*, typically by error back-propagation, aimed to minimise classification error on the training data. At this point, the network should have learnt how to recognise the *test* data (they aim to learn its structure): the output of a neural network can be arranged to be class labels. Approaches using neural nets (Muhamad, 1994) show how texture metrics can be used with neural nets as classifiers, another uses cascaded neural nets for texture extraction (Shang, 1994). Neural networks are within a research field that has shown immense growth in the past two decades, further details may be found in Michie (1994), Bishop (1995) (often a student favourite), and more targeted at vision in Zhou and Chellappa (1992). Support Vector Machines (SVMs) (Vapnik, 1995) are one of the more popular new approaches to data modelling and classification. Amongst SVMs advantages is excellent *generalisation* capabilty which concerns the ability to classify correctly samples which are not within feature space used for training. SVMs are already finding application in texture classification (Kim, 1999).

Also, there are methods aimed to improve classification capability by pruning the data to remove that which does not contribute to the classification decision. *Principle components analysis* (the *Karhunen–Loeve transform*) can reduce dimensionality, orthogonalise and remove redundant data. There is also *linear discriminant analysis* (also called *canonical analysis*) to improve class separability, whilst concurrently reducing cluster size (it is formulated to concurrently minimise the within-class distance and to maximise the between-class distance). There are also algorithms aimed at choosing a reduced set of features for classification: feature selection for improved discriminatory ability; a recent comparison can be found in Jain and Zongker (1997). Alternatively, the basis functionals can be chosen in such a way as to improve classificatiion capability. Recently, interest in biometrics has focused on combining different classifiers, such as face and speech, and there are promising new approaches to accommodate this (Kittler, 1998a) and (Kittler, 1998b).

8.5 Segmentation

In order to *segment* an image according to its texture, we can measure the texture in a chosen region and then classify it. This is equivalent to *template convolution* but where the result applied to pixels is the class to which they belong, as opposed to the usual result of template convolution. Here, we shall use a 7×7 template size: the texture measures will be derived from the 49 points within the template. First though we need data from which we can make a classification decision, the training data. Naturally, this depends on a chosen application. Here we shall consider the problem of segmenting the eye image into regions of *hair* and *skin*.

This is a two class problem for which we need samples of each class, samples of skin and hair. We will take samples of each of the two classes, in this way the classification decision is as illustrated in Figure **8.5**. The texture measures are the energy, entropy and inertia of the co-occurrence matrix of the 7×7 region, so the feature space is three-dimensional. The training data is derived from regions of hair and from regions of skin, as shown in Figures **8.6**(a) and (b), respectively. The first half of this data is the samples of hair, the other half is samples of the skin, as required for the k-nearest neighbour classifier of Code **8.5**.

We can then segment the image by classifying each pixel according to the description obtained from its 7×7 region. Clearly, the training samples of each class should be classified correctly. The result is shown in Figure **8.7**(a). Here, the top left corner is first (correctly) classified as hair, and the top row of the image is classified as hair until the skin commences (note that the border inherent in template convolution reappears). In fact, much of the image appears to be classified as expected. The eye region is classified as hair, but this is a somewhat arbitrary decision; it is simply that hair is the closest texture feature. Also, some of the darker regions of skin are classified as hair, perhaps the result of training on regions of brighter skin.

Naturally, this is a computationally demanding process. An alternative approach is simply to classify regions as opposed to pixels. This is the tiled approach, with the result

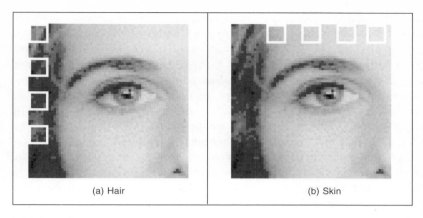

(a) Hair   (b) Skin

Figure 8.6 Training regions for classification

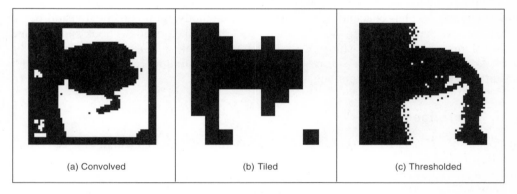

(a) Convolved   (b) Tiled   (c) Thresholded

Figure 8.7 Segmenting the eye image into two classes

shown in Figure **8.7**(b). The resolution is clearly very poor: the image has effectively been reduced to a set of 7×7 regions but it is much *faster*, requiring only 2% of the computation of the convolution approach.

A comparison with the result achieved by uniform thresholding is given, for comparison, in Figure **8.7**(c). This is equivalent to pixel segmentation by brightness alone. Clearly, there are no regions where the hair and skin are mixed and in some ways the result appears superior. This is in part due to the simplicity in implementation of texture segmentation. But the result of thresholding depends on *illumination* level and on appropriate choice of the threshold value. The texture segmentation method is completely *automatic* and the measures are known to have *invariance* properties to illumination, as well as other factors. Also, in uniform thresholding there is no extension possible to separate *more* classes (except perhaps to threshold at differing brightness levels).

8.6 Further reading

Clearly, there is much further reading in the area of texture description, segmentation, and classification as evidenced by the volume of published work in this area. There is one fairly recent survey (Reed, 1993), which is certainly more recent than the earlier surveys (Wechsler, 1980; Davis, 1981), but it is a large field of work to survey with many applications. Even though it is a large body of work, it is still only a subset of the field of pattern recognition. In fact, a recent review of pattern recognition gives many pointers to this fascinating and extensive field (Jain, 2000). In this text, the general paradigm is to extract features that describe the target and then to classify it for purposes of recognition. In vision-based systems such approaches are used in *biometrics*: ways to recognise a person's identity by some innate human properties. The biometrics of major recent interest are *signatures*, *speech*, *irises* and *faces*, though there is work in other areas including hand geometry (as used in US immigration) and gait. The first text on biometrics appeared only recently (Jain, 1999) and surveys all major biometric approaches. Naturally, there is much interest in automatic target recognition both in military and commercial applications. This naturally translates to medical studies, where the interest is either in diagnosis or therapy. Here, researchers seek to be able to identify and recognise normal or abnormal features within one of the many medical imaging modalities, for surgical purposes. This is the world of image processing and computer vision. But all these operations depend on *feature extraction*, that is why this text has concentrated on these basic methods, for no practical vision-based system yet exists without them. We finish here, we hope you enjoyed the book and will find it useful in your career or study. Certainly have a look at our website, `http://www.ecs.soton.ac.uk/~msn/book/`, as you will find more material there. Don't hesitate to send us comments or suggestions. À bientôt!

8.7 References

Bishop, C. M., *Neural Networks for Pattern Recognition*, Oxford University Press, Oxford UK, 1995

Bovik, A. C., Clark, M. and Geisler, W. S., Multichannel Texture Analysis using Localised Spatial Filters, *IEEE Trans. on PAMI*, **12**(1), pp. 55–73, 1990

Brodatz, P., *Textures: a Photographic Album for Artists and Designers*, Reinhold, NY USA, 1968

Chen, Y. Q., Nixon, M. S. and Thomas, D. W., Texture Classification using Statistical Geometric Features, *Pattern Recog.*, **28**(4), pp. 537–552, 1995

Cherkassky, V. and Mulier, F., *Learning from Data*, Wiley, NY, USA 1998

Daugman, J. G., High Confidence Visual Recognition of Persons using a Test of Statistical Independence, *IEEE Trans. on PAMI*, **18**(8), pp. 1148–1161, 1993

Davis, L. S., Image Texture Analysis Techniques – a Survey, *Digital Image Processing. Proceedings of the NATO Advanced Study Institute*, Reidel, Dordrecht, Netherlands, pp. 189–201, 1981

Dunn, D., Higgins, W. E. and Wakely, Texture Segmentation using 2-D Gabor Elementary Functions, *IEEE Trans. on PAMI* **16**(2), pp. 130–149, 1994

Gimmel'farb, G. L. and Jain, A. K., On Retrieving Textured Images from an Image Database, *Pattern Recog.*, **28**(12), pp. 1807–1817, 1996

Haralick, R. M., Shanmugam, K. and Dinstein, I., Textural Features for Image Classification, *IEEE Trans. on Systems, Man and Cybernetics*, **2**, pp. 610–621, 1973

Jain, A. K. and Farrokhnia, F., Unsupervised Texture Segmentation using Gabor Filters, *Pattern Recog.*, **24**(12), pp. 1186–1191, 1991

Jain, A. K. and Zongker, D., Feature Selection: Evaluation, Application and Small Sample Performance, *IEEE Trans. on PAMI*, **19**(2), pp. 153–158, 1997

Jain, A. K., Bolle, R. and Pankanti, S. (eds), *Biometrics – Personal Identification in Networked Society*, Kluwer Academic Publishers, Norwell Mass. USA 1999

Jain, A. K., Duin, R. P. W. and Mao, J., Statistical Pattern Recognition: a Review, *IEEE Trans. on PAMI*, **22**(1), pp. 4–37, 2000

Karru, K., Jain, A. K. and Bolle, R., Is There Any Texture in an Image?, *Pattern Recog.*, **29**(9), pp. 1437–1446, 1996

Kim, K.I., Jung K., Park, S. H. and Kim, H. J., Supervised Texture Segmentation using Support Vector Machines, *Electronics Letters*, **35**(22), pp. 1935–1937, 1999

Kittler, J., Hatef, M., Duin, R. P. W. and Matas, J., On Combining Classifiers, *IEEE Trans. on PAMI*, **20**(3), pp. 226–239, 1998

Kittler, J., Combining Classifiers: a Theoretical Framework, *Pattern Analysis and Applications*, **1**(1), pp. 18–27, 1998

Lachenbruch, P. A. and Mickey, M. R., Estimation of Error Rates in Discriminant Analysis, *Technometrics*, **10**, pp. 1–11, 1968

Laine, A. and Fan, J., Texture Classification via Wavelet Pattern Signatures, *IEEE Trans. on PAMI*, **15**(11), pp. 1186–1191, 1993

Liu, S. S. and Jernigan, M. E., Texture Analysis and Discrimination in Additive Noise, *CVGIP*, **49**, pp. 52–67, 1990.

Lu, C. S., Chung, P. C. and Chen, C. F., Unsupervised Texture Segmentation via Wavelet Transform, *Pattern Recog.*, **30**(5), pp. 729–742, 1997

Michie, D., Spiegelhlter, D. J. and Taylor, C. C. (eds), *Machine Learning, Neural and Statistical Classification*, Ellis Horwood, Hemel Hempstead UK, 1994

Muhamad, A. K. and Deravi, F., Neural Networks for the Classification of Image Texture, *Engineering Applications of Artificial Intelligence*, **7**(4), pp. 381–393, 1994

Ohanian, P. P. and Dubes, R. C., Performance Evaluation for Four Classes of Textural Features, *Pattern Recog.*, **25**(8), pp. 819–833, 1992

Pichler, O., Teuner, A. and Hosticka, B. J., A Comparison of Texture Feature Extraction using Adaptive Gabor Filtering, Pyramidal and Tree Structured Wavelet Transforms, *Pattern Recog.*, **29**(5), pp. 733–742, 1996

Porter, R. and Canagarajah, N., Robust Rotation-Invariant Texture Classification: Wavelet, Gabor Filter and GRMF Based Schemes, *IEE Proceedings Vision, Image and Signal Processing*, **144**(3), pp. 180–188, 1997

Pratt, W. K., *Digital Image Processing*, Wiley, UK, 1992

Randen, T. and Husoy, J. H., Filtering for Texture Classification: a Comparative Study, *IEEE Trans. on PAMI*, **21**(4), pp. 291–310, 2000

Reed, T. R., A Review of Recent Texture Segmentation and Feature Extraction Techniques, *CVGIP: Image Understanding*, **57**(3) pp. 359–372, 1993

Shang, C. G. and Brown, K., Principal Features-Based Texture Classification with Neural Networks, *Pattern Recog.* **27**(5), pp. 675–687, 1994

Shalkoff, R. J., *Pattern Recognition – Statistical, Structural and Neural Approaches*, Wiley and Sons Inc., NY USA, 1992

Vapnik, V., *The Nature of Statistical Learning Theory*, Springer-Verlag, NY USA, 1995

Walker, R. F. and Jackway, P. T., Statistical Geometric Features – Extensions for Cytological Texture Analysis, Proc. 13th ICPR, Vienna, **II** (Track B), pp. 790–794, 1996

Wechsler, H., Texture Analysis – a Survey, *Signal Processing*, **2**(3), pp. 271–282, 1980

Weska, J. S., Dyer, C. R. and Rosenfeld, A., A Comparative Study of Texture Measures for Terrain Classification, *IEEE Trans. on SMC*, **SMC-6**(4), pp. 269–285, 1976

Wu, C. M. and Chen, Y. C., Statistical Feature Matrix for Texture Analysis, *CVGIP: Graphical Models and Image Processing*, **54**, pp. 407–419, 1992

Wu, W. and Wei, S., Rotation and Gray-Scale Transform-Invariant Texture Classification using Spiral Resampling, Subband Decomposition and Hidden Markov Model, *IEEE Trans. on Image Processing*, **5**(10), pp. 1423–1434, 1996

Zhou, Y.–T. and Chellappa, R., *Artificial Neural Networks for Computer Vision*, Springer, NY USA, 1992

9
Appendices

9.1 Appendix 1: Homogeneous co-ordinate system

The *homogeneous co-ordinate system* is essentially the mathematics of how we relate *camera* co-ordinates to '*real world*' co-ordinates: the relation between *image* and *physical* space. Its major advantages are that it is *linear*, consistent and easy to use. Image transformations become simple matrix operations, as opposed to geometric calculations. It includes *perspective* (distance) and as such finds use in stereo and 3D vision applications and in camera control. It is not mainstream to shape analysis, since in many applications we use *orthographic projections* where spatial physical co-ordinates map directly to image space co-ordinates *ignoring* projection. But there are occasions when perspective is extremely important; as such it is necessary to have a co-ordinate system which can handle it. The homogeneous co-ordinate system has proved popular for this task for many years.

It is common to represent position as a set of x, y and z co-ordinates where x and y usually index spatial position and z is *depth*. By reference to the system arrangement illustrated in the figure below, by triangulation, the image point co-ordinate y_i is related to the focal length f and the x, y, z co-ordinate of the physical point x_p, y_p, z_p by

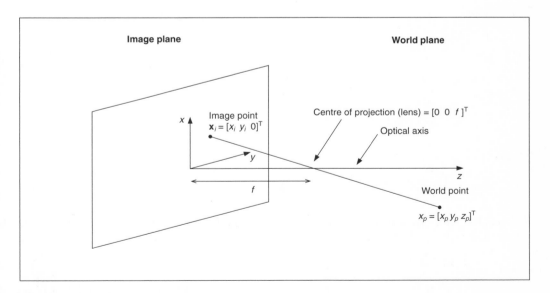

Co-ordinate system arrangement

311

$$\frac{y_p}{z_p - f} = \frac{y_i}{f} \tag{9.1}$$

Similar equations can be developed for the x and z co-ordinates. For $z_p \gg f$, as is often the case with short focal lengths, $y_i = fy_p/z_p$ is a simple approximation to Equation 9.1. (Note that the ratio z_p/f is often called the *magnification ratio*.) Unfortunately, Equation 9.1 is non-linear in z_p and f. Also, the 'world' co-ordinates are fixed to the image co-ordinates and translation and perspective are different mathematical functions (addition and multiplication, respectively). Because of these factors, many applications use the homogeneous co-ordinate system.

A Cartesian vector of co-ordinates $\mathbf{x}_c$ is given by

$$\mathbf{x}_c = [x \quad y \quad z]^{\mathrm{T}} \tag{9.2}$$

and the homogeneous co-ordinate vector $\mathbf{x}_h$ includes an extra element

$$\mathbf{x}_h = [wx \quad wy \quad wz \quad w]^{\mathrm{T}} \tag{9.3}$$

where w is an, arbitrary scalar. Accordingly, there is *no* unique representation for a point using homogeneous co-ordinates (which is consistent with imaging real-world data anyway). Conversion between the homogeneous and Cartesian co-ordinates can be achieved by division by w. A *perspective transformation matrix* $\mathbf{P}$ can be used to transform apparent distance to obtain a set of transformed co-ordinates $\mathbf{x}_t$ as

$$\mathbf{x}_t = \mathbf{P}(f)\mathbf{x}_h \tag{9.4}$$

where

$$\mathbf{P}(f) = \begin{bmatrix} 1 & 0 & 0 & 0 \\ 0 & 1 & 0 & 0 \\ 0 & 0 & 1 & 0 \\ 0 & 0 & 1/f & -1 \end{bmatrix} \tag{9.5}$$

so

$$\mathbf{x}_t = \begin{bmatrix} wx & wy & wz & \dfrac{wz}{f} - w \end{bmatrix}^{\mathrm{T}}$$
$$= \begin{bmatrix} wx & wy & wz & \dfrac{w(z-f)}{f} \end{bmatrix}^{\mathrm{T}} \tag{9.6}$$

giving

$$\mathbf{x}_c = \begin{bmatrix} \dfrac{fx}{z-f} & \dfrac{fy}{z-f} & \dfrac{fz}{z-f} \end{bmatrix}^{\mathrm{T}} \tag{9.7}$$

To shift the data (for translation), we need to add the amount of shift to each co-ordinate value. A set of transformed co-ordinates $\mathbf{x}_t$, each by an amount $\mathbf{d}$, is given by

$$\mathbf{x}_t = \mathbf{x}_h - \mathbf{d} \tag{9.8}$$

so this can be achieved in matrix form by multiplying $\mathbf{x}_h$ by a *translation matrix* $\mathbf{T}$ according to:

$$\mathbf{x}_i = \mathbf{T}(\mathbf{d})\mathbf{x}_h = \begin{bmatrix} 1 & 0 & 0 & -dx \\ 0 & 1 & 0 & -dy \\ 0 & 0 & 1 & -dz \\ 0 & 0 & 0 & 1 \end{bmatrix} \mathbf{x}_h \tag{9.9}$$

for clockwise rotation about the z axis by an angle θ, the new vector of co-ordinates $\mathbf{x}_r$ is obtained from a *rotation matrix* $\mathbf{R}_z$ as:

$$\mathbf{x}_r = \mathbf{R}_z(\theta)\mathbf{x}_h = \begin{bmatrix} \cos(\theta) & \sin(\theta) & 0 & 0 \\ -\sin(\theta) & \cos(\theta) & 0 & 0 \\ 0 & 0 & 1 & 0 \\ 0 & 0 & 0 & 1 \end{bmatrix} \mathbf{x}_h \tag{9.10}$$

If this rotation matrix is applied to an image then points will be unspecified in the rotated image, and appear as (say) black, as in Figure **3.21**(a). This is why practical implementation of image rotation is usually by *texture mapping*; further details can be found in Parker (1994). The matrix in Equation 9.10 can be used to rotate a shape, notwithstanding inherent discretisation difficulties. Other rotation matrices can be similarly defined for rotation about the x and y axes, $\mathbf{R}_x$ and $\mathbf{R}_y$, respectively. Finally, for image scaling, we derive a new set of co-ordinates $\mathbf{x}_s$ according to a scale factor s by multiplication by a scaling matrix $\mathbf{S}(s)$ as:

$$\mathbf{x}_t = \mathbf{S}(s)\mathbf{x}_h = \begin{bmatrix} s & 0 & 0 & 0 \\ 0 & s & 0 & 0 \\ 0 & 0 & s & 0 \\ 0 & 0 & 0 & 1 \end{bmatrix} \mathbf{x}_h \tag{9.11}$$

Each transform, perspective, translation, rotation and scaling is expressed in matrix form. Accordingly, in general, a set of co-ordinates of image points first transformed by $\mathbf{d}_1$, then scaled by s_1, then rotated about the z axis by q_1 and, finally, with perspective change by f_1, is expressed as

$$\mathbf{x}_t = \mathbf{P}(f_1)\mathbf{R}_z(q_1)\mathbf{S}(s_1)\mathbf{T}(\mathbf{d}_1)\mathbf{x}_h \tag{9.12}$$

Note that these operations do not commute and that order is important. This gives a linear and general co-ordinate system where image transformations are expressed as simple matrix operations. Furthermore, the conventional Cartesian system can easily be recovered from them. Naturally, homogeneous co-ordinates are most usually found in texts which include 3D imaging (a good coverage is given in Shalkoff (1989) and naturally in texts on graphics (see, for example, Parker (1994)).

9.1.1 References

Shalkoff, R. J., *Digital Image Processing and Computer Vision*, John Wiley and Sons Inc., NY USA, 1989

Parker, J. R., *Practical Computer Vision using C*, Wiley & Sons Inc., NY USA, 1994

9.2 Appendix 2: Least squares analysis

9.2.1 The least squares criterion

The *least squares criterion* is one of the foundations of *estimation theory*. This is the theory that concerns extracting the *true* value of signals from *noisy* measurements. Estimation theory techniques have been used to guide Exocet missiles and astronauts on moon missions (where navigation data was derived using sextants!), all based on techniques which employ the least squares criterion. The least squares criterion was originally developed by Gauss when he was confronted by the problem of measuring the six parameters of the orbits of planets, given astronomical measurements. These measurements were naturally subject to error, and Gauss realised that they could be combined together in some way in order to reduce a best estimate of the six parameters of interest.

Gauss assumed that the noise corrupting the measurements would have a *normal distribution*, indeed such distributions are often now called Gaussian to honour his great insight. As a consequence of the *central limit theorem*, it may be assumed that many real random noise sources are normally distributed. In cases where this assumption is not valid, the mathematical advantages that accrue from its use generally offset any resulting loss of accuracy. Also, the assumption of normality is particularly invaluable in view of the fact that the output of a system excited by Gaussian-distributed noise is Gaussian-distributed also (as seen in Fourier analysis, Chapter 2). A Gaussian probability distribution of a variable x is defined by

$$p(x) = \frac{1}{\sigma\sqrt{2\pi}} e^{\frac{-(x-\bar{x})^2}{\sigma^2}} \tag{9.13}$$

where $\bar{x}$ is the mean (loosely the average) of the distribution and σ^2 is the second moment or variance of the distribution. Given many measurements of a single unknown quantity, when that quantity is subject to errors of a zero-mean (symmetric) normal distribution, it is well known that the best estimate of the unknown quantity is the average of the measurements. In the case of two or more unknown quantities, the requirement is to combine the measurements in such a way that the error in the estimates of the unknown quantities is minimised. Clearly, direct averaging will not suffice when measurements are a function of two or more unknown quantities.

Consider the case where N equally precise measurements, $f_1, f_2 \ldots f_N$, are made on a linear function $f(a)$ of a single parameter a. The measurements are subject to zero-mean additive Gaussian noise $v_i(t)$ as such the measurements are given by

$$f_i = f(a) + v_i(t) \quad \forall i \in 1, N \tag{9.14}$$

The differences $\tilde{f}$ between the true value of the function and the noisy measurements of it are then

$$\tilde{f}_i = f(a) - f_i \quad \forall i \in 1, N \tag{9.15}$$

By Equation 9.13, the probability distribution of these errors is

$$p(\tilde{f}_i) = \frac{1}{\sigma\sqrt{2\pi}} e^{\frac{-(\tilde{f}_i)^2}{\sigma^2}} \quad \forall i \in 1, N \tag{9.16}$$

Since the errors are *independent*, the *compound* distribution of these errors is the product of their distributions, and is given by

$$p(\tilde{f}) = \frac{1}{\sigma\sqrt{2\pi}} e^{\frac{-((\tilde{f_1})^2 + (\tilde{f_2})^2 + (\tilde{f_3})^2 + ... + (\tilde{f_N})^2)}{\sigma^2}} \tag{9.17}$$

Each of the errors is a function of the unknown quantity, a, which is to be estimated. Different estimates of a will give different values for $p(\tilde{f})$. The most probable system of errors will be that for which $p(\tilde{f})$ is a *maximum*, and this corresponds to the *best* estimate of the unknown quantity. Thus to maximise $p(\tilde{f})$

$$\max\{p(\tilde{f})\} = \max\left\{\frac{1}{\sigma\sqrt{2\pi}} e^{\frac{-((\tilde{f_1})^2 + (\tilde{f_2})^2 + (\tilde{f_3})^2 + ... + (\tilde{f_N})^2)}{\sigma^2}}\right\}$$

$$= \max\left\{e^{\frac{-((\tilde{f_1})^2 + (\tilde{f_2})^2 + (\tilde{f_3})^2 + ... + (\tilde{f_N})^2)}{\sigma^2}}\right\} \tag{9.18}$$

$$= \max\{-((\tilde{f_1})^2 + (\tilde{f_2})^2 + (\tilde{f_3})^2 + ... + (\tilde{f_N})^2)\}$$

$$= \min\{(\tilde{f_1})^2 + (\tilde{f_2})^2 + (\tilde{f_3})^2 + ... + (\tilde{f_N})^2\}$$

Thus the required estimate is that which *minimises* the sum of the differences squared and this estimate is the one that is *optimal* by the least squares criterion.

This criterion leads on to the method of least squares which follows in the next section. This is a method commonly used to fit curves to measured data. This concerns estimating the values of parameters from a complete set of measurements. There are also techniques which provide estimate of parameters at time instants, based on a set of previous measurements. These techniques include the Weiner filter and the Kalman filter. The Kalman filter was the algorithm chosen for guiding Exocet missiles and moon missions (an extended square root Kalman filter, no less).

9.2.2 Curve fitting by least squares

Curve fitting by the method of least squares concerns combining a set of measurements to derive *estimates* of the parameters which specify the curve which best fits the data. By the least squares criterion, given a set of N (noisy) measurements f_i $i \in 1, N$ which are to be fitted to a curve $f(\mathbf{a})$ where $\mathbf{a}$ is a vector of parameter values, we seek to minimise the square of the difference between the measurements and the values of the curve to give an estimate of the parameters $\hat{\mathbf{a}}$ according to

$$\hat{\mathbf{a}} = \min \sum_{i=1}^{N} (f_i - f(x_i, y_i, \mathbf{a}))^2 \tag{9.19}$$

Since we seek a minimum, by differentiation we obtain

$$\frac{\partial \sum_{i=1}^{N} (f_i - f(x_i, y_i, \mathbf{a}))^2}{\partial \mathbf{a}} = 0 \tag{9.20}$$

which implies that

$$2 \sum_{i=1}^{N} (f_i - f(x_i, y_i, \mathbf{a})) \frac{\partial f(\mathbf{a})}{\partial \mathbf{a}} = 0 \tag{9.21}$$

The solution is usually of the form

$$\mathbf{Ma} = \mathbf{F} \tag{9.22}$$

where $\mathbf{M}$ is a matrix of summations of products of the index i and $\mathbf{F}$ is a vector of summations of products of the measurements and i. The solution, the best estimate of the values of $\mathbf{a}$, is then given by

$$\hat{\mathbf{a}} = \mathbf{M}^{-1} \mathbf{F} \tag{9.23}$$

By way of example, let us consider the problem of fitting a two-dimensional surface to a set of data points. The surface is given by

$$f(x, y, \mathbf{a}) = a + bx + cy + dxy \tag{9.24}$$

where the vector of parameters $\mathbf{a} = [a \quad b \quad c \quad d]^T$ controls the shape of the surface, and (x, y) are the co-ordinates of a point on the surface. Given a set of (noisy) measurements of the value of the surface at points with co-ordinates (x, y), $f_i = f(x, y) + v_i$, we seek to estimate values for the parameters using the method of least squares. By Equation 9.19 we seek

$$\hat{\mathbf{a}} = [\hat{a} \quad \hat{b} \quad \hat{c} \quad \hat{d}]^T = \min \sum_{i=1}^{N} (f_i - f(x_i, y_i, \mathbf{a}))^2 \tag{9.25}$$

By Equation 9.21 we require

$$2 \sum_{i=1}^{N} (f_i - (a + bx_i + cy_i + dx_iy_i)) \frac{\partial f(x_i, y_i, \mathbf{a})}{\partial \mathbf{a}} = 0 \tag{9.26}$$

By differentiating $f(x, y, \mathbf{a})$ with respect to each parameter we have

$$\frac{\partial f(x_i, y_i)}{\partial a} = 1 \tag{9.27}$$

$$\frac{\partial f(x_i, y_i)}{\partial b} = x \tag{9.28}$$

$$\frac{\partial f(x_i, y_i)}{\partial c} = y \tag{9.29}$$

and

$$\frac{\partial f(x_i, y_i)}{\partial d} = xy \tag{9.30}$$

and by substitution of Equations 9.27, 9.28, 9.29 and 9.30 in Equation 9.26, we obtain four simultaneous equations:

$$\sum_{i=1}^{N} (f_i - (a + bx_i + cy_i + dx_iy_i)) \times 1 = 0 \tag{9.31}$$

$$\sum_{i=1}^{N} (f_i - (a + bx_i + cy_i + dx_iy_i)) \times x_i = 0 \tag{9.32}$$

$$\sum_{i=1}^{N} (f_i - (a + bx_i + cy_i + dx_i y_i)) \times y_i = 0 \tag{9.33}$$

and

$$\sum_{i=1}^{N} (f_i - (a + bx_i + cy_i + dx_i y_i)) \times x_i y_i = 0 \tag{9.34}$$

since $\sum_{i=1}^{N} a = Na$ Equation 9.31 can be reformulated as:

$$\sum_{i=1}^{N} f_i - Na - b \sum_{i=1}^{N} x_i - c \sum_{i=1}^{N} y_i - d \sum_{i=1}^{N} x_i y_i = 0 \tag{9.35}$$

and Equations 9.32, 9.33 and 9.34 can be reformulated likewise. By expressing the simultaneous equations in matrix form,

$$\begin{bmatrix} N & \sum_{i=1}^{N} x_i & \sum_{i=1}^{N} y_i & \sum_{i=1}^{N} x_i y_i \\ \sum_{i=1}^{N} x_i & \sum_{i=1}^{N} (x_i)^2 & \sum_{i=1}^{N} x_i y_i & \sum_{i=1}^{N} (x_i)^2 y_i \\ \sum_{i=1}^{N} y_i & \sum_{i=1}^{N} x_i y_i & \sum_{i=1}^{N} (y_i)^2 & \sum_{i=1}^{N} x_i (y_i)^2 \\ \sum_{i=1}^{N} x_i y_i & \sum_{i=1}^{N} (x_i)^2 y_i & \sum_{i=1}^{N} x_i (y_i)^2 & \sum_{i=1}^{N} (x_i)^2 (y_i)^2 \end{bmatrix} \begin{bmatrix} a \\ b \\ c \\ d \end{bmatrix} = \begin{bmatrix} \sum_{i=1}^{N} f_i \\ \sum_{i=1}^{N} f_i x_i \\ \sum_{i=1}^{N} f_i y_i \\ \sum_{i=1}^{N} f_i x_i y_i \end{bmatrix} \tag{9.36}$$

and this is the same form as Equation 9.22 and can be solved by inversion, as in Equation 9.23. Note that the matrix is *symmetric* and its inversion, or solution, does not impose such a great computational penalty as appears. Given a set of data points, the values need to be entered in the summations, thus completing the matrices from which the solution is found. This technique can replace the one used in the zero-crossing detector within the Marr–Hildreth edge detection operator (Section 4.3.3), but appeared to offer no significant advantage over the (much simpler) function implemented there.

9.3 Appendix 3: Example Mathcad worksheet for Chapter 3

The appearance of the worksheets actually depends on the configuration of your system and of the Mathcad set-up. To show you how they should look, here's a typeset version of the shortest worksheet. Note that the real worksheet's appearance will depend largely on your machine's setup.

Chapter 3 Basic Image Processing Operations: Chapter 3. MCD Written by: Mark S. Nixon, 10/11/95, Last Revision: 7 August 1997

This worksheet is the companion to Chapter 3 and implements the basic image processing operations described therein. The worksheet follows the text directly and allows you to process the eye image.

This chapter concerns basic image operations, essentially those which alter a pixel's *value* in a chosen way. We might want to make an image *brighter* (if it is too dark), or to remove contamination by *noise*. For these, we would need to make the pixel values *larger* (in some controlled way) or to change the pixel's value if we suspect it to be wrong, respectively. Let's start with images of pixels, by reading in the image of a human eye.

```
eye:=READBMP(eye_orig)
```

We can view (part) of the image as a matrix of pixels or we can view it as an image (viewed using Mathcad's picture facility) as

	0	1	2	3	4	5	6	7	8	9
0	115	117	130	155	155	146	146	135	115	132
1	135	130	139	155	141	146	146	115	115	135
2	139	146	146	152	152	155	117	117	117	139
3	139	144	146	155	155	146	115	114	117	139
4	139	146	146	152	150	136	117	115	135	139
5	146	146	146	155	149	130	115	137	135	145
6	147	146	142	150	136	115	132	146	146	146
7	146	141	155	152	130	115	139	139	146	146
8	136	145	160	141	115	129	139	147	146	141
9	117	146	155	130	115	115	137	149	141	139
10	132	152	150	130	115	115	142	149	141	118
11	137	149	136	130	130	114	135	139	141	139
12	137	145	130	117	115	115	117	117	132	132

eye =

(a)

(b)

This image is 64 pixels wide and 64 pixels in height. Let's check: `cols(eye)=64` `rows(eye)=64`

This gives us 4096 pixels. Each pixel is an 8-*bit byte* (n.b. it's stored in .BMP format) so this gives us 256 possible *intensity levels*, starting at zero and ending at 255. It's more common to use larger (say 256×256) images, but you won't be tempted to use much larger ones in Mathcad. It's very common to use 8 bits for pixels, as this is well suited to digitised video information.

We describe the occupation of intensity levels by a *histogram*. This is a *count* of all pixels with a specified brightness level, plotted against brightness level. As a function, we can calculate it by:

```
histogram(pic):=   for bright∈0..255              8 bits give 256 levels, 0..255
                       pixels_at_level_bright←0   Initialise histogram
                   for x∈0..cols(pic)-1           Cover whole picture
                      for y∈0..rows(pic)-1
                          level←pic_y,x           Find level
                          pixels_at_level_level   Increment points at
                          ←pixels_at_level_level+1 specified levels
                   pixels_at_level               Return histogram
```

So let's work out the histogram of our eye image:

```
eye_histogram:=histogram(eye)
```

To display it, we need a horizontal axis which gives the range of brightness levels

```
bright:=0..255
```

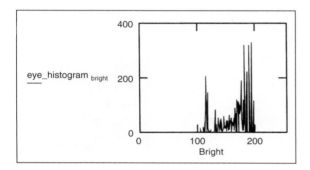

So here's the histogram of our picture of the eye image, p. The *bright* pixels relate mainly to the *skin*, the *darker* ones to the *hair*.

The most common *point operator* replaces each pixel by a scaled version of the original value. We therefore multiply each pixel by a number (like a *gain*), by specifying a function scale which is fed the picture and the gain, or a *level* shift (upwards or downwards). The function scale takes a picture pic and multiplies it by gain and adds a level

$\text{scale}(\text{pic},\text{gain},\text{level}):=$	for $x \in 0..\text{cols}(\text{pic})-1$	Address the whole picture
	for $y \in 0..\text{rows}(\text{pic})-1$	
	$\text{newpic}_{y,x} \leftarrow \text{floor}$	Multiply pixel
	$(\text{gain}\cdot\text{pic}_{y,x}+\text{level})$	by gain and add level
	newpic	Output the picture
$\text{brighter}:=\text{scale}(\text{eye, 1.2, 10})$		So let's apply it:

You can change the settings of the parameters to see their effect, that's why you've got this electronic document. Try making it brighter and darker. What happens when the gain is too big (>1.23)?

So our new picture looks like the one overleaf (using Mathcad's picture display facility):

The difference is clear in the magnitude of the pixels, those in the 'brighter' image are much larger than those in the original image, as well as by comparison of the processed with the original image. The difference between the images is much clearer when we look at the histogram of the brighter image. So let's have a look at our scaled picture:

```
b_eye_hist:=histogram(brighter)
```

	0	1	2	3	4	5	6	7	8	9
0	148	150	166	196	196	185	185	172	148	168
1	172	166	176	196	179	185	185	148	148	172
2	176	185	185	192	192	196	150	150	150	176
3	176	182	185	196	196	185	148	146	150	176
4	176	185	185	192	190	173	150	148	172	176
5	185	185	185	196	188	166	148	174	172	184
6	186	185	180	190	173	148	168	185	185	185
7	185	179	196	192	166	148	176	176	185	185
8	173	184	202	179	148	164	176	186	185	179
9	150	185	196	166	148	148	174	188	179	176
10	168	192	190	166	148	148	180	188	179	151
11	174	188	173	166	166	146	172	176	179	176
12	174	184	166	150	148	148	150	150	168	168

brighter =

(a)

Processed

brighter

(b)

Original

eye

(c)

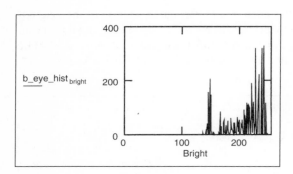

$b\_eye\_hist_{bright}$

Bright

Which is what we expect; it's just been moved *along* the brightness axis (it now starts well after 100), and reveals some detail in the histogram which was obscured earlier.

Generally, for point operators we generate a *function* which is used as a *look-up table* to find the new value of a point. Pure *scaling* is a look-up table whose graph is a *straight line* with offset set by the level. The slope of this line can be:

    (i) positive and >1 for magnification;
    (ii) positive and <1 for reduction;
and   (iii) negative (+ constant) for inversion.

Try these out!

We might also want to use a more specialised form of look-up table, say the *saw-tooth* operator. For this, we split the brightness range up into bands, and use a linear look-up table in each.

$saw\_tooth_{bright}:=mod(bright,60)$ and use the modulus operator to give a saw_tooth function

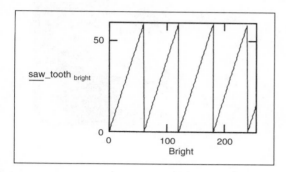

So we'll define a saw-tooth function as:

```
saw_tooth(brightness,factor):=mod(brightness,factor)
```

And as a function it is

saw(pic,modulus):=	for x∈0..cols(pic)-1	Address the whole picture
	for y∈0..rows(pic)-1	
	newpic$_{y,x}$←saw_tooth	Apply saw_tooth
	(pic$_{y,x}$,modulus)	
	newpic	Output the picture

So let's saw it: `sawn:=saw(eye,60)`

A common use of point functions is to *equalise* the intensity response of a camera. We work out the *histogram* of the camera response. This gives a function which can equalise the combined response of function*camera equal to *unity*, to give a constant intensity response. Let us suggest that the known performance of the camera is *exponential*. The equalising function is *logarithmic* since log(exp(q))=q. So let's see what it's like:

	0	1	2	3	4	5	6	7	8	9	10
0	55	57	10	35	35	26	26	15	55	12	24
1	15	10	19	35	21	26	26	55	55	15	24
2	19	26	26	32	32	35	57	57	57	19	24
3	19	24	26	35	35	26	55	54	57	19	25
4	19	26	26	32	30	16	57	55	15	19	33
5	26	26	26	35	29	10	55	17	15	25	35
6	27	26	22	30	16	55	12	26	26	26	26
7	26	21	35	32	10	55	19	19	26	26	16
8	16	25	40	21	55	9	19	27	26	21	57
9	57	26	35	10	55	55	17	29	21	19	15
10	12	32	30	10	55	55	22	29	21	58	15
11	17	29	16	10	10	54	15	19	21	19	16
12	17	25	10	57	55	55	57	57	12	12	15

sawn = (table above)

(a)   (b)

```
apply(pic) :=    for x∈0..cols(pic)-1          Address the whole picture
                   for y∈0..rows(pic)-1
                     newpic_{y,x}←floor
                     (|ln(pic_{y,x}+0.000001)|)  Apply a function (log)
                 newpic                          Output the picture
```

So let's try it out: `new_pic:=apply(eye)`

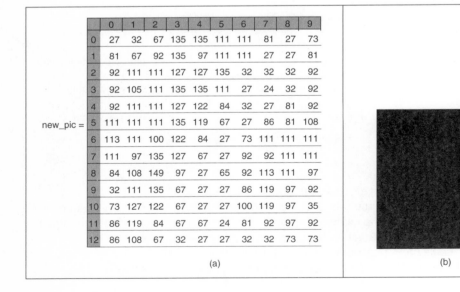

new_pic =

	0	1	2	3	4	5	6	7	8	9
0	27	32	67	135	135	111	111	81	27	73
1	81	67	92	135	97	111	111	27	27	81
2	92	111	111	127	127	135	32	32	32	92
3	92	105	111	135	135	111	27	24	32	92
4	92	111	111	127	122	84	32	27	81	92
5	111	111	111	135	119	67	27	86	81	108
6	113	111	100	122	84	27	73	111	111	111
7	111	97	135	127	67	27	92	92	111	111
8	84	108	149	97	27	65	92	113	111	97
9	32	111	135	67	27	27	86	119	97	92
10	73	127	122	67	27	27	100	119	97	35
11	86	119	84	67	67	24	81	92	97	92
12	86	108	67	32	27	27	32	32	73	73

(a)   (b)

Now we can't see *anything*! This is because there are only two brightness levels in the image (it wasn't acquired by a camera with exponential performance). In order to show up more *clearly* what happens to images, we need to be able to manipulate their histograms. *Intensity normalisation stretches* a picture's histogram so that *all* available brightness levels are used. Having *shifted* the origin to 0, by subtracting the minimum brightness, we then *scale* up the brightness, by multiplying by some fraction of full range. It's also called *histogram normalisation*. Let's say we have 8-bit pixels, giving 256 brightness levels (0..255), our function is:

$$
\begin{array}{ll}
\text{normalise(pic):=} & \text{min\_val} \leftarrow \text{min(pic)} \qquad\qquad\qquad\qquad\qquad \text{Find maximum} \\
& \text{max\_val} \leftarrow \text{..max(pic)} \qquad\qquad\qquad\qquad\quad \text{Find minimum} \\
& \text{range} \leftarrow \text{..max\_val-min\_val} \qquad\qquad\quad \text{Find range of intensity} \\
& \text{for } x \in 0..\text{cols(pic)}-1 \\
& \quad \text{for } y \in 0..\text{rows(pic)}-1 \\
& \qquad \text{newpic}_{y,x} \leftarrow \text{floor} \\
& \qquad \left[(\text{pic}_{y,x}-\text{min\_val}) \cdot \dfrac{255}{\text{range}} + 0.000001 \right] \quad \text{Map intensity values} \\
& \text{newpic}
\end{array}
$$

So let's normalise the eye image: `new_pic:=normalise(eye)`. This makes maximal use of the available grey levels.

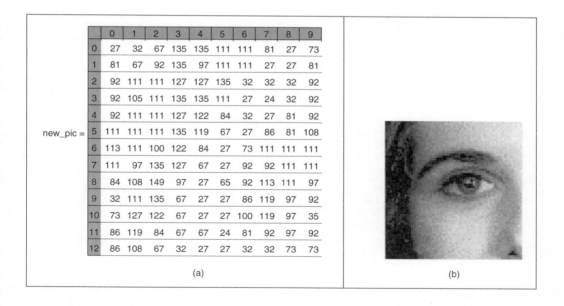

new_pic =

	0	1	2	3	4	5	6	7	8	9
0	27	32	67	135	135	111	111	81	27	73
1	81	67	92	135	97	111	111	27	27	81
2	92	111	111	127	127	135	32	32	32	92
3	92	105	111	135	135	111	27	24	32	92
4	92	111	111	127	122	84	32	27	81	92
5	111	111	111	135	119	67	27	86	81	108
6	113	111	100	122	84	27	73	111	111	111
7	111	97	135	127	67	27	92	92	111	111
8	84	108	149	97	27	65	92	113	111	97
9	32	111	135	67	27	27	86	119	97	92
10	73	127	122	67	27	27	100	119	97	35
11	86	119	84	67	67	24	81	92	97	92
12	86	108	67	32	27	27	32	32	73	73

(a)

(b)

Let's see the normalised histogram:`n_hist:=histogram(new_pic)`

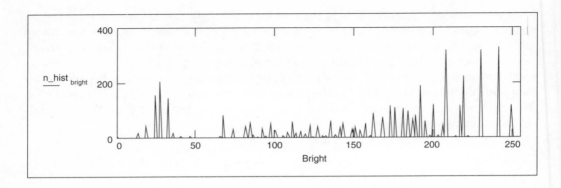

The histogram now occupies the whole available range, as required.

Histogram equalisation is a *nonlinear* histogram-stretching process. The equalised histogram is a *resampled cumulative histogram.* We first work out the histogram of the picture, then we work out the cumulative histogram. Finally, we resample the cumulative histogram, giving a look-up table to *map* original intensity levels to the equalised ones.

The main difference between equalisation and normalisation is that in *normalisation* all grey levels have the same 'weight': the process stretches the histogram to occupy the available range. In *equalisation*, the histogram is resampled or manipulated, again to cover the available range. Since the histogram is manipulated, brightness values do not have the same weight.

```
equalise(pic) :=  range←255                                    Define output range
                  number←rows(pic)·cols(pic)                   Number of points
                  for bright∈0..255
                     pixels_at_level_bright←0                  Initialise histogram
                  for x∈0..cols(pic)-1
                     for y∈0..rows(pic)-1

                        pixels_at_level_picy,x ←

                        pixes_at_level_picy,x +1               Determine histogram

                  sum←0
                  for level∈0..255
                     sum←sum+pixels_at_level_level              Form cumulative histogram

                     hist_level ←floor[( range  )·sum
                                         ───────
                                         number

                     +0.00001]                                  Make look-up table

                  for x 0..cols(pic)-1
                     for y 0..rows(pic)-1
                        newpic_y,x ←hist_picy,x                 Map input to output

                  newpic
```

So we'll equalise our eye: `new_pic:=equalise(eye)`

new_pic =

	0	1	2	3	4	5	6	7	8	9	10
0	26	35	43	78	78	64	64	47	26	45	59
1	47	43	54	78	57	64	64	26	26	47	59
2	54	64	64	73	73	78	35	35	35	54	59
3	54	59	64	78	78	64	26	13	35	54	61
4	54	64	64	73	70	51	35	26	47	54	73
5	64	64	64	78	68	43	26	52	47	61	78
6	65	64	59	70	51	26	45	64	64	64	64
7	64	57	78	73	43	26	54	54	64	64	51
8	51	61	86	57	26	38	54	65	64	57	35
9	35	64	78	43	26	26	52	68	57	54	47
10	45	73	70	43	26	26	59	68	57	36	47
11	52	68	51	43	43	13	47	54	57	54	51
12	52	61	43	35	26	26	35	35	45	45	47

(a)

(b)

This is how Mathcad displays images when you display them using the surface plot facility (which is why we're using the picture facility instead, it's faster too!). Now try equalising the image `brighter` (as defined earlier) – do you expect the result you get?

The histogram tells us what has really happened to the picture: `e_hist:=histogram(new_pic)`

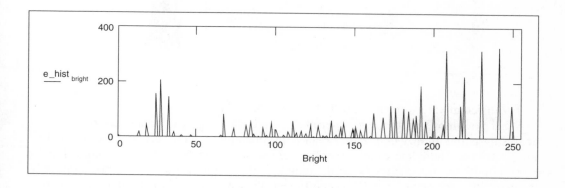

One way of interpreting this is that the histogram is now *balanced* between black and white.

If we want to find pixels with brightness *above* a specified level, we use *thresholding*. The operator is:

`threshold(pic,value):=`	`for x∈0..cols(pic)-1`	Cover the whole picture
	`  for y∈0..rows(pic)-1`	
	`    newpic`$_{y,x}$`←255 if`	Set any point above the
	`    pic`$_{y,x}$`≥value`	threshold to white,
	`    newpic`$_{y,x}$`←0 otherwise`	otherwise set it to black
	`newpic`	Return the new picture

Let's try it out: `new_pic:=threshold(eye,161)` by picking out points in the eye image brighter than 160.

So all points above the threshold are set to 255 (white), those below are set to 0 (black).

new_pic =

	0	1	2	3	4	5	6	7	8	9	10
0	0	0	0	0	0	0	0	0	0	0	0
1	0	0	0	0	0	0	0	0	0	0	0
2	0	0	0	0	0	0	0	0	0	0	0
3	0	0	0	0	0	0	0	0	0	0	0
4	0	0	0	0	0	0	0	0	0	0	0
5	0	0	0	0	0	0	0	0	0	0	0
6	0	0	0	0	0	0	0	0	0	0	0
7	0	0	0	0	0	0	0	0	0	0	0
8	0	0	0	0	0	0	0	0	0	0	0
9	0	0	0	0	0	0	0	0	0	0	0
10	0	0	0	0	0	0	0	0	0	0	0
11	0	0	0	0	0	0	0	0	0	0	0
12	0	0	0	0	0	0	0	0	0	0	0

(a)   (b)

Try different values for the threshold, other than 160.

We'll now move on to *group operators* where the new pixel values are the result of analysing points in a *region*, rather than point operators which operate on *single* points. First, we have a template which describes the region of interest and we then convolve this by summing up, over the region of the template, the result of multiplying pixel values by the respective template (*weighting*) coefficient. We can't process the borders since part of the template falls outside the picture. Accordingly, we need an operator which sets an image to black, so that the borders in the final image are set to black. Black is zero brightness values, so the operator which sets a whole image to black is:

```
zero(pic):=  │  for x∈0..rows(pic)-1
             │      for y∈0..rows(pic)-1
             │          newpic_{y,x}←0
             │  newpic
```

We shan't bother to display the results of this operator!
The generalised template convolution operator is then:

```
tm_conv(pic,temp):= │ conv←zero(pic)                              Set output pic to black

                      w←floor( cols(temp) / 2 )                   Find size of template

                      for y∈w..rows(pic)-w-1                      Cover whole picture
                          for x∈w..cols(pic)-w-1
                          │ conv_{y,x}←0                          Initialise sum
                          │ for yy∈0..rows(temp)-1               Cover whole
                          │    for xx∈0..cols(temp)-1            template
                          │    │ pic_y←y-w+yy                     Find x co-ordinate
                          │    │ pic_x←x-w+xx                     Find y co-ordinate
                          │    │ conv_{y,x}←conv_{y,x}+           Add product to sum
                          │    │    (pic_{pic_y,pic_x}·temp_{yy,xx})

                      ──────────────────────→                     Return (integer)
                      floor(conv)                                 picture
```

A 3×3 *averaging* (*mean*) operator sums the points in the 3×3 neighbourhood centred on the point of interest. This means we can't process a 1 pixel wide picture border so the operator first sets the whole output picture to black and then replaces points by the average of their 3×3 neighbourhood. A direct implementation of this process is

```
ave33(pic):=
    │ newpic←zero(pic)                                           Set output picture
    │ for x∈1..rows(pic)-2                                       to black
    │    for y∈1..rows(pic)-2                                    Address the
    │                                                            whole picture
    │
    │                   ⎡ ⎛ pic_{y-1,x-1}+pic_{y-1,x}+pic_{y-1,x+1}... ⎞ ⎤
    │    newpic_{y,x}←floor⎢ ⎜ +pic_{y,x-1}+pic_{y+1}+pic_{y,x+1}...    ⎟ ⎥     Calculate average
    │                   ⎢ ⎝ +pic_{y+1,x-1}+pic_{y+1,x}+pic_{y+1,x+1}  ⎠ ⎥
    │                   ⎢ ──────────────────────────────────────── ⎥
    │                   ⎣                    9                       ⎦
    │ newpic                                                     Output it
```

Let's apply the 3×3 averaging operator smooth:=ave33(eye)

So our smoothed picture looks like:

smooth =

	0	1	2	3	4	5	6	7	8	9
0	0	0	0	0	0	0	0	0	0	0
1	0	133	141	147	150	144	135	124	124	131
2	0	140	145	149	150	141	130	119	123	132
3	0	143	148	150	150	138	125	118	125	136
4	0	144	148	150	147	134	125	122	130	140
5	0	144	147	147	141	131	127	130	138	144
6	0	146	148	146	136	129	129	137	142	144
7	0	146	148	142	131	127	133	142	144	141
8	0	144	147	139	126	126	134	142	143	138
9	0	143	145	134	122	124	135	143	141	134
10	0	141	142	132	121	124	132	141	139	136
11	0	140	137	128	120	122	127	134	134	134
12	0	136	130	122	118	121	125	130	131	133

(a)

normalise(smooth)

(b)

This is equivalent to *convolving* a *template* which has all elements set to *unity* and then dividing the result by the sum of the template coefficients. A *general* form of an averaging template operator (which can accept any template size) is

$$
\begin{aligned}
&\texttt{ave(pic,winsize):=} \\
&\qquad \texttt{new}\leftarrow\texttt{zero(pic)} \\
&\qquad \texttt{half}\leftarrow\texttt{floor}\left(\dfrac{\texttt{winsize}}{2}\right) \\
&\qquad \texttt{for } x\in\texttt{half..cols(pic)-half-1} \\
&\qquad\quad \texttt{for } y\in\texttt{half..rows(pic)-half-1} \\
&\qquad\qquad \texttt{new}_{y,x}\leftarrow\texttt{floor}\left[\dfrac{\displaystyle\sum_{\texttt{iwin}=0}^{\texttt{winsize}-1}\sum_{\texttt{jwin}=0}^{\texttt{winsize}-1}\texttt{pic}_{y+\texttt{iwin}-\texttt{half},x+\texttt{jwin}-\texttt{half}}}{(\texttt{winsize}\cdot\texttt{winsize})}\right] \\
&\qquad \texttt{new}
\end{aligned}
$$

So let's apply it: `smooth:=ave(eye,3)`
With result:

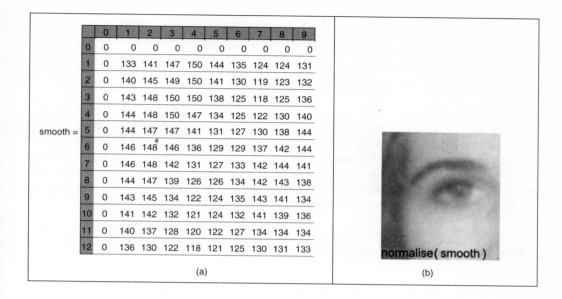

	0	1	2	3	4	5	6	7	8	9
0	0	0	0	0	0	0	0	0	0	0
1	0	133	141	147	150	144	135	124	124	131
2	0	140	145	149	150	141	130	119	123	132
3	0	143	148	150	150	138	125	118	125	136
4	0	144	148	150	147	134	125	122	130	140
5	0	144	147	147	141	131	127	130	138	144
6	0	146	148	146	136	129	129	137	142	144
7	0	146	148	142	131	127	133	142	144	141
8	0	144	147	139	126	126	134	142	143	138
9	0	143	145	134	122	124	135	143	141	134
10	0	141	142	132	121	124	132	141	139	136
11	0	140	137	128	120	122	127	134	134	134
12	0	136	130	122	118	121	125	130	131	133

smooth =

(a) normalise(smooth) (b)

Note the blurring in the result, as well as the increased uniformity of the background; this is equivalent to reducing the background noise. Try other (*odd*) numbers for the size, say 5, 7 or 9. Do you expect the observed effects? There is a mean operator in Mathcad which we shall use for future averaging operations, as:

$$\text{ave(pic,winsize)} := \begin{vmatrix} \text{newpic} \leftarrow \text{zero(pic)} \\ \text{for } x \in \text{floor}\left(\frac{\text{winsize}}{2}\right)..\text{cols(pic)} - \text{floor}\left(\frac{\text{winsize}}{2}\right) - 1 \\ \quad \text{for } y \in \text{floor}\left(\frac{\text{winsize}}{2}\right)..\text{rows(pic)} - \text{floor}\left(\frac{\text{winsize}}{2}\right) - 1 \\ \qquad \begin{vmatrix} \text{half} \leftarrow \text{floor}\left(\frac{\text{winsize}}{2}\right) \\ \text{newpic}_{y,x} \leftarrow \text{floor(mean(submatrix} \\ \text{(pic,y-half,y+half,x-half,x+half)))} \end{vmatrix} \\ \text{newpic} \end{vmatrix}$$

with the same result. An alternative is to use the centre smoothing operation in Mathcad, put centsmooth in place of mean. To use the template convolution operator, tmconv, we need to define an averaging template:

$$\text{averaging\_template(winsize)} := \begin{vmatrix} \text{sum} \leftarrow \text{winsize} \cdot \text{winsize} \\ \text{for } y \in 0..\text{winsize-1} \\ \quad \text{for } x \in 0..\text{winsize-1} \\ \qquad \text{template}_{y,x} \leftarrow 1 \\ \dfrac{\text{template}}{\text{sum}} \end{vmatrix}$$

So a 3×3 template is:

$$\text{averaging\_template(3)} = \begin{pmatrix} 0.111 & 0.111 & 0.111 \\ 0.111 & 0.111 & 0.111 \\ 0.111 & 0.111 & 0.111 \end{pmatrix}$$

and to apply it: `smoothed:=tm_conv(eye,averaging_template(3))`

Since there is a *duality* between *convolution* in the time domain and *multiplication* in the frequency domain, we can implement template convolution by using the Fourier transform. Template convolution is the inverse Fourier transform of the product of Fourier transform of the image with the transform of the template. First we need a picture of the template, this picture must be the same size as the image we want to convolve it with. For averaging, we need a 3×3 square in the centre of an image of the same size as the eye image:

```
square:=    for x∈0..cods(eye)-1
              for y∈0..rows(eye)-1
```
$$\text{pic}_{y,x} \leftarrow \frac{1}{9} \text{ if } \left[y \geq \left(\frac{\text{rows(eye)}}{2}-1\right)\right]\cdot\left(y \leq \frac{\text{rows(eye)}}{2}+1\right)$$
$$\cdot\left[x \geq \left(\frac{\text{cols(eye)}}{2}-1\right)\right]\cdot\left(x \leq \frac{\text{cols(eye)}}{2}+1\right)$$
$$\text{pic}_{y,x} \leftarrow 0 \text{ otherwise}$$
```
            pic
```

Then, template convolution is given by:

```
conv(pic,temp):=  pic_spectrum←Fourier(pic)          Take transform of image
                  temp_spectrum←Fourier(temp)        Transform template
                  convolved_spectrum←
```
$$\overline{(\text{pic\_spectrum}\cdot\text{temp\_spectrum})} \qquad \text{Form product}$$
```
                  result←inv_Fourier
                    (rearrange(convolved_spectrum))  Inverse transform
                  result                             Supply result
```

Let's see what happens: `Fsmoothed:=conv(eye,square)`

To check the result, we need to scale its magnitude:

$$\text{sc\_smooth} := \text{cols(eye)} \cdot \overrightarrow{|\text{Fsmoothed}|}$$

Now, let's see the difference

	0	1	2	3	4	5	6	7	8	9
0	142	123	130	135	138	135	130	123	121	125
1	151	0	0	0	0	0	0	0	0	0
2	157	0	0	0	0	0	0	0	0	0
3	160	0	0	0	0	0	0	0	0	0
4	161	0	0	0	0	0	1	0	0	0
5	162	0	0	0	0	0	0	0	0	0
6	162	0	0	0	0	0	0	0	0	0
7	161	0	1	0	0	0	0	0	0	0
8	157	0	0	0	0	1	0	0	0	0
9	157	0	0	0	0	0	0	0	0	0
10	157	0	0	0	0	0	0	0	0	0
11	159	0	0	0	0	1	1	0	0	0
12	159	0	0	0	0	0	0	0	0	0

$$\overrightarrow{\text{floor(sc\_smooth-smoothed)}} =$$

which shows that the difference is in the borders, the small differences in pixels' values are due to numerical considerations.

In image processing, we often use a *Gaussian* smoothing filter which can give a better smoothing performance than direct averaging. Here the template coefficients are set according to the Gaussian distribution which for a two-dimensional distribution controlled by a variance σ^2 is, for a template size defined by `winsize`:

```
Gaussian_template(winsize,σ) :=   sum←0

                                  centre←floor( winsize) / 2 )

                                  for y∈0..winsize-1
                                    for x∈0..winsize-1

                                                -[(y-centre)² +(x-centre)²]
                                                ──────────────────────────
                                                          2·σ²
                                      template_y,x←e
                                      sum←sum+template_y,x
                                    template
                                    ────────
                                      sum
```

So let's have a peep at the normalised template we obtain:

$$
\text{Gaussian\_template}(5,1)=
\begin{bmatrix}
0.003 & 0.013 & 0.022 & 0.013 & 0.003 \\
0.013 & 0.06 & 0.098 & 0.06 & 0.013 \\
0.022 & 0.098 & 0.162 & 0.098 & 0.022 \\
0.013 & 0.06 & 0.098 & 0.06 & 0.013 \\
0.003 & 0.013 & 0.022 & 0.013 & 0.003
\end{bmatrix}
$$

This gives the famous *bell-shaped* function shown here for a 19×19 window with a standard deviation of 4. Try changing the standard deviation from 4 to, say, 2 and 8 so you can see its effect on the width.

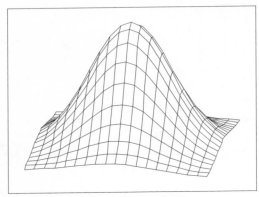

Gaussian_template (19, 4)

So let's apply it: `Gaussian_smoothed:=tm_conv(eye,Gaussian_template (3,0.8))`
And the result is:

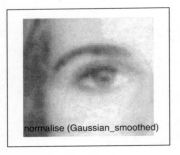

normalise (Gaussian_smoothed)

This can keep much more detail concerning image features; note here its ability to retain detail in the eye region which was lost in the earlier direct averaging. Again, it can be implemented in the frequency domain, as can any template convolution process.

The mean and Gaussian operators are actually *statistical* operators since they provide estimates of the mean. There are *other* statistics; let's go for a *median* operator. This gives the midpoint of a sorted list. The list is derived from the pixel values within a specified area. We need to provide the *sort* function with a vector, so for a *3×3 neighbourhood* centred on a point with co-ordinates *x*, *y*, we get

```
y:=3   x:=3
```

And a pointer to the nine elements is: $\text{x1}:=0..8$

And we get a vector of unsorted values: $\text{unsorted}_{x1} := \text{eye}_{x+mod(x1,3)-1,x+floor\left(\frac{x1}{3}\right)-1}$

$$\text{unsorted}^T=(146\ \ 146\ \ 146\ \ 152\ \ 155\ \ 152\ \ 152\ \ 155\ \ 150)$$

We need to sort these into ascending order: $\text{sorted}:=\text{sort}(\text{unsorted})$

$$\text{sorted}^T =(146\ \ 146\ \ 146\ \ 150\ \ 152\ \ 152\ \ 155\ \ 155)$$

And our median is the middle of the list: $\text{our\_median}:=\text{sorted}_4$
$$\text{our\_median}=152$$

So let's implement it as a general 3×3 median operator:

```
med(pic):= | newpic←zero(pic)
           | for x∈1..cols(pic)-2
           |    for y∈1..rows(pic)-2
           |       | for x1∈0..8
           |       |    unsorted_x1 ←pic_{y+mod(x1,3)-1,x+floor(x1/3)-1}
           |       | sorted←sort(unsorted)
           |       | newpic_{y,x}←sorted_4
           |
           | newpic
```

So let's apply it: $\text{our\_med}:=\text{med}(\text{eye})$

	0	1	2	3	4	5	6	7	8	9
0	0	0	0	0	0	0	0	0	0	0
1	0	135	146	152	152	146	146	117	117	135
2	0	139	146	152	152	146	117	117	117	139
3	0	146	146	152	152	146	117	117	117	139
4	0	146	146	150	150	136	117	117	135	139
5	0	146	146	149	149	132	130	135	139	146
6	0	146	146	149	136	130	132	139	146	146
7	0	146	146	142	130	130	139	146	146	146
8	0	146	146	141	129	129	139	141	146	141
9	0	146	146	130	115	115	139	142	141	139
10	0	146	146	130	115	115	137	141	141	139
11	0	137	136	130	115	115	117	139	139	135
12	0	137	130	117	115	115	117	135	135	135

our_med =

(a)

normalise (our_med)

(b)

The main function of the median operator is to remove noise (especially salt and pepper noise) whilst retaining the edges of features in an image. You can't see that here, there is little image noise. So let's add some in:

```
noisy_p:=addcondiments(eye,0.1)
```

If you make the value supplied as an argument to `addcondiments` smaller, you'll get *less* noise, larger values (0.3 say) result in greater noise contamination.

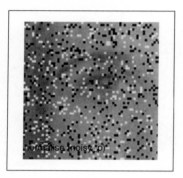

10/10 for the label of this image! Now we have introduced light (salt) and dark (pepper) points into the image. This type of noise is quite common in satellite image transmission decoding errors.

So let's see what our median operator can do with this image, in comparison with direct and Gaussian averaging:

Median	Mean = Direct Averaging	Gaussian Averaging
`nmed:=med(noisy_p)`	`nmean:=ave(noisy_p,3)`	`gmean:=tm_conv(noisy_p,`
		`Gaussian_template(3,0.8))`

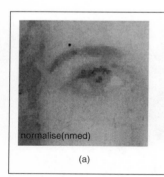
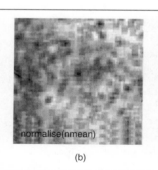
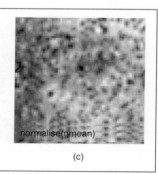

(a)   (b)   (c)

The median operator clearly has a better ability to remove this type of noise. This is because it is removed when it is placed at either end of the rank sorted list. However, in direct and Gaussian averaging, the salt and pepper contributes to the final result. To run it again, with a different selection of noise points, just select the function `noisy_p :=addcondiments()` and run it again. Each time, you'll get a different pattern of noise. Check the filtering still works.

There is of course a median operator in Mathcad, but we thought we'd show you how it worked. Median filters can be implemented in an adaptive manner, or using non-square templates (e.g. cross or line, usually for computational reasons). We can get a Mathcad median by:

```
their_med(pic,winsize):= newpic←zero(pic)
                         half←floor( winsize )
                                    (  2    )
                          for x∈half..cols(pic)-half-1
                            for y∈half..rows(pic)-half-1
                               newpic_y,x←median(submatrix
                                  (pic,y-half,y+half,x-half,x+half))
                         newpic
```

This gives you a median operator for an arbitrary template size.

Finally, the last statistic is the *mode*. This is the *peak* of the probability distribution (the value most likely to occur). One way to estimate its value is to use the *truncated median filter*. It operates by taking the median of the distribution resulting from truncation of the distribution within a window at a point beyond the mean.

Let's have a picture of an artery to work on:

$$noisy\_p:=READBMP(artery)$$

Now, here's the code:

```
trun_med(p,wsze):= newpic←zero(p)
                   ha←floor( wsze )
                            (  2   )
                   for x∈ha..cols(p)-ha-1
                     for y∈ha..rows(p)-ha-1
                        win←submatrix(p,y-ha,y+ha,x-ha,x+ha)
                        med←median(win)
                        ave←mean(win)
                        upper←2·med-min(win)
                        lower←2·med-max(win)
                        cc←0
                        for i∈0..wsze-1
                          for j∈0..wsze-1
                             trun_cc←win_j,i if(win_j,i<upper)·(med<ave)
                             trun_cc←win_j,i if(win_j,i>lower)·(med>ave)
                             cc←cc+1
                          newpic_y,x←median(trun)
                   newpic
```

To see how it works: `tfilt=trun_med(noisy_p,5)`

It's actually switched off here. To switch it on, select it, press: and then press return. Then go and make a cup of tea. It should be finished after that! So to save your time, we'll read in a processed bitmap for a 13 × 13 operator.

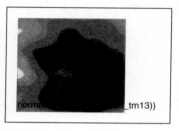

This completes our study of low-level image operators. Why not follow some of the suggestions below to extend/improve your knowledge?

Suggestions: (i) investigate the effects of *different window sizes*;
(ii) try out *different values* for the control parameters;
(iii) try adding your own *noise* to the original image, and see the effects;
(iv) try different template *shapes* for averaging and median operators;
(v) try *different* images.

Now we'll move on to finding objects in images. So far, we've modified brightness so as to control an object's appearance in an image. But the change in brightness signifies an object's perimeter or border. So this can be used as a first step in finding the object. This is a basic feature, the subject of Chapter 4, Low-Level Feature Extraction.

9.4   Appendix 4: Abbreviated Matlab worksheet

This is an abbreviated version of the worksheet for Chapter 4. Essentially, the text is a Matlab script and the subroutines called and the images provided are set into figures.

```
%Chapter 4 Low-Level Feature Extraction and Edge Detection: CHAPTER4.M
%Written by: Mark S. Nixon

disp ('Welcome to the Chapter4 script')
disp ('This worksheet is the companion to Chapter 4 and is an
introduction.')
disp ('The worksheet follows the text directly and allows you to
process basic images.')

%Let's first empty the memory
clear
```

```
%Let's initialise the display colour
colormap(grey);

disp (' ')
disp ('Let us use the image of an eye.')
disp ('When you are ready to move on, press RETURN')
%read in the image
eye=imread('eye.jpg','jpg');
%images are stored as integers, so we need to double them for Matlab
%we also need to ensure we have a greyscale, not three colour planes
eye=double(eye(:,:,1));
%so let's display it
subplot(1,1,1), imagesc(eye);
plotedit on, title ('Image of an eye'), plotedit off
pause;
```

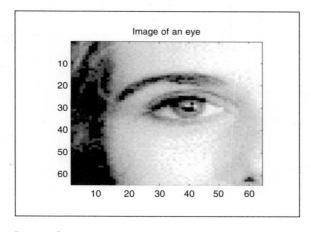

Image of an eye

```
disp(' ')
disp ('We detect vertical edges by differencing horizontally adjacent')
disp ('points. Note how clearly the edge of the face appears')
%so we'll call the edge_x operator.

vertical=edge_x(eye);
imagesc(vertical);
plotedit on, title ('Vertical edges of an eye'), plotedit off
pause;
```

```
function vertical_edges=edge_x (image)
%Find edges by horizontal differencing
%
%Usage: [new image]=edge_x (image)
%
%Parameters: image-array of points
%
%Author: Mark S. Nixon

%get dimensions
[rows, cols]=size (image);

%set the output image to black
vertical_edges=zeros (rows, cols);
%this is equivalent to
vertical_edges (1:rows, 1:cols)=0

%then form the difference between horizontal
successive points
for x=1: cols-1 %address all columns except border
  for y=1: rows %address all rows
     vertical_edges (y,x)=
        abs (image (y, x)-image (y, x+1));
  end
end
```

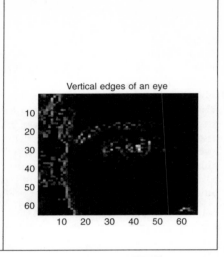

Vertical edge detection

```
disp (' ')
disp ('We detect horizontal edges by differencing vertically adjacent
points')
disp ('Notice how the side of the face now disappears, wheras the')
disp ('eyebrows appear')
%so we'll call the edge_y operator
subplot(1,2,2), horizontal=edge_y(eye);
subplot(1,2,1), imagesc(horizontal);
plotedit on, title ('Horizontal edges of an eye'), plotedit off
subplot(1,2,2), imagesc(vertical);
plotedit on, title ('Vertical edges of an eye'), plotedit off
pause;
```

```
function horizontal_edges=edge_y(image)
%Find edges by vertical differencing
%
%Usage: [new image]=edge(image)
%
%Parameters: image-array of points
%
%Author: Mark S. Nixon

%get dimensions
[rows, cols]=size (image);

%set the output image to black
horizontal_edges=zeros(rows,cols);

%then form the difference between vertical
successive points
for x=1:cols %address all columns
  for y=1:rows-1 %address all rows except border
     horizontal_edges (y,x)=
           abs(image(y, x)-image(y+1,x));
  end
end
```

Horizontal edge detection (in comparison with vertical)

```
disp (` ')
disp (`We detect all edges by combining the vertical and horizontal
edges')
%so we'll call the edge operator
all_edges=edge(eye);
subplot(1,1,1), imagesc(all_edges);
plotedit on, title (`All edges of an eye'), plotedit off
pause;
```

```
function edges=edge(image)
%Find all edges by first order differencing
%
%Usage: [new image]=edge(image)
%
%Parameters: image-array of points
%
%Author: Mark S. Nixon

%get dimensions
[rows, cols]=size (image);

%set the output image to black
edges=zeros (rows, cols);

%then form the difference between horizontal and
vertical points
for x=1: cols-1 %address all columns
  for y=1: rows-1 %address all rows except border
    edges (y,x)=abs(2*image(y,x)
        image (y+1, x)-image (y, x+1));
  end
end
```

All edges of an eye

Detecting all edges

```
disp (` ')
disp (`The Roberts operator is actually one of the oldest edge
detection')
disp (`operators. The edges are the maximum of the difference between')
disp (`points on the two diagonals.')
%so we'll call the Roberts cross operator
roberts_edges=roberts(eye);
imagesc(roberts_edges);
plotedit on, title (`Eye edges by Roberts cross operator'), plotedit
off
pause;
```

```
Function edges=roberts(image)
%Find all edges by roberts cross operator
%
%Usage: [new image]=roberts(image)
%
%Parameters: image-array of points
%
%Author: Mark S. Nixon

%get dimensions
[rows, cols]=size(image);

%set the output image to black
edges=zeros (rows, cols);

for x=1: cols-1 %address all columns
        except right border
  for y=1: rows-1 %address all rows
        except bottom border
    %top right minus bottom left point
    M_plus=abs(image (y,x+1)-image (y+1, x));
    %top left minus bottom right point
    M_minus=abs(image(y,x)-image (y+1, x+1));
    %return maximum
    edges(y,x)=max(M_plus, M_minus);
  end
end
```

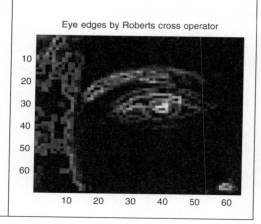

Eye edges by Roberts cross operator

Edges by Roberts operator

```
disp (' ')
disp ('The Prewitt operator includes smoothing in horizontal and
vertical')
disp ('templates')

prewitt_edges=prewitt(eye);

disp ('From these, we calculate the magnitude and direction. The
magnitude')
disp ('shows the amount of contrast, as revealed by its image')
pmagnitude=prewitt_edges(:,:,1);

subplot (1,2,1), imagesc(pmagnitude);
```

```
Function edges=prewitt(image)
%derive edges by 3*3 Prewitt operator
%
%Usage: [new image]=prewitt(image)
%
%Parameters: image-array of points
%
%Author: Mark S. Nixon

%get dimensions
[rows, cols]=size(image);

%set the output image to black(0)
edges(1: rows,1:cols)=0;

for x=2: cols-1 %address all columns
                except border
  for y=2: rows-1 %address all rows
                except border
    %apply Mx template
x_mag=image (y-1, x-1)+image(y-1,x)...
    +image(y-1, x+1)-image(y+1,x-1)-...
    image(y+1, x)-image(y+1, x+1);
    %apply My template
y_mag=image(y-1,x-1)+image(y,x-1)...
    +image(y+1,x-1)-image(y-1, x+1)-...
    image(y,x+1)-image(y+1,x+1);

    %evaluate edge magnitude
edges(y,x,1)=sqrt((x_mag*x_mag)
                +(y_mag*y_mag));
    %evaluate edge direction
    if x_mag==0
      edges(y,x,2)=sign(y_mag)*1.5708;
    else edges(y,x,2)=atan(y_mag/x_mag);
      end
  end
end
```

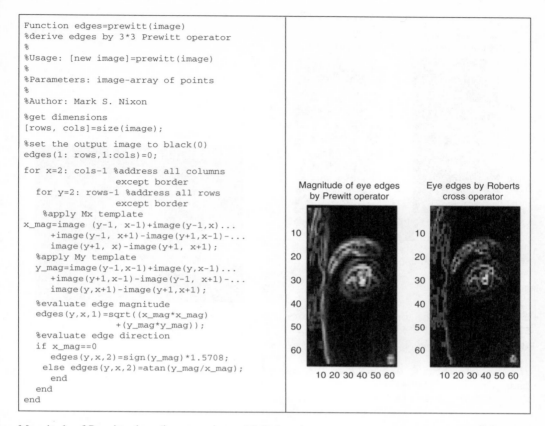

Magnitude of eye edges by Prewitt operator

Eye edges by Roberts cross operator

Magnitude of Prewitt edges (in comparison with Roberts)

```
plotedit on, title ('Magnitude of eye edges by Prewitt operator'),
plotedit off
subplot(1,2,2), imagesc(roberts_edges);
plotedit on, title ('Eye edges by Roberts cross operator'), plotedit
off
disp ('We can see that the effect of smoothing is to reduce noise in')
disp ('the edge detection process')
pause;
disp ('The direction is how the edge is changing, but this is much
less')
disp ('easy to see in the displayed image.')
direction=prewitt_edges(:,:,2);
imagesc(direction);
plotedit on, title ('Direction of eye edges by Prewitt operator'),
plotedit off
pause;
```

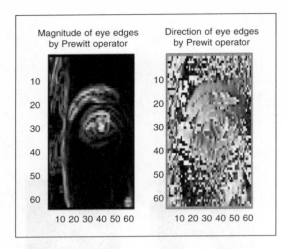

Magnitude and Direction of Prewitt Edges

```
disp (' ')
disp ('The Sobel operator includes better smoothing than the Prewitt')
disp ('operator.It is harder to see here, but is gereally experienced')
sobel_edges=sobel33(eye);

disp ('Again, we calculate the magnitude and direction. Again, The')
disp ('magnitude shows the amount of contrast, as shown in the image')
disp ('for a 3*3 Sobel operator.')

smagnitude=sobel_edges(:,:,1);

subplot(1,2,1), imagesc(smagnitude);
plotedit on, title ('Magnitude of eye edges by Sobel'), plotedit off
subplot(1,2,2), imagesc(pmagnitude);
plotedit on, title ('Magnitude of eye edges by Prewitt'), plotedit off
pause;
```

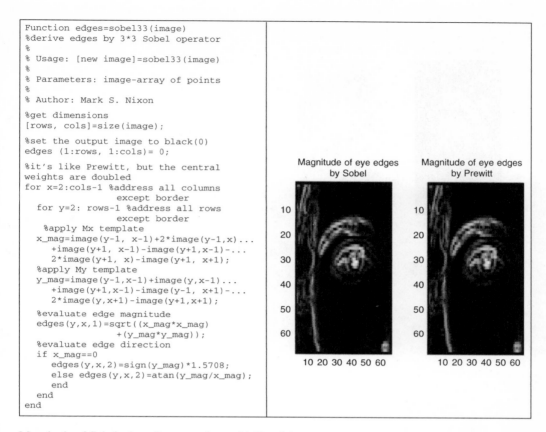

```
Function edges=sobel33(image)
%derive edges by 3*3 Sobel operator
%
% Usage: [new image]=sobel33(image)
%
% Parameters: image-array of points
%
% Author: Mark S. Nixon

%get dimensions
[rows, cols]=size(image);

%set the output image to black(0)
edges (1:rows, 1:cols)= 0;

%it's like Prewitt, but the central
weights are doubled
for x=2:cols-1 %address all columns
                except border
  for y=2: rows-1 %address all rows
                except border
   %apply Mx template
   x_mag=image(y-1, x-1)+2*image(y-1,x)...
    +image(y+1, x-1)-image(y+1,x-1)-...
    2*image(y+1, x)-image(y+1, x+1);
   %apply My template
   y_mag=image(y-1,x-1)+image(y,x-1)...
    +image(y+1,x-1)-image(y-1, x+1)-...
    2*image(y,x+1)-image(y+1,x+1);
   %evaluate edge magnitude
   edges(y,x,1)=sqrt((x_mag*x_mag)
                +(y_mag*y_mag));
   %evaluate edge direction
   if x_mag==0
     edges(y,x,2)=sign(y_mag)*1.5708;
     else edges(y,x,2)=atan(y_mag/x_mag);
     end
   end
end
```

Magnitude of Sobel edges (in comparison with Prewitt)

```
disp ('The direction is still much less easy to see!')
subplot(1,1,1), direction=sobel_edges(:,:,2);
imagesc(direction);
plotedit on, title ('Direction of eye edges by Sobel'), plotedit off
pause;
```

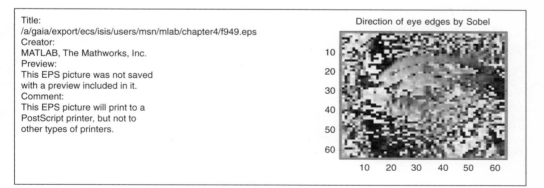

Direction of Sobel edges

Index